# AN ARMY
# AFIRE

# AN ARMY AFIRE

## HOW THE US ARMY CONFRONTED ITS RACIAL CRISIS IN THE VIETNAM ERA

## BETH BAILEY

THE UNIVERSITY OF NORTH CAROLINA PRESS

*Chapel Hill*

*Publication of this book was made possible in part by a grant from Carnegie Corporation of New York. The statements made and views expressed are solely the responsibility of the author.*

*This book was published with the assistance of the William R. Kenan Jr. Fund of the University of North Carolina Press.*

© 2023 Beth Bailey

Designed by Jamison Cockerham
Set in Scala and Langdon
by Rebecca Evans

Cover illustration: *Black Power.* "Bob Kelly, spreading a petroleum-based soil binder that covers his hand and lower forearm, in a 'black power' salute." Photographer unknown. Copyright Vietnam Soldier, https://galleries.vietnamsoldier.com/photo-gallery/black-power.

*Manufactured in the United States of America*

Complete Library of Congress Cataloging-in-Publication Data
is available at https://lccn.loc.gov/2022049609

978-1-4696-7326-4 (cloth: alk. paper)
978-1-4696-7327-1 (ebook)

*For David, always*

# CONTENTS

# ILLUSTRATIONS

# A NOTE ON LANGUAGE

In the 1960s and 1970s—the era about which I am writing—the ugliest of racial epithets were commonplace. As a historian, I believe it is important not to sanitize the past. Therefore, when the people about whom I write use such language, including the N-word, I quote exactly what they said.

In a different vein, the US Army used the term "Negro" in official documents through the end of the 1960s. This had been the term that civil rights organizations and most African Americans preferred; its use at this time was respectful. By the mid- to late 1960s, however, many young African Americans rejected that word; they wished to be called "Black," even as older officers and noncommissioned officers were often uncomfortable with the political connotations of that label. Army officers responded to this ongoing debate inconsistently. In my writing, I use our contemporary terms: Black and African American. When I quote, I use the original language.

Throughout this work, I occasionally use terms that were in widespread vernacular use during the late 1960s and early 1970s, even though I am not quoting a specific, individual source. In those cases, I enclose the words or phrases in quotation marks as a way to distinguish between language of the historical moment and my own authorial voice.

In accordance with UNC Press style, I primarily use traditional rank abbreviations rather than US Army–specific abbreviations in the text. I use army-specific rank abbreviations in the notes.

# ABBREVIATIONS

| | |
|---|---|
| AAFES | Army & Air Force Exchange Service |
| AR | Army Regulation |
| AWC | US Army War College |
| DoD | Department of Defense |
| DRRI | Defense Race Relations Institute |
| EM | enlisted man (abbreviation commonly used during this era rather than "soldier," "GI," or "enlisted personnel") |
| G-1 | Office of the Deputy Chief of Staff for Personnel, US Army |
| HBCU | historically Black college or university |
| IG | inspector general |
| LBJ | Long Binh Jail |
| MACV | Military Assistance Command, Vietnam (Department of Defense Joint-Service Command) |
| MP | military police |
| NAACP | National Association for the Advancement of Colored People |
| NCO | noncommissioned officer |
| OCS | officer candidate school |
| OER | Officer Efficiency Report |
| PX | post exchange |
| ROTC | Reserve Officers' Training Corps |
| SNCC | Student Nonviolent Coordinating Committee |
| UCMJ | Uniform Code of Military Justice |
| USAREUR | US Army Europe |
| USARPAC | US Army Pacific |
| USARV | US Army Vietnam |
| USMA | US Military Academy |

# AN ARMY AFIRE

# INTRODUCTION

*You show me a commander or leader who says he doesn't have
race trouble, and I'll show you a dumb son of a bitch.*

BRIG. GEN. GEORGE S. PATTON, 1971

The US Army was afire. Sparks had fallen in dry tinder, fanned by broader
discord: a nation riven by racial violence, mired in the death throes of legal
segregation, at odds over a failing war. Flames had ignited in soldiers' barracks and bars, found fuel in the army's own policies and practices, caught
fire in thousands of confrontations, large and small. Some burned brief;
others flared, out of control. By the cusp of the 1970s, race was tearing the
army apart.

That wasn't supposed to be the story. Many Americans, Black and white,
civilian and in uniform, had seen the US military as a model of racial progress. Flawed, sure, but nonetheless a counterbalance both to white segregationist mobs and to clashes in the streets of American cities. That belief,
like smoke, obscured the fire. It was not immediately obvious what threat
the initial outbreaks posed, or even that they were part of a larger pattern.
Not until the late 1960s did army leaders begin to directly and systematically
confront the expanding racial conflict. By the beginning of the 1970s, army
leaders had begun calling the crisis they confronted "the problem of race."[1]

n Fort Hood, Texas, August 1968, forty-three Black soldiers refused orders
to stand by for riot duty at the Democratic National Convention in Chicago.
"The people we are supposed to control, the rioters, are probably our own

race," said one. "We shouldn't have to go out there and do wrong to our own people." Some 9,000 miles away, in war-ravaged Vietnam, 200 Black prisoners seized control of the army jail at Long Binh. They burned buildings to smoldering embers, beat guards and fellow prisoners, repurposed army blankets into makeshift dashikis and improvised "African drums." Their occupation lasted three weeks.[2]

That same year, in Knielingen, West Germany, two white soldiers stabbed three Black soldiers to death. At Fort McClellan, Alabama, someone called the commander's office to warn that Black soldiers, meeting off-post, were heading back to "to burn it down." Said a second anonymous caller to the staff duty officer, "When the riot starts, tell Col Hipp we are going to turn the weapons on him. Black Power, Black Power Baby, Ho Chi Minh."[3]

In 1970, at Fort Carson, Colorado, a white soldier—working part-time as a filling station attendant—murdered the head of the local university's Black studies program. Next came a confrontation between thirty-five military police officers and 150 Black soldiers, armed with handguns and a stash of M-1 carbines. Dong Tam base camp, in Vietnam's Mekong Delta, struggled with "roving gangs" of Black soldiers who attacked white soldiers at random. And at Fire Support Base Buttons, close to the Cambodian border, a few dozen Black soldiers debated how to "force ['whitey'] to pay attention to the blacks" without injuring anyone. They destroyed two helicopters.[4]

The following year, in Pyeongtaek, South Korea, adjacent to Camp Humphreys, a hundred Black soldiers attacked a local bar that had replaced soul music with country and western, shifting its focus from Black soldiers to white. At the 1st Cavalry Division's camp in the Central Highlands, Republic of Vietnam, a first sergeant ordered a Black soldier into the field with his platoon. His response: "You stop f——king with us, rabbit. We are not niggers; niggers are scared. We are black men and it don't matter." That afternoon, confronted by the troop commander, the soldier fired an automatic burst from his M16, at close range, into the commander's head. "Don't cover the rabbit up," he shouted when a staff sergeant tried to spread a poncho over the body. "All you rabbits take a good look; that's what we are going to do to all you rabbits."[5]

By 1972, in West Germany, officers and NCOs, Black and white, had begun refusing to enter barracks unless they were armed. In Stuttgart, a group of Black soldiers attacked a police station, using knives and broken bottles. The fight lasted for five hours.[6]

*Time* magazine called it "the war within the war," and the army's problem of race did seem more urgent in the context of the controversial and failing war in Vietnam.[7] Within the war, however, among men in combat, race was usually set aside. It was at the periphery of war where conflict flourished. Conflict was most likely when soldiers had too little to do, were bored and frustrated, left with little sense for why their presence mattered. Nonetheless, racial conflict extended from fire bases in Vietnam to army posts within the United States and to installations in West Germany, Korea, Thailand, and Okinawa. It spilled into the streets of surrounding communities, both within the United States and beyond.

"Race is my problem," a white NCO told a reporter in Frankfurt, West Germany, in 1970. "Not the Russians, not Vietnam." Race.[8]

And that same year Lt. Col. James S. White, the Black officer who in 1969 had begun briefing army commands, worldwide, on what he called "the race problem," described "a war which is being fought every night in barracks and other places where our soldiers gather." He—speaking at the behest of the army's chief and secretary—insisted that the "problem" must be addressed.[9]

R acial tension—and the prejudices and discrimination that fed it—was not new to the US Army. But in the months and years following the assassination of Martin Luther King Jr., Black enlisted men (and it was, almost without exception, men), along with sozme NCOs and officers, had begun to challenge the status quo. Some offered little more than rage and the violence that accompanied it; some presented thoughtful analysis and carefully considered solutions. Most fell somewhere in the middle. But in various ways, they demanded attention to their status as Black men and to the problems they faced within the US Army. Their demands were often confrontational, those confrontations more explosive because many angry and unwilling draftees, men of all races, had little investment in the institution of the army.

At a time when escalating Cold War tensions and increasing instability in the Middle East were exacerbating an already dangerous and volatile strategic environment, key military leaders came to believe that the growing racial crisis threatened their ability to defend the nation. Thus, it demanded attention. If racial conflict undermined the institution's very reason for being, their logic went, "the problem of race" had to be addressed.

Army leaders saw race as a problem because racial conflict disrupted military efficiency. There were certainly some who saw racial discrimination in the army, or the military more broadly, as a moral or ethical failing. But it was the disruption that forced attention, the looming crisis that brought racial conflict to the top of the army's list of concerns, second only to the war in Vietnam. (The continuing Cold War remained a concern, but that only further emphasized the need to deal with racial conflict among US troops in West Germany.)

That understanding—that race was a problem because it disrupted the proper function of the army—shaped army actions. And because conflict between Black and white enlisted men drove the crisis, the "problem" was defined as Black-and-white. Although Fort Carson's commander insisted, in a communication to his troops, that white soldiers, not black, were most responsible for racial conflict, it was primarily—though not always—white men doing the defining, and it was Black men who were challenging the status quo.[10] That does not mean that whites were ignored; army programs and regulations attempted to change the behavior of white enlisted men and officers, to educate them about Black history and the consequences of both "individual" and "institutional" racism. Nonetheless, there was often slippage. Many of those in positions of authority equated the problem of race —the growing racial conflict—with the demands of Black soldiers.

And Black soldiers *did* demand change. They disrupted. They challenged. They sought assistance from external groups, took their cases to the press, to members of Congress, even to the president. Many concluded, quite reasonably, that only by posing problems that could not be ignored could they force the army, as an institution, to address the discrimination and inequality they found in their army service. Such tactical actions, along with explosions of rage and frustration, further solidified the institutional army's focus: here, "race" meant Black.

Thus, as the army confronted its crisis of race, it did not encompass the range of racial and ethnic identities in America's Vietnam-era army. Even though some programs acknowledged the existence of—and difficulties faced by—the "Spanish-speaking" and Mexican Americans, Native Americans, Asian Americans, and even Appalachians, these groups always dropped quickly from sight. In the eyes of army leadership, members of those groups might be *experiencing* problems, but they were not *causing* problems. An army staff sergeant made that point in uncomfortably direct language in a letter to the editor of *Stars and Stripes*: Japanese Americans are "'our model minority.'" Mexican Americans "don't riot." "Wounded Knee is nothing compared to Watts and Detroit." The "poor mountaineer"? "An exhausted people in an exhausted land of exhausted hope." All have legitimate claims, as minorities, he wrote. But only "Blacks . . . promis[e] retaliation against personal and institutional racism." The system's focus on Black Americans, he concluded, had "something to do with fear."[11]

He had a point. As it applied to the army, however, that fear was not simply of violence. There were complaints about white commanders intimidated by Black troops, afraid of explosions that might be sparked in so many ways. But army leaders also feared the publicity drawn by racial conflict. They feared external intervention. They feared the disruptions that undermined the army's ability to fulfill its mission of national defense.

Therefore, just as army leaders framed the problem of race as Black and white, they also framed it as male. Until 1978, women belonged to a separate Women's Army Corps and, in the late 1960s, constituted even a smaller percentage (0.8) of active-duty strength than the 2 percent limit set by law until 1967. WACs rarely disrupted order in the US Army, but even as racial conflict—including some violence—surfaced among its approximately 13,000 members, army leaders did not see that conflict as especially significant. They were not concerned that racial conflict among WACs would disrupt the combat readiness of the army.[12]

In response to what army leaders defined as a critical problem, the institution focused its resources. Those army leaders (white and Black) who were charged with solving "the problem" often were surprisingly creative. Yes, certainly, some treated Black soldiers as the problem, but many more tried to assess and address Black soldiers' complaints. That meant, at times, challenging key premises and practices of the institution. Not surprisingly, they encountered roadblocks and resistance. Some resistance was blatantly racist. Some was generational (older Black NCOs and officers often included). Some individuals were sympathetic but had other priorities; some found the proposed solutions antithetical to the army's fundamental principles of discipline, order, hierarchical authority, and uniformed service.

This book explores the army's attempts to solve "the problem of race" in the context of those fundamental principles and in the broader context of what I shorthand as "institutional logic"—the collective force of the army's culture, history, and tradition, its structure and organization, its avowed mission and purpose, its policies and practices. I argue that the US Army's institutional logic shaped the ways in which its leaders and members defined the problem at hand. It made certain proposed solutions more likely than others. It determined, to a great extent, how those attempted solutions played out: what would most easily succeed; what would more likely fail.

More broadly, I am arguing that if we want to understand the process of social change in the modern United States, we have to look beyond the movements for social change. Change, most certainly, originates in the struggles and protests and demands of the oppressed and their allies. But such demands are rarely the end point, and few activists see them as such. To make a fundamental difference, change has to be enacted into law or translated into policy, and with sufficient mechanisms of enforcement to make the change significant. Change has to percolate through culture. And most fundamentally, change has to be managed through the institutions of American life, including its workplaces, its economic institutions and its purveyors of law and order, its schools and universities, its media—and in this case, the US Army, a massive and highly visible institution that touched the lives of tens of millions of Americans in the latter half of the twentieth century.

Military experience shaped how millions of young Americans during this era came to understand racial conflict and the struggle for racial justice in the United States: 9.1 million served on active duty in the US military over the course of the US war in Vietnam. During this era the US Army (sometimes within Department of Defense initiatives) focused directly on "the problem of race." And because the US Army had "an almost unlimited control over individual action" (in the words of a highly critical study from the Congressional Black Caucus), that focus forced soldiers' attention.[13]

In its attempts to solve the problem of race, the US Army could bring to bear tools that were unavailable to civilian institutions. Unlike civilian workplaces, schools and universities, or most other institutions of American life, the army is a hierarchical institution with far-reaching authority over its members. That authority gave it—again in the words of the Congressional Black Caucus—"a unique chance to begin the work of eliminating discrimination and racism."[14] As the army confronted the growing "problem" of race, it relied on the tools of hierarchy and authority. But it went further. In surprisingly wide-ranging efforts, the US Army pushed the boundaries of its institutional logic and challenged some of its fundamental principles.

The army's struggles over racial policy and practice were rarely simple, and they were never simply two-sided. Here, the challenges were great (large numbers of young men, Black and white, many of them unwilling draftees in a failing war, forced together day and night as currents of racial division and anger tore the nation apart) and the stakes were high (the ability of the US Army to defend the nation). External pressure was also intense, as organizations including the National Association for the Advancement of Colored People (NAACP) and the Congressional Black Caucus saw the military as an efficient use of their resources; success in the military sphere, they knew, could have immediate and profound effects. As Rep. Ron Dellums, cochair of the Congressional Black Caucus's hearings on racism in the military, noted, some who sought change were now focused on changing "fundamental institutions in this country so that they relate to human pride and human dignity." "As powerful as the military is," he insisted, "it will change."[15]

And it did. With both commitment and resistance, and always with mission held paramount, the US Army changed. As an institution, the army rejected claims of color blindness, insisting that "I see only one color and that's olive drab"—even when sincerely embraced—was no better than a "cop-out." It questioned the sanctity of the chain of command, tried new methods of leadership, altered the criteria for officer evaluation. It created new approaches to training and education (some of them definitely best left in the 1970s) and offered knowledge of soldiers' different histories and cultures as a means to understanding. It recognized that army regulations defaulted "white" and changed them; it experimented with allowing its members to claim identities that went beyond "soldier" and to display symbols that expressed those identities. It confronted off-post discrimination. It reformed portions of its system of military justice. And it implemented programs of affirmative action, seeking to make the army's officer corps resemble the makeup of the nation, even if it fell short of the racial balance of the enlisted ranks.

None of these changes was sufficient, if the goal was to *solve* the problem of race. As repeated testimony makes clear, much work remains to be done. But they did vastly improve the conditions of people of color in the US Army. And the reforms did accomplish their goal: they stabilized the institution.

In the end, this is a story replete with missteps and bad faith. But it is also a story of commitment, innovation, and success.

# 1
# A TACTIC OF SILENCE

On a humid afternoon in mid-October 1968, Maj. Lavell Merritt, described by one newspaper as "a uniformed Negro," strode into the official press briefing in Saigon and passed out copies of a statement asserting that "the American military services are the strongest citadels of racism on the face of the earth."[1]

Merritt had no official business in that room. His right to distribute such a statement was unclear and vigorously contested; by 1968 the military was struggling over the legal limits of dissent by those in uniform.[2] Merritt knew he was on tricky legal ground. He knew his actions were likely to have consequences. But this infantry officer, nearing the forced retirement that would mark the end of his army career, had concluded that he had nothing to lose and much to gain—to his mind, it was his manhood that was at stake.

The next day (on the other side of the international date line), Merritt's claims made the front page of the *Chicago Tribune*, with its banner slogan "The American Paper for Americans." The *Honolulu Star-Bulletin* headlined its story "Negro Major Finds Army Racism Strong." The *Los Angeles Times* offered "Negro Major Charges U.S. Army Is Racist." Similar claims appeared from Elmira, New York, to Hobbs, New Mexico, in America's small towns and big cities alike. With few exceptions, each paper ran a photo of Major Merritt, a fit-looking man of forty with close-cropped hair and the sort of heavy, black-framed glasses that would not become fashionable for decades. The *St. Louis Post-Dispatch* captioned his photo "Maj. Lavell Merritt Calls Army a 'Racist Organization.'"[3]

Most powerful was coverage in the *New York Times*, where Merritt's complaints ("Army Denounced by Negro Major: Equality and Justice Denied to Blacks, He Asserts") seemed simply confirmation of the heart-wrenching story *Times* editors placed adjacent to it. The parents of a twenty-one-year-old soldier, here shown receiving their son's posthumously awarded Bronze Star, had learned he was missing in action the same day they heard from the wife of another son, a soldier stationed in Germany, that the couple had been unable to rent an apartment there because of their race. "'And that afternoon,'" the grieving mother told reporters, "'still heavy with the cruelty of discrimination, the Army notified us that Fred was missing in action in Vietnam.'" Major Merritt, scant column-inches away, offered the broader lesson: "'The American people have for years been told that the military leads the nation in breaking down and eliminating all vestiges of segregation and discriminatory treatment of minority groups,' he said. 'This is a blatant lie.'"[4]

None of this was good news for the army, which had gotten a fair amount of mileage from the relative calm of its integrated forces as violence erupted in the civilian world, whether in the form of murderous attacks on those who sought their full rights or of cities in flames during the long hot summers of the mid-1960s. When Frederic Ellis Davison was promoted to brigadier general in September 1968, becoming only the third Black man to reach flag rank in the history of not only the army but the entire US military, he praised the army's "unbelievable progress" in race relations.[5] That was the story the army meant to tell, and one that many of its officers and NCOs, white and Black, endorsed. Not perfection, but progress.

From that perspective: it had been only twenty years since President Harry Truman ended official racial segregation in the US Armed Forces, and even fewer since segregation had ended in fact. How could one not applaud what had been accomplished? Not recognize the positive changes the army was making? Certainly, those who embraced the story of progress would concede, there were problems. A scarcity of Black faces in positions of leadership and command? True. But they could not pull generals out of nowhere; there was no possibility of lateral hires, no fast-track from second lieutenant to brigadier general. The army was starting to grow a cohort of Black leaders, to move past the poor decisions of the past. That would take time, the story went, but it would happen.

And off-post housing? That was a perpetual issue, most particularly in the American South and in Germany. President John F. Kennedy's Committee on Equal Opportunity in the Armed Forces had highlighted the problem back in 1961. But surrounding communities were not under military control, and relationships were especially tricky in host nations. Those who saw progress acknowledged that civilian discrimination was a problem. They nonetheless emphasized the changes accomplished and to come.

What of the indignities of "boy," the outrage of "nigger," the casual racism in the daily life of the enlisted man? Many whites never registered that language, or they paid it no heed. They had come of age where such words were common, or they saw them as no different than "pollock" and "wop" and "kike" in a sergeant's vocabulary of abuse. Countering such lapses were tales of the "notable camaraderie between the races" at Fort Bragg, the insistence from Vietnam that "we don't talk or think race out here; we depend on each other too much. . . . I see only one color and that's olive drab."[6]

Such interpretations seem undeniably self-serving, especially in retrospect. They were, however, in keeping with both external and internal analysis. Sociologist Charles Moskos, who had spent a year studying the issue, concluded in 1966 that (in the words of the *Washington Post*) the army was an "Example of Integration's Success." *Time* magazine told its close to 20 million readers in late 1966 that "despite a few blemishes, the armed forces remain the model of the reasonably integrated society that the U.S. looks forward to in a new generation." Black leaders agreed, praising the military for its progress, endorsing it as a model for the nation. And where it may have mattered most, inside the army, race did not make the list of command concerns. When the secretary of defense received a top secret briefing on Vietnam soldiers' morale in July 1967, he heard about the use of "marihuana" and narcotics, rising courts-martial rates, and the extent of the black market—but not a word about race.[7]

Just two years later, by late summer of 1969, both the army chief and its secretary would put race second only to the war itself in their catalog of concerns. In this shift, as in so much else for the army and for the nation, 1968 marked a turning point.

In civilian society, by 1968, racial conflict was both pervasive and explosive. The quest for equal rights, for full integration into a color-blind society —the model for which the "only one color and that's olive drab" army got so much praise—persisted. But it was increasingly challenged by those who embraced Black power and Black pride, who rejected patience and slow progress, who, in the wake of violence that reached back to the holds of slave ships and forward to the assassination of Martin Luther King Jr., were willing to seek freedom "by any means necessary."

The army did not—could not—stand fully apart from the society it served. It had become increasingly impossible, by this point in the war, to construct and enforce boundaries between worlds military and civilian. For the war in Vietnam demanded men. US Army strength almost doubled between 1961 and 1968, increasing by more than 700,000 uniformed personnel. Not all those troops were in Vietnam; over a hundred nations had some (often quite small) US military presence in 1968, with twenty-five hosting at least 1,000 uniformed Americans. Most of the military forces not in the United States and its territories (1.9 million) or Vietnam (537,000) were stationed in West Germany (214,000), the Republic of Korea (62,000), and Japan/Okinawa (83,000).[8] But the wartime demand for men changed the shape and, to some extent, the character of the army.

It was young men, raised in the turmoil of 1960s revolt, who would swell the army's ranks over the course of this increasingly unpopular war. Whether draftees or volunteers (many of whom were draft-motivated), the great majority of these men did not plan an army career. Their long-term allegiance was not to the institution and its culture and practices. Their ties to home and the weight of their civilian identities were less fully eclipsed in the two (draftees) or three (volunteer) years the military required of them than had been the case with men who had joined before the war, and the practice of rotating individuals, rather than units, through yearlong tours in Vietnam left men bound less tightly to their brothers-in-arms.

Perhaps the army's racial problems did come from without, as army leaders would repeatedly insist. It is not likely that the army, as an institution, became strikingly more racist within the course of a single year. But as the nature of the struggles over race changed in the civilian world, those changes could not fail to touch some of those who served in uniform. And as the army inducted large numbers of young men, many against their will, most would carry with them the beliefs and prejudices of their civilian origins. Some number of them would almost certainly see continuing racism where the army claimed progress. And some of them would reject the constraints that had, in earlier years, made the army seem a model for the rest of the nation.

In 1968 the army first confronted the emerging racial crisis. That blunt claim in no way denies that racism and racial discrimination pervaded the army before that date, even if its force, by the mid-1960s, was generally less powerful than in civilian life. But it was in 1968 that the *reactions* to racism within the army began to change. It was in 1968 that race began to trouble the stability of the nation's armed forces. It was in 1968 that the army as an institution began, in stuttering and incomplete fashion, to perceive race as a problem.

What that perception meant, for the institutional army, was not yet clear. Amid all the challenges of 1968, the problem of race registered incompletely. Even as units of the Army National Guard were mobilized to pacify uprisings in America's Black inner-city neighborhoods, white army officers tended to see racial conflict within their army as isolated incidents best handled at the local level. And while a pattern of growing conflict, alienation, and violence is clear in retrospect, in 1968 leaders found some cause for optimism. The army managed to avoid widespread violence in the wake of the Reverend Martin Luther King's assassination in April—though King's murder undoubtedly fed the alienation of Black soldiers throughout the army and throughout the world, and the fact that some white soldiers had celebrated his death would not soon be forgotten.

But two very different events that year—one a minor battle of words, the other a violent conflict that left smoldering ruins and a young private dead at the hands of his fellow soldiers—forced the US Army to begin to deal with what army leaders would soon dub "the problem of race." One was Maj. Lavell Merritt's venture into that press briefing in Saigon and the investigations that surrounded it. The other was the uprising of Black prisoners in the stockade at the army's sprawling Long Binh Post, just northeast of Saigon. These conflicts were just two of many. But in each case, the responses of army authority to the actions of Black servicemen give a sense for how reluctantly the US Army, as an institution, began to confront its emerging crisis.

### THE INVESTIGATION OF MAJ. LAVELL MERRITT, OCTOBER 1968

When Major Merritt entered the press room in Saigon, he was prepared to be shut down. And as he told reporters afterward, he was ready to face whatever retribution might come "like a man," now that he had had his say.[9] In fact, no one in that room had tried to prevent Merritt from passing out copies of his statement or then to prevent journalists from asking him questions after the press briefing concluded.

At first, Merritt likely felt he had triumphed. Certainly a few reporters— most particularly those back home who transformed the Associated Press filing into articles for their local papers—ended their stories with Gen. Frederic Davison's "unbelievable progress," thus undermining Merritt's more extreme claims. Several, citing army sources, noted inaccurately that Major Merritt had been passed over for promotion twice (or perhaps thrice); the *Los Angeles Times* suggested that those decisions might be the source of his "pique."[10] But all in all, the papers gave voice to his message: despite its claims to the contrary, the army was a racist institution.

Merritt's message was, in fact, much less coherent.[11] His statement ran to eight pages of single-spaced type. It was rambling in structure and inconsistent in tone, veering between sentences seemingly well rehearsed and

Maj. Lavell Merritt made international news in 1968 when he accused the US Army of being a "citadel of racism." Here he appears on the cover of *Urban Magazine*, a Black-oriented US publication. *Courtesy Collection of the Smithsonian National Museum of African American History and Culture.*

suited to a civil rights–era pulpit and perhaps equally well-rehearsed insults and crude, sexualized claims. Merritt's anger and frustration were palpable, and they undermined portions of his message even as they gave it power.

He had begun, Merritt explained in his second paragraph, to reject "those who represent maintenance of the status quo, who beguile the people with twisted truths and slanted facts; those whose mastery of deceit and subterfuge is likely unequalled in the history of all mankind." By the fourth page, he was railing against white officers, "at least seventy five percent [of whom] were raised by black mammys." Every one of them, he continued, "was dearly loved by that mammy who was also his fathers mistress"—and thus had something in common with him, "for I was also raised by a black woman and I will admit that she too slept with my father."[12]

Black officers did not escape his ire: he branded most "accommodationists," "Uncle Toms," and "hanky heads." Merritt most directly challenged the "black general" who offered "false promises of equality, freedom and justice in the military." "I do so," he wrote, in a return to elevated language, "in the name and for the sake of truth, for the real advancement of equality, for the real advancement of justice and to hasten the attainment of freedom with the measure of dignity our constitution prescribes for all Americans."[13]

Most fundamentally, Merritt wrote of manhood—his own and that of his fellow Black officers. As Black officers, Merritt claimed, they had served as "useful pawns in the effort to maintain the facade of equal opportunity." That, to him, was a failing. The "real tragedy," however, lay in their "self-denial of manhood." "How long does it take for a man to know he is a man," he asked, forgoing question marks. "What must he feel before he feels like a man. And how much will he endure before he decides it would be better to die like a man." Ending the rhetorical sequence of questions, he asserted, "I am a man, a black American man."[14]

In Merritt's world of dawning consciousness, the path to manhood was not an individual journey of self-discovery. "Manhood" was a powerful language of racial awakening, a rejection of repeated humiliation and insult. After all, the sanitation workers' strike that brought Martin Luther King to Memphis the April night he was murdered took as its slogan "I AM A MAN." It was in that spirit that Merritt concluded his statement with a message to his sons, "who have witnessed my debasement and suffered this humiliation and indignity that I was to[o] insensitive to feel all these years": "I dedicate the remainder of my life to earn again your respect."[15]

Merritt had begun by introducing himself as "a black American now serving my country to the best of my ability as part of our Army in Vietnam." But even as his claims became painfully personal, he neglected the information that would have given his words greater weight.

Lavell Merritt had been born in Tuscaloosa, Alabama, shortly before the great economic crash of 1929, though he later moved to a poor Black neighborhood in Chicago. He had joined the army in early 1949, soon after Truman ended the legal segregation of the US military with Executive Order 9981. The young enlisted man had been selected for officer candidate school and had risen to the rank of major. In the course of his career, Merritt had been deployed overseas six times; in 1968 he was completing his second tour in Vietnam. His awards included an Army Commendation Medal for his service in the Office of the Inspector General (IG) at Fort Leonard Wood, the Combat Infantryman Badge, the Vietnamese Gallantry Cross with Silver Star and with Palm, and the Bronze Star.[16] By the metrics of the institution in which he served, Merritt had done well.

It is true that none of the officers in the Saigon press briefing had prevented Merritt from distributing his statement or from speaking with reporters. But that did not mean they ignored the provocation. Copies of Merritt's anti-army diatribe were carried back to various offices. The next day, even as Merritt prepared for the possibility of a televised discussion on NBC, the chief of staff of the US Military Assistance Command, Vietnam (MACV), initiated an investigation of alleged misconduct on the part of Major Merritt.[17]

There was a significant backstory to that investigation; it was not solely the result of Merritt's press release. And, perhaps paradoxically, it was Merritt's own recent request for command assistance, in which he cited Army Regulation 600-21: Equal Opportunity and Treatment of Military Personnel and sought "release from the psychological intimidation and harassment being perpetrated against me" that most directly prompted the inspector general's investigation. But the IG did not focus on the intimidation and harassment of Major Merritt. He focused on Merritt himself.[18]

The investigation into Merritt's alleged misconduct, records of which include not only official reports but the verbatim transcription of more than thirty interviews and highly revealing summaries of each, demonstrates what tools the army brought to bear on "the problem of race" at the start of its struggles. And the responses of the inspector general, MACV; the staff judge advocate, MACV; and the chief of staff, MACV, demonstrate how very uneasy the army was with race, made visible.

In short, the IG's office found Major Merritt to be obsessed with race. It ignored failures of leadership on the part of those who found themselves "uncomfortable" talking about race and so created a potentially unnecessary problem. It equated discussions of racial discrimination with militancy and potential violence. It failed to follow up on alleged threats against Major Merritt's physical safety, and instead sought evidence that Merritt had verbally denied both the army's "progress" on race and the significance of its recently promoted Black general as evidence of such progress. And it ignored Merritt's claims of racial discrimination, investigating, instead, how Merritt's claims about race affected his white subordinates. Within the space of a month, following up on the IG investigation, the staff attorney general had compiled a list of four potential criminal charges to be preferred against the major who had sought command assistance.[19]

Judging from both the investigation testimonies and his own words, Merritt does seem to have been a difficult man. Both peers and subordinates described him as arrogant, prone to dominate conversations, certain always that he was in the right and willing to embarrass others to prove himself so. He tended toward grand schemes, often far exceeding the parameters of his responsibility or the appropriateness of the situation, and while they were never for personal profit, they did tend to raise eyebrows.[20] It is clear that he had never fully developed the leadership skills necessary to forge men into a team, though it is worth pointing out how unlikely it was that a Black officer would find a strong mentor in developing such skills during the 1950s and early 1960s, as well as how challenging it had become to motivate troops in post-Tet Vietnam.

Even acknowledging the weight of history stacked against him, it is possible that there were reasons Merritt had not been recommended for promotion. His writings suggest a certain lack of balance, though by the time he typed both his statement and appeal he had lost any incentive to moderation. It is also certain that both institutional and personal racism had undermined his career.

What is at stake here, however, are not the successes and failures of one Black major. It is instead the ways that the army approached the problem that major presented. It is, in broader terms, how the army approached racial conflict. The investigation of Lavell Merritt demonstrates how poorly prepared the army was to face the challenges that lay ahead.

t was on the third day of the Tet Offensive in early 1968 that Major Merritt took up his new assignment as a deputy senior advisor at Dong Da National Training Center, near Da Nang. Since "rockets [had come] in and destroyed part of the building" during the Tet attacks, the training team's senior advisor, Lt. Col. Wray Bradley, invited Merritt to share his room. According to Bradley they "got very friendly," discussing "everything in the world" as they lay awake at night in their shared room, including Merritt's belief that he had been not been selected for promotion because he was Black. "Val," Colonel Bradley remembered saying, "I'd be glad to help you out and to show you my heart is on the right side and there is no malice, no prejudice, no nothing. I said I think you are imagining a lot of this and . . . I'm going to show you that my heart is on the right side."[21]

When Bradley received his next assignment he pushed Merritt for his replacement; the slot was meant for a lieutenant colonel, but men of that rank were in short supply so "they were trying to find a major who could hold it down." Bradley's supervisor was a bit "leary [sic]," noting that, in his estimation, Merritt's past record was "none too good." And, in fact, Merritt's three prior evaluations had declined precipitously from "exceptional" to "effective," with comments citing "a need for close supervision and a substandard performance of duties."[22]

Bradley, however, insisted that Merritt had done a great job for him and made that claim official, awarding Merritt an "exceptional" rating on his OER (Officer Efficiency Report), with not a word of criticism, constructive or otherwise.[23] Whether it was Bradley's recommendation or the shortage of lieu-

*A Tactic of Silence*

tenant colonels that made the difference, Merritt got the position. On the first of May, when Bradley departed, Merritt took command of Advisory Team 5.

What happened next is not completely clear, despite the hundreds of pages of testimony compiled in the IG investigation. Bradley had departed quickly, leaving an outstanding mess bill and some personal items, including a couple of enemy weapons he had had mounted for display. When the weapons arrived at his new post in poor condition, Bradley blamed Merritt. But Bradley also seems to have felt that Merritt had not been grateful enough to him; in his testimony months later Bradley kept pointing out all he had done for Merritt. He could not quite let go of the fact that Merritt never once came to visit him in Da Nang. "Well, hell no, he hasn't," Bradley said. "He could come down here. . . . I would appreciate that he did. Sort of expected him to really. Thought we were good friends. But something happened. I don't know what the hell it was."[24]

Whatever his motivation, Bradley contacted the MACV Training Directorate in June to report that things were "going to pot" in Dong Da. In the process of sorting out his outstanding fifteen-dollar mess bill, he had heard a couple of complaints about Merritt and had decided to follow up on them. The directorate took Bradley's claim seriously. In a late July briefing, officers instructed Merritt's newly assigned deputy, Maj. James Irving, to keep an eye on Merritt and report back to headquarters on Merritt's actions. Irving did not like going behind Merritt's back. But as ordered, he kept Saigon updated on the situation in Team 5.[25]

Merritt, in the meantime, had grand ideas for his command. He wanted to install a putting green and a swimming pool ("really not in keeping with the austere theme of things," noted the lieutenant colonel who later replaced Merritt as senior advisor, especially given that it rained four months a year in Dong Da). He imagined the mess—which was shared by officers and enlisted men and doubled as an open bar—transformed into something more "luxurious," offering theme nights with Spanish, French, and Italian menus.[26]

Merritt also positioned himself as a defender of Vietnamese rights. He thought the men under his command should study the Vietnamese language and learn about Vietnamese culture, and so he set up lessons—with required attendance. "Moaning, groaning, and complaining" ensued. And when Merritt got into an argument over the Seabees' use of a portion of the training center's property in late June, he told the navy officer in charge that many Americans were in Vietnam only to "feather their own nest" and were quite willing to "screw the Vietnamese people and the ARVN forces." Things became heated enough that the marine MACV chief of staff contacted his army counterpart. In response, an army team determined that Merritt's comments were "inimical" to the interests of the US military, and an overzealous lieutenant colonel proposed charging Merritt with blackmail and extortion in his dealings with the military real estate office.[27]

Concurrently, over the course of his command of Team 5, Merritt began talking more about race—about the situation of Black Americans in the United States, and of Black soldiers in the army. Capt. Richard Heroux was eating dinner in the mess soon after he arrived at Dong Da when Major Merritt dropped a copy of the Kerner report (which examined the causes of the recent civil disorder in the United States) on the table and asked him what he thought of it. Heroux tried to excuse himself, explaining that since he had not read the report or paid much attention to it he really was not qualified to discuss it, but Merritt insisted that he stay to "get educated"; that education lasted until well after midnight. After a conversation in the club with Sgt. Robert Lee Hall, who (in his own words) became "quite heated" in his condemnations of "the burning and protesting and so forth that was going on back in the states," the "problem with the racial [sic]" that was "way out of hand," Major Merritt brought him a magazine article about living conditions for "Negro personnel" back home.[28]

Merritt meant to educate, but his efforts often were not welcome. Recalled Heroux: "Once he started talking on this civil rights thing, he went kind of, well, like a man who was really fighting for a cause and tried to push it on everybody." And because Merritt was so knowledgeable, Heroux complained, "he would always have the facts to back up his particular field and made us all feel like we were kind of inferior."[29] A consensus was building in the otherwise all-white Team 5 that Merritt was too preoccupied with questions of race.

But from May to late August there was only one real confrontation, and that took place with someone outside Merritt's command when a buddy of the marine liaison at Dong Da interrupted a conversation Merritt was having with Captain Heroux. The captain had bought the marine a coffee earlier, and he wanted to reciprocate with a beer. Merritt took offense. "Besides being rude what else do you do?" he asked the man, who replied that he was first sergeant for an infantry company. Merritt persisted, and the marine pushed back: "Well, I kill gooks ever once in a while." Merritt's response, "And you probably kill niggers too, don't you?" got the reply, "Well, you said that, Major. I didn't." Although everyone had been drinking fairly heavily, it ended there; Major Merritt instructed the marine liaison to see his friend off the compound.[30]

But things came to a head on the evening of August 22. It is not clear whether Merritt simply drank too much and lost control or whether the men who shared the bar with him just got tired of the intensity of his focus on race. That night, in the course of downing "numerous martinis," Merritt "got on the racial kick." He was loud and opinionated and dominated the room, wandering from person to person, holding forth. Most of the conversation was between Merritt and Sergeant Nicely, a Special Forces NCO who had bar privileges there. The two men argued back and forth, getting heated, then backing off. Merritt, agitated, pounded his hand on the bar. Nicely once threatened to hit Merritt. At one point Merritt propelled a chair toward the bar door, though accounts vary as to whether the chair was thrown, slammed, or given an "underhanded toss."[31]

Merritt's focus on race was not solely Black-and-white. He challenged Nicely's use of the term "zipperhead" to describe the Vietnamese: Why not use it to their face?, he asked. And Nicely, every bit as drunk as Merritt, obliged. Merritt's language declined, as well. He called himself (and perhaps others, though only two other men in the room over the course of the evening were Black) "nigger"; white enlisted men got labeled "honky," "cracker," and "white trash." ("I didn't know what he meant by being crackers," one NCO from North Carolina later testified.) He referred to "lowly sergeants." And he spoke the sexually charged language of late-sixties racial pride, claiming not only that Black men were the sons of kings but that once a white woman had been with a Black man, she would never want white men again.[32]

Sgt. Jackie Bivins, the marine liaison, thought things were getting out of hand. He went looking for the deputy senior advisor, Major Irving, but Irving and the other ranking officers (all three hanging out together in one room) perhaps understandably declined to intervene. "He's the Senior Advisor," Irving said.[33]

In the meantime, Sergeant Hall, the one who had no truck with the "burning and protesting," decided—from the other end of the bar, where he was nursing a Coke—that he had had enough. Merritt had unplugged the jukebox more than once that night; he said he was getting hoarse from shouting over the music. Hall plugged it in again and dropped his quarters. Merritt got mad; he told Hall to stop the music and leave the bar. Hall asked whether that was an order, and he got an affirmative reply. When Hall did not move immediately to obey, Merritt went to find Captain Heroux, the duty officer, who then escorted Hall to his room.[34] Not much later, things trailed off.

The next morning Major Merritt was apologetic; one officer remembered that Merritt told him he had done a "'Rap Brown' routine" (referring to the

Black Power activist) the previous night to help people learn how to "combat such antics" when they got back to the States. But he definitely told more than one person that he was considering an Article 15 (nonjudicial punishment) for Sergeant Hall and would make up his mind during his scheduled R&R. Merritt left Dong Da that morning.[35]

That same morning Major Irving, along with another major and a captain, called Saigon. It was not long before two senior officers from the training directorate in Saigon, along with a representative from the MACV inspector general's office, arrived at the training center in Dong Da. Even though this was not an official investigation, the team interviewed six people, including Major Irving.[36]

The captain who had contacted Saigon began his testimony with a broad complaint about Merritt's behavior: "During my assignment to Team 5, Major Merritt has continually cajoled and harassed some of the officers and non-commissioned officers about racial problem[s] in the States, and the fact that he is a Negro Officer." Captain Miller continued: "[Merritt] stopped people in the lounge, in the mess, or other places on the compound and tried to bait them to learn of their prejudices and to get them to admit that they are prejudiced against Negroes." As evidence of Merritt's misconduct, he offered a version of the "you said that, Major, I didn't" story.[37] Other testimony focused more narrowly on the events of August 22, though all were, one way or another, about Merritt's discussions of race.

Merritt, in the meantime, knew nothing of the unofficial investigation, and members of Team 5 were instructed not to tell him about it when he returned.[38]

The senior officer from the training directorate also, while in Dong Da, decided to replace Major Merritt as senior advisor, and he did not keep that decision to himself. When Merritt returned, Major Irving let slip the news —not of the investigation, but of the pending replacement. (In other words, Merritt was informed by a subordinate that he was losing his position of command.) Within days, Merritt received official world of his transfer to Saigon. There were now a sufficient number of lieutenant colonels to fill Team 5's senior advisor position at the authorized grade, the head of the training directorate explained, while assuring Merritt that the Saigon office would benefit from his "considerable experience."[39]

Merritt reported to Saigon as ordered. And on his first day he was summoned to the inspector general's office, read his rights, and charged with conspiring to blackmail the US government (a charge stemming from the conflict with the real estate office back in June). The IG's office would not clarify the allegations, and on the following day, in a telephone call, the major handling the case told Merritt that the inquiry was "at that time dormant." Merritt did not want such charges hanging over his head; he believed they were easily refuted. But his protests were to no avail.[40]

It seems to have been the following day that Merritt received a poor evaluation for his role as senior advisor for Team 5. Feeling bitter and betrayed, Merritt submitted a request for command assistance. And he continued to stew. Two days later Merritt sat down at a typewriter and began to compose the statement that would guarantee the attention not only of MACV command but of the American public as well.

To sum up, thus far: Merritt's insistent focus on racial inequality had so disturbed two white officers under his command that they had contacted Saigon with their concerns. In response, senior officers from the training directorate and inspector general's office had come to Dong Da, knowing that Merritt was away on leave, and conducted an investigation of Merritt's behavior. They never discussed either the complaints or their findings with Major Merritt, and they ordered members of Team 5 to keep the conditions of their visit from him. Based on this visit, due to "evidence of misconduct," the training directorate decided to replace Major Merritt and appoint a new senior advisor.[41] However, the letter notifying Merritt of his transfer offered only compliments on his role at Dong Da and an offer of new opportunities.

The training directorate had decided to bury the question of race, to avoid the racial issues at the heart of this story.

But Merritt had just been called into the IG's office and read his rights, and he had received a devastating efficiency report on his sole command experience, one that virtually guaranteed he would be neither promoted nor retained in rank. He had lost faith in the story of racial progress. He was not going to be silent.

And so the official investigation began, made necessary by the request for command assistance and almost certainly shaped by Merritt's public complaints. Lt. Col. Clifford Wagner, from the MACV inspector general's office, initiated a series of interviews at Dong Da on the morning of October 16. Oddly enough, Colonel Wagner was under the impression that Major Merritt had been relieved of command, rather than transferred and replaced; Merritt's replacement, the new senior advisor, corrected him twice before his misperception registered.[42]

In gathering evidence about the night of August 22, Wagner largely focused on language used and the spirit behind it. There was, after all, no violence. No one had been injured; there were no direct consequences of the event.

Wagner asked frequent questions about Merritt's exact words: Did he say "dumb ass sergeant" or "stupid sergeant"? Did he call only himself "nigger," or did he use that word about others? Did he directly belittle individuals, or were the terms more general? Did other people in the bar use such language as well? Could the waitresses hear?[43]

"Do you remember the word 'Mother fucker,' being used in the club that night?" Wagner asked a Black cook. "Yes sir," the sergeant answered, but he made the point that seems obvious. "Occasionally sir, you sit around the table with a few guys and they get to drinking a little they will say these things. It is not that they are saying it directly to a person, it's their words of speaking." Nonetheless, the IG's office did seem authentically concerned about offensive language, as the report's appendix containing these testimonies was preceded by the warning, on an otherwise blank sheet of paper, "THIS FILE CONTAINS OBSCENE MATERIAL." [44]

But over and over, even as people testified, without hesitation, that Merritt's behavior that night was not that of an officer and a gentleman (or even of a man, one insisted, while another ventured that it was "unbecoming to a soldier or to an American or to anyone"), most also made clear that—even though Merritt often held forth about race—such unacceptable behavior was not usual or habitual. Wagner, in several instances, pushed further, "puzzled" as to why, "because of one incident," it seemed necessary to appeal to higher authorities. Wagner's demand for specific incidents of concern drew fairly lame examples from both Irving and Miller, two of the men who had called Saigon on the morning of August 23, but Miller insisted that he had made a judgment call and Irving said that he had contacted the training directorate because he felt unable to cope with the situation.[45]

Eventually, in the course of questioning, the possibility of violence did arise. It seems that one sergeant in Team 5 had been heard threatening to shoot Major Merritt. Others, too, Captain Miller ventured, might be angry enough to take physical action. And Major Irving said he thought a couple of officers were on the verge of mutiny.[46]

Merritt, it seemed, had frequently corrected two captains, often in front of other officers and even around enlisted men. According to Major Irving, the two felt "badgered, badgered, and badgered," and had complained to him about "racial overtones." Yet another major, while condemning Merritt's practice as poor leadership technique, said the corrections themselves were well deserved. These officers were new at their jobs and making little effort to learn them, he said, and they resented the fact that Merritt was pressuring them to do better.[47]

Sergeant First Class Willie Nelson concurred: too often, he reported, when Merritt issued orders, officers "would take them with a grain of salt and act on them rather nonchalantly." The issue was mainly with the two captains, Heroux and Waltman, but Merritt had also frequently corrected one NCO: Vincent Paulson, the man who later threatened to shoot him. "Well, he's not the greatest NCO in the world," admitted Irving. He "needed correcting. If [Merritt] hadn't done it, I probably would have done it myself."[48]

There were clearly problems with morale in Team 5, but people did not agree on their cause. As an Air Division technical sergeant who lived on the compound explained, the men did not have enough work to keep them busy. Maj. Richard Stanton, also from outside the team, said that he, as senior advisor, would have run the team just like Major Merritt had, "minus the arguments." The problem at Team 5, Stanton said, was not Merritt's leadership at the training center. There, he was on an "even keel." The problem was with Merritt's "constant conversations" on "race, discrimination, rioting back in the states" and his tendency to "bait" men, ensnaring them in arguments that allowed them no acceptable answer.[49]

Time and time again, the conversation came back to race. The most striking testimony on the subject comes from Merritt's second-in-command. By the time the investigator got to Major Irving, the second of his interviewees, he had figured out that the story was more complicated than he had anticipated. He grew increasingly frustrated as he questioned Major Irving, not once, but twice.

Irving assured Wagner *twice* that he and Merritt "got on famously" but stammered and stumbled as Wagner continued to press him about why, then, he did not simply talk to Merritt about whatever problem he perceived rather than make a call to higher command. "I get kind of aggravated," Irving said, "everybody telling me these things; and I figured it was my place to call somebody cause hell I just didn't want to confront the boss with it." Wagner kept working his way back to the issue, and Irving finally said it directly: "Well, there was so much racial overtone in it, sir. I've lived in Alabama just about all my life and I didn't want to let it appear that there was any differentiation there. Now a major from Alabama and a negro officer, and I'm not prejudice. . . . You understand what I mean. I tried to avoid the issue in a way, which is probably wrong. I don't know."[50]

As evidence of mounting problems in Team 5, Irving recounted a conversation he had partially overheard. Once it became clear that the conversation "had racial overtones," Irving said, he had "backed out." "I heard the words 'civil rights', what's the other one that goes along with it, 'equality', and I said oh, I don't want to hear any more of that, so I left." And when Wagner asked why Irving had not gone into the bar to intervene—as requested—on the night of August 22, Irving did not point out that his position in Team 5 was subordinate to Merritt's. He told Wagner he had been reluctant to get involved because of Merritt's "boisterous arrogant attitude," continuing, "I stated before in my tape, me being from Alabama, I just didn't want to let this appear to be a racial issue."[51]

Irving, whether "prejudice" or not, had been paralyzed by his discomfort over race. It was Irving's inability to address the problem of race that escalated the situation—both his reluctance to intervene on the night of August 22 and his eagerness to pass along responsibility to Saigon for anything with "racial overtones." Asked, at the end of his second testimony, whether he had any further comments to offer, Irving concluded, "No sir. Not really, except this is the most embarrassing situation I've ever been in."[52] Based solely on his testimony, Irving appears to have been one of the most hapless majors in the history of the US Army. But he was right. He could not cope. He lacked both natural capacity and experience, and he had not been trained for this.

Wagner wrapped up his investigation in Dong Da over the course of four days, and the final report went forward to the commander's office on October 29, following a few interviews elsewhere. But the final report was completed by the chief of the inspections division, not by Colonel Wagner. And much changed in the process. It is not that the final report was dishonest, exactly, but none of the nuance evident in Wagner's investigation appeared, nor was the five-inch-thick volume of testimony forwarded to the MACV chief of staff. Replacing the testimonies were brief summaries, as revealing for what they omitted as for what was included.

There was no mention, for example, of problems with the performance of Captains Heroux and Waltman or with the behavior of Sergeant Paulson. The physical threats against Merritt were absent. The summary of the testimony from Merritt's replacement itemized allegations he heard on his arrival: that Merritt was falsifying civilian pay records, having an affair, misusing funds from the mess association. It omitted his repeated statements that he had found no evidence for such charges. On the other hand, the new senior advisor also told Wagner that it seemed Bradley had interfered in Team 5 after his departure, undermining Merritt's command. That charge went missing from testimony to summary. And Irving's account was of racial badgering and arrogance, not of his own unwillingness to act.[53]

Every positive comment anyone had made about Major Merritt, along with any negative comment about anyone in his command, disappeared in the transition from testimony to summary—in all cases but one. An air force technical sergeant was quoted as saying that Major Merritt was the biggest advocate of Black Power he had ever seen and that Merritt told him he meant to "kill people like us" when he got home so the "colored race" could take over. But—possibly out of concern that a case so unrelenting became less convincing—the summary also included his claim that Team 5's problem was too much free time and his insistence that he found Major Merritt to be "an outstanding officer."[54]

The investigator general's report essentially dismissed the charges surrounding the real estate office in Dong Da but produced a new set of charges: Merritt had an "obsessive preoccupation with matters pertaining to racial discrimination and the civil rights movement" and had "oppressively abused" his subordinates "through frequent leading and argumentative discussions with them on these matters." The report also recommended that the IG's office begin a new investigation into Merritt's management of the mess association fund.[55]

The IG's office then recommended action against Major Merritt under the Uniform Code of Military Justice. MACV command approved the report. According to usual procedure, it then went to the Office of the Staff Judge Advocate for review and compilation of potential charges.

Col. Robert Ivey, the staff judge advocate, found four obvious incidents of criminal misconduct. First, Merritt had engaged in conduct unbecoming an officer and a gentleman in the Dong Da National Training Center's open mess on August 22, arguing with "various enlisted men about racial matters (a subject he initiated and persisted in discussing)," "contemptuously" referring to Lt. Gen. Benjamin O. Davis Jr. of the US Air Force as an "Uncle Tom," and insisting that "once a white woman had a negro she would never go back to a white man." Second, he had falsified the work report of his civilian Vietnamese secretary, crediting her with eight illegitimate hours. Third, he had released an eight-page news article to the press without proper review. And finally, when a fellow officer reminded him of the "many successful negro officers," citing two, Merritt had dismissed them as "House Niggers."[56]

Colonel Ivey's outrage was palpable, and he made clear that he was confident Merritt would be found guilty, at least on the first charge. But he immediately offered a caution. Such a trial would be time-consuming and expensive. And while it might possibly discredit Merritt with the press, it would also give him a platform. A trial would provide Merritt with more publicity, Ivey wrote. Unstated was the more significant point: it would also bring publicity to the army and its growing problem with race. And so Ivey made a recommendation that went against his own desires. "Although it hurts me to say this," he wrote, "for the overall good of the command, I recommend . . . that Major Merritt be removed from the command and retired as soon as possible."[57]

Thus Lavell Merritt was retired "contrary to [his] desire" on January 31, 1969, at the end of his twenty years of service. In the years to come, he maintained both his commitment to racial change and his capacity for grand ideas, but his focus no longer was the US Army.[58]

Shortly before he was retired from active duty, Merritt wrote to his commander in chief, President Lyndon Baines Johnson:

When I publicly accused the Military of harboring Citadels (strong holds) of racism, I knew full well the scope of the battle I was joining. I understood the magnitude of bitterness and animosity that would be heaped upon me for daring to make such an accusation. But I did not know the extent and depth of the fear that permeates the military hierarchy. Fear for loss of position or favor, fear of being identified as one who supports changes toward dignity and just treatment for all humans, fear of admitting that we do have race problems.[59]

The case of Major Merritt demonstrates how poorly the army, as an institution, was prepared to deal with the problem of race. Whatever failures accrued to Major Merritt, the failures of the institution were greater. Officers had no training in managing issues of race, even as the racial disruptions of civilian life filtered into the army. The official reports issued by the Office of the Inspector General and the staff judge advocate betray a level of insensitivity—and of racial prejudice—that would come to haunt them over years to come. And the tactic of silence, which worked briefly and partially in the case of one increasingly frustrated Black major in 1968, would soon be no more than coal on the flames.

### THE LONG BINH JAIL RIOT

It was a week, almost to the hour, from the time Major Merritt had tossed both that fateful chair and his career in the open mess bar in Dong Da. Shortly before midnight on August 29, 1968, a small group of inmates in Long Binh Jail (LBJ)—the US Army's stockade in Vietnam—overpowered a guard, relieved him of his keys, and unleashed a storm of uncontrolled violence and systematic destruction. These men were soon joined by others, and in the hours that followed, about 200 men, a number of them released from

On August 29, 1968, a group of inmates in Long Binh Jail, Vietnam, seized control of the stockade, setting fire to buildings and beating both guards and other inmates. This is what remained of the LBJ mess building on August 30. *Courtesy National Archives and Records Administration.*

maximum security cells, rampaged through the grounds, setting buildings on fire and attacking not only guards but also other inmates. By morning one inmate was dead. The stockade was a smoldering wreck. And prisoners remained in control of one of its three compounds.[60]

American newspapers paid relatively little attention, though that was likely due to timing. A minor prison riot on the other side of the world could not compete with live coverage of police and National Guard troops facing down protesters in Chicago streets outside the 1968 Democratic National Convention. And as far as violence in Vietnam goes, for perspective, 537 American servicemen had been killed in action that month alone.[61] It is not surprising that the uprising at Long Binh Jail drew little notice from the American press.

Army leaders were generally grateful for that small advantage. But army command in Vietnam was paying attention, even if the *New York Times* was not. In 1967, US Army Vietnam (USARV) headquarters had moved from Saigon to Long Binh Post. This installation would eventually span twenty-five square miles, offering an air-conditioned refuge with world-class shopping, swimming pools, tennis courts, and close to 60,000 residents. In the summer of 1968, Long Binh Jail was a significant presence there, and USARV HQ was painfully aware of the crisis it faced—as were army leaders back in the United States.[62] As days turned into weeks, with prisoners still controlling a portion of the stockade, the "LBJ riot" became one of the army's earliest experiments in managing the problem of race.

For that is what this was: a problem of race. Oddly enough, neither Associated Press–based stories or the brief piece that ran in *Time* magazine mentioned race at all. Both sources claimed that the riot had begun as a fistfight between two prisoners. That was not true. This was a racial uprising, an explosion of violence fed by inchoate rage. Black men began the revolt. Black men, joined by a handful of "Mexicans," burned buildings and chanted "kill the Chucks." Black men used improvised weapons to attack guards and white inmates. And in the aftermath of the violence, Black men occupied Compound B not only by taking physical control of it but by improvising an "African" space with makeshift dashikis, spears, and drums.[63]

These men's actions were, like Merritt's, born in anger and frustration. But that is where the similarity ends. Merritt was a forty-year-old officer with almost twenty years of army service. He had thought hard about the role of Black men in the United States and its military, and while prone to hyperbole, he commanded the persuasive language of sixties-era civil rights. He had a case to make. He was seeking change.

The men who rioted at Long Binh Jail were enlisted men. Almost all were young, many still teenagers. They were, some investigators later argued, inflamed by their own experiences both in Vietnam and in the stockade, inspired by racial uprisings in American cities, encouraged by Black Panther literature. But they made no demands. They offered no coherent critique of racism or of oppression or even of their own immediate conditions. The language this group commanded was violence. And that language was not without power.

In the years that followed, the army would have to confront charges of racism from both within and without, and it did so both more and less successfully. What army leaders found more difficult, however, were the grievances that did not find words—or not words intelligible to the army's hierarchy of complaint, in any case—but instead erupted into inarticulate and, often, seemingly random violence. Thus the riot at Long Binh Jail stands as the army's first major attempt to manage the violence that, more than any other aspect of the problem of race, worried military leaders in the Vietnam era.

The stockade at Long Binh was known to all as "LBJ," an ironic play on the initials of the president who had fully committed his nation to this unfortunate war. And throughout the US Army in Vietnam, LBJ was notorious, a place that was hated and feared, "a brooding presence in the lives and consciousness of young soldiers," in the words of its only historian to date.[64]

As the United States moved more deeply into war and as the number of US troops grew and their morale declined in the months following the Tet Offensive, LBJ was quickly stretched beyond capacity. The jail had been built to hold 400 men; by mid-1968 it housed 719. The space allotted each man had been cut almost in half, from 70 to 36.5 square feet. The dining room could seat only 200 men at a time, though it fed both prisoners and guards. There were way too many opportunities for conflict in such close quarters. The crowded conditions, wrote a Catholic chaplain, "irritated small hurts into painful wounds."[65]

Overcrowding was compounded by other shortages. Army regulations specified 282 trained guards for an inmate population of that size; LBJ had only 153. Few were adequately trained, and the story is that, in these early years, MPs were punished for their own misconduct by assignment to guard duty at LBJ. The brutality of the guards was rumored and later at least partly substantiated. Guards, in turn, recalled the challenge of keeping order in this volatile space, moving among inmates without weapons of any sort, not even a nightstick.[66]

The men incarcerated in LBJ were a mixed bunch. Some had gone AWOL or refused a lawful order, whether it was to advance into combat or to cut their hair. "Scared kids in a war zone," LBJ's second-in-command later called them. Nonetheless, according to one stockade official, in 1968 virtually none of the prisoners were first- or even second-time offenders. Officers were reluctant to take men out of the field, so it commonly took several offenses before a man was sent from his unit to serve time in the stockade.[67]

No matter how many "scared kids" got themselves crosswise with authority and ended up in LBJ, the jail also housed murderers and rapists and soldiers convicted of war crimes. Some of the prisoners were men who, in the words of the commander of the 18th MP Brigade, had "committed crimes against the population, against their own unit . . . guys [who] . . . shot and killed Vietnamese on a whim." "You've got to understand," said an officer who took command of LBJ in late 1968. "They had psychotics in there. These weren't just average black people off the streets; . . . they weren't average white people off the streets. . . . The fellows we had were sociopaths."[68]

During the year of 1968, in every month except one, Black prisoners outnumbered whites, even as Black soldiers accounted for only about 11 percent of army troops in Vietnam. Some estimates, surely inflated, put the Black population of LBJ at 70 percent, even as high as 90 percent.[69] (As a matter of policy, at that point the US military did not compile these racial statistics.) Whatever the actual numbers, the imbalance was obvious. Many Black inmates saw that imbalance as evidence that they had been treated unfairly by prejudiced officers and NCOs and a biased system of military justice.

The officer who commanded the stockade at Long Binh Post for the first six months of 1968 reported, shortly before he was rotated back to the United States, that LBJ had a racial problem. The "Negro" inmates in Compound B had an "unruly attitude," he wrote, and neither shifting prisoners around to break up disorderly groups nor increasing the number of guards had defused the situation. More likely he had exacerbated it, as he followed standard stockade practice of moving "troublesome" prisoners into less-favorable confinement—in this case the repurposed Conex shipping containers that served as individual maximum-security cells. LBJ's racial disparity became even higher in the maximum-security block, where prisoners sweltered in the 6 × 6 × 9 square-foot metal containers they referred to, collectively, as The Box.[70]

Lt. Col. Vernon Johnson, who took over LBJ on July 5, 1968, was the Military Police Corps's attempt to solve the growing crisis at the army stockade —at least as MP leaders understood that crisis in mid-1968. Johnson held a PhD in penology and, in keeping with developments in that field, he believed in rehabilitation. The officer who insisted that LBJ was populated by psychotics and sociopaths saw the situation differently. He described Colonel Johnson as a "Father Flanagan," someone who seemed to believe that "there's no such thing as a bad boy."[71]

Johnson wasted no time putting his principles into practice. In the spirit of rehabilitation, he increased recreational opportunities for inmates. He emphasized the roles of social workers and psychologists. He listened to prisoners' complaints, even supported them in the face of claims from his own correctional staff. He urged guards to get to know the prisoners, spend time talking with them, join their basketball games. He also attempted to stem the flow of illegal drugs into the jail. For many prisoners, this effort likely outweighed all the others, especially as LBJ began a highly unpopular practice of strip-searching inmates returning from work details, such as collecting and burning latrine waste, that took them outside the stockade.[72] Johnson, as those who assigned him to LBJ intended, was implementing modern penal practices. But those practices did not offer solutions to the growing problem of race any more than had the standard stockade practices he revised.

Some of Johnson's subordinates, in fact, were convinced that he had made the problem worse. One former guard remembered Johnson as "more of a sociologist than a soldier" who encouraged practices that destroyed "necessary control." Johnson's deputy said, in a later interview, that although Johnson seemed to think that he had created a good rapport with the prisoners, he had instead undermined discipline so thoroughly that the prisoners were running the jail.[73]

The riot that erupted on the night of August 29 was not spontaneous. The violence was orchestrated by a well-organized group of Black inmates who referred to themselves as "the syndicate" and controlled the flow of drugs into and through the stockade. It is possible that Colonel Johnson's attempts to stop the movement of drugs into LBJ precipitated action, but syndicate members had been talking for a while about burning the place down. There were certainly plenty of reasons for them to be angry, whether the immediate conditions in the overcrowded jail, the racial prejudice they saw as pervading the entire system of military justice, or the more general oppression of Black men in American society. They had models for inspiration, as well. Prisoners were talking about a recent disturbance at the marine stockade in Da Nang. They knew about the Ohio Penitentiary riot that had followed only a few days later.[74]

In clandestine meetings, syndicate members developed plans. They assigned tasks: one inmate was to smuggle kerosene into the jail, another to obtain a supply of Binoctal tablets (a barbituate) and marijuana to be distributed before the uprising. A broader group of inmates were alerted to await the signal.[75]

The plans were not closely guarded, and rumors had been circulating that "big trouble" was coming. In the face of such rumors, Colonel Johnson took precautions. Maj. Gerald Vessels, the Catholic chaplain in whom Johnson confided (he "often used my shoulders to complain about the problems he faced," the chaplain wrote), thought that Johnson had done everything he could. Even the stays from the ends of inmates' canvas cots had been removed, Vessels noted, after one had been repurposed to beat a white prisoner to death. (Inmates found this one more irritation, as without stays the effective length of their cots was about four and a half feet.) White men had begun telling Vessels that they were afraid of being beaten or cut with razors; Black men had largely stopped attending mass and confession. Vessels was of the opinion that the only way to forestall the coming crisis was to segregate the races. But that, he noted, was forbidden by law. The tension was palpable —and rising. And despite his best efforts, the chaplain was unable to learn the true source of the trouble to come or to pinpoint the form it would take.[76]

One inmate, Antonio Aguinaldo Gibel, both had that knowledge and was willing to share it. As he explained to the disbelieving investigator in the days following the riot ("You lived in the same area with these people?"), as his father "was in real estate" he had grown up hanging out in Harlem. Italian American Gibel had joined the army with a group of Black men—"about 50, all from my block," he claimed—and by whatever coincidence some of these men were also confined in LBJ.[77]

Gibel knew what was coming, and he had tried to warn the stockade command. "I went to Lieutenant Talps," he told investigators. "I said you have to do something. The way you are punishing them—sending all the Negroes to the box—to them it is a racial matter. The only way they can handle it is with violence, like the riot we had in New York. The way they talk is, in the next three or four days we will take care of it ourselves. . . . I said if you don't know, if you have any consideration, please do something." That night, testified Private Gibel, he heard noises, "the same war cry we have in New York, and I knew what was going on."[78]

At the signal, men in the Conex boxes lit cigarette filters they had stuffed into the locks on their doors; the heat softened the metal and at least some prisoners were able to free themselves. Over in the detainee section of Compound B, a designated group of prisoners overpowered two gate guards, taking their keys. Even though syndicate members had worked for months, previously, on a thwarted escape attempt that involved tunneling below stockade walls, this time escape was not on the agenda. This was, instead, about violence and general retribution. Black inmates tore apart bunks to create weapons, pulled boards from buildings to serve as clubs, liberated knives from the mess hall kitchen. Many prisoners, Black and white, ran for the main gate in an attempt to escape the violence. Guards fled for their lives, climbing the fence and wedging themselves through concertina wire.[79]

Groups of men dragged mattresses into piles and set them on fire; they ignited tents and buildings. One man worked his way through maximum security, releasing all remaining Black prisoners from their cells. He then poured what he believed to be kerosene around the Conex boxes, some of which still held white prisoners. The liquid failed to ignite, and he turned his attention elsewhere. Other men attacked guards, both Black and white. Some rounded up white prisoners, bound their hands and feet, and let loose with fists and feet and makeshift weapons. Unknown assailants beat one young private, Edward Haskett of St. Petersburg, Florida, to death with a shovel. In the midst of the violence a frustrated Black man paced angrily back and forth, yelling, "You stupid fucking fools, you're doing it all wrong."[80]

Colonel Johnson, banking on the goodwill he believed he had earned, went unarmed into the stockade in an attempt to talk the men down. It is not quite clear what happened; one witness said that Johnson, in gesturing to the crowd, accidentally knocked a plate of food out of an inmate's hands "and the guy took that very personal." Another insisted that Johnson, walking near the mess hall, was attacked before he had even begun to speak. And yet another remembered Johnson making his appeal to the crowd; whatever hold he had had was broken when someone yelled, "'Fire that Chuck up,'" and the crowd turned on him. Likewise, to this day, no one knows how Johnson got free. The next time he was seen was near the stockade gate, staggering and stumbling, covered in blood. When Chaplain Vessels later found Colonel Johnson at the hospital, awaiting surgery on a deep gash in his head, Johnson, agitated, told the chaplain, "We did it to them. I don't blame any of them, we did it to them."[81]

Colonel Johnson had not downplayed the violence, despite his own attempts to manage it. Army command was close at hand, so close that smoke from the stockade would have been visible at the headquarters buildings just south of LBJ. In any case, stockade staff had immediately notified Gen. Frank Mildren, deputy commanding general of the US Army Vietnam. Mildren quickly took charge. Concluding that there was no risk of a mass escape, Mildren chose not to storm the stockade. He decided to bide his time, wait until daylight, and then evaluate options.[82]

At the stockade, the chaos was gradually subsiding. Inmates who had fled the violence had been herded into a nearby field, where they spent the rest of the night—along with some of the rioters who had been rounded up —ringed by armed troops, under the glare of floodlights from helicopters circling overhead and the headlights of assembled trucks and jeeps. Wounded prisoners had been evacuated, some by troops who had gone into the chaos and others by Black inmates who had rescued guards and other inmates at risk of their own lives. The medium security compound, however, remained under inmates' control.[83]

As it would for more than three weeks.

Dawn broke on smoking ruins. Among the prisoners, rumors swirled. Colonel Johnson was dead. A hundred men had escaped. Dead bodies had been hurled by rioters onto the barbed wire fence that surrounded the stockade. Significantly, some rumors claimed parallels with violence back "in the world." Four hundred police had been killed in Chicago, some said. Vice President Hubert Humphrey had been shot.[84]

With Colonel Johnson hospitalized and in serious condition, General Mildren needed someone to take command of a very difficult situation. By first light on the morning of August 30, he had made his decision, summoning two military police officers, Lt. Col. "Big Gene" Murdock and Lt. Col. Herman Trop, to Long Binh Post. Command was given to Murdock, with Trop as his deputy. There were almost 200 inmates remaining in the medium security area. General Mildren, in consultation with Murdock and Trop, chose to wait them out.[85]

General Mildren asked, "Can you go in there and take them?" remembered Colonel Murdock. And "I said, 'Yessir.' . . . We could have gone in there anytime we wanted. . . . We'd have wiped their ass. We left them alone." Colonel Trop explained his own logic: "If we acted like gentlemen—treated them fairly as officers should treat EM [enlisted men]—we were going to deal with some of them." Rejecting suggestions that they remove the cigarettes and coffee from the C rations they provided inmates, Trop argued, "Let's don't screw around. We have to look better than they do."[86] The following day Murdock sent in several truckloads of blankets and sheets, cots, and tents.

As days passed, inmates made no demands. No spokesperson emerged. There were no negotiations. Instead, the men claimed a Black identity that transcended the history of slavery in the United States, creating an alternative "African" space for themselves in what came to be known as the "Soul Brother" compound. "We used the blankets to make African robes and the tent poles for spears," recalled a participant. "That is where our head was at the time." Wrote the chaplain, "My Rosaries were being used quite creatively." Colonel Murdock was less generous in his evaluation. "Those blacks turned native. They wore blankets and put chicken bones in their hair and tied them in their nose. Beat on barrels for drums. . . . No, I don't understand [people] who put goddam chicken bones in their nose and their hair."[87]

Nothing interrupted the delivery of food and water. But Murdock had the stockade fence covered with burlap so no one could see the men in the Soul Brother compound. "That broke their hearts," said Murdock. "They wanted to be watched." Even so, the men continued to drum and chant. Colonel Trop, who seemed to maintain his sense of humor no matter what, went to the fence one night and shouted, "Alright, this is the last time I'm going to tell you—I want you to tune that sonofabitch up!"[88]

Men whom the chaplain characterized as "the hard core of Black Power" continued to shout "their complaints against the world . . . in a language that was violent and vulgar even when judged by normal stockade standards," threatening to kill those who came close to the fence. But with no demands to negotiate or clear way forward, other inmates began pulling away from the instigators of the riot. A man who one day violently cursed the chaplain appealed the following day for help getting out of the compound. "I thought these were my people," he said, "but they aren't my people, they are all insane. They are going to start killing each other before long and I want out before they kill me."[89]

The chaplain—who believed both that the riot stemmed from profound anger and feelings of oppression and also that because "colored men" often said that white guards treated them better than "colored" guards did there was no direct racial prejudice in the stockade—saw this as a turning point. "The men," he wrote, "were beginning to separate into those who had begun to think and those who were still feeling their emotions."[90]

That may be. At the same time, Colonel Murdock had provided them an incentive. His plan—possible once the stockade's records had been salvaged from the burned administration building—was to call men individually from the occupied space and load them onto a plane bound for the army stockade at Fort Leavenworth, Kansas. No violence was involved, just a calm threat. If an inmate did not come out from the occupied space when his name was called, Murdock promised, he would be court-martialed for escape and end up with twenty years added to what was already a certain five-year sentence.[91]

Murdock's plan was effective, even though not all had faith in his tactics. As Chaplain Vessels wrote to the army's chief of chaplains on September 9, "The segregated compound is still not under control. We dare not use force because of the publicity, we dare not fire one bullet because of the publicity. What we will do, what the final outcome will be, I do not have any idea."[92]

Nonetheless, as the days passed in heat and boredom and the command's forbearance held, the remaining inmates' resolve began to fade. A small group continued to hold out. But when their numbers dwindled to thirteen, General Mildren sent in troops with loaded weapons and enough tear gas "to fill New York City." They met no resistance.[93]

The tactic of patience had, from the army's perspective, worked. Without confrontation, it was more difficult for inmates to maintain a core of committed, angry resistance. Without confrontation, the story had no purchase in the American media. And for the army, the wait had no significant cost. Inmates had burned stockade buildings in the first hour of the uprising, before Colonel Johnson or General Mildren could have sent in a reaction force.

They tore up some sheets and blankets—all US government property—in the days that followed the riot, but in terms of destruction of property, that was a pretty minor loss. And the men who held the "Soul Brothers Compound" until the twenty-first of September had not harmed anyone else after the initial hours of violence.

In the end, the uprising left one young prisoner dead. Twenty-six inmates were hospitalized for serious injury. The same number were treated as outpatients. The great majority of the injured inmates were white, and army headquarters made clear that they had been beaten by other inmates, not by stockade guards. Sixty-three MPs (correction officers, administrative staff, and reaction troops) had been injured, twenty-three badly enough to be hospitalized. Colonel Johnson never recovered from his head wound. And much of the stockade's physical plant had been destroyed. Of the approximately 200 men who planned or joined the violent uprising on August 29, 129 were individually court-martialed on charges that included murder, mutiny, aggravated assault, and willful destruction of government property.[94]

With the stockade fully reclaimed, Colonels Trop and Murdock moved on to their next assignments. In selecting a new commanding officer for the stockade, army leaders rejected the enlightened penology of Colonel Johnson. The new commander was a "Patton-type ass-kicker" who had earned his nickname of "Ivan the Terrible." Col. Ivan Nelson cracked down on the guards and on the prisoners. "Under Nelson," recalled an MP, "the place became steel and barb wire; immaculate, absolute discipline."[95]

The army takes pride in being a learning institution, and events on the scale of the uprising at LBJ almost without exception demanded an accounting of lessons learned. The army's key takeaway was most obvious in the appointment of Colonel Nelson. But the commander of the 18th MP Brigade laid out his "lessons learned" in more detail. Maintenance of discipline is crucial, he noted. Idleness contributes to unrest. Drugs must be kept from the stockade. There must be enough properly trained custodial personnel for the actual number of inmates. Overcrowding increases prisoner dissatisfaction and makes it more difficult for guards to exert control.[96]

These are appropriate lessons learned, even as the devil remains in the details. Does one combat idleness with basketball courts, or with work details? How does one maintain discipline? Most striking, however, is what is missing. In his recommendations for ways to prevent future racial uprisings, this MP commander never once mentioned race.

A s in the case of Major Merritt, army leaders at LBJ tried to deflect the problem of race. And avoidance was no more a solution in the stockade than in the public eye. Racial anger festered in LBJ. Strict discipline tamped down the violence for a while, but the underlying problems would resurface and feed broader complaints about racial injustice in the Vietnam-era army.

Major Merritt's public protest was a rare case. Few, if any, other field grade officers would complain so publicly about injustices they witnessed or experienced. But over the following years, a great many soldiers and their allies would offer compelling critiques of army racial practices and policies. And the uprising at LBJ was simply a taste of what was to come. Racially charged violence exploded throughout the army—not only in stockades and not only in Vietnam but in the barracks and mess halls and bars and communities surrounding army posts in the United States and throughout the world.

From the perspective of August 1968, however, it is hard not to have sympathy with Chaplain Vessels, who frankly admitted that the answers were beyond him. Concluding his report on the LBJ uprising (though he might well have been describing the crisis as a whole), he wrote, "Thank God it is not my job to solve the dilemma."[97]

That task would fall to army leaders, who would have no choice but to confront the problem of race.

# 2 SAME MUD, SAME BLOOD

October 13, 1969. Washington, DC.

When Secretary of the Army Stanley Resor greeted the members of the Association of the United States Army (AUSA) who had assembled at the Sheraton Park Hotel that day in the lingering heat of a DC fall, he wasted no time on pleasantries. His purpose, he said, was to "report to you, who have a deep and direct interest in the Army," about "matters of importance."[1]

First on his mind, not surprisingly, was "our situation in Vietnam." The shadow of war was unavoidable and the secretary, of necessity, addressed ongoing combat in a war that "has been difficult and frustrating" and acknowledged the spirit of those who fought. But he did so quickly, devoting a scant five minutes to the perils and promise of Vietnamization and an appeal for continued "will and perseverance." In Vietnam, he assured his audience, "time is now on our side."[2]

Resor quickly turned to the point of his speech. In language that seems understated, even in comparison to his restrained take on the future of the US war in Vietnam, the secretary of the army noted that the condition of race relations in the US Army "gives cause for concern."[3]

Resor made no mention of racial conflict in the discussion that followed. He did not refer to the headlines generated by Maj. Lavell Merritt's protests or to the uprising at Long Binh Jail. He did not mention the racial violence that had exploded at Fort Bragg, at Fort Carson, at Fort Dix, or at Fort Riley over the course of the preceding year and a half, just as he did not chronicle the incidents of racial violence that had plagued the Marine Corps and the navy. He did not discuss the special subcommittee appointed in August by

Secretary of the Army
Stanley R. Resor chal-
lenged the army's "color-
blind" model of equal
opportunity in 1969.
Awarded the Silver Star,
Bronze Star, and Purple
Heart for his service
in the US Army during
World War II, Resor served
as secretary of the army
from July 1965 through
June 1971.
*Department of Defense
official photograph.*

the House Armed Services Committee to investigate the "root causes" of racial conflict on military installations.[4]

He did not need to. This audience was aware of that context, just as its members were aware of the rising number of US military deaths in Vietnam and the massive antiwar demonstration scheduled on the National Mall just two days hence. Instead of mustering evidence that a problem existed, Resor took the next step. He offered a diagnosis of the situation and some prescriptions for its solution. "A Negro in uniform," Resor told his audience, "does not cease to be a Negro and become a soldier instead. He becomes a Negro soldier."[5]

Resor's address, in fundamental ways, created the US Army's "problem of race." That is not to say that he was the first to notice the growing racial crisis or even to speak of it publicly. The Department of Defense (DoD), under Secretary Robert McNamara and later Melvin Laird, invested significant political capital in military civil rights initiatives from the Kennedy administration forward. And some DoD leaders had come to see the long hot summer of 1967 as a potential portent of trouble to come.

Military chiefs were well aware of those concerns, and they had concerns of their own. As Resor noted in his keynote, army chief of staff William Westmoreland had issued a "personal message" on equal opportunity and individual dignity to all army personnel just ten days before. (Resor did not mention the message of the Marine Corps commandant, which had preceded that of the army.) More significantly—though this move was quiet, behind the scenes—Westmoreland also had dispatched a small team to investigate the growing racial tensions within the US Army.[6]

In both actions, Westmoreland was acting in the interests of the army, as he saw them. But his actions also were in keeping with a longer trajectory of professional experience and commitment. In 1952, during the Korean War, thirty-eight-year-old Brigadier General Westmoreland had commanded one of the first racially integrated army combat units, the 187th Airborne Infantry Regiment. And in the spring of 1967, asked to address the general assembly of his native South Carolina, the commander of US forces in Vietnam chose to tell those convened legislators—members of a body that had embraced racial segregation and white supremacy; that had, just four years previously, voted to begin flying the Confederate Battle Flag from the State House dome—that "the service of the Negro servicemen in Vietnam has been particularly inspirational to me" and that "they are a credit to their country."[7]

In investigations launched by the Department of Defense and the US Army alike, what became increasingly clear is that army officers and noncoms, from the rawest first lieutenant and freshly promoted sergeant through the highest command, men of all races and ethnicities, had been dealing with racial conflict—in growing intensity—at least since the 1968 assassination of Martin Luther King Jr. In the case of racial violence, most commanders had addressed the symptoms, not the causes: they added lights to dark stretches of army installations, increased MP patrols, administered nonjudicial punishments.[8] And when the issue of race was inescapable—when soldiers complained officially about racism or racial discrimination—investigators evaluated those complaints in relation to policies designed to foster equal opportunity in a race-blind institution.

Such policies left room for both personal and institutional racism to fester. The casual use of racial epithets was virtually never judged evidence of racism; the army entrance exams that channeled high numbers of poorly educated Black men into the infantry were simply, as designed, fostering military efficiency. In a great many cases—as with Major Merritt's complaints and the riot at LBJ—race was the elephant in the room; it was undeniable but unacknowledged. Even the army's equal opportunity program required

*Same Mud, Same Blood*

that racial identity be hidden: photographs were removed from files sent forward for promotions decisions.[9] In sum, race was meant to remain invisible.

Of course, by mid-1968, the problem of race could not be hidden. More than anything else, it was the rising tide of racial violence that drew the focused attention of army leaders. "Racial overtones," in the official language of the moment, were obvious in fights and assaults, fraggings and riots and uprisings. But race had also become visible because Black Americans insisted on its visibility, rejecting models of integration that treated white culture as the norm and claiming instead Black pride and Black beauty and Black consciousness. Proud as the institutional army was of its undeniable progress toward full racial integration and equal opportunity, especially in comparison to civilian society, its policies were geared toward the integrationist goals of an earlier era. Its race-blind approaches were not sufficient for the crisis at hand. In this context the army, as an institution, was forced to confront a new racial consciousness and a new racial pride.

Racial violence had made the army take note that there was indeed a problem. An institution at war within could not survive. And more immediately, in the current conduct of wars both hot and cold, an institution riven by internal conflict could not adequately provide for the defense of the nation. As an army statement noted in 1970, "Racial conflict is a problem which the Army must acknowledge and respond to in order to continue to remain a combat effective force."[10] The stakes could not be higher.

Secretary Resor offered no clear solution to the problem of race—to the racial conflict that seemed to threaten the army's mission of national defense—and some of his explanation embodied the contradictions that the army would struggle with in the months and years to come. But he did two things. He endorsed a positive "race-conscious" approach, and he called for a "total commitment" to solving the problem at hand. Nonetheless, even as the army began to acknowledge the problem of race as its own and turn its institutional focus to solutions, it had to contend with the fact that it was not —and could not be—fully separate from a society that was, at that moment in history, embroiled in extraordinary strife.

Although Resor formally endorsed a *positive* race-conscious approach in the fall of 1969, race consciousness was not new to the army. The US military had always been conscious of race simply because American society has always been conscious of race. And while the secretary and chief of staff of the army held extraordinary power to declare—and to enforce—racial policy within the institution, that institution was nonetheless subject to controls and pressures from outside its ranks. That is not only because members of the armed forces carry with them the prejudices and possibilities of their civilian upbringings, especially when those forces expand rapidly in times of war; it is also because the military is under civilian control, subject to civilian authority, dependent on Congress for funding and authorization. Thus, military institutions are not walled off from the nation's social and political struggles. And in the twentieth century, that was particularly true when it came to race.

Black men had fought in America's armies since the nation's beginnings. Black men, both free and enslaved, served in the Continental army during the American Revolution, mostly in integrated units. In the Civil War, Black men fought in the Union army's sixteen segregated combat regiments and served, both officially and unofficially, as laborers, cooks, and teamsters. In both cases, the army relied on Black men because it desperately needed soldiers—not because white leaders embraced notions of Black equality. But following Appomattox, Congress created six permanent Black units in the regular army: four infantry and two cavalry. This legislation, which predated the Supreme Court's *Plessy v. Ferguson* decision by more than a decade, gave federal recognition to "separate but equal" segregated forces. For most Black Americans, such permanent status was a sign of racial progress.[11]

The United States fought World War I, the war "to make the world safe for democracy," with a segregated army. In the era of Jim Crow, the question was not whether army units would be segregated but whether Black men would be allowed to serve at all. In the end, using a racially specific draft, the US Army called up 368,000 Black men, or about 13 percent of wartime draftees. Most did unskilled labor, often in dangerous conditions, but the all-Black 92nd and 93rd Infantry Divisions fought alongside French troops on the western front.[12]

Black leaders debated the proper approach to the war, well aware that they were fighting for a nation that denied them the full rights of citizenship. Most believed, along with W. E. B. Du Bois, that military service would advance the cause of equal rights. In the NAACP's official publication, *The Crisis*, Du Bois wrote, "*The Crisis* says, *first* your Country, *then* your Rights!" To those who questioned that priority, Du Bois insisted that "our loyalty in time of trial" had led African Americans from slavery to the relative freedom and prosperity of the current day, and that continued loyalty would yield greater freedoms in the future.[13]

In the years following the Great War, racial progress remained slow. But even as the Ku Klux Klan was reborn and southern Democrats in Congress repeatedly blocked passage of an anti-lynching bill, African Americans who had joined the Great Migration north after 1915 gained political power. And this time, with clouds of war looming, the NAACP was less quick to urge "*first your Country, then your Rights!*" As columnist George Schuyler wrote in the *Pittsburgh Courier*, "If nothing more comes out of this emergency than the widespread understanding among white leaders that the Negro's loyalty is conditional, we shall not have suffered in vain."[14]

The *Courier* had, in 1938, launched what became a major lobbying effort to ensure that African Americans were allowed to join the nation's military services. Some advocates of war preparedness had taken up the call, and the combined pressure began to produce results. Congress passed legislation providing that "there shall be no discrimination against any person on account of race or color" in military selection or training. All rested, however, on the definition of "discrimination."[15] And according to the doctrine of "separate but equal" endorsed by the Supreme Court in 1896, segregation was not, by definition, discriminatory.

Few Black leaders, however, still believed that the path to equality might lie in separate institutions. And as they built their campaign for equal rights in the decades following the First World War, they logically focused on "the most obvious practitioner of Jim Crow" in the federal government: the US military. When A. Philip Randolph threatened to disrupt war preparations with a civil rights "March on Washington" during the summer of 1941, he sought not only "fair employment practices" in the civilian workplace but also integration of the US military. In response, President Franklin Roosevelt issued an executive order guaranteeing fair employment. Military integration, however, found no traction. The NAACP's 1941 call for the immediate integration of the US military was, likewise, to no avail. Nonetheless, Black leaders had wielded some influence. It was political pressure, rather than perceived military necessity, that led to the creation of Black combat units in the US Army.[16]

Civilian authorities determined whether the United States would fight its enemies with integrated or segregated forces. But army leaders also resisted the calls for integration. That was not because the army was particularly bad on racial issues, given the context of the times. In that context—and a grim context it was—the army might even have been considered somewhat progressive. But army leaders (almost exclusively white) were products of their society, and they had been tasked with rapidly enlisting, training, and fielding millions of men in a war for the future of the world.

At they stood at the brink of war, America's military leaders assumed that any attempt to integrate the ranks would disrupt military order and so undermine the nation's ability to wage war. Many, often ignoring the lack of training and resources that Black units had received, argued that they had, overall, performed poorly in combat during the Great War and it was thus not worth the risk that Black combat units would undermine military efficacy in this one. Moving to broader principles, army officials commonly argued that the army was not the proper site for "social experiments," most particularly in time of war. Speaking to a group of Black newspaper publishers and editors on December 8, 1941, less than twenty-four hours after Japanese forces had attacked the US base at Pearl Harbor and other US possessions in the Pacific, a representative of the army's adjutant general's office insisted that "the Army is not a sociological laboratory. . . . Experiments to meet the wishes and demands of the champions of every race and creed for the solution of their problems are a danger to efficiency, discipline and morale and would result in ultimate defeat."[17]

It is impossible to know whether these white leaders were correct in predicting massive resistance to racial integration. The fact that the US Red Cross racially segregated blood plasma—even for men wounded in battle —suggests the extent and depth of white racial prejudice in those years. But even as the United States betrayed the principles for which it fought by denying full rights to some of its citizens, it did not avoid racial disorder. Racial conflict reached riot conditions at bases in Michigan, Georgia, Louisiana, Texas, and Kentucky. Complaints of racial discrimination—which required investigation—flooded into the War Department, most particularly as northern Black men were subjected to the racial conditions of the Jim Crow South.[18] The problem of race, during the Second World War, could not be ignored.

After war's end, civilian struggles over race continued to shape military policy and practice. For Black Americans in the immediate postwar years, military integration remained a key goal. They targeted the military in part because military service had long been a point of pride for Black Americans. The US military was also a vast and visible institution, one worth the struggle. But more than that: it was a *national* institution that practiced Jim Crow segregation. The US military was also perhaps the most practical possible target, for it could be desegregated by executive order, thus bypassing the guaranteed outrage and opposition of the southern congressional Democrats who were collectively dubbed "Dixiecrats."[19]

And executive action seemed increasingly possible. By the mid-twentieth century, African Americans had become a significant voting bloc outside the

South, and President Truman—though no advocate of "social relations" between whites and "Negroes"—relied on their political support. Prompted in part by political considerations but also horrified by stories of returning Black war veterans set upon by white mobs, Truman committed his administration to what was, at the time, a strong civil rights platform. In 1946 Truman's Committee on Civil Rights recommended the nation end racial segregation and discrimination in the US Armed Forces, though it looked to Congress for action. Given, for example, Georgia senator Richard Russell's attempt to guarantee that draftees would not have to serve in units with members of other races if they preferred not to do so, most interested parties understood that Congress was not going to be the solution.[20]

It was in that context that President Truman issued Executive Order 9981 —in the midst of the 1948 presidential election campaign. The order that ended the legal segregation of the US military never used the word "integration." It did not even specify desegregation. Instead, it ordered "equality of treatment and opportunity for all persons," regardless of race, color, religion, or national origin.[21] Key definitions had changed: no longer was *segregated* opportunity assumed to be equal.

Although it was a major milestone in the American civil rights struggle, Truman's order expressed no real urgency and stipulated that each service take the time necessary to avoid "impairing efficiency or morale." Thus it was not until the depths of the subsequent war in Korea that true racial integration began, and then due only to military necessity. The army, in particular, had dragged its feet in response to Truman's order, arguing that its existing policies already offered equal opportunity—despite the fact that only 21 of the army's 106 training courses were open to African Americans—and rejecting the notion that men should be assigned without regard to race.[22]

But on October 30, 1954, the *New York Times* noted (admittedly, in a brief article buried on page 23) that the US military had, "without any 'untoward incidents'" and "ahead of schedule," ended the practice of segregation. The "Negro serviceman," it continued, "is now utilized on the basis of individual merit and proficiency." The following day, another brief notice drove the point home: "While the Supreme Court's ruling against segregation of the races in the public schools is still a generalization unsupported by a court order, segregation in the armed services is legally extinct."[23]

That sentence, contrasting racial progress in the military with the civilian society's slower advance, provided the narrative outline for the following decade. As white mobs jeered the nine Black students who enrolled at Little Rock's Central High in September 1957 and rioted in the wake of James

Meredith's enrollment at the University of Mississippi in 1962, an array of Black and white leaders, politicians, and journalists pointed to the armed forces as a model of change.[24]

It must be said, however, that civilian pressure was responsible for most of that progress—at least until the late 1960s. As the civilian civil rights movement began to convince more white Americans of the moral force of its claims and the practical consequences of rejecting them, civilian leaders exercised their direct authority to change the policies of the US armed forces.

When John F. Kennedy stood coatless on a bitterly cold Inauguration Day, heralding the passing of the torch to a new generation, some African Americans found hope in his words. But though Kennedy soon sent a special message to Congress, calling upon it to deliver civil rights legislation, his interests and commitments lay elsewhere. On civil rights, Kennedy was cautious, not willing to expend political capital when southern "Dixiecrats" in Congress could threaten his other agendas over the issue of race. Roy Wilkins, head of the NAACP, wrote to Harris Wofford, Kennedy's special assistant for civil rights, "The Kennedy Administration has done with Negro citizens what it has done with a vast number of Americans: it has charmed them. It has intrigued them. Every seventy-two hours it has delighted them." But it had not delivered. "It is plain why the civil rights legislative line was abandoned," Wilkins continued, "but nothing was accomplished by the maneuver."[25]

Despite his slow move to commitment, the forty-first president's impact on racial policy in the armed forces was immediate and concrete—because of the man he appointed his secretary of defense. Robert Strange McNamara's legacy is forever shaped by his role in America's war in Vietnam; "Architect of a Futile War" was how the *New York Times* summed up his life in its headline to his 2009 obituary. But even as McNamara led the nation deeper into "the maelstrom of Vietnam," he pushed the nation's armed forces toward full racial equality.[26]

McNamara took his Pentagon office in late January 1961. Just less than a year earlier, four young Black men, students at North Carolina Agricultural and Technical State University, had taken seats at the whites-only lunch counter in a Woolworth's store in Greensboro, North Carolina, and attempted to order cups of coffee. By the time Americans had given Kennedy a narrow edge over Richard Nixon, his Republican opponent, in the 1960 presidential election, the sit-in movement had spread through the South and beyond; 70,000 Americans had joined to defeat Jim Crow segregation.

During McNamara's fourth month as secretary of defense, following close upon the failed US-sponsored Bay of Pigs invasion of Cuba and the Soviet

Union's successful launch (and recovery) of the first human into space, white mobs in Alabama brutally attacked "Freedom Riders" who were challenging Jim Crow segregation of interstate transportation in violation of Supreme Court rulings. An editorial in the *Washington Post*, McNamara's local paper, made the point he had certainly already grasped: "We may be sure," the *Post* editorial began, "that the beatings and brutality in Alabama have been front-page news in a great many countries of the world. The harm done to the standing of the United States by such racial violence is incalculable," particularly, it noted, in "a world that is two thirds non-white."[27]

Cold War concerns certainly provided impetus to act, but McNamara was, in fact, a longtime member of the NAACP. At the same time, although his willingness to address the issue of race in the military was not born in the violence of early 1960s resistance and concerns about the nation's image in the increasingly dangerous Cold War, the specific contemporary concerns of the civilian civil rights movement did help to shape his focus. In his new role as secretary of defense, urged on by his special assistant, Adam Yarmolinsky, McNamara quickly ordered the heads of all military services to guarantee equal opportunity for members of minority groups and to make decisions solely on the basis of "merit and fitness."[28] But he would go further.

McNamara saw the military as a site of racial progress. He knew it could improve, and he meant to foster policies of equal opportunity. But—like the leadership of the civil rights movement at that moment—he saw southern segregation as the larger problem. So did most African American members of the military. As civilians risked violence and death in their struggle against legal segregation and doctrines of separate but equal, service members wrote to complain about how they were treated when they ventured off-base. How could it be that only "a short bus ride to town" separated proud American service members from second-class citizenship? How was it legitimate that their children were restricted to segregated schools, their families barred from rental housing, denied service at local restaurants, sent to the back of the bus or to the "colored" seats in the movie theater?[29]

The more savvy among these servicemen understood that external pressure was more likely to get results than a complaint registered upward through the ranks, so many wrote to their congressional representatives or to the NAACP about their concerns. Thus it was that, in the summer of 1961, Detroit congressman Charles Diggs relayed such complaints to fellow Michigander Robert McNamara (McNamara had spent eleven years at Ford Motor Company's Dearborn headquarters and had raised his children in the university town of Ann Arbor). In a well-publicized letter to the secretary of defense,

Diggs—who had served in the US Army during World War II—reported that Black members of the armed forces were writing him with increasing frequency. Some letters, he noted, concerned discrimination within the military. But most had to do with problems that service members encountered in civilian communities outside post gates. Diggs called for a "citizens' study" of the problem, and his letter found fertile ground.[30]

The following spring, President Kennedy established the President's Committee on Equal Opportunity in the Armed Forces. The Gesell Committee, as it was also known (after its chair, Gerhard Gesell), was actually a Pentagon initiative; Kennedy's involvement, McNamara later noted, was "window dressing." Key Pentagon officials wanted an external study to justify desired actions, and they knew that a study conducted under presidential auspices would offer both legitimacy and a useful public distance from the Department of Defense. So, despite the fact that Kennedy lent his authority and his title, it was McNamara aide Adam Yarmolinsky who conceived this "president's committee," identified its members and its chair, established its parameters, and wrote its directives.[31]

Yarmolinsky, at thirty-eight, was one of the "whiz kids" McNamara brought into the Pentagon to help reform its labyrinthine systems and processes. Brilliant and arrogant in equal measures, Yarmolinsky had never mastered the art of diplomacy or figured out how to navigate DC politics. And if McNamara alienated some Pentagon staffers with his own uncompromising certainties, Yarmolinsky was more profoundly disliked. His zeal in implementing McNamara's objectives had high-ranking military officers calling him the "Cardinal Richelieu of the Pentagon" behind his back. He was also widely hated by powerful southern Democrats in Congress. For Yarmolinsky—a New Yorker who had attended both Harvard and Yale, the Jewish son of two liberal university professors—was deeply committed to racial equality and did not intend to make political concessions in his pursuit of change. Within the Pentagon, where the secretary of defense had multiple demands on his time and attention, Yarmolinsky helped keep focus on the issue of race.[32]

The Gesell Report was very much a product of its time. The committee had been appointed in the context of struggles against Jim Crow segregation —a practice the military had ended not only in policy but in practice. In that context, while the 93-page Gesell Report noted opportunities for internal improvement, it primarily focused on the "humiliation and degradation" Black military personnel suffered daily in "communities near bases where they are compelled to serve." Such discrimination, the committee stated,

*Same Mud, Same Blood*

caused "deep resentment," as "indignities and inequities" affected the morale of white and Black troops alike.[33] In other words, the Committee on Equal Opportunity *in* the Armed Forces concluded that its major problems lay *outside* the military.

The Gesell Committee had been appointed by a president reluctant to expend political capital for gains in civil rights. Its report was received by one who had committed his administration to change. After Birmingham police trained high-pressure fire hoses and loosed police dogs on children marching for civil rights in May 1963 and Governor George Wallace vowed "segregation forever" as he physically blocked doors at the University of Alabama to prevent African Americans from registering that June, Kennedy was forced to deal directly with the demands for civil rights. Speaking to the nation one evening in June, just hours after Governor Wallace had backed down in the face of federalized National Guard troops, Kennedy made his first powerful appeal for racial justice and equality. "When Americans are sent to Viet Nam or West Berlin to risk their lives for yours and mine, we do not ask for whites only," the president—himself a veteran, and speaking to a nation in which the majority of men had served—reminded his listeners, offering shared military service as justification for equal rights.[34]

In this speech, Kennedy defined the civil rights struggle as "a moral crisis." He used the same language of morality and "human decency" in his letter to McNamara upon delivery of the final Gesell Report. But President Kennedy also embraced the narrative of military superiority. The report's findings, Kennedy wrote to McNamara, showed that the "military services lead almost every other segment of our society in establishing equality of opportunity for all Americans."[35]

As intended, this "outside" study gave McNamara both cover and authority. In his reply to the president, he used the Gesell Report to substantiate his claim that "military effectiveness is unquestionably reduced as a result of civilian racial discrimination against men in uniform." With such justification, the secretary of defense issued a major directive on equal opportunity and civil rights. He created a new position, a deputy assistant secretary of defense for civil rights, and—true to his systems background—charged each military service with creating regulations, manuals, instructions, policies, and processes for gathering and reporting data. McNamara authorized military commanders to put civilian institutions that practiced "relentless discrimination against the Negro" off-limits, just as they had long done in cases of "off-base vice" that were assumed to spread venereal disease—though the complex process the regulations stipulated made such action less likely.

Moreover, McNamara's directive made clear that responsibility for ensuring equal opportunity and for preventing ongoing discrimination—both on- and off-base—fell to military commanders.[36]

Under McNamara's lead, the Pentagon had committed the US military to the fight against Jim Crow not only within its ranks but in civilian public spaces where its members encountered discrimination. Such an approach was in accord with the focus of the civil rights movement in the early 1960s, as African Americans fought for equal opportunity and against the forces of Jim Crow segregation. It fit well with the ongoing narrative—and reality —that the military far surpassed civilian society when it came to issues of race. And it put the Pentagon right in the middle of the civilian struggle over civil rights.

Of course, even as civilian authority pushed the military toward racial reform, other strands of civilian authority pushed back. Rep. Carl Vinson, the Georgia Democrat who chaired the House Armed Services Committee, called upon Congress to make any action against off-base discrimination (in other words, following the DoD directive) a court-martial offense. McNamara, Vinson charged, was trying to "impose a new social order throughout the United States through use of our armed forces"; the directive was, in his reading, a "direct invasion by the Department of Defense into local affairs." Fellow Dixiecrat F. Edward Hébert, another member (and future chair) of the House Armed Services Committee, warned that the directive was crafted with "one objective in mind—with an almost saticlike zeal—the forced integration of every facet of the American way of life, using the full power of the Department of Defense to bring about this change."[37]

Vinson and Hébert were right on one count. McNamara did mean to use the full power of the Department of Defense to bring about change. He said so directly in a 1967 speech. As the "largest single institution in the world," he told his audience, the DoD had enormous "unused potential" to alleviate "social inequities," and its role as a "powerful fulcrum in removing road-blocks to racial justice" in no way threatened its "primary responsibility" of ensuring combat readiness.[38]

I n the mid-1960s, the military *was* doing a better job than civilian institutions when it came to race, both in terms of equal opportunity and of peaceful integration. Images of white civilian mobs attacking nonviolent civil rights marchers simply drove home the contrast.

Belief that the military handled race better than civilian institutions persisted—perhaps even strengthened—as the race of the "mob" changed. *Time*

*Same Mud, Same Blood*

magazine's description of "marauding mobs in the Negro suburb of Watts," where Black residents "pillaged, burned and killed" within their own neighborhood, compared the destruction to the aftermath of war: "the atmosphere reminded soldiers of embattled Saigon."[39]

The five nights of devastation in Watts shocked the nation, but it was only a precursor of what would come. The litany of violent "race riots" and uprisings that began in Harlem during the summer of 1964 continued on: Bedford-Stuyvesant, Rochester, Chicago, Philadelphia, New Jersey. In 1965, Watts. In 1966, Cleveland, Chicago, San Francisco. In 1967, Omaha, Nashville, Jackson (Mississippi), Houston, Roxbury (Boston), Tampa, Cincinnati, Atlanta, Buffalo, the New Jersey cities of Newark, Elizabeth, Englewood, Jersey City, New Brunswick, Plainfield; Detroit. . . . By September of that year, at least 170 American cities had experienced mass violence.[40]

In late July 1967, at the request of Michigan governor George Romney, soldiers from the army's 82nd Airborne were dispatched into the urban "jungle" of Detroit to quell "looting, arson, and sniping." Soon thereafter President Johnson, who had ordered 5,000 federal troops into Detroit's streets, addressed the nation. As television cameras rolled, he stood flanked by Secretary of Defense McNamara and Secretary of the Army Resor (along with FBI director Herbert Hoover and the army's chief of staff). Reporting on Detroit, NBC's *Huntley-Brinkley Report* quoted Black militant Stokely Carmichael: "Negro groups were preparing for guerrilla warfare in American cities."[41]

One month later, NBC correspondent Frank McGee joined members of the army's 101st Airborne in Viet Cong territory west of Chu Lai, where he would spend a month embedded with combat troops reporting on race relations in the US Army Vietnam. McGee, himself an army veteran, had grown up in the southern oil country of Louisiana and Oklahoma. Race relations were not a new topic for him. In 1955, at the age of thirty-three, he had been transferred from his broadcast news position in Oklahoma City to the NBC-TV affiliate in Montgomery, Alabama. Soon thereafter, Rosa Parks refused to relinquish her seat on one of the city's public buses. McGee's coverage of the Montgomery bus boycott got him noticed, and he was soon offered a position on NBC's Washington staff. Higher-ups there, in turn, dispatched him to Little Rock to cover the integration of Central High School in September 1957. By the mid-1960s, McGee was a prominent TV journalist, based at NBC's New York headquarters.

Frank McGee was not a war reporter, and it is almost without question that he pitched NBC on his project—which required McGee and two camera crews to spend a month with combat troops in Vietnam—in the context of racial warfare at home.[42] If racial conflict was tearing the nation apart, at home, what of the troops in Vietnam, where the United States was fighting for the first time with a fully racially integrated force?

McGee's answer to that question was clear from the title of the NBC special—*Same Mud, Same Blood*—and he made that point relentlessly throughout it. He framed his special "report" around Sgt. Lewis Larry, who, as McGee noted, was "a Negro." "For this report," McGee explained early in the broadcast, "the fact that Larry is a Negro is of paramount importance. To the officers and men he serves with, it's a matter of total irrelevance." That theme, the irrelevance of race, structured his story.[43]

*Same Mud, Same Blood* contrasted the army's success with civilian society's failures, relying on Sergeant Larry to make the case most explicitly. In the army, Larry told McGee, "I'm given every opportunity to develop myself and show what skill I have to the max, and given every opportunity to—to prove beyond a doubt in anybody's mind that I'm a man and I can perform." Here, the army appears as a model for race relations nationwide. In civilian life, McGee noted, "it's still rare for whites to take orders from Negroes, especially in the South." But in the army, "Arkansas" (whom McGee described as "a Southern white serving under a Negro") saw no problem. "It doesn't seem to bother anyone to take orders from him. No one in the field, they don't think anything about it," Arkansas told McGee. "I've never heard a slang thrown at him because he is of Negro race." Comments of enlisted men and officers, woven into a coherent chorus, led directly to McGee's conclusion: "The American army is fully a generation ahead of the American public in its handling of racism."

McGee continued with a paean to color blindness: "What the Army has achieved is what America, despite bigots Negro and white, hopes someday to achieve—the elimination of race as a factor in human existence." The army McGee portrayed was the fulfillment of (a popular interpretation of) Martin Luther King's "dream": a world in which the color of one's skin was of no importance in comparison to the content of one's character.

Jim Hawkins, a "white boy from Chicago," explained the point in an irresistible sequence of video. "After you're with them so long," he said, "you're not looking at a man's color. You're looking at his intention and his job and what he's doing. You look over there and say, well, that man's picking up the shovel. You don't say that black man's picking up the shovel. You don't say, hey, colored sergeant, come here. Or hey, colored sergeant, can I talk to you?" Said Lieutenant Wilkerson, a "young Negro officer," "Just the other day, we had so many casualties. And nobody said, well, we had one colored and five —five whites. I mean, it were all casualties."

The report's final words went to (white) Capt. Anthony Mavroudis. In the army, he said, "we're all soldiers and [the] only color we know is the khaki and the green, the color of the mud and the color of the blood is all the same." McGee added a solemn postscript. Captain Mavroudis, he said, the man who believed that "the color of the mud and the color of the blood is all the same," was killed by an exploding landmine five days after the NBC team departed.

McGee's NBC special, which ran again in late May 1968, reached a broader range of Americans than any single news article, but the argument he made was neither original nor singular. African American newspapers generally heralded military progress. Urban League director Whitney Young, noted the *Los Angeles Sentinel* in 1966, had praised the armed forces' efforts on race, arguing that it was "shameful and ironical" that Black Americans find "more dignity, more security, and more chances for leadership as military men in Vietnam than in civilian life at home." The claim that appeared in a *Sentinel* story in 1966 ("the military for years [has] led the civilian sector in the matter of complete integration") by 1967 was a headline: "Military Leads the Way in Race Relations." Stated *Ebony*, in 1968, of military service: "The years of protest . . . are paying off."[44]

Articles in the white press offered the same praise for military integration, even as they often veered into sentimentality or, more often, patronizing language. White columnist Joseph Alsop wrote in the *Washington Post* about a "wiry young Negro lieutenant . . . strikingly alert, exceptionally intelligent," whose relationship with his white company commander showed how "this totally integrated new model Army should in truth serve as a model to the rest of us."[45]

*Time* magazine's 1967 "Democracy in the Foxhole" concluded that the performance of the "American Negro" in Vietnam proclaimed the truth that "color has no place in war; merit is the only measure of the man. . . . Black-white relations [in Vietnam] are years ahead of Denver and Dairen, decades ahead of Birmingham and Biloxi." (For context, these claims were embedded in a portrait of the Black soldier that included these lines: "Often inchoate and inconsistent, instinctively self-serving yet naturally altruistic, the Negro fighting man is both savage in combat and gentle in his regard for the Vietnamese"; "He may fight to prove his manhood—perhaps as a corrective to the matriarchal dominance of the Negro ghetto back home").[46] "In effect," concluded the author of a *New York Times* feature story, "The U.S. Negro in

Vietnam," while "participating in a war that pits yellow people against yellow people, America is demonstrating that its black and white people can get along."[47]

All these pieces—and there were dozens—offered the same refrain. "The only color out here is olive drab," insisted a white sergeant in *Time*'s 1967 article. A company commander from Mississippi (presumably white, as his race is not noted) told a *New York Times* reporter in 1966, "I see only one color, and that's olive drab." "[My] happiest experience" was in joining the army, said (Black) Sergeant Tapp to yet another *Times* reporter. "It was the first time I had ever been treated just like an individual." The commander of an army cavalry regiment, a Black lieutenant colonel, told a reporter for the *Chicago Defender* that if he were asked how many Negroes he had in his unit, "I couldn't answer, if my life depended on it. I don't know, and I don't want to know. All I'm interested in are men who will soldier." Noted *Time* magazine, in what was meant as a positive statement, "The Negro on duty becomes a truly invisible man." Concluded an article in the *Washington Post*, "Army Cited as Example of Integration's Success": "I see only one color and that's olive drab."[48]

It is important to remember that journalists craft stories. Frank McGee, for example, spent a month with the 101st Airborne in Vietnam, and his resulting fifty-minute television special relied on the comments of only seven men, all of whom endorsed, in various ways, a story of a color-blind army. A differently motivated reporter could certainly have put together a story on white racism and Black resentment—and some reporters did give hints of such tension. But in the mid-1960s, reports on race in the military tended to focus on the positive, if not in all details at least in their broader conclusions. That was not unreasonable. In that historical moment the military *did*, in fact, offer greater opportunity to Black Americans than did civilian society. Combat troops in Vietnam did, in fact, usually transcend racial divisions. And the phrase "same mud, same blood" was powerful, as was the wonderfully quotable and seemingly ubiquitous "I see only one color and that's olive drab."

Such monochromatic vision was also army standard. Key military officials, in efforts to ensure equal opportunity, were resolved to make race invisible. Moving beyond directives to consider only "merit" in promotions and assignments, the Department of Defense attempted to remove race from consideration altogether. Noted a *New York Times* reporter in early 1966, "Records are not kept here [Vietnam] by race. There is no place to record a

*Same Mud, Same Blood*

man's race, for example, on the Army's personnel forms 20 and 66." (In an era when roughly 45 percent of American men were veterans and 3.1 million Americans served on active duty, neither the reporter nor his copyeditor thought it necessary to explain what forms 20 and 66 were.)[49]

Race had disappeared from many official forms in the spring of 1964, when Norman Paul, the DoD chief of manpower, quietly ordered racial designations removed from the majority of DoD and individual service forms —thus ending most collection of racial data. His deputy assistant secretary of defense for civil rights did not believe the chief's initial directive went far enough; he drafted a version that would purge racial designations from all *existing* service files and collect new data only for biostatistical purposes. That revision went nowhere. But even so, the Department of Defense had gone a long way toward rendering race officially invisible.[50]

E ven as public stories of racial progress in the ranks pleased senior army leaders, most saw the problem with that narrative. Perhaps the army and its sister services were surpassing civilian society when it came to race relations, but the two worlds were never truly separate. And while the experience of combat might well have led men to rely on each other in ways that denied the divisions of race, the whole of the army, to put it bluntly, was not on the front lines in Vietnam.

In America's civilian society, the racial climate was changing dramatically in the mid-1960s. By that point civil rights activists could point to a series of successes: Truman's executive order desegregating the military; the Supreme Court's 1954 *Brown v. Board of Education* decision; the Civil Rights Act of 1964, passed by Congress in the aftermath of John F. Kennedy's assassination; the Voting Rights Act of 1965. But it was a scant five days after President Johnson signed the Voting Rights Act that Watts began to burn.

It was not solely spontaneous acts of civil unrest that marked that change, though they did give it a fearsome weight. The civil rights movement had faced profound internal divisions even before the 1963 March on Washington, and a growing group of young people—both within the movement and beyond—were becoming increasingly frustrated with the slow pace of change and the continuing violence visited on America's people of color.

In 1965, the Student Nonviolent Coordinating Committee (SNCC) reported, 92 percent of Black children in the South still attended "separate and unequal schools." In Alabama, for example, only .5 of 1 percent of Negro children were enrolled with whites in September 1965—and that was, percentage-wise, a huge increase over the .032 percent reported the previous year.[51] *Brown v. Board of Education* had been decided in 1954; this was eleven years' worth of "progress."

Moreover, despite strong national civil rights legislation, violence against those who claimed their rights had not abated. Alabama, again, provides an example. On a day that became known as Bloody Sunday, about 600 civil rights activists began a planned fifty-mile march from Selma to the state capital of Montgomery. They made it six blocks. State troopers and local police blocked the bridge leading out of Selma; when the peaceful marchers refused to turn back, police attacked with tear gas and billy clubs. The bridge, incidentally, was named for Edmund Pettus, a former US senator who had served as Grand Dragon of the Alabama Ku Klux Klan.

Despite the repeated sins of Alabama and continuing white resistance throughout the South, it was becoming increasingly clear that the South was not the only problem. Even though the rest of the nation had not written second-class citizenship into law, de facto segregation was just as real as its de jure parallel. In cities and towns far distant from the former Confederate states, a majority of Black children attended schools that were all-Black and disproportionately poor. Landlords and lenders discriminated on the basis of race, leaving people of color crowded into neighborhoods where dilapidated housing combined with poor city services. In 1965, the Black unemployment rate was 8.1 percent—almost precisely double the rate for whites.[52] But it was not only material conditions that mattered. Throughout the United States, Black Americans felt their vulnerability to white power and the inescapable pervasiveness of racism in American culture.

In this landscape, if the violence of the Watts uprising marked one sort of turning point in America's racial landscape, the emerging vision offered by charismatic SNCC leader Stokely Carmichael provided another. In June 1966, Carmichael, the newly elected chair of the Student Nonviolent Coordinating Committee, offered activists a new mantra. Speaking to the men and women who took up James Meredith's "Walk against Fear" after Meredith had been shot three times on the second day of his solo journey from Memphis, Tennessee, to Jackson, Mississippi, Carmichael proclaimed, "We been sayin' 'freedom' for six years and we ain't got nothin'. What we gonna start sayin' now is—'Black Power!'"[53]

Calls for "Black Power" alarmed a lot of people, in part because Carmichael refused to be pinned down about its definition. It was not up to him, he insisted, to define how Black people should exercise the power they had been so long denied. Still, he was well aware of its connotations, and mainstream civil rights groups hurried to distance themselves from Carmichael's calls.

That fall, NAACP director Roy Wilkins, in a letter to NAACP supporters, explicitly rejected the "strategy and tactics" of Black Power, the idea that "Negroes should stand in armed readiness to retaliate and deal out punishment on their own," and the implicit demand for "separatism" that "in a racially pluralistic society" makes all other groups "antagonists." The New York *Afro-American*, on the other hand, greeted Carmichael's move with reluctant support. SNCC's move to radicalism, argued its editors, was the "inevitable evolution of the drive for human rights in the face of a racist society in the Deep South." Its radicalism was "the offspring of oppression and race hate," they explained, "and if its table manners are not the best, its parents have only themselves to blame."[54]

Carmichael had gained a national stage. He squared off with a hostile interviewer on *Face the Nation* that June. He commanded a long feature story in *Ebony* that fall, reaching a broad national audience of African American readers. And even as the article explored the meaning of Black Power in thoughtful terms, it offered Carmichael as a model for young Black men: Carmichael was "the person sculptors would seek as a model for a statue of a Nubian god." His "disciplined wildness" had earned him the sobriquet "the Magnificent Barbarian." And he "walks like Sidney Poitier, talks like Harry Belafonte and thinks like a post-Muslim Malcolm X."[55]

Stokely Carmichael continued to give speeches around the nation, gradually honing his message. "In the past six years or so," he told an audience at the University of California, Berkeley, "this country has been feeding us a thalidomide drug of integration, and some Negroes have been walking down a dream street talking about sitting next to white people." Integration, Carmichael repeatedly insisted, was "an insidious subterfuge for white supremacy when initiated by blacks." What he meant by that was that integration came on white terms. That model of integration flowed only one way, as Black Americans sought access to white institutions. Integration never meant sending white children to Black schools or drawing white residents into Black neighborhoods. Thus integration, as a goal, implicitly defined white schools as good, Black schools as bad; white neighborhoods as good, Black neighborhoods as bad. How did that serve the needs of the broader Black community?[56]

Carmichael's call was for Black power and Black pride. "We must stop being ashamed of being black . . . we got to tell our brothers to stop kinking their hair and watching Tarzan movies, rooting for the white man," he explained.[57] The goal was not to win acceptance in white society. It was to take pride in their own.

Carmichael was in the vanguard, but he was not alone. In wildly different ways, young Black men and women began to live their own visions of Black Power. H. Rap Brown, who took over SNCC from Carmichael in mid-1967, called upon Black people to "carry on guerrilla warfare in all the cities . . . make the Vietcong look like Sunday school teachers." The Detroit riot, he told an enthusiastic audience in Detroit, was a "very good job." And as the white counterculture celebrated the 1967 Summer of Love in San Francisco's Haight-Ashbury district, members of Oakland's growing Black Panther Party for Self-Defense sent armed patrols to watch "racist pig cops" in Black neighborhoods and set up "liberation schools" for Black youth. "Political power comes through the barrel of a gun," said Panther leader Huey Newton to a *New York Times* reporter the following spring.[58]

In Atlantic City, a world away from the Panther's armed defense, a new "Miss Black America" pageant challenged "Miss America" notions of beauty. Saundra Williams, the contestant chosen as the first Miss Black America, wore a bright yellow jumpsuit with bells around her ankles as she performed an "African dance" in the talent competition. Williams told reporters, "With my title, I can show black women that they too are beautiful, even if they have large noses and thick lips." Mainstream Black magazines featured stories on Black pride and advertised the consumer goods that demonstrated it: "Are You Soul?" asked *Sepia* magazine's ad for "Soul Brother" car plates. Increasingly believing that "pride in one's racial heritage should be seen as well as heard and felt," in the words of *Ebony* magazine, members of a new "soulful generation" embraced the Afro as a sign of Black pride and identity.[59] "Say It Loud . . . I'm Black and I'm Proud," sang James Brown in 1968; his single hit the top of the R&B chart, where it remained for six weeks.

This is the world from which Black army privates were drawn: a realm of growing impatience and increasing militancy, a culture of Black pride and Black identity. Very few of these young men were members of organized Black Power groups. Not many of them yet had carefully reasoned ideological positions. The vast majority of these enlisted men were, like their white and brown counterparts, eighteen and nineteen years old. About a third of them, white and Black, had not even graduated from high school. And like their white peers, by 1968 more than a third of young Black soldiers were reluctant draftees into an increasingly unpopular war. They did not want to be in the army. They had not joined because they saw it as a site of opportunity.

*Same Mud, Same Blood*

Coming of age amid powerful assertions of "Black pride," many of these young men did not see the army's status of "better than civilian society" as acceptable. They did not mean to become "invisible," not if that meant fitting into a white-defined institution. And they certainly did not mean to put up with anyone calling them "boy" or "nigger," with racist graffiti in the latrines and rebel flags on barracks walls.

In the army, young Black draftees encountered young white draftees who, likewise, were products of a specific historical moment. They were thrown in with white men who had been raised to hate Black people, as well as with those who had had little contact with members of other races. They were made subordinate to white officers and NCOs who did not welcome challenges to their own sense of white superiority or fully embrace the notion of a color-blind army ("There's only one color, and that's o.d."). They grew frustrated with Black NCOs who had made the army a career and believed strongly in its possibilities. And they had learned lessons of Black solidarity.

Racial rumblings in the army had begun by 1967. During the fall of that year, for example, a soldier from the 4th Infantry Division in Vietnam wrote General Westmoreland to warn of a narrowly averted "race riot," the sort of action he believed might even "alter the U.S. policy in Vietnam." In a unit where clerks "display the confederate flag more than the Nation[']s flag," wrote Pvt. Curtis Monroe, "you could actually feel the tension in the air," and soldiers "were walking around with grenades in their pockets," ready to begin the "riot." Monroe concluded his letter with a plea for someone to "look into the matter" instead of assuming that "everyone is a fanatic when it comes to reporting these acts of racial disturbances."[60]

The resulting investigation concluded that there was no evidence of racial friction, even though the investigating officer noted that display of the Confederate flag could be "antagonistic in nature," as could referring to "colored soldiers" as "Boy." He also attached examples of anonymous letters received by a first sergeant "in the rear." "We have asked you for help," read one, "but they continue to Fuck with the negroes. So we are tired of asking, now we are demanding. A change is going to come and it will be very bad, because a lot of people will be hurt because we are tired of fighting Charlie and the white people too. So beware." Another threatened, "There is going to be trouble that you have never seen before if we aren't treated equal." It was signed "Yours truly, Sole Brother."[61] Yet none of these egregious examples of racism or evidence of Black frustration shattered the investigator's confidence in the color-blind army.

L. Howard Bennett, who had served in the civil rights office of the Department of Defense since 1963, had grown alarmed by rising racial tension and unrest that corresponded to the "racial conflagrations" in Newark and Detroit during the long hot summer of 1967. He saw a "disturbing deterioration" in military race relations following the Tet Offensive in early 1968 and communicated his apprehension to the secretary of defense. McNamara, concerned by rising levels of racial violence, made clear to each military service that it must take action to "preclude and prevent" further unrest and violence.[62]

The assassination of Martin Luther King Jr. in April 1968 marked a true turning point. By and large, within the army, violence was averted. "Some of the guys were angry and just wanted to hurt someone," recalled one Black man about his experience in Vietnam, "and there were some fistfights between whites and blacks, but most of the men were simply in shock."[63] Nonetheless, six outbreaks of internal violence in Vietnam were significant enough to require a "Serious Incident Report" in the days following King's murder, including one of the first fraggings reported in that war. And in Mannheim, Germany, a "racially oriented brawl" broke out in the Baden-Württemberg Confinement Facility after a "white prisoner opened up his damned trap and made a racial remark" (in the words of the provost marshal for the US Army Europe) as inmates learned of King's death.[64]

Even as conflict within the military did not begin to approach levels of civilian strife, King's assassination and its aftermath drove home McNamara's charge. Racial tensions existed. Nonetheless, army leadership seemed not fully cognizant of the growing crisis. General Westmoreland, who would command the army in Vietnam for another two months, worried that "militant groups" *might try* to spread racial conflict to Vietnam; Gen. Creighton Abrams, who would assume command there in June, wrote, "While I have no basis for feeling as I do . . . there is in my opinion a possibility that the racial unrest now exhibiting itself in our country could in some way infect our own men."[65]

Bennett himself, on an inspection tour evaluating equal opportunity efforts in Europe that May, likewise raised no immediate alarm. Instead, he told the *Stars and Stripes* that "the American military community has achieved a level of racial equality unmatched in civilian communities." The deputy assistant secretary of defense for civil rights, Jack Moskowitz (Bennett was his aide) went further. Following a conversation with Moskowitz, the head of *Stars and Stripes'* Munich bureau reported that the "racial problems which worried the Defense Department in 1964 have been solved." The army, Moskowitz said (here, in a direct quote), was the "most integrated sector of American life."[66]

*Same Mud, Same Blood*

In the summer of 1968, however, that integration was increasingly un-comfortable. Perhaps not surprisingly, racial conflict began at the margins, in places full of men who had failed to fully internalize army discipline. Stock-ades saw racial violence first. The riot at Long Binh Jail came in August 1968. The forty prisoners transferred from LBJ to an army stockade in Hawaiʻi introduced new forms of racial tension: "exchanges of profanity, fist fights, accusations, recriminations, and self-imposed separations." In the fall of 1968, the US Army stockade in the Ryukyus contended with multiple racial assaults, including one provoked by "custodial personnel" who "vilified the ethnic origin of Negro prisoners in general" in response to "verbal abuse" from Black inmates.[67]

But racial conflict also exploded in Vietnam that October at the China Beach Rest and Recreation Center, eight miles north of Da Nang, when eight Black servicemen, the majority of them marines, refused an order to surrender their weapons and severely beat an MP who attempted to force them to do so. The men took refuge in the nearby army compound, where they marched up and down the main street, weapons at ready, trailed by about fifty MPs and guards who prudently chose not to provoke what one of them called the potential for "a real Dodge City shootout." The men held out for five hours, as a group of Black soldiers expressed solidarity with them. Although the situation was defused without violence, tensions spread from the army compound to the neighboring navy and marine camps. Service-members gathered in race-based groups. The mood became increasingly ugly. Command efforts to address fundamental grievances helped, but the men remained on edge.[68]

In the wake of these events, Moskowitz and Bennett traveled to Vietnam; as they had inspected the implementation of DoD equal opportunity policies in Europe the preceding May, they were scheduled to evaluate efforts in the Far East that fall. On his return from Asia, Bennett offered an urgent warn-ing: if the Pentagon did not take immediate and significant action to deal with racial grievances and to combat racial hostility, the military would likely face "riots and demonstrations of epidemic proportions."[69]

Little came of Bennett's warnings. Reportedly, the new secretary for man-power and reserve affairs (who was, like recently departed Secretary of De-fense Robert McNamara, a white liberal from Michigan) was shocked and surprised by Bennett's claims. "Alarmist" was the word he used. Jack Mosko-witz, called into the boss's office, offered no support for Bennett's conclu-sions; he had not seen evidence, he said, of such racial strife. The source of this story, syndicated journalist Carl T. Rowan, attributed Pentagon inaction to "arrogance"—to the "notion held by some white liberals that they knew more about the problems than the Negroes who were warning them."[70] And Rowan, who had over the course of the decade thus far served as deputy assistant secretary of state, delegate to the United Nations, ambassador to Finland, and director of the US Information Agency (thus with a seat on the National Security Council), certainly had ways to know what happened behind closed doors.[71]

Oddly, Moskowitz stated publicly—to the *Washington Post*—that racial incidents in the military were "likely" to increase. "The young Negro serviceman," he said, "is expressing his black awareness and wanted to be respected. He is not going to be sloughed off. He is not going to suffer indignities." To this journalist, if not to his Pentagon superior, Moskowitz made clear where his sympathies lay. Recalling the anti-Semitic remarks he had shrugged off during his years in the army, he speculated that young Black men were no longer willing to let such comments go. "Maybe," Moskowitz said, "that's good."[72]

Rowan's sharp criticism of Pentagon leaders (in yet another layer of inside-politics) may have stemmed from simmering discontent over Moskowitz's appointment to the DoD civil rights post; in 1965 *Jet* magazine had complained that in appointing Moskowitz, McNamara had passed over three "Negro experts," including Bennett, who remained subordinate to the new deputy assistant secretary.[73] Whatever the explanation, however, Rowan was right: the Pentagon took little action. General Abrams, commander of US troops in Vietnam, did not even learn of Bennett's report on race relations until March 1969, and then only because the secretary of defense mentioned it in passing.[74]

As both Bennett and Moskowitz had predicted, the violence did not cease. And it was by no means restricted to Vietnam. In December 1968 alone, an "outspoken white segregationist" provoked "fisticuffs" in the mess line in Fort Riley's stockade in Kansas; ten "Negro prisoners" beat and forced three "Caucasian prisoners" to drink urine at California's Fort Ord; Black prisoners armed themselves with sticks to protest disciplinary segregation of three fellow Black soldiers at Louisiana's Fort Polk. The next year brought assaults on white prisoners by Black and Mexican American prisoners at Fort Hood in Texas and a series of racial fights and assaults at Fort Carson in Colorado.[75]

Meanwhile, at Fort Hood, somewhere between 60 and 100 Black soldiers of the 1st Armored Division had staged a sit-in to protest expected orders for anti-riot duty at the August 1968 Chicago National Convention. Their concern: being deployed against other Black Americans. After 43 men were charged with violating an order, the NAACP came to their aid, and the Army Special Civil Disturbance Board worried that these soldiers' actions presaged further such resistance. Public figures speculated about what might happen when Black soldiers were sent to restore order in other cases of civil unrest in Black neighborhoods. Would they stand with their brothers-in-arms, or would they turn their weapons on the forces of order in defense of their brothers-by-race?[76]

That same August, *Ebony* magazine ran a long story titled "Germany: Trouble Spot for Black GIs." Written by the editor of the notorious *Overseas Weekly* (a tabloid-style newspaper aimed at soldiers stationed in Germany and known best for its photos of topless women and headlines such as "Mickey Mouse Captain Screws Troops" and "GI Stabs Woman for Not Saying Thank You," even as it embraced a truth-telling ethos), this piece was a serious discussion of the "wide range of morale-destroying unpleasantness" that Black GIs and officers encountered in Germany. By late 1968, the growing number of GI complaints about racism, racial friction, and racial discrimination in the army was striking, even (or especially) as the inspector general's office judged almost all unsubstantiated.[77]

In 1969, news stories of Black-white brotherhood within the military—even with acknowledgment of residual tension—were being replaced with articles such as "Tensions of Black Power Reach Troops in Vietnam" and "Black Ire Erupts on Military Posts." Offered the latter, in August 1969: "It is more than an idle speculation to consider whether the percolation of racial hostility which progressed to disorders on city streets, on college campuses and high schools, has now found a new locus—on America's military installations."[78]

In some sense, the army's final straw came from the Marine Corps. Late in the evening of July 20, 1969—the day US astronauts first landed on the moon—a group of forty or so Black and Puerto Rican marines at Camp Lejeune in North Carolina began what was variously characterized as a "disturbance," a "war," and a "race fight." Shouting, "Call us niggers now" and "We're going to mess up some beast tonight," and armed with tree branches and broken broom handles, these members of the 2nd Marine Division injured fifteen white marines in seemingly random individual attacks. Cpl. Edward Bankston, who had been wounded three times in Vietnam, was surrounded by a group of thirty fellow marines who kicked him in frenzied violence as he lay prone on the ground. He died a week later of massive head injuries.[79]

The violence at Lejeune was not unprecedented. There were stories of a Black marine beaten to death by two white marines at Camp Lejeune during the summer of 1968—a murder that was apparently never prosecuted. The following November three Black marines killed a white marine on base. In the first seven months of 1969, 160 assaults, muggings, and robberies were reported, a significant number deemed racial in nature. In April, the 2nd Division commander had put together an ad hoc committee to investigate the complaints of minority personnel. But it was the violence of July 20 that drew attention. The *Chicago Tribune* reported, in a headline that summed up so much more than its author intended, "Three Marines Hurt in Fight with Negroes."[80]

Soon thereafter, the Honorable L. Mendel Rivers, chairman of the House Armed Services Committee, appointed a "Special Subcommittee to Probe Disturbances on Military Bases." Rivers charged the subcommittee with investigating the origins and extent of racial violence "on military installations," but the subcommittee, in the end, restricted its report to the incident at Camp Lejeune. However, based on 1,250 pages of sworn testimony in eight days' worth of hearings that sometimes ran until one or two in the morning, the report confidently stated that the "root causes of the race problems" at Camp Lejeune were "typical of those of any military base" and that the "tragic events" at Lejeune should serve as "strong and real evidence" of "a serious race problem . . . in all the services."[81]

As this congressional subcommittee conducted hearings into the state of race relations in the US military, the *Washington Post* weighed in. "Fragmentation, polarization and divisiveness are deplorable aspects of civilian life," the editorial stated bluntly. "For the military, given the nature of its assignment to be ready for any eventuality, they become intolerable."[82]

Pressure was coming from all directions. Within the army, "nervous commanders" tried to talk the troops down. The hands that held the purse strings—in Congress—demanded solutions. The new secretary of defense, Nixon appointee Melvin Laird, had placed race relations high on the draft of "people objectives" he had circulated to all service secretaries and chiefs of staff that summer, and a new deputy assistant secretary of defense for civil rights had claimed a public voice. Black civilians were weighing in, from the collegial pressure of mainstream organizations such as the Urban League and the NAACP to the furious insistence of more radical groups that Vietnam was nothing more than "the White Man sending the Black Man to fight the Yellow Man to protect the country he stole from the Red Man."[83] The press was chronicling the outbreaks of racial violence and the frustrations of Black soldiers, pointing to the racial failures of a military service that was also struggling in a failing war. And within the army, as anger grew and morale declined, those who led men (and women) tried whatever seemed plausible, offering a proliferation of ad hoc solutions to a problem that had yet to be officially recognized.

Thus in the summer of 1969, Gen. William Westmoreland—now chief of staff of the army, his command in Vietnam given over to Creighton Abrams in June 1968—charged a small team with investigating the state of race relations in the army. This was the summer following the debacle of the army assault on Hill 937 in May, won in ten days' close battle, only to be immediately abandoned. A total of 56 Americans had died in repeated assaults, with 420 wounded. Sen. Edward Kennedy, on the floor of the US Senate, said of "Hamburger Hill" what many Americans had begun to believe: "American boys are too valuable to be sacrificed for a false sense of military pride."[84]

This was the summer that *Life* magazine ran the "Faces of the American Dead," photographs of 242 young men who were only "one week's toll." It was the summer that Westmoreland waited for the results of an army investigation into former helicopter gunner Ronald Ridenhour's report of "something rather dark and bloody" in Vietnam: the massacre of hundreds of unarmed Vietnamese civilians in Pinkville (My Lai hamlet) the previous spring.[85] And it was the summer that the cascade of racial incidents could no longer be forced into the traditional framework of equal opportunity in the "I see only one color and that's olive drab" army.

Lt. Col. James S. White, who became the public face of that investigation team, briefed the chief of staff in mid-September. Westmoreland's calendar shows that he devoted an hour and forty-five minutes to White's "Briefing on Assessment of Racial Harmony in the U.S. Army" on a day in which he also delivered a speech, juggled twelve other meetings, allotted five minutes for lunch at his desk, and managed both a haircut and a tennis match "with Stevie" (his daughter). A week and a half later, on a Saturday morning, Westmoreland accompanied White to meet with Secretary Resor. Resor's briefing, which lasted for an hour and twenty minutes, appeared in Westmoreland's calendar as "Briefing on Assessment of Racial Tension in the Army." It is hard to imagine that anyone had seriously offered "harmony" as a description, even as a topic to be assessed. "Tension," in Resor's briefing, better fit the reality. The term White used, however, was "war."[86]

In that context, the secretary of the army decided to focus on race in his October address to the members of the Association of the United States Army. And Resor, who had been awarded a Silver Star for his actions during the Battle of the Bulge before he returned to Yale Law and his subsequent career at a top New York firm, spoke as one who understood the history, culture, and logic of the US Army.[87]

The army, Secretary Resor told the assembled crowd, had for years been "far ahead of civilian society." In the army, he said, "black and white soldiers were living, eating, and fighting side by side well before the Supreme Court's first decision on school desegregation." But even though the army had offered Black Americans the chance "to be treated as an equal, to rise or fall on [their] own efforts and abilities," he argued, that was not now sufficient. The army was not able to insulate itself from the upheavals of social change, as soldiers not only came to the army shaped by their lives to date but also —because of changes in media and communications—maintained ties to civilian society in unprecedented ways.[88]

"The Negro soldier in particular," said Resor, "is different from his counterpart of ten years ago." In that earlier incarnation, Black soldiers had met racial discrimination "only with hard work and endurance." Today, in contrast, that Black soldier would be likely to "make his resentment known." Today, he continued, the young Black soldier showed "more personal and racial pride, more bitterness at real and imagined injustice." Like his white peers, he wanted to "retain his personal identity," his "individuality," of which his race was a part. "A Negro in uniform," Resor proposed, in a sentence worth quoting a second time, "does not cease to be a Negro and become a soldier instead. He becomes a Negro soldier."[89]

In powerful terms, Resor rejected the premise of a color-blind army. Black soldiers, he said, confronted "difficulties in the Army which are directly tied to their race." They experienced "subtle discourtesies" and were "abused with racial epithets." They suffered discrimination, sometimes open, sometimes unspoken, when they left post. They found regulations enforced more strictly against them than against white soldiers, and gatherings of Black soldiers were treated with suspicion, harassed or dispersed by military police. They resented "the imperfections in the country they are defending with their lives."[90]

And so, Resor insisted, the Black soldier deserved "to know from his leaders where they stand . . . whether they are willing to accept him without asking that he reject his heritage." He needed a commander who "recognizes such slogans as 'black is beautiful' as the gestures of pride, comradeship and solidarity," a commander who was not quick to "write off the spirited ones" but could see in them the potential for leadership.[91]

And thus he offered a call for race consciousness. "Occasionally," said the secretary of the army, publicly rejecting the proud refrain, "one hears a commander say, with the best of intentions, 'for me, there's only one color, and that's o.d.'" That pledge, he continued, must remain. Army policy must be to treat all its members fairly and equally, regardless of race. "But putting black and white soldiers in green uniforms," he insisted, "does not relieve the commander of the responsibility to recognize the differences in racial background—and consequently in experience and outlook—among the troops." Equity and equality would not come from insisting there was no difference between Black and white but from recognizing and embracing the significance of difference. Only thus, he concluded, could the army build "a degree of racial understanding and respect for human dignity of which the Nation can be proud."[92]

# 3 DEFINING THE PROBLEM

When the secretary of the army devotes a high-profile speech to a single issue, his comments obviously carry weight, both within the army and beyond. In Secretary Stanley Resor's case, this was especially true. Resor, in keeping with his reputation for "quiet efficiency" in dealing with the problems plaguing his army, commonly kept the press at a distance; he held only two press conferences over the course of his six-year term. (His public reticence is interesting, for Resor likely learned about shaping public perception at his mother's knee: his parents had, together, revolutionized the field of advertising while building J. Walter Thompson into a major international firm.)[1] That day in DC, however, Resor spoke on a matter of urgency. And as headlines about race relations in the military shifted from praise to alarm, Resor offered the army's first significant public response.

Even as Secretary Resor's October speech gave shape to "the problem of race," his comments betray their origins in multiple, shifting, and contradictory efforts to define the "problem"—efforts that did not end with Resor's pronouncement. Resor's words reflect the influence of other crises his institution faced at that moment and nod toward some of their proposed solutions. And even as he challenged the primacy of "only one color, and that's o.d.," he continued to rely heavily on the institutional logic of the army.

Furthermore, as Resor and a host of army leaders struggled to define the problem and to propose solutions, they were not acting in isolation. The most important pressure came from the Department of Defense, which had confronted racial discrimination well before the army began to acknowledge the growing crisis. Like his recent predecessor Robert McNamara, Richard

Nixon's secretary of defense, Melvin Laird, directly addressed the problem of race—though in a radically different environment.

It is not that Laird put equal opportunity at the top of his list of priorities. A hawkish man whose "broad, blunt features, receding hairline and severe crewcut suggested the visage of a Marine drill sergeant" (in the words of his *New York Times* obituary) and who was sometimes portrayed by political cartoonist Herblock as a human H-bomb, Laird was fully focused on the war in Vietnam. He was crafting and defending his "Vietnamization" of the war, managing the withdrawal of troops, contending with massive cuts in budget and personnel, planning for the advent of the all-volunteer force, and, bottom line, dealing with President Nixon's lies and paranoia.[2]

Nonetheless, as race relations in the military deteriorated, Laird was forced to confront the growing crisis. In March 1969, Robert Brown—Nixon's special assistant for civil rights—had begun to push for action, and a White House memorandum offered pointed questions about racial discrimination in the military. That same month, National Urban League director Whitney Young sought assurance from Secretary Laird that he would work toward "affirmative accomplishments," including for military personnel. Soon thereafter Laird issued a statement on equal opportunity in the armed forces, pledging to all personnel that he intended to remove "every vestige of discrimination," and began circulating drafts of an expansive "Human Goals Charter." Throughout this era of racial turbulence, the DoD steadily exerted pressure on the individual services—sometime privately, sometimes quite publicly.[3]

External pressure and DoD directives mattered enormously. But it is also critical to understand that, by the time the army secretary publicly acknowledged the racial crisis in the fall of 1969, local commanders had been dealing with it for a while. Much racial conflict was minor, easily subsumed into the petty sorts of indiscipline that NCOs handle as a matter of course. Other times it rose to the notice of command, mostly when someone was killed or a complaint drew attention from a congressional representative. In such scattered instances, *this* sergeant or colonel or general did a better job handling the problem; *that* one did worse. But in all cases their responses were immediate and contingent, because the army—as an institution—had not yet officially recognized "the problem" of race.

As the army, at the behest of its secretary and chief of staff, turned its institutional focus to race—racial violence, racial discontent, racial tension, racial discrimination, and flat-out racism—it did two things, both of which conformed to normal army practice. First of all, official attention made the problem visible. All the racial conflicts that had been simmering and erupting over the previous months now were categorized as "racial." Such incidents were newly subject to official report, in standardized form. Specific actions were prescribed. Regular evaluations were required.

Second, the army tried to define the problem. What were its origins? Its manifestations? Its solutions? It is not that people had not been grappling with those questions, in various ways, before the secretary's speech, most particularly from 1968 forward. But from October 1969 on, those efforts took new significance. In true army fashion, the newly named problem prompted studies and investigations, consultancies and evaluations, briefings and reports. It generated mountains of paper. Out of these, in the way of bureaucracy, a set of ideas developed. Phrases were adopted and repeated without attribution, again and again and again, until they seemed nothing more than common sense.

From this process, within the space of just over a year, emerged a set of claims and principles that shaped army actions over the course of this army-defined crisis. And as those charged with managing the problem narrowed their definitions of its origins, they remained quite ecumenical when it came to solutions. It is tempting to claim that they threw everything at the wall to see what stuck; the process was not that random, but the solutions explored were strikingly diverse and, in a few cases, seem completely at odds with the institutional logic of the army itself.

In that process, as well, men scrambled for advantage. As the problem of race was now deemed significant, successful solutions could advance careers. Intriguing proposals could bring resources. Being in the right place at the right time could be useful. Likewise, failure now mattered as it had not before. Some now sought to control the terms, to define the parameters, to guard their positions or to defend past actions. Who would define the problem? And who, within the institutional structure of the army, would gain or suffer in that process?

D uring the summer of 1969, as it became ever less possible to dismiss instances of racial violence as either isolated or random, and with the House Armed Services Committee launching its own investigation of the emerging crisis, Gen. William Westmoreland had begun the official internal army process. Seeking information, he ordered the army staff to assess the level of racial tension in the institution. Westmoreland's charge, in the midst of the US war in Vietnam, was in itself revealing: to identify problems that "could negate" the army's "past accomplishments in racial harmony" and "impair the army's ability to accomplish its mission."[4]

The staff did what competent staffs do: it gathered information to the desired end. Staff members assembled and analyzed complaints of racial discrimination and reports of racial incidents. They made fact-finding trips to Fort Bragg and Fort Riley. They reviewed reports from army representatives on DoD fact-finding trips conducted between 1966 and 1968, examining interviews of soldiers "of all grades and races" and commanders at all levels, both within the United States and at six major overseas commands. And they took a "hard look" at statistical data, trying to determine whether complaints about assignment, promotion, and punishment were backed up by the numbers.[5] (Given that the army had purposely dropped many racial identifiers in the interest of color-blind equality, this last was a challenge.)

By mid-September they were ready to brief the chief of staff. Though their report reflected the work of many, it was a single man—a Black officer—who was tasked with speaking for them. It was he who would deliver the message, first to Westmoreland and then to Resor, and then to commanders around the globe. James S. White was a thirty-seven-year-old lieutenant colonel, recently returned from Vietnam. White had been commissioned in the army in 1954, just days after graduating from Baltimore's Morgan State College. Soon thereafter he married a girl from Philadelphia, spent the tail end of the 1950s in Bamberg, West Germany (1st Battle Group, 15th Infantry), and then was graduated from the Infantry Officer Advanced Course in the summer of 1960. He put in time on the ROTC (Reserve Officers' Training Corps) staff at Florida A&M; survived a helicopter crash as part of an 82nd Airborne Test Unit at Fort Bragg; had been stationed in Korea; had fought in Vietnam. The Black press noted his progress, as it did in the days when Black officers were few and such achievement seemed to demand public recognition.[6]

White was an extraordinarily competent man. He would go on, after leaving the army, to earn advanced degrees and serve as managing director of the city of Philadelphia in the difficult years after city officials ordered the bombing of the MOVE house in West Philadelphia. He had been appointed to the position in part because he was the only person who was trusted by "both" sides in the bombing. White was good at building consensus, "quiet, calculating, and fair-minded," in the words of a later admirer.[7]

In addition to those qualities of character, White offered credibility. First and foremost, he was a Black officer. In the eyes of most of those he briefed on race relations, his own visible racial identity granted him authority. His

Lt. Col. James S. White, accompanied by his wife, Juanita A. White,
receiving the 1969 Department of the Army Pace Award for
Exceptional Service for his work on army race relations.
*Courtesy Gary A. White.*

military appearance also mattered. It is true that in the late 1960s and early
1970s, military officers assigned to the Pentagon wore civilian clothes most
of the time, a custom traced back to President Dwight D. Eisenhower's complaint that there were so many uniforms in DC that the city resembled an
armed camp. That practice had some advantages in those years, when uniforms drew unwelcome attention from the growing number of anti-war
protesters who often targeted the Pentagon. But White would have worn his
uniform to conduct briefings in the Pentagon and, subsequently, in Europe
and Vietnam, and that uniform displayed a set of key facts that signified a
different form of authority or, at the very least, legitimacy: infantry, service
in Vietnam, awarded four Bronze Stars.[8]

Colonel White's briefings, almost certainly by design, gained power from
their delivery. White warned army leaders that it was "indefensible" to ignore
the racial "fears, hostilities and misunderstandings," the "signs [that] can
be read in the racial obscenities" written on latrine walls, the complaints of
Black troops who suffered injustice solely because of their race. "I can verify
from my own experiences," White told the chief of staff and the secretary of
the army, and then commanders in the continental United States and the

*Defining the Problem*

US Army Europe (USAREUR), the US Army Pacific (USARPAC) and MACV and USARV, "that the cries of the Negro soldier . . . have never been so loud."[9]

These briefings, delivered by a Black man speaking in the first person, offered the army's initial definitions of the problem of race. In these repeated briefings, which (in the version presented to commanders outside the United States) on paper stretch to nineteen pages of type and six pre-PowerPoint charts, White explained the origins and manifestations of racial tension in the army and offered some potential solutions. The presentation was not especially clearly organized. It began strong, but by the end the order seemed haphazard, with scattered points occasionally interrupted by powerful, quotable lines. Nonetheless, the key claims of the army staff weave through the document, and from the distance of decades their underlying assumptions are almost painfully obvious.

To begin, White posed a question: "Does the Army have a race problem?" His answer was an unequivocal "yes." He likened the problem to an iceberg, much remaining below the surface, unseen. He rejected reports from the field that labeled racial conflict "spontaneous," with no real impact on discipline or morale. "We feel that it is not to be taken lightly," he said, "when, in a military environment, men, regardless of geographical location, begin fighting men of another race." And while he believed the "serious" problem was "not hopeless," he also acknowledged that no immediate solutions may exist.[10]

The origins of the problem, White explained in a line that would be recycled for years, did not lie within the army. They lay outside, in American society. "The Army has a race problem," he said, "because our country has a race problem." Young soldiers entered the military as products of society, their racial attitudes and experiences shaped long before they put on a uniform. "Putting black and white citizens in green uniforms," White noted, did not obliterate those attitudes and experiences. "A Negro in uniform," he wrote, "does not cease being a Negro and become a soldier instead. He becomes a Negro soldier." Here, in White's original briefing, is the origin not simply of Resor's claim but of his exact words. But White, unlike Resor, continued: "White troops, also, are not instantly cleansed of years of experience and attitudes."[11]

According to White's assessment, the sources of racial tension were not only societal, but generational. "The young Negro soldier," said White, "as well as the young Caucasian soldier, is much different than his counterpart of ten years ago." (As almost always happened in military comments on race, the young white soldier quickly disappeared from discussion.) In the past, said White, when confronted with discrimination the Black soldier's "typical response was hard work and endurance" (see Resor, once again). In contrast, the current young Black soldier reacted with "more personal and racial pride; more bitterness at real or imagined injustice; and often," White continued, with "a chip on the shoulder."[12] (And again, Resor, though he wisely dropped the phrase "a chip on the shoulder.")

In the end, White presented two linked messages. Although "the roots of the race problem lie outside the army . . . the tendrils have spread within it" and so "must be recognized and dealt with." The solution he offered made perfect sense within army culture and logic: the problem of race could be managed through "outstanding leadership." In the months ahead, army commanders, at all levels, must begin to address the "root causes" of racial unrest, from racial slurs and overt discrimination to the influence of "both the black and white racists," from racial inequities in assignments to the administration of nonjudicial punishment. And, insisted White, they must be trained to do so.[13]

In that effort, White argued, army leaders' best tool would be "proper communication." It had been, he said repeatedly, a failure of communication, "a lack of mutual understanding," that had inflamed the racial tension and distrust that young men carried into the army, that had sparked the racial violence. To manage the problem, the army must improve communication between Black and white soldiers, most particularly as young Black enlisted men claimed racial pride and Black consciousness. The army must improve communication across ranks so that commanders did not overreact to "spirited" Black soldiers, thus writing off "potential leaders" as "troublemakers and militants." (Of course, he noted, his years of army life showing, "discipline is not discrimination.") And leaders must do a better job explaining the rationale for their actions. Even as "Negro" complaints were frequently identical to those of "Caucasian soldiers," White said, "the Negro blames discrimination while the Caucasian soldier blames the Army as a whole," for Black soldiers have "lost faith" in the army system.[14]

Just as passages from White's briefing turned up word-for-word in Resor's October address, the briefing also shaped the message sent that month by the army chief of staff. Westmoreland noted the spreading "tendrils" that must be dealt with, even as the "roots of the race problem lie outside the army"; he saw the solution in "outstanding leadership"; he endorsed the need for "effective communication" and cautioned against "overreaction."[15] Westmoreland trusted White's analysis. He also clearly trusted White, for he made him his messenger: Westmoreland put Colonel White in front of the House

*Defining the Problem*

Armed Services Committee and dispatched him to brief army leaders in both Europe and the Pacific.

Congress came first, and hitting the right tone before the House Committee was not easy. Members were upset. They were angry. They saw the military's problem of race as just one more crisis in a nation marred by violence and division, floundering in a failing war. In these hearings, committee members required a combination of mea culpa and reassurance; in White's testimony, for the army, a good deal was at stake. Colonel White offered his now-standard briefing and at the very least survived the experience. His analysis, however, got no public notice. The testimony on racial conflict in the military was closely guarded. Syndicated columnist Jack Anderson—who in late September exposed secret testimony that some military bases were every bit as "dangerous" at night as "encampments in the middle of Viet Cong territory" —reported that, once transcripts of the hearings had been typed up, both shorthand tapes and typewriter ribbons were confiscated and burned. Anderson saw the Pentagon's influence there. Civilian attitudes toward the military were bad enough in 1969; service and DoD leaders knew such stories of racial violence would not help. Anderson's column, in fact, was titled "Military Chiefs Accused of Race Trouble Coverup."[16]

While White's briefings got little press coverage, they did spark internal maneuvering, as those in the path of the new institutional focus on race began constructing their defenses, scheming to use this new concern to their advantage, or simply figuring what the new directives would mean for their own workload and for day-to-day life in the units for which they were responsible. Race was now a problem, but "the problem of race" might well be an opportunity.

Traveling west first, to Pacific Command, White briefed Gen. Ralph Haines, commander in chief, US Army Pacific, in early January 1970. Writing from USARPAC headquarters in Hawai'i, Haines put his personal authority behind White. White was knowledgeable and offered "food for thought," Haines told top commanders in the Pacific, and he urged them to make sure White's onsite briefings got appropriate attention.[17] White now had the imprimatur of the secretary of the army, its chief of staff, and the commander in chief of USARPAC.

But Haines's attention to race had preceded White's January USARPAC briefing. In the wake of Westmoreland's message and Resor's speech, he had circulated a memo on "equal opportunity and treatment of military personnel" to key officers in the Pacific Command. At least one officer seized the opportunity implied. Ben Sternberg, the commander of the US Army Hawai'i, took proactive measures, addressing what he saw as the root causes of racial unrest: the marginalization of and disrespect toward Black soldiers. He also documented his efforts in a November 1969 letter to General Haines.[18]

To note that Sternberg saw an opportunity is not to suggest that he was not committed to racial equality; perhaps, like Jack Moskowitz, his experience as a Jew in the army had made him particularly sensitive to the struggles of Black soldiers. This veteran of three wars also had an impressive record of initiative. At the age of sixteen, as a new high school graduate, he had had to delay entry to West Point because of his youth. By the age of twenty-eight, Sternberg was a lieutenant colonel; even by the standards of promotion during World War II that was strikingly young. And as an infantry officer, he had earned both a Distinguished Service Cross and a Silver Star.[19] Nonetheless, in his letter to Haines, Sternberg was staking a claim, positioning himself to shape USARPAC's response and to receive credit for so doing.

Sternberg's November letter to Haines detailed his command's efforts to make sure that the US Army Hawai'i had an effective program "not only on paper but in fact." Sternberg highlighted the importance of leadership. He emphasized the significance of culture, from "Afro-natural" haircuts and Black-oriented merchandise in the PX (post exchange) to soul music in jukeboxes and Black entertainers onstage. He documented the addition of Black officers and NCOs to promotion boards and to the inspector general and judge advocate staffs and of Black soldiers to the military police. He pointed out his new junior officer councils and training in race relations. He informed Haines of his outreach to civilian groups who might help make Black soldiers more welcome in local communities. And, like everyone else who worried about the problem of race in the army, he stressed the importance of communication.[20] Sternberg must have been preternaturally attuned to army currents, for the actions he outlined corresponded almost exactly to the ones the army would eventually embrace.

Haines, in turn, distributed Sternberg's letter throughout the Pacific Command. But Sternberg's communication was clearly meant for his commanding officer, not for his peers. To demonstrate how seriously he took the issue, for example, Sternberg explained that he himself had carried the first load of Black-oriented merchandise from the mainland to Hawai'i—on General Haines's aircraft.[21] In Vietnam, Sternberg's letter did not find a warm reception.

In Vietnam, G-1's (Personnel) request that officers evaluate the "fruitful areas we can exploit" from Sternberg's letter drew resistance. Few officers in Vietnam saw this as an opportunity; for most, it seemed a diversion from their primary mission. An information officer's response was the most positive but noted only what his office already did right: "black pin-ups and black soldier characters in cartoons" appeared in the *Command Information* newspaper. The provost marshal acknowledged the "merit" of adding "Negro military police" but made clear that was a problem for the MP training brigade at Fort Gordon, Georgia, rather than for him. The staff judge advocate had no "legal objection" to requiring that all courts-martial include a Black officer or NCO but questioned such a requirement's feasibility: Was there a sufficient number available for such detail? he asked.[22]

Most responses offered the minimum necessary reply. That was not true of the Office of the Inspector General. The initial response from Col. Willard W. Hawke, the IG behind the case against Major Merritt, while not brief, was largely dismissive. The IG's office had received some complaints that corresponded to Sternberg's proposed solutions, Hawke acknowledged, but they were of no significant number and certainly not sufficient to justify creating programs to address them.[23]

But the inspector general did not leave it there. In response to G-1's request, the IG's office examined 1,000 files that contained complaints and requests for assistance received over the past six months. In them they found little to support Sternberg's analysis. Of 1,000 cases, only 61, or 6.1 percent, were tied to race. And of those 61, only two charges of racial discrimination or prejudice had been fully substantiated by the IG's office.[24]

Here the IG's report went further. The issue was not simply lack of evidence for Sternberg's concerns; it was a troublesome pattern the IG staff perceived. Soldiers who alleged racial prejudice, they argued, tended to be those who were "already in trouble or under pressure." Rather than racial discrimination, these officers saw immaturity and lack of self-control, messy personal lives, refusals to follow legitimate orders. They also found it significant that complainants aimed high and distant. Almost two-thirds of complaints went to high officials in Washington; the president was a favorite for appeals. Members of Congress, the attorney general, and the army chief of staff received their share. In Hawke's account, this was evidence that the complaints were not legitimate—not that soldiers did not trust the system.[25]

In the end, the IG's office pushed back hard against Sternberg's model. Sternberg's approach, Colonel Hawke asserted, would likely backfire. In army bureaucratese, the IG's office insisted that "the approach to the development of prevention and elimination programs be based on an understanding of the nature of the problems." And from Hawke's perspective, Sternberg's sensitivity to the desires of "a small vocal group" was not an appropriate understanding of the problem. Some of Sternberg's specific suggestions "could create more disharmony than they would eliminate," concluded the IG. For example, "command sanctions for special hair styles, 'black-oriented' merchandise, soul music, [and] Negro entertainment may well serve to polarize even more the whites and blacks."[26]

With impressive institutional savvy, the IG mined Secretary Resor's address for support in his reply to G-1. Resor "struck at the heart of the problem," wrote the IG. In Hawke's version of Resor's address, however, the problem was not the root causes of racial strife but the preferential treatment of Black soldiers and the disruptions they caused. Hawke offered his claim in Resor's words and in so doing transformed Resor's caveat into the fundamental point of the speech: "I do not suggest that the Negro soldier receive preferential treatment," Hawke quoted. "Nor should he be held to anything less than traditional standards of performance and discipline."[27]

Soon thereafter, the inspector general provided a short article on "racial understanding" for the *USARV Commander's Notes*. The substance of the article, Hawke noted, came from Secretary Resor's remarks. "Since today's Negro seeks to retain his personal and racial identity, racial conscientiousness [*sic*] should not be understood as militancy," he wrote, in words drawn from Resor and thus indirectly from White. But much depends on order and stress, and Hawke's final words changed the emphasis of the message. Resor had concluded with a call for "racial understanding and respect for human dignity." Hawke offered, as final words, the following: "On the other hand, militants and troublemakers who allege racial discrimination as a ploy must be dealt with calmly and fairly—discipline is not discrimination."[28]

Here, the inspector general had offered an alternate definition of the problem, and he had brought his best evidence to bear. It is not surprising he pushed so hard, as the problem of race would bring unwelcome attention to the entire IG system and, in Hawke's estimation, make the job of the IG's office more difficult. In retrospect, it would not be fair *not* to concede that the IG's office was sometimes right about the motivations of men "already in trouble," just as it would not be fair not to point out the institutional racism that shaped assumptions and procedure. The IG's office endorsed the status quo, and the status quo had found no evidence of racism in the use (presumably by white NCOs and officers) of "nigger" and "boy" to address African American soldiers.[29]

Just as Hawke's response reveals the force of institutional racism, it also reflects the army's vaunted belief in color-blind equality. In its most generous reading, Hawke's rejection of "preferential treatment" belongs to that tradition, just as it reveals its limits. The case for color-blind equality appeared elsewhere, too, as others responded to Sternberg's letter with a sense of moral commitment. Outlining the requirements for service on promotion boards or court-martial panels, one colonel noted that "none of the considerations . . . is contingent on the color of the soldier's skin" and insisted that compelling "any minority group to accept a lion's share of this type of duty eliminates the 'equal' from the phrase 'equal opportunity and treatment.'" In his response to Sternberg's letter, the deputy adjutant general cited DoD Directive 5120.36, which in 1963 had removed racial identifications from most military records. He bristled: "It is ironic that certain actions being taken by US Army, Hawaii actually violate this long standing directive and premise that all will be treated equally." Duty rosters, he noted, "are not maintained by race," and to do so would be "tantamount to 20 years regression in the Army's efforts toward racial equality."[30]

Resor's address offered a fundamental change in the army's color-blind approach to racial equality: identity matters. But the address was not a directive. Nor was it a clear and pointed statement. After all, Hawke's takeaway was "discipline is not discrimination." Other readings were possible, too: the problem is the generation gap; leadership offers the solution; we must focus on better communication. Sternberg's letter, on the other hand, detailed efforts to put race consciousness into practice. It could not be read differently. Still, the pushback might seem surprising, even given that General Haines's support had inadvertently made Sternberg a target in officers' ongoing jockeying for advantage.

Here, though, context matters. Sternberg's letter hit desks in Vietnam in the immediate wake of a visit by L. Howard Bennett, who (following the departure of Jack Moskowitz) served briefly as acting deputy assistant secretary of defense for civil rights. Many army officers felt themselves under the microscope, judged for racial conflict they saw as imported from civilian society and largely beyond their control. Bennett, of course, had made a similar trip as Moskowitz's aide the previous year, visiting Europe as well as Southeast Asia. Still, things were different in 1969. Perhaps most significantly, it was no longer possible to dismiss racial conflict in the military as isolated, sporadic events.

The 1968 trips had drawn no notice and disappeared with scarcely a trace; in 1969 newspapers heralded the visit of an "eight-man Pentagon team accompanied by a special presidential aide." That aide was supposed to be Bob Brown, an African American special assistant to the president who worked closely with Nixon on issues of race. Instead, for reasons never publicly explained, it was Bruce Rabb, a twenty-eight-year-old white staff assistant who had recently graduated from Harvard Law. But Brown and Bennett were working in concert. Shortly before Bennett's November trip to Asia, the two men had traveled together to inspect a military post in Mississippi; in Biloxi, Brown and Bennett had been turned away from an off-post tavern that catered to military personnel. "We don't serve colored here," they were told by the "woman manager."[31]

By late 1969, Bennett had been at the heart of Department of Defense approaches to civil rights and race relations for six years. Although he chafed against the limits he confronted and was repeatedly passed over for the position of deputy assistant secretary of defense for civil rights, eventually serving as aide to a man half his age, he spanned the terms of three secretaries (McNamara, Clark Clifford, and Laird) and three presidents (Kennedy, Johnson, and Nixon). As with other actors, Bennett's background helps to explain his approach to the problem of race.

Lowell Howard Bennett, born in Charleston, South Carolina, in early 1913, was the grandson of enslaved men and women and a minister's son. He graduated cum laude from Fisk University in 1935 and began the hard work of civil rights advocacy, eventually leaving the South for Minneapolis. He was not in uniform during World War II, serving instead as a regional director for the USO. After the war Bennett worked with future presidential candidate Hubert Humphrey—then mayor of Minneapolis—to set up a council on human relations and then moved on to the University of Chicago, where, as a Julius Rosenwald Fellow, he earned a law degree and a master's degree in political science. Back in Minneapolis, Bennett combined the practice of law with directing the local branches of the NAACP and the Urban League and raising the daughter he had with his wife and college sweetheart, Marian. In 1957 Minnesota's governor appointed Bennett to the municipal bench as the first African American to serve. Defeated in his reelection bid two years later, Bennett then defeated seven other candidates for a seat on the Minneapolis school board in 1963—again, as the first African American to serve. That role did not last long: Jack Kennedy, just weeks before he was assassinated, tapped Bennett for a DoD position focused on race relations in the armed forces.[32]

Bennett came to DC in 1963 as an accomplished fifty-year-old. His origins were in the elite circles of Negro society; his life structured by education and professional advancement; his activism anchored in the law and policy, in the venerable institutions of the NAACP and the Urban League. He counted Martin Luther King Jr. as a friend; likewise Hubert Humphrey. Everything in his experience—including the setbacks—validated the traditional means and goals of the early civil rights movement: hard work, education, respectability, integration. Yet he did have a daughter who came of age in the 1960s, and perhaps her experiences offered him some different insights. In 1965, twenty-one-year-old Marian Bennett was arrested for trespassing, as part of a racially integrated group, in a Charleston, South Carolina, beach park that the state legislature had shut down to prevent its racial integration. The incident was widely covered. Headlines such as "U.S. Official's Daughter Booked" were likely uncomfortable for Bennett.[33] Nonetheless, perhaps the fact that his daughter's arrest was for nonviolent protest undertaken by university students with the goal of racial integration provided him some comfort.

Bennett struggled with the turn to violence and anger, as well as with the tenets of Black Power. In the graduation addresses Bennett delivered at Black colleges and universities, we see the beliefs that would inform his DoD analysis of race. In 1964, at the South Carolina "coed Negro college" Allen University, Bennett warned that violent demonstrations—what he called "a futile exercise in calisthenics"—harmed the cause of civil rights. In 1968, as youth embraced Black pride, Bennett wove disparate impulses into an inspirational call. Addressing the ninety-ninth graduating class of Atlanta University, he asked, "Who among you is willing to condemn the resort to violence? Who among you is willing to embrace Negritude, and appreciate the heritage of Negroes . . . ? Who among you is willing to witness against . . . the folly of separation? Who among you is willing to say you believe in . . . an integrated and inclusive society . . . ?"[34]

As L. Howard Bennett once again addressed the problem of race in the military, traveling first to Vietnam and then to Europe in 1969 and 1970, he brought these understandings to bear. Just as White (initially by way of Resor and Westmoreland) had offered phrases and concepts that framed the military response to race, Bennett did likewise. But Bennett also carried with him the weight of a Pentagon now more concerned with the problem of racial conflict inside the military than with the issue of off-post discrimination. Internal army memos warned that Bennett was "highly critical" of the management of his visit the previous year. "For your information," an army talking paper noted, "Mr. Bennett alleged that it was evident from his discussion with one group in one of our unit's last year, that the personnel selected to talk with him were hand picked."[35]

In a brief trip, beginning in late November 1969, Bennett and the men who accompanied him evaluated race relations in Vietnam, Thailand, Japan, Hong Kong, and Hawai'i. Bennett heard eighteen major command briefings: army, navy, air force, marines. He and his team spoke with more than 600 enlisted men, including those incarcerated at LBJ. He also asked for—and got—a detailed listing of all significant race-linked "disturbances" that had taken place in the army over the previous twelve months.[36]

In his initial overview and the more formal reports that followed, Bennett identified all the complaints that were consolidating: failures of communication; distrust of the inspector general's office, the military police, and the entire process of military justice; unfair assignments; the reluctance of commanders to acknowledge problems. He focused, particularly, on the importance of cultural symbols. He offered some sensible interventions as well as a couple that should have been left in the brainstorming phase. But Bennett's analysis, this time, was endorsed by the DoD, and it was circulated to the chiefs of staff and service secretaries. One report went to civilian journalists, though it is not clear whether it was a leak or an official release. In stark contrast to the previous year, the results of Bennett's 1969 investigation reached key military leaders, and his insights—both those they adopted and those they ignored—helped to define "the problem of race."

Like White, Bennett laid responsibility outside the military. The armed forces, he explained in the report that went to the Joint Chiefs of Staff, "mirror and reflect the patterns of black-white relationships that exist in the nation's civilian communities." Those patterns had been intensified in the military as the Vietnam era draft swept up "short-timers" who had been exposed, whether actually or vicariously, to the "racial turbulence in American cities." Even worse, wrote the man who valued education so highly, that "civil disorder" had moved from the streets to the schools—the schools that had educated the young men swept into America's lengthening war.[37]

Bennett, like White, attempted to define the heart of the problem. And Bennett, like White, pointed to the generation gap. In many ways their shared concern is predictable: use of the term peaked in American newspapers in 1969, along with extended meditations on the nature of this unusually troublesome "generation." In his musings on the nature of contemporary youth, Bennett offered language of the sort that would soon suffuse army efforts to imagine the path to an all-volunteer force. These young men, he wrote in his initial overview, were better educated and more articulate than enlisted men in the past. But they were also more cynical, more "questioning and challenging," and more "aggressively anti-institution" than "any like generation in American history." They "hold little reverence for dictums simply because they are based on tradition or proceed from some exalted height." No surprise, then, Bennett concluded, that they would "produce dissonance" in an "institution which has traditionally depended on unquestioning obedience, a rigidly enforced hierarchy, de-emphasis of the individual, and a reverence for tradition."[38]

The youth of this new generation, conscious of themselves as such, did not trust their elders. They did not trust authority. And according to Bennett, this mistrust was not an issue of Black or white; it was an issue of age. But race, Bennett explained, added an additional layer. Just as young men in the late 1960s belonged to a generation unlike any that came before, Bennett wrote, young Black men were newly "sensitive racially, and proud." Black youth were conscious of the discrimination that had shaped "the black man's experience," and for them that experience was "widely shared and deeply felt." Bennett continued: "This young black is demanding recognition of himself as B*L*A*C*K (not ersatz white), different but completely equal. He is groping for a cultural identity and a set of black- (not white) developed and black- (not white) approved norms and goals on which to establish his racial individuality and identity. . . . He is aggressive about this fledgling identity and its symbols, demanding respect for them, and rebelling against, even retaliating for real and perceived aspersions cast on them."[39]

Bennett was not without sympathy, and perhaps his approach was an effective way to translate the actions and attitudes of young enlisted men to senior military leaders. "Many officers," he noted in his initial overview, "insightfully expressed the recognition" that the problems they faced with "young blacks (indeed, with all young troops)" were the same problems they had "trying to interact with their own teenage children at home."[40]

In defining this generational shift, Bennett sought to explain both the "New Breed Black" and the "new young white, both in rebellion against adult society, and poised in conflict with one another." Bennett's relatively sustained attention to the role of white youth is notable; most often when defense officials and military officers discussed "the problem of race," what they really meant was "the problem of Black youth," and in fact Bennett's team met with very few white enlisted men during their trip to Vietnam and Thailand. Bennett's attention to the parallel and intersecting roles of Black and white youth, however, led him to draw another parallel between the two groups. "Racism," wrote Bennett in a report that was endorsed by the DoD and sent to all service secretaries and chiefs of staff, "was being practiced by both blacks and whites."[41]

In his attempts to change the racial attitudes and practices of the US military, Bennett brought insights resulting from decades of civil rights work, long years spent navigating the Pentagon as the most senior Black civilian in the DoD, and legal and academic training from a top-ranked university. His official reports must be read in that context. Bennett clearly hoped to reframe the discussion of race, shifting the official story from a narrative of racial conflict to a story of racial integration. In "Command Leadership," the report that fell into journalists' hands, Bennett argued that the US military had gone through three clear historical periods in managing "the presence of people of different races, nationalities, ethnic backgrounds and religious beliefs" in the armed forces: segregation, desegregation (1948–55), and "functional integration" (1950–69). Functional integration, however, was not sufficient. From here forward, he wrote, the armed services must seek "fraternal and spiritual integration" in which "there will abide a true brotherhood among comrades in arms."[42]

Bennett's inspirational vision gained little traction, nor did his repeated insistence that the problem concerned "men of all races, faiths, backgrounds and stations in life." Neither fit the developing narrative or the increasingly pressing reality of Black-white conflict. And Bennett's calls for mutual understanding were too easily parodied. Journalists, given Bennett's eleven-page "Command Leadership" report, skipped over his historical analysis and inclusive vision of diversity, instead zeroing in on his most out-of-touch ideas. Bennett had, in fact, suggested that "group activity" could lessen racial tensions, offering examples that clearly showed which side of the generation gap he inhabited: in the era of soul, funk, and rock 'n' roll, he suggested "group singing" and "group dancing (Negroes could learn the polkas and schottisches and the whites the Charleston and the Cake Walk)." Newspaper headlines such as "Pentagon on Race Tiff: 'Sing' Troubles Away" made his report a laughing matter. It was anything but.[43]

Even as Bennett failed to shift military leaders' attention from the problem of racial violence to the promise of fraternal integration, he did help to shape the emerging conversation. The phrase "B*L*A*C*K (not ersatz white)" began to appear in internal army documents. The term "New Breed Black"—legitimated by Bennett's use—slotted into military memos and newspaper articles. And the notion that racism was practiced by Blacks as well as whites, validated by a highly placed Black civil rights officer, took on a power well beyond Bennett's initial use or, most certainly, his intent.[44]

And by early 1970, because the Department of Defense could not ignore the growing racial crisis and escalating racial violence in the US military, Bennett's recommendations had power. Thus when he proposed education as a solution, envisioning "the entire complement of the military hierarchy" being trained in "human relations," the army would develop that training.

As he insisted that the "signs and symbols" of youth were a "new language" that could not be left a "foreign tongue," that "relevant literature and . . . relevant sound" were "the heart of the search and thrust for identity which Blacks now seek," he conferred authority on those who decided what music and magazines were available to troops and those who understood the power of cultural symbols. And because Bennett saw human relations councils—which stood apart from the chain of command—as effective ways to foster communication, commanders of army installations worldwide would be directed to establish and support them.[45]

Bennett, in his travels to US military bases throughout the Pacific, represented Pentagon oversight; his recommendations would filter down to army command from the Department of Defense. But the army had one of its own in Bennett's party. Arthur Sussman's report focused squarely on the "Army's race problem," and his conclusions were alarming: "The potential for racial violence is present at every Army installation . . . in both Vietnam and Thailand."[46]

Army commanders, Sussman reported, were aware of "their race problems" and were taking "definite actions" to deal with them—even as he noted that quite a few of their equal opportunity messages barely predated the DOD team's visit and some of the signs on Equal Opportunity Officers' doors were "freshly painted." Sussman meant to make clear that awareness was not sufficient. In the current context, he wrote, even the most "insignificant appearing incidents" could "trigger large riot situations." He had no problem with earlier studies and suggestions but insisted that the army must move more quickly to "develop the necessary aids for the commander in the field."[47]

In his report, Sussman listed most of the same complaints that Bennett did, though in less inspirational language. "The young soldier," wrote Sussman, "believes the Inspector General System is a farce." And, he noted, there was sometimes "the tendency to use latrines as cathartics for expressing latent hostilities." Sussman ended his report with sixteen recommendations for action that ranged dramatically in scale, scope, and ease of implementation—or at least one assumes that it would be easier to clarify army policy on haircuts (recommendation 10) than to restore confidence in the entire system of military justice (recommendation 6).[48]

Sussman offered a necessary sense of urgency. That, in part, was his job. But he also squared a troublesome circle. When Secretary Resor rejected the "o.d." path to equality, he did not really explain how race consciousness (even if necessary) would create racial equality in the army. How to answer that question? How to respond when skeptics—whether white supremacists or I-have-a-dream integrationists or confused NCOs—suggested that young Black soldiers were demanding special treatment?

Sussman, with all the confidence of a twenty-something-year-old white man who had recently graduated Harvard Law, explained Black demands to the assistant secretary of the army for manpower. "The black soldier," he wrote, "is more aware and proud of his blackness than ever before. Triumphantly he proclaims 'I am different' and wants his difference to be admitted and honored."[49] However, Sussman noted, even as Black soldiers proclaimed their difference, they demanded that the army treat them the same as it treated their white peers.

"'We are different'; 'We want to be treated the same as whites.'" Were Black soldiers' claims a "demand for special treatment," resented as such by white troops and by "commanders who persist in the concept of the 'olive drab Army'"? And didn't these claims (different; the same) conflict? Sussman struggled to find words to explain how different and the same were, well, the same, or at least "really not different." He began incoherently—"The demands based on the 'We are different' theme are the fact that blacks want the same consideration generally." Still, one might identify, in his tortured prose, nascent understandings of institutional racism and white privilege. Sussman argued that contemporary youth—Black and white alike—wanted their respective "identities" recognized.[50]

Equal treatment, then, required that the army acknowledge difference. The o.d. army *was*, in fact, color-blind. It failed to see its non-white members; it offered goods and services that catered almost solely to the "needs and tastes" of whites. For Black service members to be treated equally—to have the army offer goods and services that catered to their own "needs and tastes"—argued Sussman, they had to make their difference visible, to claim that "we are different." Only by asserting their difference could Black soldiers be treated the same as whites. It is important to recognize that "needs and tastes" did not simply refer to what music was available in jukeboxes; Black soldiers also "needed" Black representation in the military police and on promotion boards and court-martial panels; they needed a voice in policy decisions that might affect white and African American soldiers differently.[51]

Sussman submitted his call for urgent action in mid-January 1970, just three days before Colonel White arrived in Vietnam. Bennett (and Sussman) had traveled to Southeast Asia to evaluate race relations. White, in contrast, was there to offer MACV and USARV the same briefing he had provided to the chief of staff and the secretary of the army. The officers he briefed asked

*Defining the Problem*

HARAMBEE *RHC*

Volume I, Number 4     Fort Carson, Colorado 80913     2 September 1971

*Harambee*, an arts and opinion magazine published at Fort Carson in the early 1970s, included drawings, poetry, short stories, and essays portraying the culture and history of Black, Latino, and Native peoples. *Harambee* translates from Kiswahili, Kenya's national language, as "all pull together." *Courtesy US Army.*

thoughtful questions. Gen. Creighton Abrams, commander of MACV, wanted to know how best to train junior officers and NCOs to discuss racial problems. Gen. Frank Mildren, deputy commanding general, USARV, asked how to decide whether or not to classify an incident as "racial." Notes from the briefings show that White, in discussions, emphasized communication as both problem and potential solution. He made recommendations that were quickly translated into a to-do list for USARV staff.[52]

Oddly enough, it was from Saigon—rather than from Washington, DC —that the army made its first public report on race relations. Perhaps that is because Vietnam had initially represented success: the first US war fought by an army integrated from its start, a war fought by men who found brotherhood in combat, whose gut-level understanding of "same mud, same blood" transcended their pasts. Or maybe it was because most military leaders understood that it was in Vietnam that racial conflict would be most immediately disruptive.

Whatever the logic, in late January 1970, army officials gathered journalists in an auditorium in Saigon, where (in the words of *New York Times* reporter Ralph Blumenthal) they were informed of the state of race relations in the US Army "by a tape-recorded voice coming from loudspeakers in the ceiling." The voice from the ceiling was Colonel White's; the tape recording was of his briefing to army commanders, minus the question-and-answer period. Oddly, as Blumenthal informed his readers, "official sources refused to permit publication of the name of the man who briefed the commanders," even though (as Blumenthal noted) the Associated Press had reported earlier that week that Lt. Col. James S. White of the Department of the Army had come to Saigon to address army commanders on racial tensions.

Journalists were frustrated. Some wondered whether they were getting the entire briefing. Could not portions of the tape have been erased? And the voice from the ceiling referred to charts that seemed to contain "comprehensive statistics" (though in fact they did not), but no charts were provided. And finally, despite the explosive news—that "widespread racial violence in the Army" was likely within the year if action was not taken—these correspondents were not given the chance to ask questions, to follow up, to do what they had been trained to do. When pushed, an official spokesperson for the army told them that access had been restricted because of the "delicate nature" of the topic—and because "the briefer was not equipped to deal with the press."[53]

Nonetheless, White's unattributed words made front-page news throughout the United States. "Negro Losing Faith?" asked the Indiana edition of the *Louisville Courier-Journal*. "Blacks Have Lost Faith," asserted the *Washington Post*. In contrast, the African American *Chicago Daily Defender* titled its account "Racism in the Army." "Of course Negroes are losing faith in an army system that allows junior and non-commissioned officers to call them 'stupid black niggers,'" the author wrote, angrily dismissing White's eagerly embraced and frequently repeated claim that "the army has a race problem because American society has a race problem." "Yes," he wrote, in response to that claim, "but the army," unlike civilian society, "is supposed to be a disciplined body with wide jurisdiction over the lives and behavior of those who serve under its authority." The problem was the army's, insisted the *Chicago Defender*, and it "MUST" be solved.[54]

Even as army leaders increasingly acknowledged the problem they faced, racial violence continued to grow—and because race relations were now an official concern, individual incidents were cataloged and compiled. In Vietnam, for example, army officials reported 348 cases of aggravated assault in the eleven months beginning in July 1970, and while they listed only about a quarter of them as racially motivated (by whites against Blacks or by Blacks against whites), well over half of the 348 cases were "Negro" attacks on "Caucasians" —well out of scale given that African Americans made up about 11.5 percent of US military troops in Vietnam.[55]

*Defining the Problem*

As the war ground on, race relations in Vietnam remained the army's primary concern, but racial violence elsewhere increasingly demanded attention. After all, the war in Vietnam could well be seen as part of the larger Cold War, and US troops in Germany were not simply holdovers from postwar occupation; they served a significant strategic purpose. Shifting press focus from Vietnam to Germany, *New York Times* journalist Thomas Johnson described the anger and growing bitterness that threatened to "undermine the combat efficiency" of the Seventh Army, Europe's first line of defense against the USSR. "There is no doubt," a white senior infantry officer said flatly, "that race is our most serious internal problem," and Johnson offered evidence of a growing crisis not only in the rear but in combat-ready units along the East German and Czechoslovakian borders.[56]

In recent months, he wrote, Germany had been the site of the army's most serious racial disorders. In Bad Hersfeld, three Black soldiers had attacked the MPs who were escorting a Black soldier to the stockade for pretrial confinement. In Frankfurt, a white officer was shot and killed as he entered the "black-frequented" Corso Bar; in Ulm, a white NCO shot a Black soldier who was holding a loaded pistol on two white officers; in Crailsheim, fifteen Black soldiers attacked MPs who were transferring three other Black soldiers to the stockade; in Berlin, a fistfight between Black and white soldiers at McNair Barracks escalated into a full-scale riot. Johnson's chronicle of violence was certainly incomplete, for, as he noted, reporters for *Stars and Stripes* had been cautioned to "avoid racial stories," and the editor of the tabloid *Overseas Weekly* was confident he had lost his job because he so insistently covered them.[57]

Johnson reported Black bitterness with sympathy, making clear that anger was often well founded. He chose to quote a veteran of Vietnam, now stationed "10 miles across the cabbage fields from East Germany," who insisted that "America should deserve my life if I'm going to give it," and another young man who asked, "How can you fight for America when every morning you read about black people being killed?" The Ku Klux Klan, Johnson reported, had a presence in Germany, and the Confederate flag was "prominently displayed" in the window of the MP headquarters in Heidelberg. "The burnings of crosses on military bases," he continued, burying what perhaps should have been his lede, "has goaded the young blacks." The situation was summed up by a Black sergeant first class with eighteen years' service: his infantry outfit, he said, "no longer functions like an Army platoon but like two street gangs."[58]

As racial violence escalated, the Nixon administration had dispatched a "team of investigators" to Europe. Nixon, said an administration official, was "deeply concerned" about the "growing racial problems" in Europe and, given that they showed no sign of abating, had decided to take action. Nixon's "race probe" was not as much a departure as it seemed; once again L. Howard Bennett was at the heart of the team, accompanying his new boss, Frank Render II, who had been named deputy assistant secretary of defense for civil rights in July 1970.[59]

Frank Render seemed to come out of nowhere. While newspapers described the thirty-four-year-old as a lecturer at Le Moyne College and a senior research associate at Syracuse University, it seems likely (reading between the lines) that he was a graduate student at Syracuse, working toward a PhD in the field of mass communication. Like Bennett, Render had no military experience. He had served briefly as executive director of the Syracuse Human Rights Commission but resigned from that position in August 1969 to run —as a Republican—for the Syracuse City Council. He lost.[60]

It could not have been easy for Bennett to relinquish his acting position to a man who was, in Bennett's own words, "young enough to be my son." In a moment of indiscretion, Bennett told the Minneapolis *Star Tribune* that Secretary Laird had nominated him for the position, but that was "more than the White House could handle"; Nixon, he said, "needed a black Republican." And *Jet* magazine's reporter evidently could not quite believe that the new "highest ranking Black civilian in the Department of Defense," a man charged with ensuring equal opportunity for "a total empire" of 20 million people, was thirty-four years old. The August 1970 issue—its front cover asking "Will Success Spoil the Jackson Five?"—quoted the *forty-four*-year-old Render's pledge of "total commitment." "The responsibility that I have started to take is awesome," Render said, as he took the oath of office.[61]

Bennett was a professional, so his public rumblings of dissatisfaction were quickly silenced. Nonetheless, he either showed extraordinary good grace in the face of adversity or Render soon won him over. By September, Bennett was portraying an exemplary partnership, one that succeeded *because* of the generational divide. Some young Black men, he told a reporter, "look at me and wonder what the hell does this gray bearded fellow know about my problems?" Some, he said, figured that his age had relegated him to "the Uncle Tom position," that a man of his generation could not possibly understand "this new insistence for all freedoms right now." But when he and Frank Render talked with them *together*, Bennett said, "I think they get our reactions, our feelings, and that we're genuine."[62]

These new partners, at Nixon's behest, departed for Europe on September 12, 1970. They spent three weeks evaluating race relations at US military installations, and while those installations included an air force base in England and naval stations in Spain and Italy, their visit focused on USAREUR —the US Army Europe—in Germany, where they met with 5,000 army officers, NCOs, and enlisted men.[63]

Render meant to shift the armed forces' approach to the problem of race. He had explained, soon after his appointment, that he thought it more important to change behavior than to change attitudes. In keeping with that "philosophy," he began his report to the secretary of defense by dismissing the framework Bennett had offered. "There is no attempt herewith," Render wrote, "to belabor philosophic variances on how much or to what degree there should or should not be a functionally and fraternally integrated military. We have cut this message from the core with the hope the use of direct comment and unflowered prose will further emphasize the sharpness of our focus on the issue."[64]

Render failed to offer "direct . . . and unflowered prose" (he began one section as follows: "At this point in time as we reflect on the overt manifestations of feelings about the treatment of people and without the considerations of race, it becomes apparent that the core of the problems and the greatest amount of difficulty relates to the negative interface between black and white personnel"). But he certainly did not sugarcoat his conclusions. The Render Report was no measured expression of concern. Render's message was urgent: if the US military intended to "maintain highly effective" combat units, it must change the behavior of its members.[65]

Render validated the usual list of problems and complaints: military justice, promotions and assignments, misunderstandings of "the thrust for identity," the display of "offensive" symbols, problems with communication. All, he acknowledged, required attention. But Render wanted the secretary of defense to understand that things were worse than anticipated. "The problems are not unlike the media have made them appear," he wrote.[66]

Render was prepared for "racial unrest, tensions and conflict," and Bennett had seen it all before. But neither anticipated the "degree and intensity" of what they found, the "acute frustration" and "volatile anger" of Blacks, the "somewhat lower level of frustration evidenced by young whites." Men had come to the DoD team's meetings for no reason other than to "[cast] incredulity" on their visit. Some used "verbally inflammatory language rank with profanity and obscenities." In Mannheim and Karlsruhe, Render and Bennett had found "alienated blacks who could not be reached," men who said they had no place "fighting in a white man's Army and in a white man's war" when they belonged back home, "[in] New York, Chicago, Atlanta, Detroit, Jacksonville, where they could fight to liberate and free their black sisters and brothers from the dirty, stinking, teeming ghettos and from all forms of racial bigotry and oppression. They told us they wanted guns, ammunition and grenades because they felt 'whitey' understood no approach other than that of violent confrontation. They accused us of coming over to brainwash them."[67]

Render insisted that, in most cases, reason would triumph and "firm control" could overcome "uncivil manifestations." But some of the men, he acknowledged, had so lost faith in "the establishment and the system—the establishment of the Armed Forces and the system that represents the American way of life"—that they could not be reached.[68]

In many ways, Render was joining the chorus. Poor communication was the problem, improved communication a big part of the solution (after all, Render's academic training was in the field of "communication"). Like others, he identified "civilian society" as the source of racial conflict in the military, while—in keeping with the *Chicago Defender* editorial—he held the armed forces to a higher standard. After all, he made clear, the military services had much greater authority over their members' lives and actions than did civilian institutions. Render, like his predecessors, identified the generation gap in addition to the racial divide.[69]

On the other hand, Render was much less interested in cultural symbols than was Bennett, who had been credited with "softening" military approaches to Afros and other such symbols of racial pride. And while he wholly signed on to the educational programs that Bennett had proposed, he saw education as a way to increase "knowledge" about the "problems of human and race relations" rather than a means to change the attitudes of the men and women of the US military.

Render intended to change the discussion in two key ways. First, he emphasized structural change and mechanisms of enforcement. He sought a "human relations machinery built into the military," as well as a service-designed "mechanism" to ensure effective communication.[70]

Second, Render pointed to commanders. Slipping back from the straightforward anger he had channeled in describing Black men's frustrations, he offered his first "principal concern": "Perhaps the most overriding single factor about which there can be generalizations regarding the visible shortcomings of the Military Services in dealing with the present human relations–race relations problem is the failure in too many instances of command leadership to exercise its authority and responsibility in these areas." Clearly it was not easy to call out general officers. But Render did not completely bury his point in convoluted prose. He titled this section "The Failure of Command Leadership," and he proposed that the services institute mechanisms for relieving officers and NCOs "who are bigoted and irresponsive relative to equal opportunity."[71]

Back in the United States, Render spoke publicly about his findings in November; the Department of Defense released his findings to the press in mid-December in conjunction with a new set of directives drafted in response. Over the following years, the DoD would both monitor and command the actions of the individual services, and the US Army's attempts to solve its problem of race were always within this framework.

On November 17, 1970, at the direction of army chief of staff William Westmoreland, the Department of the Army held a major four-day race relations conference at Fort Monroe, Virginia. All major army commands sent representatives, as did the US Air Force, Navy, and Marine Corps. Westmoreland addressed the assembly, as did Secretary of the Army Resor. Frank Render spoke for the DoD. Colonel White offered "Remarks." L. Howard Bennett joined a panel discussion, along with officers from the air force, navy, and Marine Corps. The army's deputy chief of staff for personnel offered closing remarks. Participants were briefed on efforts in progress. They viewed four films that had been developed for race relations training. They listened to panel discussions and, in small work groups, discussed the nature of the problem and its potential solutions.[72]

In those four tightly scheduled days in late November, military leaders discussed the problem they faced. All the key actors were there, all the gradually consolidating narratives in play. Those who had shown initiative got credit. Those seen as part of the problem got warning. And the massive institution of the US Army set its path. Through leadership, education and training, acceptance of different cultures, attention to off-post discrimination, reforms of military justice, and programs of affirmative action, the army pledged to solve the problem of race.

# 4 LEADERSHIP

As the institutional army began its struggle to solve the problem of race, it increasingly confronted a profound tension. On the one hand, the army could bring extraordinarily powerful tools to bear. This was an institution built on principles of command, of rank hierarchy, of obedience. When superiors issued orders, subordinates were required to obey them. As the army created specific and detailed regulations, its members were required to follow them. Failure to do so had consequences. Nothing in civilian society compared to the power or reach of military command: soldiers belonged to the army twenty-four hours a day. Imagine the possibilities. A commander, intent on solving the problem of race, might not change hearts and minds. But he (and in this case, it was almost always "he") certainly could change behavior.

Command, rank hierarchy, and obedience. These principles were fundamental. The centrality of command was a given, an essential piece of institutional logic and organizational practice. All solutions worked from that unnamed premise. As army leaders struggled with their racial crisis, however, some began to realize that army structures of command—for all their utility—were not an unmixed blessing.

In this system, so much depended on leadership. On command. And commanders—whether they led a platoon or a brigade—were human. They were products of a society divided by race. Anyone with significant authority in the army at the cusp of the 1970s had come of age before the Civil Rights Act of 1964 and the Supreme Court's 1954 *Brown v. Board of Education* decision. They had been well into military service when Rosa Parks refused to move to the back of the bus, when four college students sat down at Woolworth's segregated lunch counter in Greensboro, North Carolina, when a quarter million Americans came together in the March on Washington for Jobs and Freedom. Those few senior officers who were Black had risen in rank through talent and ability—but part of that ability was to navigate a white-dominated institution.

The vast majority of officers, white men, had grown up in a nation where white superiority was assumed. By the end of the 1960s, some of these men wholeheartedly supported racial justice; some of these men were unapologetic white supremacists. The surviving records suggest that, if we plotted white army officers on a continuum from white supremacy to racial justice, we would most likely get something approaching a bell curve. Senior officers (based on public comments, at least) tended to fall distinctly on the positive side of the midline. But even those well into positive territory were shaped by their upbringing, both individual and institutional, and it is difficult not to be shocked today by relatively common blind spots and insensitivities.

Army leaders, of course, had authority over those below them on the chain of command. Sometimes that structure allowed leaders to circumvent or minimize the individual prejudices of subordinates. That was a plus. But the chain of command also offered a *structural* problem. Each step down the chain of command offered potential for things to go awry. After all, the truth of the matter lies in implementation, not intention. And each step up the chain of command offered officers a chance to shift a narrative, to obscure a problem. There was no reward for noting that the sky was falling, even if it were true. There was ample incentive to downplay the negative, sidetracking complaints and minimizing crises, just as there was incentive to inflate body count in combat or to exaggerate the success of a mission. Communication suffered. And, as those charged with solving the problem frequently insisted, failed communication lay at the heart of the army's racial crisis.

More than anything else, however, those who sought to solve the problem pointed to a generational divide. If the senior leaders of the army had come of age before the movement for civil rights reshaped the law of the nation and the beliefs of millions, the young men (and women) they led had come of age in its ferment. The eighteen-year-old drafted in 1970 was still in elementary school when Martin Luther King Jr. offered his "dream" from the steps of the Lincoln Memorial. More immediately, during their high school years, these young men experienced the aftermath of that hope: assassinations, anger, the growing frustration that left cities in flames. This shared context created more division than connection among a cohort of youth. How young people understood these events was shaped by race and region, by the influences of family, of education, of belief, by all the contingent contacts and events that help to determine the nascent politics of the young. But even as this shared context divided youth among themselves, it also divided the young from their elders.

As the politics of race divided youth from their elders, so too did the politics of youth. This cohort of youth—white, Black, and other—generally found itself more comfortable with the watchword "question authority" than with the army's required "yes, sir." Young men saw no virtue in blind obedience. Leaders struggled with privates who wanted to understand *why* they were being told to cut their hair or to take a hill, men who refused orders or were willing to circumvent the chain of command in search of an answer. "Don't you ever tell me what to do," a new recruit yelled at his drill sergeant in 1971. "You ask me. I'm a human being."[1]

In this world, many Black officers and NCOs were appalled and perplexed by the claims of Black youth. Many young Black soldiers dismissed these men as "oreos" (black on the outside, white on the inside) or Uncle Toms.

From the beginning, army leaders assumed that the problem of race was a command challenge and that the solution lay in the actions of leaders. As they struggled to contain the forces that threatened to tear the army apart, they learned that the power of command, in the context of the era, required rethinking in ways that challenged the army's institutional logic and culture.

O n May 21, 1970, in Germany, the 26th Battalion, 1st Infantry Division (Forward), was conducting maneuvers about sixty miles from the Czech border. Such maneuvers had purpose, for the Soviet Cold War threat remained strong at the cusp of the 1970s, and US troops stationed in Europe were well aware that it had been less than nineteen months since half a million Warsaw Pact troops, mobilized by the Soviet Union, had invaded the Czech Republic. Even though the United States and the USSR had begun negotiations to limit nuclear arms, the United States remained wary of Soviet power. As one US commander said, the following year, of the Warsaw Pact nations, "They stand poised behind the Iron Curtain."[2]

Since the mid-1960s, however, the US Army had been intently focused on Vietnam. Men, equipment, funding, attention—all had shifted from Europe to Indochina. The Pentagon increasingly treated the Seventh Army in Germany —the highly disciplined fighting force charged with holding the line against Soviet invasion of Europe—as a reserve, of both men and equipment, for the US war in Vietnam. By the late 1960s, many units in USAREUR—the US Army Europe—carried barely half their authorized strength. The officer corps was hollowed out. Majors were especially scarce, down by half, and (in the words of a later commander in chief) "it was common to find a battalion commanded by a Lieutenant Colonel who had a Captain for an executive officer and Second Lieutenants for company commanders." NCOs were likewise in short supply and too often "shake 'n' bake," "instant" sergeants with little time in uniform. Experienced officers and NCOs were in high demand, which meant they were frequently reassigned. Both continuity of leadership and unit cohesion suffered. Equipment for training was increasingly scarce. Enlisted men lived in barracks that one officer compared unfavorably to the Nuremberg Zoo. Troops were bored and frustrated. Morale was poor. Discipline was weak. Violence, now common on post, spilled into neighboring towns.[3]

On the 1st Division's Augsburg installation, the southern anchor of the Seventh Army, racial tensions were high. Perhaps, as a *Washington Post* reporter claimed, that was simply because men in this front-line combat unit were thrown in constant close contact, the sort of "rubbing against each other" that "experienced army men" know tends to "[breed] the kind of situation where people get on each other's nerves and tempers flare easily." More likely it was because Black soldiers had become less willing to put up with racism and the discrimination that accompanied it.[4]

Throughout Germany, Black soldiers were tired of graffiti about "niggers" and the KKK. They were angry about the disproportionate number of Black men sent to army stockades or given an Article 15. They were fed up with German discrimination against them off-post. And they were frustrated that every gathering of Black soldiers, for whatever purpose, drew officers' suspicion.

It is not that officers' suspicion was entirely unfounded; radical groups of Black soldiers, often led by charismatic and relatively well-educated Black draftees, had begun to emerge in Germany the previous year. German student activists fostered "revolutionary alliances" with some such groups, offering them support in dealing with "their situation in the military" and emphasizing its link to "the struggle being waged today inside Babylon (Amerikkka)."[5]

Local commanders in Germany had, overall, handled these groups poorly. Some refused to acknowledge the Black "study groups" and their talk of revolution, just as they largely discounted those with specific complaints about racial discrimination. Others came down hard on dissent. In the 1st Infantry Division, as racial discontent moved well beyond what could be ignored, the commanding general instituted what came to be known as "midnight specials": he had those he characterized as Black "militants" and

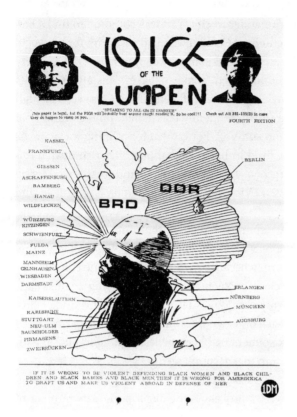

The West German Black Panther Solidarity Committee, founded in 1969, facilitated connections with Black GIs. Working with a small number of Black activists, the committee began publishing the underground paper *Voice of the Lumpen* in 1970.

"troublemakers" pulled out of their barracks in the middle of the night and sent where they would no longer make trouble—for his command, in any case. Such action did not go unnoticed. His superiors summarily halted the midnight specials, and a new commander arrived in March 1970. But the racial climate in the 1st had not improved. Black troops' anger and resentment stayed high.[6]

On that May night in 1970, forty or fifty Black GIs massed outside the headquarters building, demanding to see the commander. The captain on duty recalled their spokesman threatening violence; four times, he said, the Black sergeant told him that if they did not get to meet with General Garth there would be trouble. But Maj. Gen. Marshall B. Garth, reached on the phone by that highly unsympathetic aide, decided not to engage the group. Instead he sent his inspector general and a unit chaplain, both majors, to hear the men's claims.[7]

These Black soldiers were not pleased to be passed off to officers of lower rank and lesser authority. There was shouting. Some men walked out, brought back to the table only through the efforts of the group's leader, Sgt. James Hobson, a man whom Garth's aide described as "the Pied Piper," able to calm or to incite his men at will.[8]

The meeting with the battalion chaplain and inspector general—both white—went on for over two hours, though not all the men stayed. Around 9 p.m., someone tossed a hand grenade through the window of the unit mess hall, injuring fully half of the twenty enlisted men and officers, white and Black, who had gathered there after a softball game. Discovered nearby was another grenade, still in its canister and seemingly discarded, along with makeshift explosives: a burning broom with its handle in a truck's diesel tank and a Molotov cocktail, not yet lit. A third hand grenade went off under an unoccupied tracked personnel carrier.[9]

The fragging brought General Garth to headquarters, where he was confronted by a furious Sergeant Hobson. Hobson told General Garth that if he had just come down to meet with the soldiers, none of this would have happened. He raised his voice. He called his commanding officer "incompetent." He threatened to report "the problems of racism" to the "proper authorities."[10]

Shortly thereafter Hobson was arrested on a separate charge, accused of disobeying an order to take his men into the field for training. Before long, however, Hobson had also been charged with attempted murder and conspiracy, identified as the ringleader of a group of Black militants who had planned and carried out the fragging and the attempted arson. It turned out the sergeant had been a gang leader on Chicago's West Side; known by the street name "Caveman," he had fought his way up the ranks in the notoriously violent Vice Lords while he was still in his teens. James Hobson had cycled through thirty-one foster homes in less than seven years, slept on the streets from the age of sixteen, been convicted by the same judge in the Cook County Boys Court forty-three times for crimes of theft, battery, burglary, and mob action. If racial unrest was—as many white army leaders hoped and believed—due to a few militant troublemakers rather than to the underlying conditions in which Black soldiers served, Hobson was a perfect example of the problem they faced.[11]

This fragging, however, was not a story of Black militancy. It was instead a cautionary tale about the failure of leadership, and some came to see it as such at the time. Speaking to a journalist the following September, General Garth confessed that "race problems" had been "the furthest thing" from his mind when he took command that March: "I had just never given it a thought. Then bang. We had that hand grenade incident . . ."[12] That claim, if true, was indefensible. If Garth did not realize that race relations were explosive in his command, he was badly out of touch with his men. If, on the other hand, he saw the problem but did not take it seriously, that, too, was a failure of leadership.

Garth may well have been justified, according to army best practice, to refuse the summons of an angry group of soldiers on that May night; in subsequent years, army race relations advisors would conclude that meeting with aggrieved "crowds" in racially charged situations only lent legitimacy to such tactics. But sending out a couple of majors in his place was pretty clearly a bad move. The Black soldiers saw it as dismissive. In many ways it was.

But Garth's greatest leadership failure was in discounting *Hobson's* leadership. Yes, Hobson had been abandoned at birth, grown up unwanted, joined a gang at the age of fifteen. In that gang, however, Hobson had made a group of ill-disciplined and violent young men see him as their leader. And by the age of twenty he had walked away from the Vice Lords—despite the physical threat entailed—when two young Catholic nuns offered him a different path. Joining the military was his way out of Chicago, but given his record it took a fair amount of influence to get him into the army. The Boys Court judge had been one of his strongest sponsors, writing to President Johnson on Hobson's behalf. And once in the army, Hobson had volunteered for Vietnam, leaving behind a safe post as acting drill instructor at Fort Jackson, South Carolina. The former gang member came home with two Bronze Stars and the Vietnamese Cross for Gallantry; Chicago had welcomed him back from Vietnam in early 1970 with its Medal of Honor. Hobson, who had marched with Dr. King in Marquette Park in 1966, told Mayor Richard J. Daley and the Chicago City Council about the "racial problem" in Vietnam. It was "bad," he said. "It's second only to the war."[13]

Twenty-four-year-old Hobson was a shake 'n' bake sergeant, not a lifer. No one would mistake him for an Uncle Tom. His qualities of leadership long preceded his time in the army. And he was not one to let things ride. So when he ended up in the worst of USAREUR's racial mess in the spring of 1970, Sergeant Hobson emerged as a leader. On the May night in question, Hobson had been, without question, on the side of the men who massed outside of headquarters. But he had accompanied them to headquarters in an attempt to prevent violence—not by undermining the men's claims, but by seeking change. Hobson had tried to make the general's aide understand that the situation was serious, that it might easily erupt. But all the white captain could hear was a Black man threatening violence. And so it went.

In the end, Hobson was acquitted of attempted murder and conspiracy, the most serious charges, convicted instead (despite a chaplain's eyewitness testimony to the contrary) of disobedience and stripped of rank. Those who believed Hobson innocent of the disobedience charge thought, perhaps with reason, that the charge stemmed from his outburst at General Garth. Sergeants do not call generals incompetent to their face and walk away unscathed. Given the immediate context, Hobson's supporters in Chicago did not trust the military justice system. They raised over $7,000, much of it through blood drives, to hire a civilian defense attorney for Hobson's trial. One supporter and friend, appearing as a character witness at that trial, carried a message from Mayor Daley to the court: "Jim is a good boy," she quoted the mayor. "I want him back in Chicago. I want to send the young man to college. I need him in the ghetto."[14]

No one had been killed in the "hand grenade incident," but it "sent tremors" (in the words of one reporter) "from Bremerhaven to Bavaria," through the entirety of the Seventh Army. In the 1st Division, General Garth directly confronted the problem of race, insisting publicly that "any commander who thinks he doesn't have a racial situation is a fool." Moving forward from the attack, even as Sergeant Hobson remained incarcerated, charged with conspiracy and attempted murder, General Garth fundamentally changed his approach. Garth, an officer under his command told members of a visiting delegation from the NAACP the following year, was "a rabid exponent of fairness in regard to justice, promotions, and awards." He had made it his business to speak personally with every Black soldier in the division "so that the men can get to know him" and can say that "they heard it from the Man." He continued, perhaps with some ambivalence: General Garth's door was "wide open—so wide that he cannot get his gate work done because it is open to everybody." But this officer also offered a compelling description of the changes Garth had made in the division, from a Black study seminar to military justice reform to the enlisted men's councils established in each battalion. These councils vented pressure as tension rose, but they also were meant to bypass the chain of command, offering low-ranking enlisted men direct access to the commander.[15]

Perhaps Garth had come to believe that Sergeant Hobson was right, that if he had come to talk with the men he could have prevented the explosion. Perhaps he realized he had not done well to rely on his aide's analysis of the initial situation. Or perhaps, post-fragging, Garth heard some version of what another Black sergeant in the division told a reporter the following fall: "Your commanders may have the best intentions in the world, but they don't come down the chain of command without getting balled up by bigots and rednecks all along the line."[16]

In the final analysis, however, it was violence that got General Garth's attention, and it was violence that would command the attention of the US Army Europe. Young Black soldiers were angry, and their actions were often not carefully calibrated or directly proportional to offense. In Baumholder and Friedberg, reported the *Washington Post*, "mobs of black soldiers roamed the streets destroying property and beating and terrorizing white civilians and GIs in their path." With white and Black GIs forced into proximity and racial tensions high, battles broke out in barracks and mess halls. At McNair Barracks in West Berlin, a white soldier called a Black soldier a "nigger." A different Black soldier then walloped a different white soldier with a piece of wood. The fight escalated. Men poured from surrounding buildings to join the fray, dividing by color, setting to with rocks and clubs and pipes. By chance—by luck—a unit was at the same time returning from the field in full battle dress. They were sent in, bayonets fixed, to break up the brawl.[17]

Day-to-day interactions were so explosive that one battalion required every company-size unit to post a junior officer and a senior NCO, with side-arms, in the enlisted barracks every night to keep the men from fighting.[18] But men could not be supervised at all times, and confrontations over small matters—cutting in the mess line, music played too loud, even inadvertent slights (as opposed to purposeful provocations)—quickly turned to violence. And while Black soldiers were frequently provoked to violence, it was not always the one who had done the provoking who felt their wrath. Groups of Black GIs attacked random whites. White soldiers moved in groups for self-defense. Tensions continued to rise.

Military leaders also worried about organized violence, as radical groups worldwide began to embrace notions of violent revolution and revolutionary justice. From 1969 forward, a portion of the more radical fringe of German student activists had become increasingly captivated by the Black Panther Party's revolutionary stance, most particularly its claim that it was time "to pick up the gun." (In contrast, the sort of Panther programs that offered community schools and free breakfast for Black children drew little attention.) German activists imagined great revolutionary potential in Black GIs and devoted themselves to building connections. Women activists, designated "brides of the revolution," sought out Black GIs at clubs, danced with them, talked Black Power. One group created an "instructional sheet" on how to talk with Black GIs, advising German students to approach them with "genuine humility," even if their own English was "probably better than that of the Negro."[19]

In November 1970, German student activists near Frankfurt, along with a few Black US military veterans, began publishing the *Voice of the Lumpen*, an underground newspaper meant to bring Black Panther ideology to American troops. *Voice of the Lumpen* embraced violence, equating it to "revolutionary justice." An issue from October 1971 described people "pitching lye and glass into the faces of bus dispatchers, mistaken for pigs [police]," as a "spiritual manifestation" of such revolutionary justice and celebrated the "machine-gunning of two fascist Storm Troopers" (bodyguards for a US district attorney) as a "fitting way" to mark Malcolm X's birthday. This issue, focused in part on US military stockades in Germany, portrayed "brothers" who "turned their guns against their racist officers, their true enemies," as political prisoners; praised the Black GIs who repudiated "their role as puppets and cannon fodder for the US ruling class and their military authorities"; and carried a "Warning to the West German Government" from Black Panther leader Eldridge Cleaver: "Death to All Fascist Imperial Pigs."[20]

German student radicals, working with African American military groups such as the Unsatisfied Black Soldiers, organized rallies and protests. Black GIs and student activists marched through the streets of German cities during the spring of 1970. On July 4, close to 700 Black GIs and German allies gathered in the University of Heidelberg's largest auditorium, calling for freedom and presenting their demands and grievances. *About Face*, the underground paper published by the Unsatisfied Black Soldiers, publicized the event as a "trial" of the US Army staged by American Black GIs. Army leaders, concerned, confined units to post over the holiday weekend, designating them rapid reaction forces on call in the event of a race riot. That fall, more than a thousand "Black Panther" GIs, most in the black berets that had come to symbolize the Panthers' revolutionary stance, rallied together with German activists in the small town of Kaiserslautern.[21]

Not long thereafter, a shooting at Ramstein Air Base further raised the stakes. Three Black Panther activists, US military veterans who had remained in Germany following discharge and who worked on the *Voice of the Lumpen*, drove to Ramstein Air Base, where they intended to hang posters publicizing a talk by Black Panther communications secretary Kathleen Cleaver. (Cleaver was to speak in the stead of her husband, Eldridge Cleaver, who had been denied entry into Germany by the nation's foreign ministry, which called him a "common criminal.") They were stopped and denied access by a civilian German guard; one of the men shot the guard and then the three fled into the surrounding woods. Two of them, captured and arrested by the German police, said they had acted in self-defense.[22]

By 1970, virtually all US Army leaders in Germany were forced to contend with racial conflict. And as that conflict spilled over into German communities or gained headlines in German papers, high-ranking German officials shared their concerns. Black soldiers, on the other hand, wrote to their congressional representatives or to the NAACP in increasing numbers, complaining about rampant discrimination both on- and off-post. Tensions rose to the point that the White House dispatched a team that September, led by the Department of Defense's Frank Render, to evaluate the situation; soon thereafter the NAACP determined to conduct its own independent investigation of the racial crisis.

Such external attention forced army command to act more decisively. Shortly following Render's visit, Gen. James H. Polk, commander of USA-REUR, escalated his efforts to address the complaints of Black troops. Polk, who (inauspiciously, given the situation he confronted) counted Confederate general Leonidas Polk as a great-uncle, had served in Europe for all but three of the prior sixteen years. He had led within USAREUR when it was a highly disciplined, professional force and was well aware of both the army's own decline and its decline in the estimation of the German public.[23]

Beginning in 1970, Polk had piloted a program to bring German youth and young American service members together (he did not have the union of German radical youth and potential Black Panthers in mind); the "Kontact" program was intended to overcome stereotypes on both sides and to lessen American soldiers' sense of isolation. More pointedly, Polk launched a new initiative just one week after Render departed Germany: "flying squads" of investigators would begin making unannounced visits to company- and battalion-size units, checking for evidence of discrimination against Black service members—whether that discrimination took the form of promotion, leaves, passes, punishments, or duty rosters. "We don't know if it will work," he told a New York Times reporter. "It is experimental. I see it as putting teeth in my statement that there will be no discrimination in this command."[24]

In the end, it did not matter. Within months, General Polk's career would founder on the problem of race. In mid-December 1970, Render's report made headlines: the "acute frustration" and "volatile anger" of Black service members threatened the combat mission of the US military in Europe. Render's team listed "the failure of command leadership" first among their "principal concerns," and though they later noted (under "affirmative findings") that "general and flag officers in practically every area were strong, sensitized individuals who had affirmative attitudes in this area," their leadership undermined by "strictures in the channel of communication," that caveat carried little weight.[25] USAREUR was Polk's responsibility.

The Department of Defense accompanied its overview of Render's report with new directives on racial discrimination. Key among them: officers could be removed from command if they failed to deal with racial problems. At the Pentagon press conference, Frank Render was joined by Roger Kelley, assistant secretary of defense for manpower, who made clear that the DoD was serious about race. The new directives, he said, make it "abundantly clear" that the secretary of each military service was responsible for easing racial tensions and that he would be "held accountable for results." In turn, the service secretaries were given authority to "impose effective sanctions . . . against individuals who fail to produce satisfactory results." That meant, Kelley clarified, "appropriate action" such as "removal of the individual from his command post." Clarifying further, the *Post* journalist noted, "Presumably, racial disturbances at a military base would jeopardize the future of the base commander." Significantly, the same day in October that General Polk had announced his "flying squads," the army's deputy personnel chief, Gen. Walter Kerwin, wrote his second-in-command, "I would like recommendations as to how we can cut down on turbulence in general and USAREUR in particular." He added a postscript: "I anticipate Q's from CSA [chief of staff of the army]."[26]

Whether or not General Polk was a "strong, sensitized individual" with "affirmative attitudes" about racial justice, he was failing to produce satisfactory results. It was not only the racial violence. He also had not won over young Black soldiers, though whether any white officer might have done so at that moment is an open question. *About Face*, the underground paper published by the Unsatisfied Black Soldiers organization in Heidelberg, pronounced in September 1970, "We are unsatisfied because there is Racism being practiced and sanctioned right here in the Military at all levels from Head-Pig Gen Polk down to Racist 1st Shirts."[27]

It was not only the Unsatisfied Black Soldiers who dismissed General Polk. An ambitious young army judge who would, in the not-so-distant future, claim Frank Render's job as DoD equal opportunity chief, also had General Polk in his sights. Capt. Curtis Smothers was twenty-eight years old, a graduate of the historically Black Morgan State University and of American University's school of law, where he had held a position in the Student Nonviolent Coordinating Committee. In 1970 he was the youngest judge in the US Army and one of the few who were African American.[28] Smothers brought the passion of youth to his work, especially as it tied to civil rights advocacy. He also had a youthful certainty that he knew best about pretty much everything.

Speaking with the NAACP's Nathaniel Jones, who had traveled to West Germany to investigate charges of discrimination against Black GIs, Smothers made clear he would do whatever it took to assist him. But he also offered a caution. What, he asked, was the NAACP going to do? "Are they going to come out and do a Render type of thing? If that's the case, over and above this, it isn't worth my time." Moderating a bit, he told Jones, "I have to be honest with you because that's the only way you can deal." And when Jones, who had served in the Army Air Corps during World War II, queried him about his army career, Smothers flatly rejected the notion that he was a token and offered a purported quote from his supervisor as evidence. When asked why so many people wanted Smothers to defend them, Smothers told *the general counsel of the NAACP*, "My boss in essence said because Smothers is a god."[29]

Smothers's arrogance shines from the pages of the transcript of his conversation with Jones. But perhaps such—well, let's call it confidence—is what it takes to challenge an entrenched system, to buck the chain of command. And in his willingness to condemn those who worked within the system, who had made their way in a white-dominated world, Smothers also exemplified the generational divide that so complicated the problem of race. It is worth reiterating: the division was not solely between Black and white; it was also between youth and their elders.

Nathaniel Jones, in his autobiography, described his trip to West Germany in some detail. He and his colleagues had been taken "off guard" by the military's "eagerness" to cooperate with their mission, and they approached military officers in Europe with a bit of "paranoia." On their initial arrival in West Germany, the NAACP contingent was met at the airport by Col. Andrew Chambers, an officer who showed them "a mix of military formality and cordiality" and whose racial identity was not immediately clear. Jones, curious whether Chambers was "Black or white," posed "a test question": he asked Chambers, "Are you a frat man?" When it emerged that Chambers, like Jones, belonged to the African American fraternity Kappa Alpha Psi ("Training for Leadership since 1911"), the two "exchanged the 'grip,'" and thereafter—according to Jones—"the remainder of the trip took on a level of trust that led to a productive inquiry."[30]

Smothers (who, for whatever it is worth, belonged to a different historically Black fraternity, Omega Psi Phi: "Lifting as We Climb") had no use whatsoever for Colonel Chambers. Sliding into his version of jive talk shortly into his discussion with Jones, Smothers dismissed USAREUR's equal opportunity officer: "I swear one cat if you believe one word he says—just consider me counterfeit and don't believe a word I ever say to you again. Chambers. That is the worst excuse for anybody. Of course you know Chambers ain't never been right . . . but now Chambers is our representative and Chambers aint shit."[31]

Noting that he had heard that Chambers had been "passing for white down in Atlanta Georgia and places like that" while in the army, Smothers continued: "Chambers is absolutely dangerous. Watch him because he is their house nigger. He's shaky for some reason. Well he's got a lot of reasons. . . . This dude is the man's man. . . . He is a Tom, an oreo, he is untrustworthy. Yeah, Tom kind of shuffled a little bit. He talks a little slow. But they look at Tom as safe."[32]

Smothers offered a litany of grievances against Chambers, whom he saw as stymying Smothers's own heroic efforts to bring change to the army and giving credence to official efforts that were too little, too late. General Polk's flying squads? "Tom," charged Smothers, had taken the phrase and run with it, putting it into the press before the squads were even created. And then there were the commercials, "jingles" run on army FM radio promising "the flying squads are coming," commercials with General Polk publicizing his "open door policy": "He had it on the radio man. You got a problem, open up brother, and all this soul music come on. We've got to communicate. Listen to the words of the song James Brown sung," how "he got Afrosheen in the PX and all that shit. It's a big lie."[33]

But Captain Smothers, for all his attitude, was willing to do the hard work necessary to foster change within the system. He had spearheaded an investigation of military justice in 1968 that became the basis for eventual reform and did the analysis that made the numbers stick. He might not have been good at building coalitions, but he clearly saw the big picture. And he was willing to put his military career on the line for change he believed in. On December 25, 1970, Smothers and a few of his colleagues officially requested a court of inquiry into USAREUR command's failure to address off-post housing discrimination in Germany. Smothers's act caused a brief rift between the Department of Defense and the Department of the Army. And the court of inquiry was never convened.[34] But in February 1971, General Polk announced that he would be seeking "voluntary retirement" at the end of March.

The US Army publicly said all sorts of nice things about Polk, most especially emphasizing all the efforts he had made to combat racial discrimination. But in the context of the moment—the new DoD regulations holding service secretaries responsible for racial conflict and giving them authority to remove commanders who failed to produce satisfactory results; the media coverage of racial turbulence in Germany; Smothers's call for a court of inquiry and the NAACP's new focus on USAREUR—it was obvious to all that Polk had been pushed out, especially as his replacement, then assigned to a post in Vietnam, was not available to assume command for three more months.[35]

Demonstrating how highly charged the situation had become, and how far beyond direct army concern it reached, one of the cofounders of the Congressional Black Caucus rose in the House five days before Polk's retirement to offer his take on the situation. General Polk, Rep. Bill Clay claimed, while offering no evidence, was "a bigot," a "racist in high command." Asserting that "it was obvious" that "the racial situation would never improve in Germany so long as General Polk was in command," Clay commended Secretary of Defense Melvin Laird's "action in this case." But the freshman representative from Missouri also had a complaint. He argued that the army had sacrificed the power of that action by allowing Polk to retire "instead of filing formal charges." Rather, said Clay, the army should have publicized "the real reason" behind Polk's retirement, "making it loud and clear to all other bigots within the armed services that such practices will not be tolerated." Some, he concluded, "have suggested a Medal of Honor for General Polk. I strongly recommend a general court martial." Shortly thereafter, Smothers chimed in, telling a reporter that he "resented" army efforts to "protect" General Polk.[36]

Contrary to Clay's assertion, nothing in the public record suggests that General Polk was a racist or a bigot. But Polk had clearly failed to cut down on turbulence, to ease racial tensions, or to convince Black GIs and their allies that he was doing all he could to make a difference. And so he lost his command. Throughout the army, commanders at all levels understood what that meant.

A s the institution of the US Army confronted the growing racial crisis, it began to articulate what had been an unvoiced assumption, one in keeping with its long-standing institutional culture: leadership was key. Army chief William Westmoreland, in his initial 1969 message on race relations, called for "continued, aggressive command action" to prevent racial turbulence. Army secretary Stanley Resor, soon thereafter, emphasized the "personal responsibility of each leader for racial harmony among his men."[37] Polk's replacement in Europe, Gen. Michael S. Davison—who was white —summoned his commanders to action with a quote from 1 Corinthians (and Gen. Maxwell Taylor): "For if the trumpet give an uncertain sound, who shall prepare himself to the battle?" With these words, he told them, "I am trying to give you in this theater a very clear blast on the trumpet": the "fight to achieve racial harmony" must be "top priority" for army leaders.[38]

That emphasis on leadership as solution, however, also implied that leadership might be the problem. Davison, interviewed by the *Washington Post* on the state of the army and "the dimensions of the present crisis," said it publicly: "I think the toughest problem we have, and this is almost too frank to say, is the leadership problem within the Army." Earlier that year, another general officer in West Germany made the same point in private, telling NAACP representative Nathaniel Jones that "we have got problems . . . problems in leadership."[39] In Vietnam, the USARV Human Relations Council— charged with managing race relations—decided in the fall of 1970 to broaden its focus; recent studies had shown, noted the council, that the problems at hand were "not strictly racial in nature" but also reflected a failure of command.[40] And within the United States, Fort Carson's commander looked back from 1971 to a recent period in which "clumsy handling" by commanders had unnecessarily inflamed conflict and even "well-intentioned" efforts had failed, leaving young soldiers convinced that the army chain of command was not "seriously concerned with social justice, but only in keeping peace on post through whatever means is necessary."[41]

When it came to leaders, of course, not all were equally "well-intentioned." When the NAACP's Nathaniel Jones discovered heightened racial tensions at the Robert E. Lee Barracks in Mainz, West Germany, he concluded that the source of the problem "could be pinpointed right at the Commander." Of course the name of the barracks, in itself, shows that the source of the problem was not limited to command, and Jones did note that Black GIs "again and again" pointed out that the barracks were named for a Confederate general; that "over again" they complained that even its walls were painted a "Confederate grey." But here Jones was adamant: the individual leader mattered. This commander had not adequately implemented the army's equal opportunity policies. He allowed white soldiers to fly Confederate flags while deeming Black Panther and Black Liberation flags "subversive." And when Black soldiers presented him with a list of demands, he had "brushed them off." As a result, Jones wrote, there had been a series of racial incidents at Lee Barracks: cross burnings, marches, shootings, killings, "any number of fights." The solution, Jones argued, required just "one move": getting rid of this commander.[42]

As General Davison took on the problem of race in the US Army Europe, he was surprised by the level of command resistance. "I mistakenly thought," he told an interviewer years later, "that all I had to do was to make a policy pronouncement, promulgate the policy, and since everybody realized that it had my personal interest, they'd get with it." That, however, was not the case. Davison had scheduled an equal opportunity conference for November 1971, roughly five months after he took command. Commanders—from corps level on down—were not required to attend, but he expected they would. After all, Davison himself was planning to be there for the whole event. The two corps commanders showed up for the duration of Davison's speech; otherwise only the equal opportunity officers, whose attendance was mandated, were present. At that point, said Davison, "it became clear to me that I really had to get that mule's attention." And, of course, the only way to get a mule's attention "is to hit him over the head a couple of times with a two by four." He "read the riot act to them in a very forthright way," one senior officer remembered.[43]

Davison understood quite well what his mandate was, and he was willing to use the tools at hand. At the equal opportunity conference, General Davison's deputy chief of staff for personnel, Maj. Gen. Frederic Davison, offered the headline quote: "It won't be long before every cotton-picking commander knows his neck is on the line. Just watch and see the fur fly."[44]

As a necessary aside: command in USAREUR was confusing. Four-star general Michael S. Davison was commander in chief; two-star general Frederic Ellis Davison was deputy chief of staff for personnel. Major General Davison was "a short, bouncy man," stocky and "salty-tongued," described by junior officers as "feisty and 'mentally very fast on his feet.'" He was also the highest-ranking Black officer in the army, the first Black general to have commanded infantrymen in combat. This Davison credited his rise to "the right wars and the right schools"; he was a strong defender of the army's record on civil rights—the Black general whose "false promises of equality, freedom and justice in the military" Maj. Lavell Merritt had so angrily dismissed back in 1968. And while Davison unequivocally supported racial equality, like many Black officers of his generation, he had little use for what he considered "militancy." The two Davisons, united to combat the racial crisis, soon became known as "Salt" and "Pepper." Of the two, "Salt" was more open to the demands of youth.[45]

Soon after he arrived in Germany, "Salt" Davison let it be known that he had removed USAREUR company and battalion commanders who had failed to adequately manage race relations. Soon thereafter, Frank Render at the Department of Defense publicly announced that, beginning in December 1970,

In 1971 the two Generals Davison—Gen. Michael S. Davison (*left*)
and Maj. Gen. Frederic E. Davison—were tasked with de-escalating
the growing racial crisis in the US Army in West Germany.
*US Army official photographs.*

action had been taken against military officers in cases where commanders
"clearly . . . had been negligent." Ten or twelve high-ranking military officers
—no service specified—had been relieved of command because they had
not followed civil rights regulations. Render declined to name the officers;
"I don't believe it would serve any useful purpose to give their names—to
embarrass them," he said. But he did offer some specifics: "There are people
who wear stars, bars[,] oak leaves and birds on their shoulders who have been
relieved of duty." Pentagon officials were not pleased by Render's statement,
but the spokesman who refused to confirm or deny Render's claim nonetheless said, without caveat, that understanding race relations was "a leadership
requirement—if you can't understand race relations, you can't be a leader
in today's Army."[46]

Here, "understanding" race relations was not simply academic. That
understanding had to be manifested in one's command: minimizing racial
turbulence at the least; improving the unit's racial climate at best. But at that
moment in the army's history, racial conflict and division were virtually universal. Wallace Terry, former deputy Saigon bureau chief for *Time* magazine,
pushed that "leadership" test to its logical conclusion in his 1971 testimony
for the Congressional Black Caucus's hearings on racism in the military. "As
the old adage has it," he said, "if you ground a ship in the Navy you can forget

about being an admiral. Well, I believe if you have a cross burning on your base or a race riot, you could forget about being an admiral or a general."[47] But in the early 1970s, it would have been hard to find a post that had *not* experienced racial turmoil. What did that fact portend for this "leadership requirement"?

With continuing pressure from the Department of Defense, the army incorporated a version of this requirement. Officers—and eventually NCOs —would be held responsible for the racial climate in their units. In April 1971, the month following General Polk's "voluntary" retirement, the army institutionalized its command focus on race. That month the army changed its regulations to allow, "as appropriate," superiors to comment on how well officers managed race relations in the Officer Efficiency Reports (OERs), the "all-important" evaluations that have "a vital bearing on the success or failure of a soldier's military career." Ten months later, it required that evaluation. "Race Relations to Go on the Record," reported *Stars and Stripes* in February 1972. Curtis Smothers, pulled out of the uncomfortable situation in Europe and awarded the top military civil rights post in the Pentagon (replacing Render), had pushed the move. Equal opportunity, he said, was now in the rewards system; "the Army is making it profitable to do something about race relations for the individual's own reasons."[48]

In broad terms, the army decision to evaluate officers on how well they handled a key institutional problem was congruent with traditional army practice; commanders are responsible for the performance of the men under their command and are evaluated on that basis. The OER put teeth into equal opportunity programs and gave commanders incentives to perform. But that a four-star general was, at least seemingly, forced to retire because he had failed to manage race? That unnamed officers with "stars, bars oak leaves and birds" had been relieved of command for the same reason? That raised the stakes. It also potentially solved some of the problems.

Army leaders, recognizing not only that they confronted an intractable problem but that they would be evaluated on how well they handled it, sought guidance. Given, as they assumed, that racial conflict in the army had its roots in American society, and given, as some pointed out, that the source of Black grievance reached back hundreds of years, to the enslavement of Africans—how should a commander address the crisis?[49]

Evolving army wisdom, echoed through the world of army equal opportunity/human relations, gave two linked answers. The first looked to junior officers and NCOs; the second, to senior command.

Even as army discussions focused on the visible and active commitment

*Leadership*

of top-level command, most army leaders who were charged with solving the problem of race understood that the "real army," for most young enlisted men, was at company level or below.[50] If the NCOs, lieutenants, and captains failed to manage—or, worse, exacerbated—the problem, there could be no solution. But the situation on the ground was explosive, and few thought that young officers would instinctually handle problems that had defeated more experienced ones, most definitely including the hapless Major Irving (the officer who was both unprepared and unwilling to deal with Major Merritt and his claims about race).

In December 1969, one of several biracial, cross-rank seminars assembled at Fort Leavenworth to discuss the problem of racial tension focused on "immature leadership at the company level." Many junior officers, seminar participants asserted, lacked the necessary "training, patience, maturity, and understanding" to manage the problem at hand. That same month, the commanding general of the US Army Hawai'i wrote to the head of the US Army Pacific: "Frankly, I consider that our junior commanders and NCOs are too inexperienced to deal with all aspects of this complex problem."[51]

In turn, the army's 1969 special study, "Racial Harmony in the Army," made the same point: young officers had not been adequately prepared to deal with the "complex and sensitive issue of racial harmony." But while General Sternberg, in Hawai'i, seemed to dismiss those junior officers, this study emphasized their importance. The study's authors agreed that while public support from the secretary of the army and its chief of staff was crucial, it was even more important that the troops hear a commitment to racial equality "'straight up' eye ball to eye ball by their immediate officer superiors." Thus, the study concluded, the army had to train junior officers to handle matters of race. When Lt. Col. James White briefed MACV, the commander of US military forces in Vietnam, Gen. Creighton Abrams, asked only two questions. One focused on junior officers and NCOs: How well equipped to handle racial conflict were they, he wanted to know, and could the army train them or assist them to do better?[52]

In Germany, General Davison (Salt, not Pepper) laid out the underlying logic of this approach. Most young men, he explained, had little direct experience with members of other races when they entered the army. That fact created different challenges for white youth and for Black, but it helped to explain why the young white commander "may feel unequipped to cope with racial tension in his unit." And, Davison continued, because in the case of race relations, "as in almost every worthwhile thing the army does," it was the captain, the lieutenant, or the sergeant who "has to carry the ball," that lack of preparation mattered. "Let me make it clear," he told his audience, "that I am not trying to fix the blame for lack of adequate progress to date on these junior leaders." What blame existed must fall on senior commanders, who had not sufficiently prepared their subordinates. "We taught them to check blisters on their men's heels," Davison explained, the "marking on their equipment, the length of their hair, and what such things imply about discipline and readiness. We failed, however, to make them aware of the implications, for the whole unit and its cohesiveness, of the color of the soldiers' skins."[53]

In the face of a growing crisis, the army began to offer official guidance. L. Howard Bennett, reporting on his DoD study of race relations, recommended minimizing "Olympian hymns to fairness and equality" and instead coming up with effective techniques: a "how-to manual" for "the man on the firing line." Colonel White, conducting his standard briefing in Vietnam, recommended that a leaders' guide be created and transmitted to the field as an "immediate aid"—and a "commanders' guide" did, in fact, circulate in both Germany and Vietnam. In Vietnam, where "the nature of combat" prevented more traditional approaches, army leaders started distributing "lessons learned" for managing racial conflict. And in a more centralized fashion, the army inserted race relations modules in officer and NCO training.[54]

These were all reasonable moves, and more adequate training could certainly have prevented some problems. For example, there was the army captain in Cam Ranh Bay, in 1967, who posted a notice offering a $100 reward for information leading to the "unknown negro soldiers" who had committed a series of assaults. Journalist Ethyl Payne described the resulting discontent in the *Chicago Daily Defender*. It was the lowercase *n* in "Negro" that particularly disturbed her, along with some of the men in the unit; she had had to explain to the base commander that African Americans had struggled for the capital *N* and saw it as a "matter of dignity, pride—and proper English."[55] The white captain in question needed to know that fact, just as he needed to be made aware that if he was to use racial identifiers in a description, he needed to use them consistently across the board, not only when the suspects were identified as African American.

And training could have certainly improved the actions of the host of white junior officers and NCOs who—whether purposely or unwittingly—called men "boy" or labeled as militant any Black man who complained. But these attempts to prepare junior officers came pretty late in the game. By the early 1970s, the term "Negro" in and of itself gave offense, and while racial epithets frequently set off physical conflict, division and anger far exceeded their immediate triggers.

Senior officers all too often naively suggested that if junior officers were simply fair, all would be well.[56] That was patently false. First of all, because young Black soldiers regularly confronted racism, whether the institutional version that housed them in barracks named for a Confederate general or the immediate and personal version of racial epithets and latrine-wall graffiti, it was difficult for them not to see everything that was wrong, every frustration or disappointment or inequity, as further evidence of a racist system. And these young Black soldiers were angry about conditions that went well beyond their immediate command, even if a lieutenant or captain seemed its most immediate face.

How was Martin Luther King's charge that Vietnam was "a white man's war, a black man's fight" under the control of a lieutenant? How was a captain to compensate for the Chicago police murder of Black Panther Fred Hampton or the shooting of students at (historically Black) Jackson State University? How was he to handle the anger that manifested as seemingly random violence or engage the arguments offered by men who had been reading Black Panther Eldridge Cleaver and Algerian revolutionary Frantz Fanon?

Of course good leadership mattered, and in volatile situations poor leadership could be catastrophic. But the problems that junior officers and NCOs confronted often surpassed the ability of an inexperienced twenty-two-year-old to manage—whether because he lacked experience or because he lacked sufficient authority or because the problem at hand was larger than the company or the brigade or the army itself.

Junior officers and senior NCOs became increasingly frustrated as their best efforts yielded little positive result. One "lessons learned" case study on race relations described a junior officer's frustration. He had struggled with a Black private first class who "failed to respond to numerous counseling sessions, while becoming increasingly insubordinate to his superiors." The soldier had become "obsessed with the idea that I was prejudiced against him because he was a Negro," and while the officer had "tried at great lengths to show him through words and actions that I was in fact not prejudiced," he eventually asked for the private to be transferred to another unit—for "rehabilitation." The first sergeant from another unit (patronizingly described as "an impressive and mature Negro") also confessed frustration. Blacks, he said, "demand promotions, preferential treatment, exclusion from punishment, and plush jobs as evidence that the commander is not prejudiced against Negroes," and he made clear he believed that "both he and the commander were being manipulated by young blacks."[57]

The lesson drawn from these cases was that such frustration undermined the larger goal: if junior officers and NCOs continued to be discouraged and disturbed by such experiences, they might become unwilling to take action at all. Further complicating the situation, this "lesson" encountered a roadblock up the chain of command, as a senior officer noted that it could be interpreted as "all blacks are bad and make false allegations" and suggested both examples be deleted unless the authors could change their "tenor."[58]

Despite the commanders' reasonable concerns in this case, plenty of army leaders were drawing a similar lesson. Perhaps relying so heavily on junior commanders and on NCOs was not the best solution to the joint problem-solution of command.

In this instance another piece of emerging army wisdom came to the fore. After all, the underlying problem—according to a claim that far surpassed its origins—was "the failure to communicate." That problem manifested in the chain of command, but it also was a problem *of* the chain of command. Senior commanders were out of touch with their men. They had relied too heavily on subordinates, not only to manage problems but also for information. Subordinate officers had no incentive to admit to problems beyond their capacity or to pass along complaints, especially those that reflected poorly on themselves.[59]

These claims easily found traction, as concern about leadership reached well beyond the problem of race. In the wake of the My Lai Massacre and subsequent cover-up, army chief of staff Westmoreland had ordered the US Army War College to evaluate the "state of discipline, integrity, morality, ethics, and professionalism" in the army. This study of the "heart and soul of the Officer Corps of the Army" revealed fundamental institutional failings. "The Army has generated an environment that rewards relatively insignificant, short-term indicators of success," read the *Study on Military Professionalism*, "and disregards or discourages the growth of the long-term qualities of moral and ethical strength on which the future of the Army depends." The study's authors noted the "tenuous" state of communications between junior and senior officers, as well as the perception that senior officers were "isolated, perhaps willingly, from reality."[60] Such failures of communication—and thus of leadership—were particularly visible when it came to race. Time and again, commanders of army posts were caught short, unaware of simmering tension until it exploded in violence.

Here, again, though, it is important to remember that the army did not exist in a vacuum. Through the 1960s and into the 1970s, large portions of American youth had rejected hierarchy and authority, embracing, instead, radical visions of participatory democracy and knowledge borne of immediate experience. Such stances, no matter how much at odds with army culture and practice, could not be ignored. As one young Black NCO told the *Washington Post*, "If we're good enough to get killed over here, we're good enough to be listened to and without having to go through a chain of command."[61]

Neither donning a uniform nor surviving boot camp erased the previous beliefs and experiences of youth, and as the army struggled to figure out how it would convince 20,000 to 30,000 young people to join the army *every month* when the draft ended in 1973, it tried to directly contend with young people's desire for individualism and their reluctance to accept seemingly arbitrary authority. Thus, the army's second version of leadership-as-solution fit into a broader set of actions.

Facing growing threats of racial violence, some commanders began to experiment with something that directly violated traditional army practice: they began bypassing the chain of command. Initially, and with a bit of pressure from the Department of the Army, commanding generals instituted an open-door policy. Whether during set hours or on demand, any soldier could take his problem directly to top command (as in General Polk's "you got a problem, open up brother" radio announcement). And when enlisted men complained that even though the door was open that did not mean no one was blocking it, some—like General Garth, in West Germany—went directly *to* young enlisted men, asking to hear their concerns. But that had its own drawbacks, not the least that it diverted senior leaders from broader concerns. "A dude went up to Gen. Garth . . . the other day and complained about his breakfast," complained platoon sergeant Wade Jackson. "That's no way to run an Army."[62]

The next move, emerging piecemeal and then "recommended" to all, was the creation of race relations councils. These councils institutionalized direct access, even as they restricted its range. Councils put a clearly defined set of low-ranking enlisted men into close contact with the commanding general. (The how-to guide published at Fort Carson, Colorado, advised the commanding general to meet with council members daily.)[63]

There were good reasons to bypass the chain of command. Young white officers, most senior officers agreed, were not capable of managing the situation. And as the DoD's L. Howard Bennett argued in his 1970 report, NCOs

—white or Black—offered little better. NCOs, after all, were the ones who "harass [their men] about reading Eldridge Cleaver, wearing a slave bracelet, or exchanging the black power salute; it is the NCOs who assign the dirty details, who break up groups of Blacks talking in a 'hooch.'" In such cases the generation gap trumped race. Just as young Black GIs disdained "whitey," they dismissed older Black NCOs as "Uniform Tangos," "Oleos," "Oreos," and "Uncle Toms." They did not trust them. Bennett concluded that, even as NCOs were the "professional backbone of the Armed Forces," they weren't the solution to the problem of race. Top commanders had to talk directly to troops; otherwise they risked an "'out of the blue' racial eruption."[64]

In 1970, Fort Carson's commander went all-in. At that point Fort Carson was a challenging command, full of Vietnam returnees filling out their last weeks in service, men who cared little about the army and its traditional hierarchies and means of authority. Race relations had been bad and worse. Violent confrontations were commonplace.[65] And if that was not sufficient impetus, commanders were being held accountable for failure to manage the problem of race.

Fort Carson, at that moment, offered a case of the right person in the right place at the right time. Maj. Gen. Bernard Rogers, Rhodes Scholar from Kansas, would go on to serve as army deputy chief of staff for personnel, chief of staff of the army, and supreme allied commander of NATO. He had come to Fort Carson from a stint as commandant of the US Military Academy at West Point; before that he had been awarded the Distinguished Service Cross in Vietnam for physically leading a counterattack against an enemy camp. General Rogers—faced with crises that went beyond race—confronted the alienated Vietnam returnees and the simmering-to-boiling racial conflict in ways that had outraged traditionalists: he offered them less "chickenshit," created councils that amplified the voices of enlisted men, and lowered barriers between their lives and the powerful youth culture from which they came.[66]

Fort Carson's race council had its origins in a heated discussion between General Rogers and "a large group of articulate, talented and concerned young blacks, whites and Chicanos" in the spring of 1970. Rogers registered one fundamental complaint: that the army was not "seriously concerned with social justice" but was simply trying to keep peace on post "through any means whatever." Perhaps that was true, and perhaps that was not even bad. ("I don't care how you feel about this," "Salt" Davison was prone to tell those under his command in USAREUR, "but bigoted behavior will not be tolerated.")[67] Nonetheless, Fort Carson's commander meant to prove them wrong.

That angry conversation prompted General Rogers to create a standing "Racial Harmony Council" and to give it extraordinary access to top levels of command. The council itself would reveal an unexpected resource: a talented specialist 4 with extensive community organizing experience.

Like James Hobson, Darnell Summers had leadership qualities. And like Hobson, Summers carried a complicated history. He arrived at Fort Carson in the summer of 1970; like so many others, he was there to finish out his term of service following a tour in Vietnam. Summers had not been a reluctant draftee; he had joined the army in 1966, at the age of eighteen. His path to Fort Carson, however, was not directly from Vietnam: Summers had spent the past thirteen months in civilian prison, sentenced in connection to the shooting of two police officers during four nights of "racial unrest" during the summer of 1968. The "unrest," in response to the closing of a youth center "operated by young Negroes" in the Detroit suburb of Inkster, included the murder of an undercover police detective as he sat in his unmarked car. Minutes later a phalanx of police opened fire on a fourteen-year-old Black youth who had "something" in his hands (it was his shirt).[68]

Summers, who was at home on leave before his tour in Vietnam, was one of the "young Negroes" working to build the Malcolm X Cultural Center, and he had successfully argued before the Inkster City Council for Black culture programs "to instill a sense of dignity and pride in black people" and for investigations of police harassment in Black communities ("It gets to look like we're not being protected but occupied," the twenty-year-old GI told the Inkster City Council). Summers deployed, as scheduled, to Vietnam, where he served as personnel officer for a helicopter support unit. There he was charged with the murder of the undercover detective back in Inkster, arrested and confined to Long Binh Jail—within months of the LBJ uprising —and then returned to Michigan to stand trial. Those charges were dropped (without prejudice, meaning they could be reinstated) after the sole witness recanted, but Summers nonetheless was convicted in June 1969 of conspiracy to destroy police property.[69]

Summers served his time. But when he walked out of the civilian prison in which he had spent the last thirteen months, army MPs were waiting. It was a mess, and not only because Summers had not a single free breath before he found himself locked in the local county jail, waiting while the MPs rounded up AWOL soldiers from all over the state of Michigan. And at that point, no one was quite sure what to do with him. The army could not charge him with an offense similar to the one for which he had done time. There was no army misconduct to charge. And Summers himself was determined to stay in the army. He wanted his GI Bill benefits, and he was not about to have a less than honorable discharge on his record.[70]

Summers made his case, with letters from the Inkster mayor and police chief and from his battalion commander in Vietnam. According to his account, the army lawyers at the retention hearing were sympathetic, leaning left and anti-war. In the end, the hearing went his way: he was reinstated with both rank and secret-level security clearance intact. Because his time was so short, he was sent to Fort Carson rather than back to Vietnam. The 517th Medical Company would be his last duty station.

The obvious move, at that point, would be to keep his head down. But that was not Darnell Summers's nature. He was still (in his own words) a "brash, outspoken Black soldier, complaining about everything" when he arrived at Fort Carson. No one knew that yet, when he drove his blue Chevy up to the hospital barracks that first day. But observers did register that he was not alone; his German girlfriend and future wife, Erika, was in the passenger seat. A Black soldier. A white woman. And his records had not even arrived.

Even worse, given time in service and grade, he was at the top of the list of those eligible for promotion. Company leaders were less than thrilled. Summers saw a broader pattern of discrimination against Black soldiers. He went to the Racial Harmony Council. He brought his intellect and education to bear. ("I went to Catholic school," he said, later. "The nuns prepared me for any eventuality; I was well read, well versed.") He showed his activist roots. It was not long before he was elected to the council and then to its chair.

At Fort Carson, Summers gained the support of the assistant division commander, Brig. Gen. DeWitt C. Smith Jr.—one of the most decent officers in the US Army. Later in the 1970s, Smith would serve as the commandant of the Army War College and as the army's deputy chief of staff for personnel; he became known as a "defense intellectual" who confronted difficult questions about the role of the military in a democracy. But at that tumultuous moment in army history, Smith was overseeing Fort Carson's Project VOLAR (VOLunteer ARmy), a program meant to figure out how to transition the army to an all-volunteer force. He was a hands-on leader, not only in Project VOLAR's experiments with ending reveille and allowing beer in the barracks but in developing and working closely with the Racial Harmony Council.[71]

General Smith did not seek Summers out; Summers had been independently elected to head the Racial Harmony Council. But he did recognize Summers's ability, and he gave him a great deal of latitude. Summers spent his last months in the army working for racial justice. He led the council

Specialist Darnell Summers (*center*) and Brig. Gen. DeWitt C. Smith (*right*)
at a meeting of Fort Carson's Racial Harmony Council.
*Courtesy Darnell Summers.*

in crafting proposals for reform, but he also went into units with bad racial
problems in an attempt to "implant" the idea that a race relations council
might be worthwhile. He was not always welcome, particularly when he insisted on speaking with Black GIs; on several occasions unit commanders
had him arrested for haircut violations or "anything else they could come up
with." But he had command support, and his work continued. Armed with
a letter of passage from General Smith, Summers ventured into units with
hostile commanders, authorized to investigate complaints and—as a low-
ranking enlisted man—to require company commanders and their executive
officers to meet with him.[72]

During this process, both Smith and Rogers became increasingly convinced that the chain of command was "ill-suited" to respond to the current
situation. It had been Fort Carson's "unwillingness" to address racial conflict "outside the context of military identities, ranks and organizations," another internal evaluation asserted, that had originally exacerbated its racial
problems.[73]

This new, non-chain-of-command model was not without problems.
"Attention given to the blacks by the command group," noted a Fort Carson
report, "has been sometimes misunderstood and sometimes resented by
some whites." And some young members of the race councils, suddenly (in
their minds) placed above all those who had been telling them what to do,
given direct access to the commanding general, tended to push the bound-

aries. Guidelines insisted that communication should be frank and direct; white commanders sometimes had not bargained for what "direct" sounded like. (The *Washington Post* described one young Black soldier calling his division commander—a general—"a pig." To his face. "I burned buildings in Chicago and shot whitey," said the young man, "and it doesn't bother me one bit. And I'd just as soon shoot at whitey as the VC.") Noted the Fort Carson report: it had been necessary to "accept the abrasiveness of some of the natural black leaders as a very small price for their cooperation in a dynamic but volatile and delicate area of human relations."[74]

Internal resistance was a greater problem. A commanding general might decide to tolerate the posturing of youth. He might discover "natural black leaders" who understood the issues at hand, men whom he could trust and who might come to trust him. But what of charges that he had undermined the day-to-day authority of junior officers and NCOs? The new model solved one issue: complaints no longer got lost on their way up the chain of command. But how does an institution built on obedience offer subordinates an alternate path?

The platoon sergeant who had complained about General Garth's excessively open door said it directly: "They're breaking down the whole command structure." Frank Mildren, the deputy commanding general of USARV, was so distressed when Howard Bennett proposed such direct communication that he resorted to all caps in a letter to those under his command: "The advice 'TAKE YOUR COMPLAINTS THROUGH THE CHAIN OF COMMAND' is as sound in this modern army," he wrote, "as it was in earlier times." But General Davison, in *his* usual direct fashion, rejected the premise. Speaking to students at Fort Leavenworth's Command and General Staff College, Davison entertained the notion that "open door" policies and race relations/enlisted men's councils undercut the chain of command. But, he countered, "I can only point out that if every officer and noncommissioned officer were fully and professionally discharging his responsibilities as a leader, there would be no need for these innovations."[75]

And from Fort Carson came a more practical endorsement. The Racial Harmony Council demonstrated its potential to "bear real fruit," according to a Fort Carson report on race relations, when a "militant member" of the council warned Fort Carson's chief of staff that a "serious riot" was brewing and the command, in turn, put "a great deal of faith in the black soldier's insight and trustworthiness [and] acted on his advice" to prevent the explosion. The point? The Racial Harmony Council was not simply an attempt to co-opt Black "militants." It was mutual trust that made the difference.[76] And to build mutual trust, it was necessary to violate the chain of command.

In the end, despite their fundamental violation of army practice, the race relations councils were leadership-based solutions. At Fort Carson and elsewhere, commanders sought natural, "charismatic" leaders among the young Black enlisted men. Recognizing their unofficial roles, commanders offered them standing and a form of authority. This may have been co-optation, but it came with the ear of the commanding general and a very un-army ability to speak frankly. The drawback, of course, was that these men were not lifers. Army leaders faced a constant struggle to identify and cultivate the next "natural" leader, and the next, and the next.

I n 1981, an army officer using the pseudonym "Cincinnatus" published what was heralded as a "scathing" critique of the US Army in Vietnam. *Self-Destruction* reaped positive reviews and a featured spot in the Military Book Club before its author was revealed to be an army chaplain who taught military history at the University of South Florida and had never served in Vietnam. He had, however, attended Fort Leavenworth's Command and General Staff College, and what he said of that experience is useful here. "In military classrooms," Cincinnatus wrote, "instructors ask the rhetorical question 'Who has the responsibility?' And students respond in chorus, 'The commander.' It is a sacrosanct, inviolable, and appropriate doctrine within the military."[77]

Faced with crisis, army leaders embraced that inviolable doctrine and its associated precepts. The commander had the responsibility, and the commander would be held responsible, evaluated on his ability to manage the problem of race. Of all the army's actions, that one may have mattered most. As a solution, it was the most in keeping with army tradition and practice; endorsing command responsibility was neither bold nor disruptive. Nonetheless, in service of that most traditional principle, commanders were willing to challenge the traditional army principle and practice of always observing the chain of command.

# 5 EDUCATION AND TRAINING

Army leaders defined the racial crisis as a command problem, first and foremost, and saw leadership as a (perhaps *the*) key solution. But here, of course, we pause to remember Major Irving, the officer who threw up his hands as Maj. Lavell Merritt tossed insults and a chair one August night in Dong Da, uncertain how a white son of Alabama could address the issue of race without seeming "prejudice." And as lengthy interviews with a member of the inspector general's office made clear, he had a point. He had not been trained for that.

That point, more broadly, was amply clear to those assigned to manage the problem of race. Wrote the deputy assistant chief of staff for personnel, US Army Vietnam: "I agree that leadership is the answer to how this problem is to be handled. But just like one is taught to be a leader, so must our leaders be educated on how to handle this politically sensitive and potentially explosive area."[1]

If the US Army expected its officers and NCOs to rise to that challenge, it had to prepare them to do so. That is how the army works. The mission of the US Army is made possible through education and training, and during the Vietnam era the vast and largely self-sufficient institution trained members to fill hundreds of different military occupational specialties (known as MOSs), from 11B Infantry to 94E Pastry Baker, from 3111 Urologist to 02H Oboe Player, and from 44C Welder to 74F Software Analyst. And as it attempted to help officer candidates "discover in [themselves] the magic power of leadership," the army educated officers and NCOs in the increasing responsibilities that came with rank.[2]

Simply put, the army is a massive educational institution. In the late

1960s, as Secretary of the Army Stanley Resor—addressing the racial crisis
—called for "total commitment to this necessary goal," the institutional army
boasted twenty-seven service schools and seventeen training centers within
the continental United States. And it celebrated its educational mission.
"Except in name it is a university," proclaimed *The Spirit of Fort Benning*, an
army-produced film from the era. Home to a "towering" statue of a rifleman,
Fort Benning (according to the film) was nonetheless a "massive educational
plant" that made its own video training tapes and boasted an around-the-
clock printing shop to meet the needs of military education, a site where on
any given weekday 12,000 officers and enlisted men filled the classrooms of
Infantry Hall and thousands more completed exercises in one of 1,222 problem sites spread across its "vast" 620-square-mile reach.[3]

As demand for men had grown along with the scope of the war, the army's
training infrastructure had expanded in kind. By 1966, fifteen additional
bases had joined Forts Bragg, Campbell, and Lewis in offering basic training.
More than a quarter million men were inducted into the army in 1969; close
to 200,000 volunteered. All these men had to be trained, "transform[ed]" (in
the words of a different official army video) over the course of eight weeks
"into soldiers." Institutional logic dictated that the army, confronting a problem, would see education and training as a solution.[4]

And so it did. In September 1969, shortly after Colonel White briefed
him on "racial harmony," the army's chief of staff made race relations training mandatory throughout the army educational system. The institution
moved expeditiously, given the challenges involved. Within a year, the army
had developed, approved, and instituted a four-hour block of race relations
instruction for officers, warrant officers, and NCOs, as well as for the Special
Forces basic enlisted course. Weeks later, it was piloting a four-hour block
of instruction in basic combat training. The Department of Defense soon
stepped in. Requirements continued to expand. Before war's end, in addition
to the formal training, every army unit was directed to hold eighteen hours'
worth of "RAP seminars." ("Rap," in the early 1970s, was hip youth slang
for a conversation, and one sees the hand of army acronym-crafters in the
officially titled "Race Awareness Program.") In the space of three years, the
US Army moved from silence or stopgap, semiofficial efforts to a program
it described as "the largest effort in number of people and hours of training
ever made by an organization to provide education in race relations."[5]

Two things are important to understand here. First, adding four new
hours of instruction to basic combat training meant there would be four
fewer hours devoted to something else—at a point when many army leaders

worried that training time was not sufficient for the young men headed to combat in Vietnam.[6] General Westmoreland's order represented a significant statement of priorities.

Second, as in the case of bureaucracies in general, a simple directive (add race relations training to army education) required a seemingly endless and interconnected set of decisions and precipitated an equally overwhelming number of subordinate changes. Training required instructors. How many instructors were necessary? Would this new charge require additional personnel? If so, from which budget line would funding come? How would those instructors be selected? How would their specialization be designated? Was it an MOS or simply an SQI (special qualification identifier)? What impact would this role have on the designated individuals' military careers? Who would train the instructors? Where would the training take place? Would an individual instructor or a team be most effective in the eventual classroom? If a team, did it require diversity of race? Of rank? Who would evaluate the training, and on what grounds? And so on and so forth.

All those questions, though, are primarily about structure. What about content? What would be taught? How did the army, institutionally, imagine that it could defuse racial tension through education and training?

The army's approach was highly contingent, at least initially. As army units throughout the world were torn by racial violence, people sought solutions. A chaplain in Vietnam, inspired by a story in *Reader's Digest*, set up an informal seminar meant to help "destroy the misconceptions which breed the suspicions and mistrust leading to racial tension." A brigade commander at Fort Bragg sent all his junior officers a list of books by and about African Americans, charging them to inform themselves about "racial problems." A psychiatrist at Fort Benning tried group therapy.[7] Efforts were local, haphazard, and institutionally incoherent, but successes, even limited ones, drew notice. And those people who, due to whatever fluke of army logic, were in the right place at the right time found outsize influence.

The army's definition of the problem also shaped its approach. As an explanation for racial tension, "failure of communication" gradually transformed from analysis to assumption to fact. In the unsettled culture of late-sixties America, the language of civility, the measured and restrained, all appeared dishonest, uptight, insincere: a failure of communication. In this climate, army instructors were taught to foster free and frank discussion, to encourage men to talk about how they *really* felt, what they *really* thought, to push men of all races to confront the sources of anger and division, to reveal internal prejudice even if such prejudice had never been visible in their actions. Despite repeated claims that the army sought to change behavior, not attitudes, race relations training and education increasingly relied on the potentially explosive techniques of "T-groups" and sensitivity training. ("T-groups," or "training groups," employed psychological techniques built on intensive group encounters.) As such, the army was embracing what some saw as the forward-thinking strands of humanistic psychology, demonstrating just how flexible and creative it could be when confronted with a problem of the magnitude of race. And at the same time, these race relations courses *were* targeting attitudes. They were risking explosion. Poking the bear. And they were challenging the institutional logic of the army.

**M**aj. Avrom Carl Segal, in 1967, was a newly credentialed Jewish psychiatrist from Philadelphia who had just finished up a year at Harvard, and he definitely never intended to end up in the pine barrens of southwest Georgia. Neither had his wife; when she learned they were headed to Fort Benning, she broke down and cried. In retrospect, Segal's assignment to Fort Benning was an abrupt reminder of how the army functioned. "I'd been in the army for years," he later said, "but I'd never really been *in* the army."[8]

Segal had joined the army well before the United States committed ground troops to Southeast Asia. In 1961, no war in sight, he found himself in medical school with a wife, two kids, and not much money. The army had seemed a good solution. And mostly it was. He graduated from Philadelphia's Jefferson Medical School and took an army internship in Tacoma, Washington, and then a residency at Walter Reed Army Medical Center in DC. When he expressed interest in community mental health, the army sent him to Harvard to study with the psychiatrist who was defining the field. All seemed on track until he got orders for Georgia.[9]

Carl Segal was not one to give up on his goals, so—while still at Harvard, immersed in heady conversations about social structure and mental health—he began charting out plans for a comprehensive mental health community center at Fort Benning. But he was shocked by what he found there. Segal had completed his medical internship in Washington State, at Fort Lewis, before the wartime buildup. It was a good experience, at least as much as a medical school internship could be; he and his wife had hoped to return there. Fort Benning, in late 1967, seemed a different world. The pressure of war was obvious, and it hit close to home. The post was supposed to have five psychiatrists; Segal brought the count up to two. And the 197th Infantry Brigade, to which he was assigned, seemed tense, unsettled. Men training for combat in Vietnam combined with men back from combat in Vietnam, six months to discharge, bored, frustrated, and *done* with the army.[10]

And it was the South, less than three years after the Civil Rights Act of 1964 put a legal end to Jim Crow. It is not that Segal had never encountered segregation before. Of the 147 students in his Philadelphia medical school class, none were Black. Or female, for that matter, though there was a student from Thailand, one Japanese American, and a considerable number of Jews.[11] But segregation worked differently in the North. There were no Blacks in his classes, certainly, as he came of age in north Philadelphia, but no water fountains marked "white" and "colored." At Fort Benning, there on the Georgia-Alabama border, Black troops who ventured off-post sometimes found that white civilians did not see only olive drab.

Major Segal became increasingly aware of race. When two young men under his care, both schizophrenic, were pulled over and arrested in Alabama while on a weekend pass to visit family, he and another psychiatrist took an army helicopter to Alabama to "rescue" them. "It felt like we were flying across enemy lines," he recalled. "Two Jewish men, two African Americans." It was such "serendipitous" events that made him sensitive to racial issues. He had an equally serendipitous connection to the post's Black community. After an African American captain had a breakdown, sold his shoes and watch to get money for gas, and drove 800 miles to Walter Reed hospital, the last place he had felt safe, Segal pulled the strings he could, flew to DC, brought the man home to Fort Benning—and to his wife and family. The captain's wife, who worked in the post library, was grateful. She and Segal got to know each other; she gave him access to a different world, one in which race always remained visible.[12]

Segal's experience as chief of mental health services for the 197th was making him professionally interested in the problem of race. It was hard not to notice the number of African American enlisted men sent to him for "behavioral disorders." Most had gone to the hospital's internist complaining of headaches, backaches, other minor physical ailments; frequently, Segal recalled, they had said something like, "The sergeant's really riding me because I'm Black." With increasing frequency, the internist referred those men to the post psychiatrists. Dr. Segal had mixed feelings about that. He was confident that social systems had psychological impacts on individuals and that physical ailments were sometimes psychological in origin (or, in his words, were "somatic complaints that seemed to be associated with tension caused or aggravated by racial prejudice"). But he also understood that sending men

*Education and Training*

who complained about racial discrimination to a psychiatrist suggested the problem was in their heads.[13]

Sometime during his first year at Benning, Segal heard a story about a fight at a post enlisted men's club. Black and white soldiers battling each other with pool cues seemed clear evidence to him that the percolating tensions were coming to a boil. When those charged with handling the matter denied that race had anything to do with it, Segal went to the brigade commander and asked permission to look into the matter. That permission secured, he turned to the commander of the battalion in question: "I think there's a problem here," he told him, one that was having "an impact on the mental health and morale of the unit." With command blessing, Segal began meeting with small groups of men—focus groups, more or less, though the term was not yet coined. Although he was once reported by another officer as a "suspicious character"—a white major hanging out with Black enlisted men—he got people talking. And it was as he suspected: there was a great deal of racial tension in the 600-man battalion.[14]

At this point, the army was still claiming only-one-color, same-mud-same-blood, led-the-nation status. Segal was pressing to confront a problem that had not yet been officially acknowledged. Nonetheless, he pushed ahead. He told the battalion commander he wanted to lead a group therapy session for the battalion. There was a large building that housed the tanks and armored vehicles; he figured they could set up a platform—something like a boxing ring—in the middle and circle the men around it. The battalion commander agreed. But it had to be everyone in the unit, Segal said. All the enlisted men, all the noncoms, all the officers. There he got some pushback, but that is what happened. Every member of the battalion was ordered to attend a four-hour meeting, most likely the largest group therapy session in history.[15]

People were quiet at first, aside from the scripted remarks of the social work officer. But a question or two broke the ice. People started talking. The four hours passed. It was 1700 hours. Time for dinner. But people did not want to leave. A suggestion emerged that they come back after dinner, on their own time, and Segal promised he would be there as long as they wanted. At that dinner, Segal said, Black and white EMs sat together, still talking. And 400 men returned at 1830. They started up again: where they had lived, how they had been brought up, relationships they had had. Come 2100, Segal proposed stopping. People were getting tired, he said. And they said no. "*I'm* getting tired," said Segal. "We have to stop now."[16]

Segal had gained a lot of credibility. Next step, he began holding discussions with company-size units—100–200 men—throughout the entire brigade. In retrospect, he described one meeting as especially tough. No one wanted to talk. White EMs were sullen: "Why are Black soldiers complaining? We have it just as tough as them." An hour passed. They had hit the halfway mark with nothing much happening. And then a man who had been silent to that point, a Black first lieutenant, stood up and walked to the front of the room. "Let me tell you what it's like to be Black," he said.[17]

The lieutenant was an infantry officer, recently returned from Vietnam, a combat veteran and father of a new baby. At Christmas he and his wife had decided to drive to his family's home in Mississippi so his parents could see their grandchild. Somewhere in Alabama his wife said they needed milk for the baby, so he pulled up to a small store. "We don't serve niggers here," the proprietor told him. The officer paused. "I didn't know what to do," he said. And then he told the men what he *had* done, in his frustration and rage: he had walked around to the side of the building, out of sight of his wife, and urinated on the wall. "I'm not proud of what I did," he said that day. "But I *could* have killed him. And that's what it means to be Black in the United States." Segal carried that moment with him, evidence that communication could make a difference.[18]

Command of Fort Benning changed in September 1969. Brig. Gen. Orwin C. Talbott arrived on post September 9. He walked into one of the most highly charged crises facing the US Army: not race, in this case, but the massacre of Vietnamese civilians that in the United States came to be known, in shorthand, as My Lai. On March 16, 1968, members of Charlie Company —part of the American Division's 11th Infantry Brigade—had allegedly killed hundreds of civilians, mostly women and children, who had offered them no resistance. There had been an internal cover-up, foiled only by former army door gunner Ron Ridenhour's commitment to justice. On September 5, 1969, former platoon leader William Calley was charged, at Fort Benning, with the premeditated murder of 109 civilians. General Talbott took command five days later. An Article 32 investigation (the military equivalent of a grand jury inquiry) was underway, but army officials largely managed to keep specifics out of the press.[19]

On November 12 the story broke in the national press, as investigative journalist Seymour Hersh published a wrenching account of the atrocity. Three days later, more than a quarter million people gathered at the Washington Memorial to demand an end to the war in Vietnam. The protest was not precipitated by Hersh's story, but Charlie Company's actions at My Lai certainly gave credence to protesters' claims. That fall General Talbott, as Fort

*Education and Training*

Benning's commanding officer, had Calley's fate in his hands. He chose, on November 24, to sign the murder charges, beginning the process of what the press referred to as a "'life or death' court-martial."[20]

Talbott insisted later that he had no conversations with his superiors about Calley, that he was under no pressure as he made his decision. Nonetheless, he clearly understood the stakes. Just back from Vietnam, where he had commanded the 1st Infantry Division, he had seen the signs of failing morale. He read the papers; he understood that the American public was losing respect for its military. And he had been in DC in April 1968, American tanks in the streets of the nation's capital, swaths of the city still smoldering in the wake of violence following Martin Luther King's assassination. Benning's 197th had been sent to DC then, ready to intervene as arson and looting spread through the city. Troops under Talbott's command were on line for future civil disobedience, even as pundits began speculating about whether Black soldiers might put racial brotherhood ahead of military obligation and turn their weapons on their brothers-in-arms.[21]

This, then, is the context that shaped the direction of army race education. General Talbott was a man of character: brave, certainly, as attested to by three awards of the Silver Star (two in the Second World War and one in Vietnam), along with three Purple Hearts. And committed to his army. Like some other army leaders, he had begun to believe that something had gone wrong, not simply with the war but with the institution of the army itself. As a reminder: in the spring of 1970 General Westmoreland, the army chief of staff, would order the commandant of the US Army War College to study the "state of discipline, integrity, morality, ethics, and professionalism" in the army, most particularly among its officer corps.[22]

Talbott, thrust into the midst of the My Lai crisis, had begun more locally. Speaking in 1971 to *Washington Post* journalists who were writing about race relations education for a series they had titled "The Army in Anguish," Talbott explained the steps he had begun in 1969. "I am the man who signed the charge sheets and referred to [trial] Lt. Calley," he said, "and I did it in absolute conscience." His intent, he said, was to "[bring] home" the understanding "that each man is responsible for his actions at all times." Talbott said then that the US Army must "clean our house": "If we are straight and if we are loyal and if we are constructive as far as the country is concerned, I'm absolutely convinced the American people will consider us as such."[23]

In the fall of 1969, as he considered what to do not only about Calley but about the institution to which he had devoted his life, Talbott called Major Segal into his office. As Segal remembered it, Talbott asked, "Do we

have a race problem here?" And Segal replied, "You certainly do, General."
(Segal's choice of pronoun may suggest how he perceived his relationship
to the army.) The conversation that day initiated a post-wide race relations
program. Talbott was "creative and willing to take risks," recalled Segal, and
"sensitive to the needs of the men." There could have been a commander
"who squashed everything," he said. "Everything is serendipitous."[24]

By the following March, Benning had five full-time personnel devoted
to race relations. The Race Relations Coordinating Group, as the staffers
were called, advised Talbott on racial issues. In particular, the group focused
on race relations seminars. The army, meanwhile, sent Segal to the Walter
Reed Army Institute of Research. Though he would not see it happen, the
piecemeal seminar program he had begun in 1968 became the heart of race
relations efforts post-wide.[25]

As General Talbott launched his race relations efforts at Fort Benning,
Westmoreland had, at Department of the Army level, mandated race relations education and training army-wide. Westmoreland had designated
CONARC (the CONtinental ARmy Command) headquarters to undertake
the task; it, in turn, instructed the US Army Infantry School to create the
course of instruction.[26] The infantry school, of course, was at Fort Benning,
and General Talbott was its commandant. Benning's experience with race
relations seminars influenced the blocks of instruction the infantry school
produced for integration into army training; it also helped to shape army-
wide programs of race education.

In November 1970, key army leaders gathered at Fort Monroe, Virginia,
for a four-day race relations conference. As army secretary Stanley Resor explained, the conference was "a key step in our plan of action" to address the
problem of race; conference participants were meant to carry the ideas and
ad hoc programs developed over the past year back "to worldwide army commands." Three of ten major presentations were on instruction and education
—all tied directly to Fort Benning.[27]

On the final day of the conference, Major Segal was on the program. Now
in the Division of Neuropsychiatry at the Walter Reed Army Institute of Research, Segal was growing increasingly disenchanted with the army. He had
found strong support at Fort Benning, not only for his race relations efforts
but for an alcohol abatement program he had begun with General Talbott's
support. In DC, though, trying to address the growing problem of drug addiction, he had gotten crosswise with authority and found himself banned from
Fort Meade. Segal's army career was almost over; he would resign six months
later when his private and then public attempts to prevent Operation Golden

*Education and Training*

Flow—which required GIs returning from Vietnam to first pass a drug test or be held in confinement, for detoxification—failed. He did not know that future, but by late 1970 he was certainly not mincing words.[28]

Segal arrived at the conference planning to offer a "programmatic" description of race relations seminars. By the time he spoke, he saw little point. Too many empty claims, he thought, too little willingness to confront the problem. He had spent three days there, Black and white people talking to each other about race, and not once had he heard anyone call anybody a "motherfuck." It was all too civil. Was anything worthwhile happening? So Segal ditched his original talk. He offered instead "The Name of the Game," a speech with a refrain: "Is the name of the game reality? Or is it bullshit?" Is this meeting nothing more than a token response? Or are we really going to do something? Segal remembers getting the loudest applause of the week at the end of his hourlong presentation. And then the moderator stood up and said, "No questions."[29]

Looking back, Segal believed that the army, as an institution, did take up the challenge of race, and that perhaps his refrain played some small role in making that so. But Segal's challenge to the army in 1970 was confined to the conference room. No hint of "or is it bullshit" appeared in the official record. The conference "after-action report" noted Segal's call to replace "attitudes and behaviors based on deep-seated prejudice, black or white in origin," with "more constructive ones, based on empathetic understanding of the hopes, wishes, and human needs of others." It also recorded his caution that race relations seminars without "trained moderators . . . left in the hands of inexperienced men given inadequate resources" might "be worse than none at all."[30]

The Fort Benning program—first on the ground, highly visible at the Fort Monroe conference—was the closest thing to a model the institution offered. The official conference summary included the forty-one-page report from Fort Benning as an attachment, and its reach is confirmed by an annotated version that survives in USARV files. More significantly, when the Department of the Army crafted "support materials" for commanders, who were meant to focus on race relations in their required monthly "Commanders Call," Fort Benning's program was its exemplar. This program, noted the lengthy document, "is described here because it is well organized, flexible and imaginative—and it works."[31]

So what emerged from the Fort Monroe conference? If nothing else, army leaders understood that they were required to address the racial crisis and that education and training had been deemed critical to that project. They also encountered an emerging set of assumptions that fit uneasily with army ways. Such tensions did not emerge only from the struggles over race. Army intellectuals, by the late 1960s, were trying to figure out how the troubled institution could possibly recruit tens of thousands of young people a month when the US military, in the near future, became an all-volunteer force (AVF). They were trying to understand the nature of contemporary youth. Young people, these officers frequently claimed, had no patience with "cop-outs." They—America's youth—insisted on honesty. On "telling it like it is." When someone told a young man to do something, he wanted to know why. "Question authority" did not easily yield to "yes, sir." How was the army to appeal to these young men, once it could no longer rely on the draft?

The nature of youth also bedeviled the army intellectuals charged with solving the problem of race. And they, like those focused on the transition to an all-volunteer force, looked beyond the boundaries of military life for solutions. As the AVF-intellectuals considered policies and programs, they relied on psychologist Abraham Maslow's theories of human motivation. The race relations intellectuals, in turn, drew heavily on the Maslow-influenced human potential movement.[32]

By the late 1960s, the human potential movement was taking the nation by storm. Encounter groups, T-groups, sensitivity training: by whichever name, it was showing up in fast-multiplying "growth centers," in universities, corporations, church basements—and all over the national press. Sensitivity training had emerged from the sixties counterculture by way of the Esalen Institute at Big Sur; the retreat center used group encounters to break down social inhibitions and create honest, open, "authentic" communication. By stripping participants of defenses, forcing them into the "here and now" and emotional intensity of the encounter, sensitivity training promised catharsis, transcendence, self-awareness. Some at Esalen, in the midst of the racial uprising of 1967, imagined interracial encounter groups as a means to transcendence. The first "Racial Confrontation as Transcendent Experience" encounter was explosive and ultimately cathartic, inspiring Esalen to offer group interracial confrontations at its Big Sur campus and beyond. As a later critic noted, "authenticity" here was narrowly defined: Blacks must enact their rage; whites must come to recognize their own racism and experience guilt. Other responses were deemed inauthentic. Cop-outs.[33]

The army officers and consultants charged with figuring out how to get through to alienated and hostile youth knew that young Americans had no patience with "cop-outs." Thus sensitivity training, heralded in *Time* magazine as "the most significant social invention of this century," embraced by psychologists, and offering the "authenticity" that youth desired, was an obvious model. And it was not such an institutional reach. Before sensitivity training was transformed by the counterculture, corporations saw it as a way to improve group outcomes. Even as Fort Benning worked to craft its race relations program, sensitivity training was underway at American Airlines, IBM, General Electric, Eli Lilly, and Standard Oil.[34]

Sensitivity training was the answer Fort Benning offered attendees at the 1970 race relations conference. "Gripe sessions" were unproductive, the presenters told army leaders. Seminars should instead focus on "collective decision making," with recommendations for improving the racial crisis, or they should seek "attitude change." "Involved here," the Benning report explained, "are various racial awareness exercises (e.g. racial role reversals) and encounter group or T-group techniques designed to examine one's personal prejudices and stereotypes." Declaring, somewhat immodestly, that "we feel that we have one of the best programs within the military," these officers emphasized the "important part" sensitivity training would play in a race relations program, "if any degree of attitude change is expected."[35]

This move took the army into tricky territory. Sensitivity training, first of all, was potentially explosive. Pushing eighteen-year-old conscripts into racial confrontation was not the same thing as provoking confrontations among men and women who had sought that experience as a path to transcendence or self-awareness. And Major Segal had a good point: How was the army to provide enough experienced and perceptive moderators?

But the trickiness was more than the potential for explosion. It was the move from behavior to attitudes and beliefs. When it comes to behavior, the military has an advantage over civilian society. The US Army is an authoritarian institution; designated members have the ability to issue an order and to discipline those who violate it. When it comes to racial conflict the military can, at least in theory, control behavior.

So why shift from behavior to belief? Because it had become clear, by this point, that orders were not sufficient. Fights and riots and fraggings and beatings and arson all violated the Uniform Code of Military Justice, but they were happening, and they were often tied to race. Punishing transgressors, in turn, seemed often to escalate racial tension as Black enlisted men lost all faith in military justice. In short, the army's core tool—authority—seemed insufficient in the face of the racial crisis.

By January 1971, the army had instituted the infantry school–developed curriculum throughout its training and service school system. In Basic Combat Training, the idea was to "grab the men as soon as they come into the

Army and to let them know that we have certain policies and programs that don't condone racial discrimination." But "policies and programs" made up only a small portion of the training. Of four hours, two went to lecture: minority contributions to the United States and its military; the legacies of slavery; army equal opportunity policies. And two hours went to a sort of managed provocation. At Fort Dix, Sergeant First Class Frederick Steen— who was, according to the *New York Times*, "a Negro from Jackson, Miss." —explained that the point of the course was to "broaden experiences" of new inductees and to "open communication" between Blacks and whites.[36]

He began with projected images of a clenched fist salute and a Confederate flag, then showed the trainees, on closed-circuit TVs, a series of staged incidents of "racial friction": White soldiers, singing along to country and western music, clashing with Black soldiers who wanted soul music. Black and white soldiers in a fistfight over women at a dance. Black soldiers refusing to go on riot duty: "The hell with that honkie"; "They killed our brothers." Steen pushed the men to respond to these conflicts, then proposed "communication" as the solution.[37]

The instruction block intended for junior officers and NCOs, "Leadership Aspects of Race Relations," pushed further. Students were told to prepare for their four-hour "formal instruction" by discussing a series of claims with their classmates in advance:

- There are roughly twenty-two million Negroes in America today. They own more cars and refrigerators than all black Africans and all Russians combined. What more do they want?
- In 1969 there was one black general in the Army.
- A return to good, old fashioned discipline will solve society's racial problem as well as the Army's problem.
- Riots in Watts, Detroit, Washington, D.C., etc., were merely an excuse to loot stores and express other forms of latent criminality.
- America has a racist society.
- Equality in education will solve most of our problems.[38]

In the classroom, instructors refused color blindness and rejected the language of civility. "Today," said a Black major, introducing himself to a room full of junior officers, "I'm going to be the Nuf—nigger up front." He was joined by that day's "Huf," or "honkie up front," in an attempt to "stretch the minds" of future army leaders. "The first thing you have to do," Maj. Tyrone Fletcher—the one who had called himself "the Nuf"—told his audience, "is to admit to yourself that we basically are racists. We come from a racist society. And color means certain things in our society. Once we admit that, then we will be able to deal with it and develop normal relationships among people of all races." Curriculum designers intended the instructors to get racism on the table, to force the men in the classroom to acknowledge its pervasive force. Only then, the designers thought, could the men speak honestly, could junior leaders confront their own "preconceived ideas" and consider how those prejudices might affect their actions and thus the function of their units.[39]

Major Fletcher and his white partner, Maj. Alfred Coke, had been trained in a "pronounced sensitivity type group" developed for instructors who would teach the "Leadership Aspects of Race Relations" blocks. This training attempted to prepare them for the desired "free-wheeling" environment through T-group techniques and extended role playing. How might instructors respond to a "militant, individual racist, a liberal and an uncle tom"? Reflecting that training in his classroom that day, Major Fletcher urged understanding—of white EMs. "He might come from a home," Fletcher (the son of a Baptist preacher) offered, "where in his home, in his environment, in his school, nigger is a household word. . . . [He] might have grown up in a home where, if the maid drank out of a cup, the cup was boiled before anyone else used it." Such history, he preached to a captive audience, would inevitably affect that man's functioning in the army. And as leaders, "you must face up to them."[40]

Junior officers and NCOs were the heart of army training efforts. Senior leaders understood that high-level actions mattered little if they were thwarted or undermined lower on the chain of command. And, as is clear from the previous chapter, senior leaders had little faith in the ability of junior officers and NCOs to manage racial crisis. A recently discharged army public relations officer wrote in 1970 about the race relations seminars at Fort Bragg: one member of the committee charged with establishing the seminars worried about requiring young officers—even at company level—to lead them. That was an "awfully awkward position to put a young captain in," he told the committee. "I mean, let's face it, my son could be a company commander." It was true, mused the author in a *Washington Post*–syndicated article, that some captains were in their early twenties. "But no one seemed struck by the irony that a 'young captain' could, as a matter of course, be placed in charge of, say 150 men in combat . . . but could not be expected to handle a heated argument."[41] The army, at the direction of its chief of staff, meant to train them to do so.

Army race relations training—the four-hour instruction blocks inserted into training and orientation—was surprisingly flexible, given how army training normally functioned. Nonetheless, instructors were provided centrally produced lesson plans, complete with detailed learning objectives, along with videos of staged confrontations to be shown on closed-circuit television.

But army leaders had also mandated continuing, unit-focused *education*, meant to address possible tensions among existing groups and to improve unit function. That education varied enormously. Much depended on how those in authority perceived the problem. Was it a problem of permissiveness, to be solved by consistent discipline? Was it a problem of militants unsettling a basically sound system? Was conflict due to individual racism, or to institutional racism? Was racial conflict an immediate and fundamental threat, or were the mandated actions simply another piece of the army's endless bureaucracy?

At Fort Carson, the commander insisted that social justice, not simply equal treatment, was the goal. In his view, that demanded not only uncomfortable honesty ("There is no room for people who pretend that the races are not different, that there is no problem," he wrote; "all of us must face the conflicts which arise among our different cultural groups squarely and 'tell it like it is'") but also "hard, researchable facts and information." A military psychiatrist at Fort Carson presented the results of a "penetrating survey" on enlisted men's opinions. A Black chaplain—a Presbyterian graduate of Duke University Divinity School—"told it like it was." A Denver University professor, who turned out to be a blond, blue-eyed, white South Carolinian, offered a lecture on African American history. "These presentations, frank and professional," concluded a highly optimistic command report, demonstrated that the commanding general "meant business."[42]

In Chu Lai, by contrast, Americal command paid little attention. Ordered to teach weekly race relations courses, one NCO—a former LRRP (member of long range reconnaissance patrol) on his third tour in Vietnam—substituted his Randall knife for curriculum. "I bled on a dare," he remembered. "The essence of it was that I would jab myself, then dare first the black troops to do the same and show me that they had different blood and then, when they got through being furious, I'd taunt the rednecks the same way and let them get furious. Then the point: same blood, so knock this shit off. Worked well."[43]

And then there was the anti-racist documentary *Black and White: Uptight*. The publication *Commander's Call* recommended it; the army infantry school created a discussion guide; the film was shown so often that some confused it with an army training film. Its origins, in fact, were definitely not military.

*Uptight* was produced by the small California studio Avanti Films, part of a series on social problems aimed at 1960s youth. *Marijuana*, narrated by Sonny Bono, costar of the *Sonny and Cher Show*, was 1968's offering; 1969's *Uptight*, in turn, was narrated by Robert Culp, Bill Cosby's white costar on the then-hip 1960s television series *I Spy*.[44]

The film was unflinching in its condemnation of white racism, from lynching and bombings to "Some of my best friends are Negroes." In its exploration of American life, it validated Black rage and endorsed Black pride. Here, again, army education delivered the message gleaned from its foray into sensitivity training: White racism is universal. It is present in all whites, even the most progressive. Black rage is justified; Black pride necessary; Black power essential.

As the film begins, a white mother plays "eeny-meeny-miny-mo / catch a nigger by the toe" with her baby and the narrator asks, "Where does . . . hatred begin?" We see overt racism (white man in a gun shop: "Can't wait for those coons to start rioting"; white girl: Blacks are "dirty" and "scary") and then, in the narrator's words, "prejudices [that] masquerade as tolerance." There is a segment on the recent "race riots" ("called rebellions by many Black people"): "No, baby, they weren't kidding when they said burn baby burn and that's at least one good reason we'd better get straight on where it's really at while there's still time." A glimpse of the tasteful and spotless home of a middle-class Black family and then of the challenges posed by poverty and discrimination, the "barren world most ghetto children see" and carried with them for the rest of their lives.[45]

And finally, Black pride. Some Black people may be ready to fight "whitey," said Culp, but "unlike ever before, they are proud of their identity as Black people." Black Power, he explains, "basically" calls for Black people to gain a greater share of power in politics and in the economy. The film, at its conclusion, circles back to white racism, as a young white man declares, "One of them niggers will be wanting to marry your sister." Responds the narrator, over a shot of the 1963 March on Washington, "All of these people could not have been wanting to marry your sister." And then to an image of Martin Luther King: "And neither did he." "What can *you* do?" asks the film. "What do *you* say?" Army discussion questions asked, in an attempt to drive the point home, "Why do you think it is difficult for a prejudiced person to recognize that he is prejudiced?"[46]

Despite such strong messages, the unit-focused race relations education was inconsistent, not only in content but in frequency and command support. Lieutenant Barksdale, who had obtained a copy of *Black and White:*

*Uptight* to show in the Dong Ba Thin Training Battalion in Vietnam, was outraged when a white captain aired it while Barksdale was in Saigon, preventing him from conducting an accompanying "rap session" that offered "at least half of the desired effect." Barksdale, who meant to use that rap session to discuss problems within the battalion, noted that he had been told by the battalion adjutant that the only reason the battalion held human relations meetings was to "satisfy the requirement" and keep headquarters "off [its] back."[47]

Instructors often found a marked lack of enthusiasm among the troops. "They gave me a choice between coming to the seminar and going out to the field to fire the M-14, so here I am," one white GI said. A survey conducted at Fort Hood, most likely during the summer of 1972, found that 72 percent of whites and 61 percent of Black respondents said they had never attended an army race relations seminar, and—even more revealing—68 percent of white and 46 percent of Black respondents did not "personally know" anyone who had participated in one.[48] As was clear not only in the sphere of education, policy and implementation were far from identical.

The army initially left commanders a great deal of latitude in their race relations education programs. Such flexibility—and the resulting inconsistency—would not last long. It was not in the nature of the institution. And as early as January 1970, the Department of Defense had begun claiming authority. The army was ahead of the curve; the DoD's move to standardize race relations education across the military departments would not gain concrete form until the fall of 1971.[49] Much of what the DoD imposed looked a lot like the army's initial efforts.

L. Howard Bennett, at the heart of the DoD's civil rights efforts from 1963 forward, had great faith in education, and from his first months in DC he had relentlessly emphasized its potential. Bennett's January 1970 report, sent forward at a moment of crisis, proposed that "the entire complement of the military hierarchy" should be trained in "human relations." And this time, his emphasis on education found traction. The crisis clearly demanded action, and at that point any plausible action seemed worth considering. But a change in leadership mattered as well. The new secretary of defense, Melvin Laird, put enormous weight on his statement of "Human Goals." "*People,*" Laird told his staff during the summer of 1969, "constitute the most precious asset of the Defense Department." (The army responded: "To put the 'personal' back into 'personnel' has been and is an objective of the army.")[50] Laird's people-oriented agenda had ample space for education.

As Laird was circulating drafts of his "Human Goals" agenda—the incontrovertible "God, motherhood, and country" nature of which prompted the new secretary of the army, Robert Froehlke, to respond, "Terrific. And I love my mother too"—a congressional subcommittee was investigating the outbreak of racial violence at the Marine Corps's Camp Lejeune. And while the subcommittee report, issued in December 1969, blamed both "permissiveness" and "a few militant blacks" for the violence that left one dead and thirty-one injured, the subcommittee's first recommendation was to "institute a program of education on race relations at all levels of command, with particular emphasis on the platoon and company levels."[51] The recommendations were specific to Camp Lejeune, but the Department of Defense read them more broadly—as the congressional subcommittee clearly intended.

The report was dated December 15, 1969; six weeks later Laird created an interservice task force on race relations education. Chaired by air force colonel Lucius F. Theus, an expert in accounting and finance who at that point served in the Directorate of Data Automation, the committee had representatives from all services, both enlisted and officer ranks. It sought input broadly, visiting service schools and examining their existing programs and approaches to "communications techniques." The task force produced a five-volume report; a key recommendation was to create a mandatory program in race relations education for all military personnel, along with a "Defense Race Relations Institute" (DRRI, pronounced "dry") to develop curricula, train instructors, evaluate programs, and conduct research.[52]

With a June 1971 DoD directive, Laird established the "most comprehensive race relations education program ever instituted by any major institution in this country." The fledgling DRRI, with an initial budget of $740,000, had just seventeen weeks to locate and establish its campus, build and train its staff, and develop the seven-week training course capable of producing 1,400 race relations instructors within a year's time.[53]

DRRI would find a home on Patrick Air Force Base on Florida's "space coast," about thirty miles south of what was then called Cape Kennedy. Despite the borrowed prestige of the last days of the Apollo program, the immediate surroundings were rural Florida, and the racist nicknames "Watermelon University" and "Razor Blade Tech" make clear how many local residents felt about the race relations institute and its multiracial faculty moving into their community. The institute itself was initially assigned an old wooden post office building, though it soon moved to another structure, described in the local civilian newspaper as "no glamour campus with ivy-covered hall donated by wealthy alumnus" and somewhat implausibly painted with touches of pink.[54]

Appointed director of DRRI was Edward F. Krise, a forty-six-year-old white army colonel with a doctorate in social welfare from the University of Chicago. Krise, in turn—on the recommendation of Bennett—brought a Black civilian sociologist on board as research director. Richard O. Hope would go on to have a distinguished academic career. But at that point he was a thirty-year-old newly minted PhD with no military experience, teaching at Brooklyn College and protesting the war in Vietnam. When offered the position, he was skeptical. DRRI's creation, he later wrote, implied that "the largest institution in the United States was prepared to undertake major change in its policies, procedures, and practices." Any "sound sociological criticism," he was certain, "would question the sincerity of any institution that purported to go contrary to the basic survival tendencies of most established organizations."[55]

That is the story Hope told in his 1979 book, *Racial Strife in the U.S. Military*, one of measured reaction and scholarly concerns. His immediate response, however, was much more direct and much more uncompromising. When Colonel Krise called him the first time, Hope recalled decades later, he told Krise that he was not "interested in your illegal war" and then hung up on him. In the end, Hope joined the team, but only because Krise persisted ("I'll be kicked out of the military if you don't talk to me," Hope remembered Krise saying). To seal the deal, DoD's L. Howard Bennett stepped in, calling on connections he and Hope shared to Fisk University and the civil rights giants who had assembled there. But in the end it all almost fell through, because Richard Hope could not find housing off-post that would accept a Black family.[56]

DRRI's key purpose was to train instructors who would be assigned in two-person teams—representing both majority-minority and enlisted-officer —to every brigade-level unit throughout the US military, where they would be responsible for race relations education and training. The men (and woman) charged with creating the program to train the trainers understood that they were responding to crisis. They assumed that their educational program had to interrupt both "black militancy" and white resistance. But none of them knew how to do that. Hope delved into current research on "intergroup interaction and behavioral change." The group agreed fairly quickly on what techniques *did not* work: programs that "relied on the traditional 'bleeding heart' approach"; time spent explaining the importance of "understanding" one another.[57]

More research and more wrangling yielded two key principles. First, culture mattered. Black service members demanded an emphasis on "cultural identity," and white service members needed to understand Black culture. Second, individuals must be confronted with their own prejudices. No one would be allowed to "hide"; intense, "gut-level" communication would be the basis of DRRI training. As it evolved, DRRI instructor training looked almost identical to that developed at Fort Benning—training the DRRI team had observed—although they also depended on materials developed at a race relations institute that was established at Fisk University during the 1930s. Here, contingency played a role; Hope had worked at Fisk's race relations institute while he was an undergraduate at Morehouse College, and that experience proved useful for DRRI. And while Hope later claimed that DRRI methods should not be "confused" with sensitivity training or T-groups, leaders from the National Training Laboratory in Bethel, Maine, where the T-group originated, traveled down to work with the DRRI development group.[58]

All that said, creating the world's largest race relations education system in the space of seventeen weeks was little short of a miracle, and initial efforts showed more dedication than clarity. Some saw that as a strength. After all, it was the early 1970s. The goal was honesty. Authenticity. Only then, believed the program designers, might participants gain self-awareness and take the first steps toward resolving the problem of race.

The pilot DRRI seminar convened on schedule: November 1, 1971. The first class was selected from installations where racial tensions were particularly explosive—the sooner to have DRRI-trained teams prepared to intervene. It also served as a group guinea pig, as faculty and staff refined approaches on the fly. These men, from sergeant to lieutenant colonel, spent seven weeks, eight hours a day, "arguing, studying and learning more about themselves than about the history of ethnic groups, institutional racism, or other facets of the course," in the words of a *Stars and Stripes* article.[59]

Despite the focus on self-discovery, the seminars did have content. Participants learned about the history and culture of American ethnic groups, including white Appalachians; they studied instructional techniques and how to moderate DRRI-type seminars; and they spent forty hours in "actual ghetto-type areas" (the language comes from a *Stars and Stripes* article that DRRI faculty found particularly problematic) in Miami in order to better understand "a black community."[60]

In fact, in subsequent iterations, DRRI students would be sent to various spaces and communities. The focus on impoverished African Americans was consistent, but what DRRI instructors called "the Miami experience"

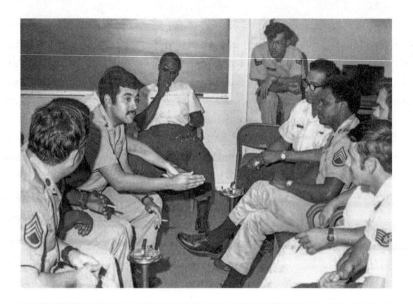

The Defense Race Relations Institute—DRRI—trained personnel to serve as race relations instructors and to provide support for equal opportunity initiatives. In December 1971, when these photographs were taken, the DRRI staff was test-flying the initial curriculum. *Courtesy of Defense Equal Opportunity Management Institute.*

would quickly evolve into what was both a carefully constructed *and* an un-safeguarded seventy-two hours designed to push students out of their comfort zone. Various class "experiences" sent students to spend time with migrant farmworkers, with hippies and street people, in Latino neighborhoods and (using an anachronistic description) LGBTQ bars. But early "experiences" were focused on impoverished Black communities, and that, along with the scripted Black-white confrontations, was highlighted by the press.[61]

*Stars and Stripes* introduced its readers to the Defense Race Relations Institute in February 1972 with the headline "One White Officer's Reaction: 'I Feel a Little Blacker . . . ,'" that line drawn from "blue-eyed, red-haired" 1st Lt. Earl R. Albright, twenty-three. Albright confessed that he found his time in the "ghetto" a real "eye-opener," but he thought the first week of the seminar most interesting: "We were all strangers and it got to be sort of a sensitivity session where everybody's personal feelings were put on the table." Research director Richard Hope, described in another *Stars and Stripes* article as someone "who looks like a white man and often startles visitors when he says, 'by the way, I'm black,'" called those initial sessions "very heated and emotional." For example, he explained, an individual who said something obviously prejudiced might be "isolated by the group" for several hours, gaining from that "peer-group pressure" a "heightened and occasionally discomforting awareness of racial prejudice." The institute's internal history, written in a very different moment in time, noted that the initial seminars began with the assumption that all were "closeted bigots," and the role of seminar leaders was to force them out of the closet and "recondition" them.[62]

Descriptions of DRRI training lend credence to that analysis. "The words rolled smoothly from the young white sergeant's lips," began a long piece in *Stars and Stripes*, "until he came to the one that's so hard to say in front of a black man. He hesitated a moment, then it burst out—'nigger.' A few feet away, the black sergeant smiled a bit and nodded his understanding, that he knew how hard it was for the white soldier to describe his feeling when he got a 'Dear John' letter in Vietnam telling him his girl back home had fallen for a black man." Here, at DRRI, field instructors were practicing the techniques they would take into the field, leading eight sergeants—seven white, one Black—through a mandatory three-day training. The man who had received the Dear John letter confessed that he had wanted to take his M-16 and "go out and kill the first black guy I saw," but (the journalist explained) honest communication in the seminar helped him understand that reaction. It was "just his masculine ego" being hurt.[63]

In this case, perhaps, the DRRI technique had worked. The instructors had pushed one young white sergeant until social constraints failed and his underlying racism was exposed, and in the process he had gained self-awareness and begun to communicate authentically and honestly. And honest communication, according to emerging army common wisdom, was the first and fundamental step in addressing racial strife.

But plenty of army NCOs and officers saw the DRRI approach as a huge gamble. What if this were not a practice group of sergeants in the DRRI's pink and gray building near Cocoa Beach, Florida, but instead a platoon in Vietnam, or Germany, or Korea, a platoon that *to that point* had been functioning well? What if Black participants did not "smile a bit and nod" when the instructors got a white participant to confirm his deep-down racism and blurt out the N-word? What if whites did not acknowledge their guilt? What if Black rage threatened violence? What if the instructors were not capable of managing what they unleashed? What if forcing latent white racism and latent Black anger to the surface did not foster solutions to the problem of race but instead undermined unit efficiency?[64]

"We often," noted one of the instructors, "walk a thin line between what's reasonable emotional argument and what's a transgression on military discipline." Argued an officer at Women's Army Corps basic training: before the race relations class her recruits "got along fine." "Then they saw the problems they were supposed to have, so they developed them. It took a while to get straightened out."[65]

By the late 1960s, this sort of approach—practiced in churches, prisons, factories, schools, and corporations, as well as in the "human growth centers" spreading from California to the rest of the nation, and called variously "sensitivity training," "T-Groups," and "encounter groups"—had become both popular and controversial. In late 1970, *Time* magazine chronicled the "explosive" growth of the human potential movement, and in its first Sunday magazine of 1971, the *New York Times* offered a long and critical piece on what its author termed the "encounter cult."[66]

In fact, the emerging mass movement had attracted opposition in Congress dating back to 1969, when John Rarick, a hyper-conservative Democrat from Louisiana, launched a campaign against what he considered "a tool to indoctrinate the masses." Rarick was joined, in early 1971, by Democratic senator Sam Ervin of North Carolina, a member of the Armed Services Committee and an ardent segregationist. Rarick was and continued to be appalled that Americans voluntarily subjected themselves to what he considered "brainwashing." Ervin's concerns were narrower. Contacted by a federal employee who had been required to attend an encounter group session intended to help employees better understand equal employment practices for minorities, Ervin meant to end "compulsory sensitivity training." Labeling the seminars "tyranny over the mind of the grossest sort," Ervin complained that they subjected federal employees "to a probe of their psyches, to provoke, and indeed require disclosure of their intimate attitudes and beliefs, during emotionally charged situations which are deliberately set up by psychologists for the manipulation of human relations."[67] (In fact, seminar leaders were rarely credentialed psychologists.)

The Defense Race Relations Institute and its planned encounter-group techniques quickly drew congressional notice. "Race relations—the new priority," Rarick lamented, shortly after Secretary Laird announced his plans in March 1971. "Billions for disarmament and race relations but not one copper for national defense." But Rarick's key concern was the DRRI approach. "Military Brainwashing by the Numbers—Race Relations," he titled his comments, and he included a news article in which DRRI director and "Army social worker" Edward Krise described plans for DRRI: "The important aspect of any kind of education is the modification of attitudes, the necessary change of emotional response, one to the other, and it is really through this discussion that the real kinds of change will take place. . . . We hope to be able to utilize this approach to enable our people to engage in a meaningful communication so that each can understand and appreciate the other."[68]

Senator Ervin, meanwhile, launched investigations into "Touch-and-Tell" sessions reportedly mandated for employees in the Department of Health, Education, and Welfare, the Department of Agriculture, and the General Services Administration. In the summer of 1971, Ervin informed the Pentagon he had heard complaints that service members would be forced to participate in sensitivity training. In response, the DoD reiterated its commitment to race relations training but told Ervin that "no attempt will be made to produce 'sensitivity trainers' or 'group psychotherapists.'"[69]

The race relations institute launched its first pilot program less than two months later. And despite Laird's unequivocal statements of support, the Pentagon joined Congress in suspicion of DRRI. Curtis Smothers, by then in the civil rights office, sought control; he gave DRRI five working days to provide him with copies of all its curricular materials. According to Hope, the DoD sent investigators, posing as students, to determine DRRI's legitimacy. Krise had gotten himself crosswise with Ervin and many in the DoD when he publicly emphasized "the modification of attitudes, the necessary change of emotional response." In fact, one of the original guiding directives instructed the institute to aim "to modify interracial behavior rather than to seek to change attitudes directly." In March 1972, Ervin described DRRI's purpose as "official attempts to manipulate people's minds"; the DoD insisted that the institute dealt "with behavior, not personal attitudes," on "how someone acts rather than how he thinks."[70]

By the summer of 1972, Krise—who was not yet halfway through his term and who, according to Hope, had inspired DRRI staff to work eighteen hours a day—had been forced out by conservative elements. His replacement was a white air force colonel, a jet pilot with a degree from Harvard's graduate management program. Krise's replacement had gotten the message about keywords. "Attitudes," said Col. Russell Ryland, "by themselves . . . seldom cause trouble. It is the individual behavior patterns that cause the flare-ups, but we know that we can change those."[71] Nonetheless, Ryland made no obvious changes to DRRI's curriculum or approach.

With the creation of the Defense Race Relations Institute, the Department of Defense consolidated control over race relations education throughout the military. The army adopted the DoD's standard eighteen-hour race relations curriculum in January 1972, specifying that all brigade-size units have a two-person team of DRRI-trained instructors. But DRRI, working at top capacity, could not meet demand. As of November 1972, DRRI had produced 287 teams—for the entire US military. A Vietnam chaplain noted, in handwritten notes from a "Human Relations" briefing, that there were "only 9 in country who have received training. Remainder doing best with what they have."[72]

Curtis Smothers, following a "compliance monitoring visit" through the Pacific Command, complained that the army's "decentralized approach toward training" was yielding "uneven results" but acknowledged that the problem was a lack of trained instructors. In response, the DoD pushed DRRI to step up production and ordered the services to "implement interim measures" in the meantime. To build capacity, the army and navy both began their own schools, modeled on DRRI. Fort Shafter, on Oʻahu, graduated eighteen members from its first "USARPAC Race Relations Discussion Course," which was established to "boost" DRRI's output. The Eighth Army in Korea graduated seventy-one discussion leaders during the fall of 1972; its goal was a two-person team for every battalion (rather than for every brigade). USAREUR began a school at Obergammerau, Germany, and was the first command to reach the army's two-instructor-per-brigade goal.[73]

By 1972, race relations blocks were integrated into army training at all levels, and the unit-focused race relations education program was well launched, even if unevenly implemented. DRRI staff—which, after all, had moved from DoD directive to worldwide program in the space of seventeen weeks—quickly began to evaluate their program's impact. First reports were not positive. Some commanders complained that personnel—especially whites —returned from DRRI as racial militants. Richard Hope, DRRI's director of research, did not dismiss their concerns. Some commanders, he knew, were failing to address the racial crisis and saw the DRRI graduates as a threat. But many of the graduates returned to their units (to use an anachronism) "woke." The emotionally intense experience at the race relations institute had—for some—profound effects. These DRRI graduates, in Hope's words, saw themselves as "legitimate . . . change agent[s]," given "formal responsibility to change the largest bureaucracy in the United States." And often they saw no need for "patience and diplomacy" in their quest to eliminate racism from the US military.[74]

When Gen. Michael Davison addressed the first class of USAREUR race relations school graduates, he warned them that commanders might be "indifferent, hostile, or even racist, whether consciously or unconsciously." Their charge, Davison insisted, was to summon "tact and wisdom" in their efforts to prompt even "an insensitive commander" to change his thinking. "Remember also," he told them, that observers in higher headquarters were monitoring the program and "the commander who is less than enthusiastic will soon be detected." Efforts to solve the crisis through leadership and through education were here interwoven.[75]

But command response was not the only obstacle. The DRRI research arm understood that evaluating a fledgling program was a fraught process, but a problematic narrative was emerging. Researchers found that the "shock treatment" sensitivity-training approach put whites on the defensive; it created white backlash. It also threatened to undermine the chain of command, as Black privates felt licensed to threaten white officers, to call them names. And instructors too often found themselves unable to manage the situation. The DRRI's approach was, institute leaders concluded, "somewhat overzealous."[76]

And congressional suspicion—most intense on the part of southern segregationists such as Ervin—had not subsided. In late 1973, the House Appropriations Committee cut 700 race relations instructors from the military allocation—400 of them from the army alone. The committee was not shifting emphasis to service-based schools; it deemed the service-based schools an "unnecessary duplication of effort" and ordered them "disestablished."[77]

While funding efficiency was its stated goal, the committee made clear that it also meant to challenge the broader race relations program. "The Committee has learned," the report noted, "that race relations training designed to promote harmony among service members may have seriously weakened discipline." In some cases, training had "degenerated into rap sessions where the private calls the colonel and general by their first names and proceeds to 'chew' them out." The report then quoted a Marine Corps directive that instructors should cease using techniques that did not foster "self-discipline or organizational unity," including "encounter groups, sensitivity training sessions, emotional confrontation, informal cross-rank address, unstructured rap sessions, touch-feel games, [or] transactional analysis."[78]

The congressional report—with its budgetary implications—forced race relations education in a different direction. That was possible, in part, because of larger changes. The last US combat troops had left Vietnam on March 29, 1973. The last American draftee had entered the army on June 30, 1973. The level of racial violence within the military was dropping, even as racial discontent remained. No longer was the army facing an immediate crisis.

Congressional criticism and its budgetary implications mattered a great deal. But DRRI faculty and staff had their own concerns. In 1973, based not only on external pressures but on the analysis of its own faculty and staff, the institute adopted a new approach. It stopped the "culture shock" tactic, getting rid of the emotion-laden confrontations in its own instructor training and eliminating sensitivity training from the field techniques being taught. Accusations of individual racism were no longer acceptable in training sessions, and some faculty proposed that the term "racism" itself was "divisive, guilt-laden, and antagonistic to whites." Said one instructor in Germany, "The guilt feeling is out. . . . It's a different program this year." "Last year," explained an article in Stars and Stripes, "rap sessions between black and white participants sometimes led to angry accusations and name calling. Whites attending often felt personal guilt was being unfairly thrust upon them. Resentment followed." That "shock treatment approach" was over; the new tone was "studious and calm."[79]

In the new DRRI, according to its leaders, the approach was "positive"; "racial harmony," previously dismissed as a "cop-out" or even inherently racist, became the goal. Two race relations instructors (these in the air force) explained, "We're interested in dialogue and constructive change." The days when race relations seminars were "a kind of haven for militant blacks and whites with a guilt complex" were gone. No more "dwelling on the past." The institute's new model would be "How do we solve this problem?"[80]

The race relation institute's struggles and reinvention had structural implications. With the original DRRI approach under fire, the army had sought additional control. The service branches were not identical, military leaders insisted, whether in their policies, their cultures, or their personnel. The DRRI one-size-fits-all approach was insufficient. In response, DRRI expanded the length of its training, turning more than half of it over to the individual services.[81]

This shift, however, was part of a broader transformation. Carl Segal's mass encounter group, the US Army Infantry School's initial experiments with race relations seminars, the Fort Monroe conference's embrace of education, the rapidity of DRRI's creation: all were responses to an institution in crisis. But as an army researcher noted, "from a military viewpoint" such crisis-born programs tend to lose force as the initial conditions subside; for the program to continue to exist, it must become part of the army's normal, routine function, built into army practices and procedures.[82]

That process was already underway. By late 1972, the Department of the Army issued a "force structure plan" for equal opportunity and race relations, designating a general officer position for its director, authorizing sufficient manpower, creating a career-field MOS, and locating race relations/equal opportunity positions within unit organization. After the US Army Training and Doctrine Command was established in 1973, it began the process of standardizing the race relations curriculum, creating lesson plans, defining student outcomes and goals, and crafting objective tests for individuals completing training.[83] The army was weaving race relations education into its bureaucracy, into its fundamental framework. This was no longer a response to crisis. It was a part of army life.

W hat came of the army's attempt to solve the racial crisis through education and training? On the cusp of the 1970s, the military began what was, in fact, the largest and most comprehensive effort to teach race relations in US history—an effort that soon reached US military installations across the world. The army pioneered that effort, its "learn-by-doing" approach based on a few leaders' commitment to solve the problem but equally on "intuition, best guess, and trial and error."[84]

While the path was not direct, Segal's mass group therapy at Fort Benning led to 50,000 graduates of the Defense Race Relations Institute and its successor, the Defense Equal Opportunity Management Institute (DEOMI), over the course of slightly less than fifty years, and to millions of men and women in uniform trained to work—at first—across divisions of race, and then of ethnicity, gender, sexuality, religion, region, and nationality.[85]

Did the education work? Both DRRI and the US Army Research Institute for the Behavioral and Social Sciences did their best to evaluate the ongoing process. Initial DRRI findings suggested that emotion-laden seminars were misguided; later research found that DRRI graduates made the greatest difference through leadership, helping to create a more supportive racial climate within their units. Participants, surveys tended to discover, tended to rate the seminars "somewhat useful."[86] Certainly not earthshaking. But we have yet to come up with a vastly superior approach today, as any employee who has recently completed an online sexual harassment or diversity and inclusion training can attest.

And while the army's initial devotion to human potential movement techniques—an approach then adopted by DRRI—seems in retrospect ill-considered, it was also a sign of the army's openness to change. Such approaches were taking the United States by storm, adopted by forward-thinking corporations and public institutions as they confronted divisions of race. That the army—the largest and potentially most conservative institution in the nation, one predicated on hierarchy, authority, and discipline—was willing to force the emotional intimacy of "authenticity" among men of disparate rank suggests just how seriously it took the problem and how creative it was willing to be in seeking solutions.

But even if creatively defined, education and training—like leadership—were obvious tools for the institution of the army to address the racial crisis. And, as with leadership, they would prove insufficient. So even as the institutional army took steps that made perfect sense within its institutional culture, it adopted others that directly challenged its institutional logic.

# 6 CULTURE AND IDENTITY

Confronting the problem of race, army leaders turned first to the institution's usual tools: leadership and authority, education and training. In the end, though, there was little usual in their approach. Army leaders were surprisingly creative in their attempts to manage the escalating crisis, even as they and others worried about how their efforts might undermine both the chain of command and the good order of their troops.

Officers' willingness to set up processes that skirted the chain of command or to listen to the "emotional truths" of young Black privates stemmed from a tenuous but increasingly powerful understanding that the army could not frame solutions based on the experiences of senior military officers. Instead, it had to address the problem of race as it was defined by the institution's most junior members, some of whom were drawing attention to army failings and some of whom appeared, themselves, to *be* the problem.

How *did* these young men define the problem? What was it that they wanted? Here, again, the army employed its usual tools in an attempt to answer those questions. The army's massive bureaucracy began to mandate reports, gather data, and report findings. Complaints, these investigations discovered, were widespread and wide-ranging. Some took the form of violent outbreaks; others were carefully crafted in the language of civil rights or Black Power.

Some Black soldiers charged that an individual officer or NCO was racist; others offered evidence of structural racism in army systems of promotion, assignment, and military justice or pointed to discrimination off-post, both in the United States and abroad. What surprised army leaders, however, was how frequently the complaints were about culture and style. Many Black soldiers wanted the right to wear an Afro and a "soul bracelet," to hear soul music in army clubs, to raise a clenched fist, and to dap with their brothers. Even as they insisted on equality in all spheres of army life, young Black soldiers also made clear that they cared desperately about their right to symbols of Black identity.

As army leaders confronted the army's racial crisis, many were quick to point to its civilian origins. And while that move too often excused—or at least shifted attention from—the army's own failings, they did have a point. The civilian movements for equal rights and social justice indisputably shaped the ways that reluctant, short-term soldiers understood their conditions. And as movements for Black pride and Black power emerged from the frustrations of broken promises and the growing awareness of what would be lost if the price of integration was assimilation into a white-defined world, young African Americans embraced a Black identity, rejecting "white" standards and seeking unity in their African roots and a culture of "soul."

Even as the secretary of the army rejected "only one color and that's o.d." and insisted that the army's putative color blindness was a weakness rather than a strength, young Black soldiers embraced difference. But unlike Secretary Resor, who primarily meant to acknowledge the ways that prior experience shaped the men who entered the army, these young soldiers claimed an essential Black identity that transcended not only background but military status. "The demeanor of many younger Black soldiers," reported the *New York Times* in late 1970, "is far more black than it is military. They risk punishments with displays of varied and ever-changing symbols of dissent."[1]

But was the Afro a symbol of dissent? Was the raised clenched fist? Or was the first simply a natural expression of identity and the second a symbol of the unity necessary for Black men to survive? Might it be worth some flexibility if allowing symbols of Black identity lessened the roiling anger in the ranks? Or did visible symbols of an identity and a solidarity that transcended the military undermine the fundamental principles of order, discipline, and uniformity necessary for the army to function?

As leaders debated those questions, some components of the army saw opportunity. The Army & Air Force Exchange Service (AAFES; pronounced "A-fes"), including the retail system commonly known as the PX, for example, moved quickly to position itself at the heart of army initiatives to recognize Black culture and identity. The PX system was, at that moment, being investigated by Congress in the wake of a major financial scandal, and by positioning itself as part of the solution to the problem of race, it sought to gain both credibility and resources. For PX officials, broadening PX stock and services

*Culture and Identity*

to meet the consumer desires of minority soldiers and their families was an easy call. Adding Afro Sheen, dashikis, and the Supremes to PX shelves worldwide in no way conflicted with the mission or usual procedures of the massive exchange system.

Some of the army's other efforts to accommodate cultural symbols, however, posed a direct challenge to its institutional logic and standard procedures. Militaries depend on policy and regulations—regulations that are laid out in often excruciating detail, subject to enforcement, and universally applicable. Thus, if the army decided to recognize the importance of Black identity and accepted the use of various cultural symbols, it could not limit the use of cultural symbols to African Americans alone. So when the army began, tentatively, to accept symbols of Black identity, it opened the door to a variety of claims about identity and expression that went well beyond its original intent—and sometimes created a whole new set of racial conflicts.

And army leaders struggled with the logic of identity, even as at least one high-ranking white officer committed to learning his local version of the dap handshake. Sensitive to charges that Black soldiers were demanding—and receiving—special treatment, the army often advised its NCOs and junior officers to manage racial tensions by acknowledging men's "individuality." Framing identity as individuality is a masterful solution to the problem of difference. If each and every soldier is recognized as an individual, no individual or group is receiving special treatment.

Individuality, moreover, was officially in vogue in the army. Misguided as the strategy seems, the army was attempting to convince young Americans to enlist in the coming all-volunteer force by offering to let them maintain their individuality. "Today's Army is willing to pay this price," reassured a 1971 recruiting ad.[2] But how was it "individuality" if the identity claimed was collective? Officers fretted over the apparent paradox.

Many, attempting to follow official guidance, latched on to Resor's notion of "the Negro soldier," weaving his acknowledgment of the importance of race together with Black soldiers' claims of difference. The "New Breed Black" had a flurry of visibility, as white officers debated why young Black men seemed so different from their elders. What rose to the fore, however, was racial, not generational, difference. As officers and NCOs were instructed to foster better communication with and among their men, the army provided materials meant to help them interpret the meaning of cultural symbols and understand "the Black experience."

And as many young Black soldiers claimed a collective Black identity, many army publications, in turn, essentialized that identity. An article titled

"The Minority Mental Process" made the rounds. DRRI sent its trainees to live with families in Miami's Black "ghetto" so they would better understand Black culture. And while efforts to bridge the "communication gap" were often well intentioned, the list of available materials for a course in Black studies began with the filmstrips *Anthony Lives in Watts* and *Jerry Lives in Harlem*.[3] Black soldiers proclaimed their difference, insisting that "Black is beautiful." The institution, often acting in good faith, imagined that difference in ways that were far from beautiful.

In the end, army leaders concluded that the institution's brief acceptance of nonmilitary identities and the symbols that expressed them was a wrong turn, fundamentally incompatible with the proper function of the US Army. What survived, however, was substantial. The enormous retail system of the PX had been forced to recognize the specific needs and desires of its non-white customers. Army leaders had a productive debate about what was and was not central to the identity of the soldier and the foundations of good order. And the army emerged with a stronger awareness that, when it came to culture and style and presumptions about identity, the army could no longer simply default to white.

In the late summer of 1969, less than a month after a "race fight" between white and Black soldiers at Fort Bragg, North Carolina, sent twenty-five men to the hospital, an assistant secretary of the army dispatched a small team of men to Fort Bragg and to Fort Riley, Kansas, with instructions to figure out what was going on. The report they submitted would help to shape the briefing that Lt. Col. James White provided the army secretary and chief of staff: racial tensions were endemic and the army must take action to address them. But the trips to Fort Bragg and Fort Riley yielded a second memorandum. "Subject: Haircuts" was no more than a side note to the larger report, submitted separately, and its four pages contained only two brief mentions of race. Its author, however, wrote with a sense of urgency and exasperation. Culture matters, he was insisting, even if not in those words.

The memo's author, John Kester, was the newly appointed deputy assistant secretary of the army for manpower. He had come to his current position by way of a *Harvard Law Review* presidency and a clerkship with Supreme Court justice Hugo Black, followed by a position in the army's Judge Advocate General's (or JAG) Corps. Though he had just passed the magic line of thirty (as in "don't trust anyone over the age of"), Kester *was* relatively young. He was also white, and though that fact did not seem to register with the Office of the Secretary of the Army, it likely did with the enlisted men

*Culture and Identity*

he interviewed in the course of his work. Kester's race certainly affected what he was told, and it probably shaped what he heard. What he reported, however, was about the importance of *age*. Kester argued that commanders failed to understand the way that young enlisted men saw the world and their place in it and that the "generation gap" over hair policy ultimately worked against "the best interest of the Army."[4]

"During our recent trips to Fort Bragg and Fort Riley to gather information on race relations," Kester's memo began, "our discussions with enlisted personnel time and again turned to a subject which none of us had previously taken seriously: haircuts." Young soldiers, Kester reported, hated being forced to wear their hair short—"much shorter," in fact, than "fashionable civilian men." The "literally dozens" of complaints from "otherwise-good-natured servicemen of both races" had convinced him that army policy on hair was creating a problem that demanded attention at the highest Department of the Army level.[5]

One can assume, given Kester's background, that he understood how to write a brief, and his memo began and ended with terms and topics that would resonate with army leadership: army regulations and the need for consistency, the necessity of further study, morale, lack of monetary cost, and the pending all-volunteer force. The internal paragraphs, however, betrayed his awareness of the gulf between young men and their elders. "Commanders' defensiveness," he titled one paragraph. "Generation gap," he headed another. Under the heading "Girls," he reported soldiers' concerns that short hair "reduced their esthetic and biological appeal to the opposite sex." His most extended charge came under the heading "Individualism." "The modern young man," Kester wrote, "is extremely jealous of his individuality in what he has been told is a big, impersonal world. He regards hair style as an expression of himself, and a harmless expression at that. In addition, to Black soldiers the Afro style is a mark of self-confidence and pride." Young men, Black and white, Kester explained, believed that the army was refusing them the "minimal dignity" of an "attractive appearance."[6]

What John Kester discovered in North Carolina and Kansas was echoed by soldiers—as well as by marines and sailors and airmen—worldwide. When, following army-wide instructions from General Westmoreland, the commander at Fort Bragg set up race relations seminars in late 1969, participants were reportedly preoccupied with the "haircut problem." And Kester's instincts were confirmed when, in March 1970, almost two-thirds of soldiers surveyed at Fort Carson, Colorado, ranked hair among their top four concerns, while one in five ranked it first.[7] Less than ten months after the battle of Hamburger Hill, and as stories on the My Lai Massacre—made public in November 1969—still appeared on the front pages of American newspapers, 20 percent of a representative group of American soldiers saw *hair* as the army's biggest issue.

But even as Kester's memo portrayed hair as a concern of youth, the institutional army chose to focus on hair because it figured so prominently in the growing crisis over race. "The question of hair" mattered immensely to Black soldiers, journalist Wallace Terry testified during the Congressional Black Caucus's 1971 hearings on racism in the military. Terry, who had served as deputy bureau chief for *Time* magazine in Vietnam, put hair below only two other issues—slow promotions and disproportionately dangerous assignments—in his list of soldiers' concerns.[8]

Some soldiers, moreover, saw army hair policy as a purposeful insult. Men in one of the mandated RAP groups meeting within the United States argued that army policies on Afros were "an attempt to undercut racial pride" —a comment then reported in the news article "The Army's Efforts to Ease Racial Tension." And in Germany, where the Afro was a frequent topic in *Stars and Stripes*, especially in letters to the editors, a Black army deserter interviewed by *Der Spiegel* explained that he had deserted because of racial discrimination. The evidence of discrimination he offered? Hair policies.[9]

Part of the problem, army observers agreed, was that the institution's hair policies exacerbated racial tensions between Black and white soldiers. A UPI story in May 1970 quoted an unspecified report on army race relations: "There probably is no single thing that exacerbates and fosters ill will more than the topic of haircuts."[10] Concurred a staff sergeant stationed in Seckenheim, Germany: "Though the problem may seem trivial, it is one of the major causes of white backlash in the armed forces today."[11]

Despite the fact that army hair regulations were uniform—or at least intended to be so—they nonetheless drew charges of unfairness and preferential treatment from both Black and white soldiers. In May 1969, *Jet* magazine reported on a "flood" of letters from Black soldiers, who complained that though they were banned from wearing "Afro-bush" styles, white officers "look the other way" when "shaggy-haired white soldiers pass." White soldiers at Fort Carson complained that "current policy permits the Negro soldier to remain inconspicuous in the civilian community while complying" with regulations (because Afros could compress to appear acceptable), while Black soldiers in Vietnam told Terry that if "you grew your hair too long, never as long as some White boys are able to wear their hair and get away with it, you risk thirty days in jail," in part because (as an army staff sergeant

*Culture and Identity*

in Germany explained), under uniform regulations, "with the same length hair, Black hair sticks out from [the] cap while white hair doesn't."[12]

For most young Black servicemen, however, the symbolism of the Afro mattered more than the potentially unfair results of uniform regulations. As a senior air force NCO in Wiesbaden, Germany, put it in his letter to the editors of *Stars and Stripes*, "the Afro look" gives young Black men "a feeling of completeness far deeper than an unthinking individual would believe."[13]

Claims about the significance of the Afro were made in American popular culture, asserted in informal conversations among service members, and debated in the world of military policy. In late 1970 when the official US Army magazine, the *Army Digest*, discussed army efforts to address racial conflict, it broke no new ground when it identified the Afro as a key element of young Black soldiers' "desire to be identified with a new black pride, for which they are constantly seeking historical evidence and visible symbolism." Breaking free of "the white man's culture," the author wrote, "means feeling black pride, regaining manhood, and a type of soul-cleansing that they cannot otherwise obtain by continuing in the ways of their forebears."[14]

In a similar vein, the defense in the first court-martial case over an Afro hairstyle portrayed the Afro as a key symbol of Black identity. Airman First Class August Doyle of New Mexico's Cannon Air Force Base had been charged, specifically, with failing to obey a legal order to cut his hair, but much of the case turned on his right to wear what was an exceptionally modest Afro.[15]

In his testimony, expert witness Charles Becknell portrayed the Afro as a constitutionally protected form of communication. But Becknell, who was a historian, also repeatedly cited what he described as "our newly [e]merging black culture." In slavery, he explained, it was the cutting of a man's hair down to the skin that helped "distinguish him as a slave." The Afro, in contrast, was an "assertion of manhood." Becknell's call back to the injustice of slavery was likely tactical, even as he strongly believed in his claims about manhood. In that courtroom, Becknell was not likely to help Doyle's case by explaining that Afros (or "naturals") had emerged in the mid-1960s not only as a sign of Black pride but also as a rejection of white standards of appropriateness or beauty.[16]

Thus, as white military officials came to understand and then to inform one another, the Afro was not simply a haircut. It was an expression of Black pride, the most visible of the cultural symbols that had come to matter a great deal to young Black servicemen. Army major general Woodrow W. Vaughan, who first authorized the wearing of the Afro in Germany, endorsed it as "one of the most important if not the most important matters of concern to the Negro soldier . . . a source of great pride and identity to the Negro." (As context, Vaughan warned officers in the same memorandum not to refer to Black soldiers as "Nigger" or "Boy.") The DoD report in which L. Howard Bennett explained that the young Black man sought recognition of himself as "B*L*A*C*K (not ersatz white)" pointed to symbols such as "the Afro, the dashiki, the black power handshake and salute, slave bracelets, etc."[17]

The army's official race relations handbook for leaders explained that "today, many blacks have . . . gained pride in their own uniqueness and have adopted their own standards of beauty. They wear the Afro because it is a *black* hairstyle, not a white one; they wear the dashiki because it is a *black* style of dress, and not a copy of the white man's style. Blacks are saying they are different and proud of it—they are not just second-rate, imitation white people." And a Fort Leavenworth seminar, assigned by headquarters in late 1969 to discuss key problems facing the army, concluded that "the wearing of an AFRO haircut is an expression of black culture and symbolic of the black soldier's dedicated and renewed interest in developing racial pride" and should be recognized as such.[18]

By the early 1970s, military officials commonly included hair policy in their race relations efforts, sometimes assigning it great importance. Here, perhaps surprisingly, the Marine Corps led the way. After racial clashes at Camp Lejeune and in Hawai'i during the summer of 1969 left one dead and thirty-one injured, the Marine Corps commandant issued ALMAR (All Marine Corps Activities) 65, authorizing the Afro. It is quite possible the officially sanctioned Afro would not have been recognized as such on the street; confronted with an image of the approved US Marine Corps Afro at the Camp Lejeune barbershop, a Black combat veteran was perplexed. The *New York Times* reported his reaction. "That ain't an Afro," the man, recently returned from Vietnam, told the barber (who was, according to the *Times*, "also a Negro"). "I thought we were going to get to have Afros." "Yep, that's it," the barber replied, with what the *Times* described as a faint smile. Said the sergeant: "Well, to hell with it, then," and he stalked out of the shop.[19]

But even as Black marines publicly described the authorized Afro as "a big laugh . . . especially [to] us Africans," word of the Marine Corps policy circulated among the other services, in part because military publications covered it extensively. It was not long before an army representative, assigned to assess interracial relations in Southeast Asia, found Black soldiers complaining that they were being "harassed" about haircuts and asking about the significance of ALMAR 65, the Marine Corps's message on hair, for the army.[20]

The army did not initially offer a coherent, army-wide response on the Afro. But two months after the Marine Corps's action, in November 1969, the army's commander in Hawai'i issued "guidance" to "insure that reasonable 'Afro-natural' hairstyles" were allowed in his command. (The meaning of "reasonable," of course, was very much open to interpretation.) In Vietnam, after Black soldiers complained to Bennett's DoD team about commanders prohibiting "the 'Afro' or 'Bush' hair cuts," the commanding general of the US Army Vietnam announced in the next *Commander[']s Notes* that "Afro-bush" and "'mod'" styles were allowed, so long as they "conformed to pre-scribed USARV standards." The following spring, the head of the European theater's army support command issued his own authorization of the Afro style. A small-town US newspaper's headline on the shift correctly identi-fied a key point: "Army OKs 'Neat' Afro Haircuts, but Hippie Hair Styles Are Out."[21]

In other words, the army was concerned about managing claims of Black pride and racial identity, not with accommodating itself to youth culture, regardless of race. And by 1970, one point had become clear in both public discussion and internal communications: young Black soldiers valued what they defined as Black culture and meant to claim a Black identity—most often, and most visibly, by growing their hair into an Afro style. Such alter-nate claims of identity, which in their very existence challenged the primary identity of soldier, and such visible rejections of uniformity, which signaled that challenge, did not mesh easily into army ways or with army values. (It is essential to recognize that those "ways" and "values" were not racially neutral; the term for the uniform haircut—a "whitewall" or "white sidewall" —clearly referred to white skin and was a slang term for white soldiers.)[22]

So how did the army attempt to reconcile such claims of Black identity with the traditional logic and practices of the institution?

Here both organizational structure and standard procedure would come into play. Army organization is complex, the subject of endless flow charts that carefully illustrate lines of authority and divisions of responsibility. From major commands down to individual soldiers, responsibilities are specified in detail. Thus the way the problem was defined would dictate which ele-ments of the army would be responsible for solutions. "The problem of race" would find purchase throughout both institutional and operational elements, but the initial organization-wide proposals centered on the Afro came from the Army & Air Force Exchange Service, including the PX retail system and the army clubs that AAFES administered.

The significance of the Afro was initially claimed by servicemen themselves: Afros, to most young Black soldiers, were symbols of identity and of Black pride. Army leaders, acknowledging such claims, were willing to experiment with more lenient policies on Afros and other cultural symbols, even though often reluctantly and only as one among many attempts to solve the broadening racial crisis. (I hasten to add, here, that the war in Vietnam continued to overshadow all other concerns, with the continuing Cold War not far behind.)

In turn, AAFES leaders had their own reading of the issue, one in keeping with their assigned role of providing consumer goods to servicemen and servicewomen on US military installations throughout the world. As they saw it, Black soldiers who faced post exchange barbers with little knowledge of Black hair and shelves full of shampoos that promised to "bring out the highlights" and "natural softness" of their hair felt excluded within the army. *That* problem, AAFES leaders were confident, they could solve.[23]

As the spokesman for AAFES explained to the assembled officers at the first Department of the Army race relations conference in late 1970, AAFES "is aware that providing products and services required by these important customers [Black servicemen and servicewomen and their dependents]" helped to fulfill the charge to improve race relations set forth by the secretary of the army in his October 1969 speech. Col. John Florio, the AAFES spokesman, attributed some of the success he claimed to "greater command interest."[24] Greater command interest, institutionally, translated into resources and increased support.

Some context is useful here. By the late 1960s, the PX system had become, in the words of a *New York Times* headline, "One of the Most Powerful and Least Visible Retailing Enterprises" in the world. With approximately 5,000 outlets in forty countries, AAFES was the nation's—and probably the world's—third-largest retail chain.[25]

In Vietnam, in particular, the PX system had grown dramatically; the 300 retail outlets established there as the US presence escalated, along with mobile PXs and PX catalogs, did $35 million in sales every month. As PXs sold everything from cameras and watches to magazines, record albums, and shampoo, companies that produced those goods recognized what placement on PX shelves meant for their sales and ultimately for their bottom line. The PX sold about $50 million worth of records every year, for example, and selection as the Army & Air Force Exchange "record of the month" often propelled an album to gold-record status.[26] But whether a company man-ufactured expensive electronics or snuff, a PX contract was lucrative. And anything defined as a "must stock" item—the PX, like everything else in the military, had layers of such bureaucratic definitions—could be a gold mine.

The possibilities for corruption are obvious: a bribe here, a kickback there, free lodging in a luxurious six-bedroom villa (which was paid for, it turned out, by the vendor for Jim Beam whiskey in Vietnam) for a few. Such poor choices by army personnel may simply have stemmed from human nature, but a legal loophole made corruption more likely. Because AAFES was not government funded, it had been largely protected from civilian oversight and executive review. In early 1969, however, the *Washington Post* reported that AAFES was "nervously awaiting" its first public investigation by Congress since 1948.[27]

AAFES had reason to be nervous, though not about that investigation. Mendel Rivers, chair of the House Armed Services Committee, made clear that he would not be conducting an investigation, but a "review." Rivers had long positioned himself as a friend of the military and was, in fact, a close friend of Brig. Gen. Earl Franklin Cole, the army officer who had overseen the PX and club system in Vietnam before taking over the club and exchange system in Europe. As news circulated that the Senate Permanent Subcom-mittee on Investigations was looking into charges that PX officials were tak-ing bribes and kickbacks—and into Cole, in particular—Rivers tried twice, in 1969, to block a Senate inquiry into army PXs. (The army dealt with Cole internally; he was recalled from his position as PX commander for Europe in late 1969, stripped of his medals, and allowed to retire.)[28]

It was not until late 1971 that the Senate subcommittee issued the report of its three-year investigation, the details of which Illinois senator Charles Percy condemned as "this amazing, bewildering story of fraud, mismanagement, bribery, kickbacks, favors and easy, high living," in which members of the US military had "exploit[ed] this tragic war."[29] But the *Washington Post* had reported the existence of at least one ongoing investigation in early 1969. As the army began, that year, to seek solutions to the emerging problem of race, there was no way that AAFES officials did not see an opportunity—even if they did not circulate a memo suggesting that highly visible efforts to address the complaints of Black service members might improve AAFES's public stand-ing. AAFES's concerted efforts to address the needs of Black service members began in September 1969, the same month that Rivers twice tried to block investigation of the PX.

In true bureaucratic style, AAFES began by researching Black consumer desires. (In the words of its report, "extensive research was made.") AAFES personnel were sent to observe what Black patrons bought in New York, Atlanta, Houston, Detroit, Dallas, and Washington, DC, department stores, where they also surveyed the "stockage of black-oriented products." AAFES representatives scrutinized national advertising aimed at African Americans. They solicited information from "major producers of toiletries" about "Negro customer usage and preferences." They visited US post exchanges to obtain "black customer comment and recommendations."[30]

In the end, they produced a detailed list of "Merchandise in Support of Negro Customers" that specified more than 200 personal care items (including Ebonaire scalp cream, Afro Sheen, and nut-brown liquid foundation) to be regularly stocked in all exchanges worldwide. The list also identified a set of "never out" items that required an "in-stock efficiency percentage of 95%." The deputy commander of the Korean regional exchange realized what a challenge that would be when the 500 Afro combs ordered for one store sold out in a matter of minutes. That response, however, the bureaucracy took in stride, pledging to continually monitor consumer demand and update its stock according to consumer preferences.[31]

In his report to the 1970 race relations conference, Colonel Florio defined Black consumer needs broadly. PXs, he informed his audience, had begun featuring "'soul food'" menus once a week. They had expanded their collections of "pre-recorded tapes that depict 'soul,' (or rhythm and blues music)." They had begun stocking "colorful high fashion clothing" similar to that portrayed in a recent issue of *Ebony* magazine and were acquiring "a distinctive Afro type shirt more commonly called the dashiki." And, finally, he assured his audience, 5 percent of the dolls stocked for the Christmas season would be Black. In response to army concerns about racial conflict, the third-largest retail enterprise in the world had committed itself to serving Black consumers.[32]

Meanwhile, AAFES had identified the "urgent requirement" to improve hair cutting and styling services for Black service members and their dependents. In this case its research led to thirty-year-old hair stylist Willie Lee Morrow. Morrow, as AAFES officials told *Ebony* magazine, had first come to army attention because of his book, *The Principles of Cutting and Styling Negro Hair*. That may have been true. However, the Marine Corps recently had spent $140 to bring Morrow and four male models to Camp Pendleton. Corps officials, in the wake of ALMAR 65, wanted to know whether Afro haircuts could conform to regulations. Could they appear neat? Would they

San Diego barber Willie Lee Morrow, hired by the Army & Air Force Exchange Service, traveled to US military bases throughout the world, teaching local barbers and beauticians how to cut Black hair. This stop, in Tokyo, was part of his 1970 Pacific tour: Korea, Japan, Okinawa, the Philippines, Guam, Alaska, and Hawai'i.
*Photograph by Katsuhiro Yokomura /* © *Stars & Stripes, all rights reserved.*

allow the proper wearing of headgear? But they were also concerned about efficiency and cost. Service cuts normally cost under a dollar, while Morrow's Afro cuts usually went for $25 (or roughly $175 in 2020 dollars). Morrow, seemingly at risk of undermining willingness to pay his regular charges, demonstrated that he could turn out Afro cuts in ten to twelve minutes each. "I showed it can be done," Morrow told the Associated Press reporter who was documenting the event. That AP story got a fair amount of play, including in *Stars and Stripes*.[33]

Morrow, who hailed from Alabama hill country and ran two successful barbershops in San Diego, was a skilled barber and an excellent self-promoter, and AAFES cast its lot with him. Army lines of authority created a brief holdup for Morrow's mission; *Stars and Stripes* reported in mid-February 1970 that AAFES was prepared to bring a "top-flight black hair specialist" to Germany to train barbers on cutting Black hair but could not do so until USAREUR decided "which style of Afro haircuts are permitted."[34]

By mid-March, Morrow was on the road, accompanied by the chief of AAFES Personal Services Division. An AP article on the program began, "The United States is sending Willie Lee Morrow around the world at government expense to bring bushy, round Afro haircuts to black soldiers," and charted his journey: three weeks in Germany and England, where he instructed 750 barbers and 300 beauticians, with an upcoming forty-day whirlwind through Alaska, Hawai'i, and Southeast Asia.[35]

Lines of authority once again engaged: in Vietnam the article, with the handwritten tag "Racial Tensions," was circulated with a note demanding, "G-1! What do you know about this?" An officer in G-1 (Personnel) explained that AAFES headquarters had initiated the trip and had secured "theater clearance" for mid-June. He recommended that USARV "neither endorse nor criticize this project." It had, after all, garnered significant support outside Vietnam. Meanwhile, Morrow made clear that he understood what the Afro meant to young Black soldiers. "The black soldier today wants his blackness recognized," he told a reporter from *Pacific Stars and Stripes* as he demonstrated Afro cuts in Seoul, "and I'm here to be part of that recognition."[36]

AAFES, in using command concern about racial conflict to secure high-level support for its expanded role, had framed the problem around consumer goods and services. Black soldiers, overall, welcomed the soul music and soul food, as well as the dashikis and Afro picks that now claimed space on PX shelves. AAFES efforts on behalf of the Afro were likewise well received, especially as army barbershops began charging "regular" rather than "special" rates for Afro cuts. Some things, though, did not change: enlisted men across racial lines continued to complain bitterly about the quality of haircuts in army barbershops.[37]

But for all its efforts, AAFES offered only a partial solution to the cultural demands of Black soldiers. Black pride could not be purchased from the post exchange or contained by its offerings. As one Black officer said in 1970, putting "chitterlings and Afro-Sheen in the commissary" was not sufficient. Thus as racial tensions grew and anti-military sentiment spread within the army, Black soldiers wove "soul bracelets" or "slave bands" out of bootlaces. They offered Black Power salutes, raising clenched fists, and greeted one another with the dap, a complicated and evolving set of moves one soldier in Germany called "a song of brotherhood, pride and struggle for unity."[38] In an era of emerging cultural nationalism, these cultural symbols carried great importance. More and more, young Black soldiers saw them as essential signs of Black pride and Black identity.

Cultural symbols, in turn, created a dilemma for the army. Better-targeted

In 1971, the popular comic strip *Beetle Bailey* captured the ambivalence some army leaders felt about regulations allowing Afros. One officer clipped this strip and filed it under "Race Relations." Cartoonist Mort Walker had introduced Lieutenant Flap, the strip's first Black character, in 1970. *Beetle Bailey* © *1971 Comicana Inc. Dist. by King Features Syndicate, Inc.*

consumer goods and increased barbering expertise at the PX fit neatly into army organization and practice. The role of the post exchange was expanding, and to most observers such visible commitments to serve all soldiers seemed fitting and not at all disruptive. The use of cultural symbols, on the other hand, violated a whole range of army regulations and practices. Signs of individual or group identity—the Afro, the soul bracelet—were by nature in conflict with the uniformity central to a uniformed service and to the primacy of military identity.

And some such symbols defied the logic of military order and its emphasis on discipline, hierarchy, rank, and regulation. The dap could disrupt the hierarchy of rank with claims of racial brotherhood (does the sergeant dap with a private? Does a captain?). The clenched fist salute could signal defiance rather than respect. And tolerance for the cultural symbols of some groups but not others violated military principles of consistent policy and equal treatment—and was also likely to cause resentment among those not so favored.

Army leaders were conscious of the potential difficulties from the beginning. The after-action report on the army's initial race relations conference in November 1970 emphasized the "immediate need" for commanders to enforce "standards of appearance, proper wear of the uniform, discipline and military courtesy." "The lowering of the standards traditional to the United States Army," it specified, "should not, under any circumstances, be included in a commander's program for improved race relations."[39]

More pointedly, an inspector general investigation of a "racial incident" at Camp Baxter, Da Nang, identified command tolerance of such cultural symbols as part of the problem. "Black soldiers at Camp Baxter," it noted, "were permitted to abuse the use and public display of the outward symbols of 'black power' or 'black unity.'" The dap was allowed to disrupt normal activity; Afros "trimmed to excessive lengths" were tolerated; and "unauthorized 'black power' symbols were permitted to be worn as part of the uniform." White soldiers, the report concluded, had come to see Black soldiers who employed such symbols "as a threat."[40]

Despite the frequently reiterated official explanations that these symbols of Black power were "symbols of unity" rather than threat (a claim accompanied, in the race relations handbook for leaders, by the statement that "black power . . . does not mean that black people are planning to turn the tables and force white folks to live in the ghetto with the rats and the roaches"), young Black soldiers often intended to express both. Many young Black men in Vietnam, writes historian Kimberley Phillips, "meant to convey a threat as they held up mess lines" to dap; they, like the white soldiers they inconvenienced, saw the elaborate ritual as "display[ing] the menace of a collective black male power."[41]

Nonetheless, in the face of a growing and intractable problem that seemed particularly significant in the context of the continuing war and geopolitical volatility, the army had become increasingly lenient about such displays. As AAFES pushed its Afro-cutting education programs, thus requiring official decisions on hair policy, the army accommodated "neat" Afros, making what was widely characterized as a "major concession" on the "Afro style." By early 1971 in Vietnam, "unity bands" were authorized for wear in the 23rd Infantry Division, and other "symbols" were deemed acceptable so long as they were worn inside the uniform. Individual commanders sometimes went further: Maj. Gen. Woodrow W. Vaughan, the white USAREUR deputy chief of staff for logistics who had initially endorsed the Afro, dapped in front of reporters.[42]

In a set of broader claims, USAREUR's commander in chief, Gen. Michael S. Davison, portrayed acceptance of such cultural symbols as a critical step toward racial reconciliation. Speaking in 1971, Davison told army officers that "Black power salutes, dapping, Afro haircuts, black bracelets, and similar accouterments advertise a need to belong where one feels accepted, and, of greater significance, a pride in being black. I do not view these signs and symbols as being anti-establishment. Rather, they point to an establishment defect. Have we truly accepted the black soldier? As our efforts continue, communication channels open; understanding improves; identification of the black soldier should turn toward the Army and its life style, with a reduced need for such symbolism."[43]

*Culture and Identity*

General Davison portrayed such symbolism as a temporary step in the full integration of Black soldiers into the army, not as an acceptable or desirable long-term path. But an institution that relies on official policies does not easily adapt to short-term approaches or unofficial leniency. By late 1972, the army was officially considering a policy that would allow troops, Black and white, to wear "culturally oriented items" while in uniform.[44] That, however, would prove an institutional step too far.

Here, again, institutional specifics matter. Because army leaders believed that racial conflict threatened the army's ability to provide for the national defense, the institution—from individual officers and NCOs through its military secretary and chief of staff—offered Black soldiers unprecedented freedom to display the symbols of Black pride, most particularly by wearing (modest) Afros. But while the urgent "problem of race" provided justification for that leniency, the issue of hair stretched well beyond the Afro style, and cultural symbols reached well beyond Black pride. That fact matters because militaries depend on policy and regulations—regulations that are laid out in often excruciating detail, subject to enforcement, and universally applicable.

If army leaders decide to accept the use of cultural symbols, that authorization must be universal; the army cannot allow one group to use cultural symbols and deny such use to all others. Thus when army leaders chose to recognize the importance of Black identity and allow Black soldiers to display various cultural symbols, even to a very specific end, it could not limit the use of cultural symbols to African Americans alone. "The army must adhere to one standard for all personnel regardless of race, creed, social background or political belief," a brigade commander in Vietnam noted in his 1971 race relations report. "We cannot make exceptions for some groups, without the same consideration for others."[45] That basic premise was clear in the late 1972 discussion of authorizing "culturally oriented items"; it specified that the policy applied alike to all soldiers, not solely to African Americans. Thus when the army began to accept symbols of Black identity, it created space for a variety of claims about identity and expression that went well beyond its original intent and at times created a whole new set of racial conflicts.

If one group's cultural symbols are acceptable, why aren't those of any other group? Where is the line drawn? If Black soldiers can display pride in Black identity, can white soldiers display pride in white identity, or perhaps in (white) southern identity?

The US military had tolerated or even embraced informal use of the Confederate Battle Flag since the flag's resurgence in the 1950s, and some local efforts to circumscribe its use during the 1960s had drawn heated responses from southern members of Congress. (The biggest flap was over a Marine Corps officer's order to end display of the Georgia state flag, which—adopted in 1956, in resistance to the civil rights movement—was just a whisper different from the battle flag of the Confederacy.)[46] No matter the history or rationale, however, it was inescapably clear that allowing use of the Confederate flag would not improve race relations in the ranks. Nonetheless, army leaders—not only whites but also Black race relations officers—frequently treated all forms of cultural symbolism as equivalent.

The report on the army's 1970 race relations conference, in its concluding section, noted that white soldiers often perceived "the widespread appearance of black symbols" as threatening, even as "the display of the Confederate flag and the use of racial epithets by white soldiers" was "equally offensive to black soldiers." Its proposed solution was to educate soldiers, Black and white, on the "origins, nature, meaning, and possible misinterpretation of these symbols." This equivalency was echoed throughout the army. In the race relations course at Fort Dix, the DRRI-trained instructor, Sergeant First Class Cleofies Jackson—a Black man raised in Owassa, Alabama—began by projecting slides of a clenched fist salute and a Confederate Battle Flag onto the screen at the front of the room. The clenched fist, he told the trainees, "does not always mean revolution nor that black people want to beat you about the head and shoulders, nor does the Confederate flag mean a man belongs to the Ku Klux Klan."[47]

The army's race relations handbook for leaders, which carefully explained the concept of institutional racism, reassured its audience that "black power insignia" were "no more threatening than school rings, rebel flags, or unit tatoos [sic]." And even the commander at Fort Carson, where an official memo insisted that "nothing exposes the deep prejudices of the white majority more than the view that racial harmony depends on solving 'the Black problem' or 'the Chicano problem'[; o]ur basic problem to be solved is our 'WHITE PROBLEM,'" put display of the Confederate flag into the same category as symbols of Black power and Black pride. Fort Carson's response to a 1971 army query on race relations noted that "there are no restrictions on black unity bracelets or the display of Confederate flags."[48]

Once again, however, from the institutional perspective of the army, the entire point of accommodating cultural symbols was to lessen racial tension. And no matter how many officers equated Black Power salutes and Confederate flags, young Black soldiers did not see the two as equivalent, and the display of Confederate flags undermined the larger goal. The army's solution —at least in Vietnam—was in keeping with army practice: it endorsed uniformity and regulation. Rather than distinguishing between the two groups and their chosen symbols, the army turned to existing military regulations that transcended the issue at hand.

A pamphlet that Military Assistance Command, Vietnam, began distributing in 1970 offered the usual equivalencies: while the "'Dixie' flag" was "particularly irritating" to Black servicemen "because of the slavery aspects of the Civil War, and its more recent use in anti–civil rights demonstrations," for some whites, the flag was a "deeply cherished" symbol of the "courage and sacrifice of Americans for a cause" and, furthermore, was incorporated into several state flags. Continuing the paragraph with no comment on the relative legitimacy of those opposing claims, the pamphlet stated MACV policy: "Within MACV the only flags authorized to be flown are those of the United States, the Republic of Vietnam, and the Minuteman award. On special occasions or holidays when the installation commander deems the display of state flags appropriate, they may be displayed in tastefully arranged groupings if all states are represented. If the flag of each state is not available, none are to be displayed."[49]

The same document suggested a vision of social change that resonated with its approach to education and training. While it might not be possible to change attitudes, the authors wrote, "we can require a change in actions and hope that a change in attitude will follow." Thus a specific policy, constructed without reference to race or meaning, could deal with the problem of the Confederate flag. Army leaders understood the policy in those terms. As evidence of efforts to handle racial tension, the commander of the 23rd Infantry Division noted in his April 1971 race relations report that the "provisions of MACV Dir 600-12 . . . with respect to the display of flags are being strictly enforced."[50]

In the preceding instances, army leaders had tentatively recognized racial identity and accepted symbols of racial pride in hopes of advancing racial comity or, at least, of calming racial tensions that found expression in violence. They had at least partially circumvented the problem posed by the Confederate flag. But what about other forms of identity—those not based in race—and their associated cultural symbols? If soldiers could wear Afros as symbols of Black identity, could soldiers likewise demonstrate that they belonged to "youth"? To the cool or the hip?

By the late 1960s, as countercultural styles merged into America's youth culture, young men had embraced long hair. If, for Black men, Afros signaled masculinity and Black pride, for many young white men, long hair laid claim to a meaningful identity, as well. And just as Afros seemed to challenge the primacy of military identity, so, too, did flowing locks. Not all agreed that the challenge was absolute; when John Kester wrote his memo for the office of the secretary of the army in 1969, he advocated loosening hair policy overall, in keeping with the fashion of the age.

Commanders, Kester wrote, did not seem to recognize that their men shared the goal of looking "neat and handsome" but understood those terms differently. "The commander sees a soldier after a haircut," Kester wrote, "and thinks, 'There, he certainly looks better.'" But that same soldier "looks at himself in the mirror" and thinks, "'I have been disfigured.'" Continuing his case for loosened regulation, Kester claimed that longer hair had become so generally accepted that it no longer had any political significance, despite commanders' associations with "filth, hippies, war protesters and draft resisters." Besides, he noted, with an attempt at humor, "They are not asking to look like the Beatles."[51]

That was clearly true, as Kester's memo more or less coincided with the release of *Abbey Road*. By 1969 the Beatles were on the leading edge of the "freak revolution," a far cry from the innocent-seeming mop-tops who had sent teenage girls into a frenzy five years before. But the haircuts of the "I Want to Hold Your Hand" Beatles also exceeded the tolerance of most NCOs and officers, and therein lay the problem. Hair was frequently a subject of contention across lines of rank. It was a source of cross-service sniping, as soldiers complained about sailors sporting long hair and beards, their pseudo-civilian look first authorized in 1970 by Admiral "Bud" Zumwalt's celebrated Z-grams.[52] And within the army the legitimacy of a haircut was always open to interpretation. A soldier might pass inspection in the morning, only to be disciplined by a different officer or NCO before noon.

There was not much the army could do about the wayward navy and its controversial admiral, but the internal confusions were just another nail for the army's hammer. This was an institution that would specify the color and brand of paint (Bone White, Benjamin Moore) to be used in all recruiting offices, along with the number (three) of toy tanks, helicopters, GI Joes, and the like allowed on each recruiter's desk.[53] Regulation was the lifeblood of the institutional army. Over the course of four years, regulations governing hair expanded from 1967's vague "present a neat and soldierly appearance" to a 37-word statement in 1969 to 1970's eventual solution: 569 words that detailed not only the permissible length or bulk of hair but also the shape of sideburns, extent of mustache, and conditions allowing the wearing of wigs. Throughout the decade, regulations required that posters portraying

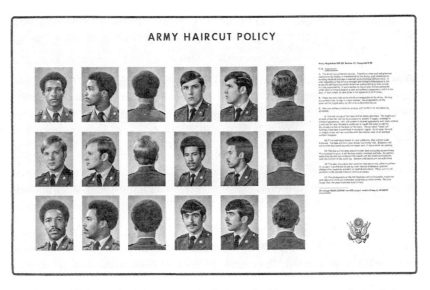

ARMY HAIRCUT POLICY

By 1971, US Army regulations governing haircuts had become extremely detailed. Nonetheless, those in authority often interpreted the specifications differently, and a man who passed inspection in the morning might find himself ordered to get a haircut before noon the same day. This army poster, which pictured front, side, and rear views of acceptable haircuts, was meant to solve the problem.
*Courtesy US Army Center of Military History, Fort McNair, Washington, DC.*

acceptable hairstyles be "prominently displayed" on unit bulletin boards and in barbershops and offices.[54]

Despite the expanding regulations, army hair policy had become more liberal by the early 1970s. Civilian hairstyles, however, were moving to the extreme. Military notions of "neat and well-groomed" were the antithesis of civilian male 1970s fashion, even if those who adopted '70s styles believed themselves, in Kester's phrase, "handsome." In this era of extremism, despite the army's best attempts to employ its usual tools and some extraordinary ones, struggles over hair policy continued to roil the institution.

A somewhat humorous example pitted the US Army Recruiting Command against the institution's chief of staff. Faced with the end of the draft and anticipating the daunting task, beginning in 1973, of attracting tens of thousands of recruits each month to the new all-volunteer force, a group of army leaders sought creative solutions. One such effort targeted unnecessary "irritants," otherwise known as "chickenshit." In this spirit, the recruiting command acknowledged how much young men, at the beginning of the 1970s, cared about their hair.

But the recruiting ad that promised "We care more about how you think than how you cut your hair," along with a photo of a young man with somewhat longish hair, pushed General Westmoreland over the edge. The army tried to recall the ad, but it was already in print. So instead an internal memo explained to all concerned that the young man pictured in this ad represented a civilian who might join the army. "It does NOT repeat NOT," continued the memo, "illustrate a soldier meeting the standards set by the Army."[55]

There was also a series of messy courts-martial cases, complete with extensive media coverage, during the early years of the all-volunteer force. News stories with titles such as "Army's Hair War Jabs Old Wounds" did nothing to help the army's reputation, which continued to be poor in the aftermath of the Vietnam War. In 1974 Senator Birch Bayh (D-IN) sent his legislative counsel to Germany to investigate the crisis over hair. Rep. Les Aspin (D-WI), who would later serve as US secretary of defense, called for a congressional investigation that same year. "Apparently the Army is willing to jeopardize our military readiness in Europe over a silly issue like the length of a man's hair," he wrote—in a press release. "That's incredibly stupid even for the Army." The Honorable Pat Schroeder (D-CO) committed herself to the cause in 1975, beginning a series of exchanges with Secretary of the Army Bo Callaway that moved from courteous to frigidly polite.[56]

But as the army saw it, none of these confrontations was about race. And almost all of the soldiers involved were white.

By the mid-1970s, as the strength and visibility of the Black Power movement had receded in civilian society, claims of cultural nationalism no longer held much sway among young enlisted Black men. Many still valued a well-cut Afro, but hair no longer carried great symbolic weight. Complaints about hair now came primarily from young white soldiers who were concerned about their ability to "pass"—as civilians. Some lamented that short haircuts made it hard to meet girls. Short hair marked them as military, claimed others, making them the targets of civilian antagonism off-post. "The young soldier," insisted a second lieutenant in 1975, "feels as if he is being viewed as a modern day member of the Hitler youth."[57]

The most extreme claim, in a petition to Congress, was that "the only reason the brass attempts to maintain this situation is to seperate [sic] us from our civilian brothers and sisters in order, to some day, make easier massacres such as Jackson State and Kent State." Such concerns betrayed problems at the heart of the new "Modern Volunteer Army," as recruits discovered the gulf between army promises and their own experiences and faced lingering public hostility in the wake of the war in Vietnam.[58] But they also show how fundamentally struggles over hair policy had changed.

The army had initially focused on hair because young servicemen suggested that hair policy exacerbated the racial conflict that, army leaders believed, threatened military readiness and efficacy. It had offered greater leniency as African American soldiers demanded recognition of Black identity and symbols of Black pride. But the fundamental logic of the institution was at odds with such actions. Yes, cultural symbols might be accommodated in a moment of crisis, the matter of hair treated with unusual forbearance as one piece of a broad, army-wide effort to contain the racial violence that many believed undermined army efficacy in an era of frightening geopolitical instability. By the mid-1970s, however, racial conflict no longer seemed so likely to overflow into violence: "Confrontation Era Over," a *Stars and Stripes* headline proclaimed in 1974, quoting the 1st Armored Division's race relations officer.[59] And army leaders did not see the haircut woes of young white soldiers as a major threat to army efficacy or to the stability of the free world—no matter what Les Aspin said.

Thus, with the question of hair separated from the problem of race, the army evaluated lessons learned. As an institution, it had never been comfortable with its limited embrace of cultural symbolism, including hairstyles; it had experimented only because it was desperate for solutions to endemic racial conflict in the ranks, and ground-level acceptance of such efforts was always spotty and contested. Now the army reasserted the claims of tradition. As an official letter on hair policy developed in 1975 explained, the army was "not merely an extension" of American society "but rather a separate and unique institution. Consequently," it continued, "the Army must retain basic standards of appearance and dress."[60]

The challenge to army hair policy was ultimately put to rest in mid-1976 by the US Court of Military Appeals, following a Supreme Court decision upholding the right of civilian police departments to regulate the hairstyles of their members. In this trial, army lawyers argued that there "is a pride and spirit in being a recognizable force, and a force whose appearance requires uniformity," and stressed the importance of discipline within that institution.[61]

When the Court of Military Appeals upheld the army's right to regulate the hairstyles of its members, it endorsed army claims about the importance of traditional institutional values of uniformity, order, and discipline. In the end, both internal army policy and the military court validated notions of military exceptionalism and rejected the right of soldiers to express alternate identities through their hairstyles. Both concluded that the US Army was a uniformed service, separate from civilian society, and based in principles of order and discipline. Self-expression through hair too directly violated the institutional logic, practices, and culture of the army. Ultimately, what was at stake was the right of a military service to enforce its regulations—something the army claimed was absolutely fundamental to the institution, regardless of the subject of those regulations.

I n the realm of race, however, the army's brief experiment with Afros and the cultural symbolism of Black pride would have long-lasting significance, helping to shape the ways that this massive institution dealt with demands for social change. In an age of cultural nationalism, Black soldiers had insisted on the right to express Black pride; they had embraced the Afro as a symbol of Black identity in an overwhelmingly white institution. As the army confronted their demands in the context of impending crisis, it tested its own institutional limits. Some of what it learned (or verified) was that the institution possessed a surprising flexibility. In the face of crisis, the army could respond creatively; it could bend—at least when under threat of internal violence and external failure.

The institution also drew lessons about the tools available for managing social change: in the military, hierarchy is clear, authority reaches well past the boundaries of civilian employers, and orders are orders, with mechanisms for enforcement. That mattered, for (as the comments on Confederate flags by MACV officers noted) it may be that forcing changes in behavior will prompt changes in attitudes. Nonetheless, as General Vaughan's instructions to avoid racial epithets when addressing Black soldiers reveals, there is often great distance between policies and their ground-level implementations.

Finally, in this process, the army confronted its institutional limits, the ways in which the weight of organization, culture, history, tradition, logic, policy, and practice fundamentally define what will more likely succeed and what will more likely fail. It was relatively easy to change what stocked the PX shelves, and those changes would be long-lasting. It was much more difficult to accommodate symbols of identity that transcended that of soldier. By the late 1970s the institution had returned to fundamentals: military identity must take precedence over all others; uniformity, order, discipline, and regulation must be paramount.

Regulations, however, do continue to evolve. In 2021, army hair policy was updated by a panel consisting of fifteen female and two male soldiers,

*Culture and Identity*

which was advised by two army dermatologists, an army psychologist, and an army equal opportunity officer. The results ran to more than 2,300 words. In large part, changes recognized the cultural desires and physical needs of women of color. "Our identity is important," said the senior enlisted leader of the army's uniform policy branch. "If we care about people first and the Soldier as a whole, we have to care about the many aspects to who they are as well. This is a small, but significant change that positively impacts a considerable size of our force."[62]

# 7 OFF-POST DISCRIMINATION

The US Army, as an institution, struggled to deal with cultural demands. Some resistance was generational—especially the conflict over hair—but the real issue, in the end, was that young soldiers saw cultural symbols as expressions of identity that (many army leaders believed) challenged or transcended the identity of "soldier." Still, most cultural demands could be handled through existing programs and processes. The army bureaucracy might pull its (collective) hair out over young soldiers' insistence they be allowed to wear Afros or "hippie" styles, but haircuts were regulated by Army Regulation (AR) 600-21. The provisions governing hair, as they grew increasingly detailed, caused conflict. But the army could—and did—claim authority to decide the appropriate length and style of soldiers' hair.

Army authority, which covered most elements of enlisted personnel's lives, became more tenuous at the boundaries of military space. Army regulations applied to its members 24/7, of course, and were implemented outside military bases to the extent that commanders were willing to exercise such authority and devote resources to enforce it. When it came to race relations off-post, however, command decisions were complicated. A commander might emphasize—and enforce—racial integration and equal access in the space under his command, whether in work details or in barracks or in clubs. But what if young men chose to self-segregate when they ventured into town? What if Black soldiers sought the comfort of a Black-oriented space? Was that acceptable?

Lt. Col. James White, whose briefing shaped the army's initial response to the racial crisis, argued that it was. "Persons of the same color, same social background and same cultural evolvement," he said in early 1970, "like to be together. Pride in shared origins is something to be valued as long as it does not result in mass polarization between races in a constricted environment." Those charged with managing army race relations continued to worry about Black and white soldiers parting ways at installation gates, but in general their answers echoed a basic claim: an individual should have the "prerogative of choosing his friends and conducting his social affairs as he so desires."[1]

But what about when off-post segregation was not driven by the choices of Black soldiers? What about when segregation was imposed by the surrounding community? In 1918, when an African American sergeant and his wife were turned away by the manager of a movie theater in Manhattan, Kansas, which neighbored Fort Riley, the head of the 92nd Division issued Bulletin No. 35. "It should be well known to all colored officers and men," Maj. Gen. Charles C. Ballou began the statement, which was read to all men under his command, "that no useful purpose is served by such acts as will cause the 'color question' to be raised." Men should, he wrote, "refrain from going where their presence will be resented," even when legally in the right, for the "GREATER WRONG" is "ANYTHING, NO MATTER HOW LEGALLY CORRECT, that will provoke race animosity." In the same vein, in 1944, when twenty-five-year-old 2nd Lt. Jack Robinson, stationed at Fort Hood, Texas, argued with the white civilian bus driver who ordered him to move farther back in the bus, the army preferred charges—against Robinson. (He was acquitted in the general court-martial proceeding, due in part to the skill and commitment of his army-appointed defense attorney, a white Texan.)[2]

Discrimination against African American men in uniform was in no way unusual, and not only in parts of the nation where Jim Crow was law. As the army moved from segregated to integrated units, and as the Defense Department committed itself to pursue equal opportunity even as nonviolent protesters were confronted by white mobs and fire hose–wielding police, post commanders were forced to contend with the divide between federally controlled military installations and surrounding communities. What could they do if local restaurants refused to serve African American soldiers? If landlords would not rent apartments to Black soldiers and their families? The army had no authority.

That claim, of course, was disingenuous. The post commander could not order civilian businesses and landlords to serve all soldiers equally, but the institutional army—and even more, the institution of the US military—had a great deal of power, should it choose to exercise it. It was a question of priority.

Military leaders, reasonably, saw the potential problems with using military might (in this case, its economic might) to force change in civilian society. And some white leaders had no problem with racial separation, racial hierarchy, or white supremacy. But organizations such as the NAACP worked to leverage military commitments to secure local change. And in the wake of the Gesell Report, the Department of Defense pushed all military departments to confront off-base discrimination. In the end, US military efforts helped advance the cause of open housing throughout the United States.

Off-post problems became even more difficult outside US borders. In both West Germany and South Korea, army investigations found, racial turmoil was fueled by local residents' discrimination against Black soldiers. But if the limits of authority presented problems within the United States, that was doubly true overseas. The risks of seeming to intervene in another nation's domestic affairs weighed heavily. And as the internal racial conflicts of the US military spilled out into the surrounding cities and towns, they affected international relations and decisions about global security.

Army attempts to manage problems off-post, where leaders exercised no direct authority, make clear just how much authority commanders exercised *within* the institution. Here, the results of army efforts to end off-post discrimination were mixed, the outcomes closely tied to the actions of external organizations, from the NAACP and the Congressional Black Caucus to the governments of West Germany and the Republic of Korea. And once again, the institutional army best handled issues that could be addressed by policy and through the existing channels of army authority. It largely failed when confronted by Black troops who made demands through violence, in an inarticulate language of rage.

I n 1960, the year four Black students from North Carolina A&T sat down at a whites-only lunch counter in Greensboro, North Carolina, and accelerated the civil rights movement's path of direct action, 2,300 women passed through the gates of Fort McClellan, Alabama, to begin basic training for the Women's Army Corps. Roughly 300 of these trainees were Black, not all of them accustomed to southern Jim Crow. On-post, at least, the army was officially committed to integration. Off-post, military personnel were subject to local law.[3]

Off-post, for most purposes, meant the small city of Anniston. One could drive to Atlanta from Fort McClellan in a couple of hours and to Birmingham a bit quicker, but Anniston provided for the basic needs of Fort McClellan and the large army depot on the other side of town. About a third of Anniston's residents were Black, almost all the rest white. By 1960, Anniston claimed both an active branch of the NAACP and an aggressive klavern of the Ku Klux Klan. And like most southern towns and cities, Anniston enforced legal segregation in all aspects of public life.[4]

That fact was inescapable, and Women's Army Corps battalion policy required "the Segregation Lecture" to be "read verbatim" to all personnel within six days of their arrival. Unlike the other policies presented in orientation—on alcoholic beverages, on punitive articles, on precautions against larceny—the segregation lecture was classified. Instructors were required to secure all copies "in accordance with paragraph 83, AR 345-15."[5]

In October 1961, however, an official letter from the commander of Fort McClellan supplanted the classified lecture. Addressed to all incoming military personnel, the letter began with a hearty "Welcome to Fort McClellan, Alabama!" But the commander, an infantry colonel, quickly shifted tone. "Before commencing your processing," he wrote, "I feel it vitally important that you be advised of local laws and customs in the civilian communities surrounding Fort McClellan. As a result of the publicity currently being given to integration and segregation in Alabama, as well as throughout the entire South, these laws and customs are being enforced more vigorously and emphatically than ever before by the local citizens."[6]

Col. Lon Smith had reason to issue a warning. The previous spring, on Mother's Day, a mob of white Anniston residents had attacked the Greyhound bus carrying the first "Freedom Riders"—a small group of Black and white civil rights activists traveling by bus through the South to test the 1960 Supreme Court ruling that segregated interstate facilities were unconstitutional. Anticipating their arrival, Anniston had closed its bus terminal that Sunday afternoon. Instead of passengers waiting to board the Greyhound to Birmingham, the bus was met by a group of about fifty white men, mostly members of the Klan. They surrounded the bus, shouting insults, smashing windows, slashing tires. Anniston police were nowhere to be seen.[7]

The police, when they arrived, made no attempt to control the mob. Instead, they escorted the damaged bus to the town limits; thirty to forty cars and pickup trucks followed. People still in their Sunday church clothes, men in suits and ties, some with children, joined the caravan. The bus pulled to the side of the road about six miles outside Anniston, just a few hundred yards from the Anniston Army Depot; it could drive no further on the slashed tires. Once again the mob surrounded the bus. Klansman "Goober" Llewellen hurled a firebomb through a broken window. Others blocked the exit. Men yelled, "Burn them alive," and, "Fry the goddamn niggers." The passengers were choking, struggling to breathe. They escaped only because an exploding fuel tank drove the attackers back.[8]

Anniston, in the days that followed, made headlines as far away as Australia. City leaders condemned the action but in language that offered little reassurance. The editors of the *Anniston Star* were primarily upset about how bad the "small group of scofflaws" made their town look, but they did insist that law enforcement should have prevented the violence. "And while this paper holds no brief whatsoever for the bus riding contingent that came down South in defiance of known prejudices," the newspaper opined the next day, referring to the Freedom Riders as "bus riding nitwits," "they were within the law and should have been protected accordingly."[9]

Fort McClellan, likewise, focused on the law. "While the Army does not countenance [segregation] on military reservations," Colonel Smith explained in his letter of welcome, "we have no authority over local government. It must be realized that, once we depart Fort McClellan and are in the civilian communities, we are subject to all local laws and customs and we are expected to comply with them." What advice did he offer for dealing with local law and custom? "Common sense and discretion." Like the Anniston city leaders, Smith was concerned about publicity. He urged new personnel "to prevent possible unfavorable publicity being directed against the military establishment." "If it becomes your unfortunate experience to become involved in an incident," Fort McClellan's commander wrote, "simply do as you are requested and, above all, do nothing which might bring discredit to you or your uniform." In "the event of any restraint," military personnel were advised to request permission to contact the military police.[10] Colonel Smith's concern about unfavorable publicity reflected the concerns of army bureaucracy. Commanders were required to submit "Blue Bell" (and later, Serious Incident) Reports for significant crimes or incidents that, if publicized, might "result in embarrassment" for the Department of the Army.

While Anniston was particularly violent in its defense of white supremacy, installations throughout the South dealt with conflict between army policy and local law. In 1960, many of the army's largest installations were in states that mandated or legally allowed racial segregation: Fort Bragg, North Carolina; Fort Campbell, Kentucky; Fort Benning, Georgia; Fort Hood, Texas; Fort Riley, Kansas (*Brown v. Board of Education* was, after all, *Brown v. Board of Education of Topeka*).

Soldiers whom the army ordered to these installations had no recourse if denied service at a restaurant or refused housing for their families off-post. Beyond the army, off-post discrimination was increasingly recognized as a fundamental problem; the Gesell Committee reported in 1963 that Black members of the armed forces were "daily suffering humiliation and degradation in communities near the bases at which they are compelled to serve" and that installation commanders not only lacked specific directions on how to deal with such discrimination but often did not see it as their responsibility.[11]

Secretary of Defense Robert McNamara was intent on changing that approach. As he explained in 1967, looking back to his early efforts, the "festering infection [of racism] in our national life" affected military personnel in ways that civilians were spared. Soldiers "on limited compensation and under military orders" were forced to move every few years, and to places not of their choosing. "While defending their nation," McNamara insisted, Black service members "are singularly defenseless against this bigotry." A Pentagon study ordered by McNamara in the fall of 1963 bore out those claims. Of the 305 military installations surveyed, north and south, east and west, 90 percent reported that adjacent communities discriminated against Black service members and their families. In all, forty-eight army installations or "activities" were in areas where public schools were segregated.[12] Jim Crow practices (as opposed to laws) extended throughout the land.

McNamara issued the first Department of Defense directive on equal opportunity in summer 1963, soon after the Gesell Committee submitted its report. Directive 5120.36 stipulated that military commanders must oppose discriminatory practices not only in areas under their direct control but also in places that service members "may live and gather in off-duty hours." The army's equal opportunity regulation, AR 600-21, came the following year; it likewise addressed equal opportunity both on- and off-post. At the same time, the new army regulation made clear that commanders had "no direct authority" over civilian communities and held the local community, not commanders, responsible for a "final and effective resolution."[13]

AR 600-21 was, in fact, the Department of the Army's line in the sand. In 1964, soon after the army issued its new regulation, the Department of the Army (DA) laid out its concerns in a classified, high-level briefing. The DA had "nonconcurred" on multiple recommendations of the 1963 Gesell Report but was particularly concerned about its stance on off-post discrimination, for which (the briefing complained) "the most radical recommendations were made." The 1964 briefing likewise portrayed the subsequent DoD directive, which extended the commander's responsibility "into the social patterns and customs of . . . communities when soldiers or their families are discriminated against because of their race," as "a radical departure from the traditional military-civilian relationship."[14] The DA had a point about departures from tradition, but it is also clear that in this case "tradition" was not on the side of the angels.

"We consider it inappropriate, if not impossible," the briefing continued, "to attempt to coerce or force civilian communities into eliminating segregation by applying 'off-limits' or other economic sanctions" when a "persuasive" approach was less likely to jeopardize commander-community relations. In contrast, the briefing stated clearly, AR 600-21 was built both on the "firm belief" that civilian communities must be persuaded to "voluntarily" end discrimination and on a calculated refusal to create a set of "hard and fast rules to be universally applied" in the "widely differing conditions throughout the nation."[15]

However, while AR 600-21 offered commanders no hard-and-fast rules for action, it did specify a hard-and-fast limit. The post commander's traditional tool for dealing with recalcitrant local communities—the authority that extended outside post gates—was the off-limits sanction. AR 600-21 forbade commanders from imposing sanctions without prior approval of the secretary of the army, and then only if all other "reasonable alternatives" had failed; it thus rendered this tool essentially useless. Commanders could not respond quickly to problems, for any request for sanctions had to work its way up the chain of command. And what commander wanted to draw the secretary of the army's attention to his failures? These obstacles were intentional, for—again, according to the classified briefing—making sanctions a last, and difficult, resort was "in keeping with our policy of encouraging and assisting rather than forcing change on a community."[16]

The obstacles were also in keeping with DoD policy. McNamara had endorsed the Gesell Committee's proposal that the military use off-limits sanctions to combat off-post segregation and discrimination that affected service personnel. But the DoD directive, like the army regulation, denied post commanders that tool. By restricting that authority to top civilian leadership, the DoD signaled that sanctions would be a last resort, infrequently employed. That move was clearly politic; in congressional hearings over the directive, still-powerful segregationists argued that such new demands on commanders "can only be detrimental to military tradition, discipline, and morale" (Sen. John Stennis, Mississippi), or that such a narrow focus on civil rights elided the question of whether it was proper to use the armed forces "to enforce a moral or social, rather than a legal," matter in civilian society (Rep. Durward Hall, Missouri).[17]

In this context, army efforts were uneven. There was some Department of the Army support. In 1967, for example, the executive secretary of the army's Open Housing Steering Group oversaw a program designed to encourage equal access to housing: the secretary or undersecretary of the army was made available to dine with key real estate and community leaders on local army posts. Army guidance went so far as to specify optimal seating arrangements. And because the DoD required regular reports on off-post discrimination, army commanders monitored the situation—though their reports were perhaps unrealistically optimistic. "Problems regarding race are being worked out together by responsible citizens and officials of both races," Georgia's Fort Gordon noted in 1966, while Fort Leavenworth (Kansas) described "informational" programs that made housing discrimination "unpopular and financially hazardous." Some commanders attempted in all good faith to exert "moral persuasion" and build "persistent, persuasive . . . contacts with community officials." Others did little to nothing. As of mid-1970, no more than six base commanders within US borders—from all military services combined—had sought permission to use off-limits sanctions for racial discrimination.[18]

The fundamental problem with this voluntary approach came into focus at the DoD's 1966 Executive Seminar on Civil Rights. Discussing off-post discrimination, Defense Department officials sought a direct reply: Should the "force and thrust" of command response be determined by the community's willingness to grant "local Negroes" their civil rights? That, of course, was the issue. "Complete uniformity of procedures" was impossible, AR 600-21 stipulated, because different community "situation[s]" required "local solutions." And an army representative in that room had just finished explaining to seminar participants that the army saw "persuasive action adjusted to the circumstances in each community" as its most effective approach to off-post discrimination.[19]

Working from those premises, the only plausible answer to the DoD was "yes": community willingness would shape command response. The army representative was not quite that blunt, of course, and he showed that he understood the politics involved. "The commander should be a step ahead of the off-base community's willingness to accord local Negroes their civil rights," he replied to the DoD query. "But," he continued, "he should not exert the force and thrust too far ahead of local community attitudes and mores—certainly not to the extent of the army acting as an agency for the enforcement of civil rights laws."[20]

That position, of course, meant that the army would knowingly assign Black soldiers to places where they would face blatant discrimination off-post and that commanders would base their actions on the racial attitudes of civilian communities rather than on the needs of their soldiers. That approach might keep the peace so long as most Black soldiers saw the army as a refuge from civilian discrimination. In 1966, that was not a good gamble.

Fast forward to November 1967. Just over two weeks after more than 100,000 Americans marched on the Pentagon in the massive national protest against the US war in Vietnam, and in the wake of the urban uprisings of the long hot summer of 1967, Secretary of Defense McNamara delivered a speech on "social inequities" and the US military. "I put the matter to you bluntly," he said. "Our nation should not, and will not, ask a Negro sergeant, for example, to risk his life, day after dangerous day, in the heat and hardship of a jungle war, and then bring him home and compel him to remain separated from his wife and his children because of the hate and prejudice that parades under the pomposity of racial superiority. And yet," he admitted, "that is precisely what has been happening in this country." The voluntary programs he had charged commanders to begin in 1963, McNamara said, had "failed, and failed miserably"; they "floundered and fell apart." And McNamara publicly blamed himself. The Pentagon, he said, had turned its attention to other problems, and top leadership—himself included—had not made off-post discrimination a sufficient priority.[21]

Under McNamara's leadership the DoD had already begun acting, first imposing off-limits sanctions in Maryland, and then for housing within a three-mile radius of the Pentagon. The undersecretary of the army, signing on to the campaign, publicly denounced racial discrimination in communities surrounding Fort Lee, Virginia, where owners of eighty-two of the ninety-four rental units said they would not rent to a Black service member.[22]

When McNamara gave that speech, his days as secretary of defense were already numbered; President Johnson announced McNamara's resignation only three weeks later. But McNamara's replacement, Clark Clifford, pressed forward. Following a 1968 Supreme Court decision that such housing discrimination was illegal, Clifford (who served for less than eleven months) forbade members of the US military to rent apartments or space in trailer courts where landlords discriminated by race, and he extended the threat of off-limits sanctions nationwide. On the first day of 1969, the Defense Department claimed striking progress, suggesting what concerted effort could accomplish. When McNamara began his push in mid-1967, only 22 percent of rental units near military bases were open to Black service personnel and their families. A year and a half later, 93 percent were open-occupancy. "While this is an impressive achievement," said Secretary of Defense Clifford, " . . . nothing short of 100 per cent success can be acceptable."[23]

While the most significant actions came from the Pentagon, at least some in the army were questioning priorities. Black soldiers were increasingly, and angrily, refusing to accept the sort of "constructive relationship" between commander and community that left them second-class citizens off-post. In late 1968, members of the army's advisory seminar on "racial tension" at the Command and General Staff College argued that "rejection" by civilian communities "embitter[ed]" Black soldiers, who then carried "hostility" into their military interactions. This group strongly recommended that the army put "more teeth" into AR 600-21 by allowing post commanders to impose off-limits sanctions. Here, Pentagon policy was the holdup, and that did not change until late 1970, when Frank Render's report on the "frustration and anger" among Black GIs in Germany forced its hand.[24]

As in the United States, Black soldiers in Germany faced discrimination off-post. That surprised many. In the years following World War II, the story told in churches and bars and at kitchen tables was that Black GIs had found acceptance in Europe, even in a nation that had killed millions in the name of racial "purity" and Aryan supremacy. As the United States defended democracy with a segregated army, those who meant to make a point emphasized, Black GIs had found more freedom in *Germany* than in the United States. There was "more friendship and equality" for Black GIs "in Berlin than in Birmingham or on Broadway," pronounced *Ebony* magazine in 1946, in a time when "democracy has more meaning on the Wilhelmstrasse than on Beale Street in Memphis."[25]

That freedom, in the form of a love affair between a Black GI and a white German woman, structured journalist William Gardner Smith's debut novel. Smith loosely based *Last of the Conquerors* on the eight months he spent— while still in his teens—as a clerk-typist in the US army of occupation in Berlin. "Here, in the land of hate," Smith's protagonist muses, looking out at a lakeside beach where Black GIs and their white German dates went unremarked, "I should find this one all-important phase of democracy." Says another: "I like this goddam country, you know that? It's the first place I was ever treated like a goddam man." Smith would go on to write significant novels of Black social protest, but in 1949 *Last of the Conquerors* became one of the first Signet paperbacks, complete with racy cover art. And it did not fade away with the US occupation; new editions were published in 1963, 1965, and 1973.[26]

Postwar Germany was not a model of racial tolerance—as Smith and others sometimes acknowledged—and most stories contrasting the two nations were more concerned with pointing out US failings than with rehabilitating the reputations of former Nazis. But in the aftermath of the war, with cities in ruins and people starving, the occupying army offered Germans—particularly German women—opportunity, whether as an immediate source of food and other scarce goods or, sometimes, for marriage and an escape to the United States. There was powerful prejudice against Black GIs; wartime German propaganda had used derogatory cartoonish images of American Blacks to illustrate the degradation and depravity of the United States. But white German women consorted with Black US soldiers, who found them-selves (or perhaps their dollars) welcome in spaces that would have been segregated back home. Like white GIs, Black GIs had the status that came with relative wealth and power.

That was no longer true in the late 1960s, and the situation for American GIs only grew more difficult. The German population was "highly affluent," NAACP officials were informed in a high-level briefing when they visited Germany in early 1970, and had "significant ill feeling" toward American GIs. German prosperity and the devaluation of the dollar, an "old-timer" who had worked for the army in Germany for a quarter century told a reporter in 1972, had undermined the status of the GI, Black and white alike. "It used to be when a GI went downtown, the dollar made him king," he said. That was no longer true. And *Ebony*, in early 1974, bemoaned the effect of this shift on the morale of the 30,000 Black service members serving in USAREUR. Germans, the author wrote, were now "well-heeled, sovereign, and far from being underdogs," and they no longer needed "black friends and American cigarettes."27

And in fundamental ways, German society made life more difficult for Black soldiers. Within the United States, even as widespread racial prejudice and the ghosts of legal segregation forced "degradation and humiliation" on service members who ventured—or lived—off-post, at least in the United States most knew how to read the landscape. And almost everywhere there were local Black communities for support, places they knew they could find housing, restaurants, bars, churches, and barbershops that were African American spaces. They might well encounter prejudice off-post, but they also knew how to avoid it.

That was not true in Germany. Bars tended to serve distinct clienteles —and woe to the one who violated the unwritten rules. But there were no local Black communities for support, no neighborhoods where Black GIs were assured of finding housing, even if in a segregated neighborhood or in substandard lodging. It was not only that housing in the cities and towns near American military bases was not "open"; it was that every encounter with a potential landlord offered the possibility of a humiliating rejection.

In Germany, as in the United States, housing discrimination demanded the attention of army leaders. The *New York Times* article that lent credence to Maj. Lavell Merritt's complaint paired the death of one son in Vietnam with a second son's struggle to find an apartment for his small army family in Frankfurt. A chatty letter from Margarita, the wife of twenty-three-year-old Private First Class Elvin Williams, had recounted the exchange: "If you were three-quarters white," the apartment's owner had told Williams, "I would give you the apartment." A follow-up in *Ebony* quoted a friend of the couple: they had run into "medieval superstition" on every attempt to find a place for themselves and their six-month-old daughter; at one place, they were turned away because German women believed that their babies would "be born colored" if a Negro lived in the same residence.[28] The Williams family was by no means alone. Black servicemen complained regularly about their difficulty in finding housing off-post.

By 1970, the seemingly omnipresent stories about racial conflict in West Germany had drawn the attention of the NAACP. Perhaps not surprisingly, the NAACP's fact-finding mission to West Germany in early 1971 focused on the sorts of issues that had long concerned the organization within the United States, and its representatives concluded that housing discrimination was "the most pervasive problem" that Black GIs faced in West Germany. More than anything else, the NAACP report argued, it was housing discrimination that "caused blacks to regard Germany as an unfriendly country and to wonder aloud why they should be stationed there." Not everyone welcomed that analysis. When *Pacific Stars and Stripes* ran "Negro GIs Rate Germany Hostile Nation—NAACP" that spring, rather than burying a rebuttal deep in the article it offered an adjacent piece: "Calls Bias Reports Magnified." Reports of racial discrimination by German landlords, said an army spokesperson in West Germany, were "grossly blown out of proportion."[29]

The NAACP, however, had purposely crafted a strong relationship with senior leaders in both the army and the Department of Defense, and Defense Secretary Melvin Laird required all services to report to him about how they planned to implement the NAACP's recommendations. The army deputy chief of staff for personnel, in turn, wrote directly to NAACP director Roy Wilkins, thanking him for the report and letting Wilkins know that he had implemented, at least "to some degree," twenty-three of the twenty-four recommendations that addressed issues under his command.[30]

Even as some army officials pushed back against the charges, others amplified them. Curtis Smothers, the extraordinarily confident twenty-seven-year-old captain who was at that point the sole Black judge in West Germany, believed current USAREUR leaders were not taking off-post housing discrimination seriously enough and demanded that the army convene a court of inquiry to investigate the issue. (Courts of inquiry deal with problems deemed too complex for the usual judicial procedures or with charges against very high-ranking officers.)[31]

Smothers had focused on housing discrimination for years; he was almost certainly the "young Negro officer" who in 1968 told *Ebony* magazine that the army's attempts to fight racial discrimination by maintaining lists of acceptable off-post housing were "a joke." For as little as ten marks, he said, German employees in army housing offices would refer white tenants to unapproved landlords "through the back door." The Pentagon was not happy with Smothers's demands, and he was summoned to DC. But a week's worth of talks there left the commanding general in West Germany taking early retirement and Smothers on his way to the position of deputy assistant secretary of defense for civil rights—although without the court of inquiry he had requested.[32]

Certainly some army commanders cared too little about off-post discrimination. Others may not have known how to intervene, for if off-post housing discrimination within the US was a difficult issue—and it was, as the heated response of congressional-segregationists-turned-states-rightists to the issue showed—it was a nightmare outside the nation's borders. US military troops were in foreign nations by invitation and were in most cases governed by "status of forces" agreements that specified the conditions under which US military personnel could operate, as well as their legal status in respect to that nation's laws. While the 1964 classified briefing expressed concern about the limits of command authority within the United States, it labeled the notion that commanders might intervene in "the social patterns or customs" of a host nation "highly improper" and essentially dismissed the prospect.[33] Germany was a particularly touchy case, critical to the US Cold War strategy. Everyone involved understood it was important that the US military not appear as an occupying force—most particularly since every German adult could remember the postwar US occupation, which had lasted until 1955.

When it came to off-post housing, the army faced a dilemma. If US military officers intervened in the domestic arrangements of a host nation, that was likely to spark government-level protest. At issue were international relations. But if racial tensions continued to grow, sparked at least in part by anger over housing discrimination, with violence spilling out of military bases into German streets, well, that too would have consequences. The United States was responsible for the conduct of its troops, and West Germany—even with the Soviets on its border—was not willing to tolerate a US race war in German territory.

The army's dilemma was complicated by its current condition. The US Army Europe was stripped bare by the war in Vietnam. Units lacked stable leadership. Most were dramatically understrength, without the equipment necessary for sustained training or a clear sense of mission. And young American GIs suffered the results of West Germany's continuing *Wirtschafts-wunder* (economic miracle). Germans had little need for their dollars, and where once American soldiers felt rich, now they barely managed to live "on the economy."[34]

USAREUR officials had a somewhat different take on the problem of housing than did Captain Smothers or the representatives from the NAACP or even the army spokesperson who called the issue "grossly blown out of proportion." They tended to point to German law, which defined discrimination as a crime only when committed by public authorities. According to German law, individuals could not be charged with discrimination unless they also attacked the "human dignity" of another by slandering or "viciously despising or defaming" that person. German courts had been specific on the question of housing: landlords could refuse to rent on any basis so long as they did not accompany their refusal with "slanderous" remarks. In other words, a landlord could repeatedly turn away Black GIs while accepting white GIs; unless he or she also said something along the lines of "I don't rent to dirty black people," that landlord could not be charged with discrimination.[35]

This law meant that USAREUR could not rely on German officials to police the choices made by German civilians. USAREUR also faced an intractable structural problem. On-post housing was almost uniformly dreadful, with dilapidated barracks and family housing that had long ago seen better days. Even so there was not sufficient housing on-post, and faced with too many demands the army gave preference to those of higher rank and with most time in service. Off-post housing was equally scarce, so GIs competed with Germans in a very tight market, even as Black GIs competed with white GIs. Army officials calculated that 25,000 married GIs lived "on the economy" in 1971, while the off-post "adequate housing inventory" was a mere 10,000 units.[36]

German landlords reasonably wanted to rent to people who could sign long-term leases, and all things considered, they opted for families with the fewest children and no pets. Landlords saw American service members as poor prospects because they often moved at short notice, sometimes after only two or three months in residence. "Turbulence," the army called it. And as one army report admitted, American tendencies to be "loud" and "to litter the premises" did not endear military tenants to German landlords. There were more than enough German applicants for available apartments, so landlords expected less-attractive tenants—military families—to pay a premium. The less tactful phrase was "rent-gouging." Low-ranking enlisted men with families might pay half their monthly salary for a stove-heated cold-water flat.[37]

The NAACP committee had offered a possible solution. In its scenario, the Pentagon would take over off-post housing in Germany, leasing tens of thousands of apartments from German landlords and then subletting them to married service members. German landlords would have no choice when it came to tenants, and so no individual landlord could discriminate on the basis of race, even if that discrimination appeared in the "subtle" form of requiring a longer lease than the soldier's tour or declining families with small children or pets. Perhaps not surprisingly, that proposal got no traction. But USAREUR did act, and more expeditiously with the arrival of the two Generals Davison, Michael S. and Frederic Ellis (with the predictable nicknames, "Salt" and "Pepper"). It beefed up its housing referral offices, replacing German staff with "minority" NCOs when possible to avoid the "back-door" bribery. It put more effort into investigating complaints. And travel orders now *required* personnel to work through housing offices, which listed the facilities declared "off-limits" because they discriminated against Black soldiers.[38]

Human nature continued to complicate the process. Plenty of GIs—particularly those with German wives—found work-arounds, rejecting army control over yet another portion of their lives. Most were confident that army bureaucrats would not spend the time and effort to track them down. Army-approved lists, likewise, had little power over German landlords. It is not like apartments would stand empty without US military tenants. And many landlords were happy not to rent to American GIs, no matter their color, race, or creed. Nonetheless, army leaders had publicly committed themselves to open housing, including a major campaign in the German media.[39] The difference in rental practices may have been marginal, but visible action mattered to many Black soldiers.

But not to all. African American soldiers in Germany were not a coherent group, any more than white soldiers were. The married soldiers living on the economy with wives and often children had different concerns than the single men in army barracks had, no matter the similarity in race or rank. And it was these young men, Black, white, and other, who caused the problems that most alarmed the army. Violence stemming from racial conflict was frequent, and common, but it took place in a broader context of low morale and high frustration.

As the often outrageous tabloid *Overseas Weekly* suggested in its usual over-the-top prose, plenty of American GIs in Germany existed in a state of general misery and boredom. One 1969 article described the "desolate, mountainous Army training center" at Graf as "the worst hell-hole in GI Europe" and Graf itself as a "cow town" whose "Sin Strip" was a "joke," its "gaudy neon oasis of cheap nightspots" always mobbed because there was nothing else to do, no other place to go. "Put a lot of lonely guys in a hell-hole like Graf," another article concluded, "and you're bound to have trouble."[40]

But the more measured *Baltimore Sun* found trouble elsewhere. Heidelberg is "a nice town," a journalist reported in 1972, but younger soldiers were bored and homesick, their misery compounded by the feeling that "they are not wanted." This journalist nonetheless judged soldiers in Heidelberg lucky compared with those stationed near Darmstadt, where streets were deserted by 10 p.m. except for "a few aging prostitutes." And then there was Geinhausen, a town of about 10,000 surrounded by 3,000 US troops. The options were grim. Even in larger and more cosmopolitan Stuttgart, however, soldiers frequented (in the words of "Salt" Davison) an "especially seamy center of bars, prostitution, and drug trafficking." Part of the problem was that, as a later newspaper article noted, most American soldiers stationed in West Germany experienced Germany as "a nation of taxi drivers, barkeepers and bar girls." Very few American soldiers spoke any German; too few made it past the "sin strips" that served American GIs. Germans, in turn, often let the behavior of the most unruly and undisciplined servicemen shape their attitudes toward American soldiers as a whole.[41]

John Kester, at this point deputy assistant secretary of the army for manpower, reported from Germany in the fall of 1970. "American soldiers," he wrote, "are probably less welcome in Germany now than they were a few years ago" because Germans, now prosperous, no longer needed anything from Americans. Kester described "a good deal of inhospitable treatment" toward American GIs, emphasizing that "where there is discrimination against Americans there usually is even more intense discrimination against blacks."[42]

Kester, attempting to tease out the roots of racial conflict in West Germany, saw part of the problem as structural: the market for "available girls" was as tight as the rental housing market. Many unmarried young soldiers wanted to meet young women—"nice girls," in particular. But as Kester noted, American soldiers were "no longer economically attractive in prosperous Germany," and many German women would have nothing to do with them.[43]

Once again, race mattered. "Where the girl market is tight for soldiers, it is especially tight for black soldiers," wrote Kester. Twenty-year-old Pvt. Melvin Turner's description of the "girl market" was more graphic. "If a Vilseck girl had the choice of going out with me or a duffle bag full of pig shit," he said, "she'd choose the pig shit every time." A member of the NAACP delegation, presumably with less direct experience, described the situation differently. Young German women, attorney Melvin Bolden wrote, "the larger percentage of whom approach the American dream of fair, sexy and voluptuous," have "from all indications . . . shown a distinct preference for the young, aggressive blacks."[44]

Despite their different takes on the situation, however, Kester and Bolden agreed that competition for women created racial conflict. "Whites who are likely to be understanding about most things," Kester noted, even as he refused to explore the "complex psychology operating" in this realm, may "feel their own interests threatened when there aren't nearly enough girls to go around and then the blacks capture some of them." Both Kester and Bolden urged military leaders to find ways to bring more Black American "girls" to Germany, even though (Kester again) the "quantitative impact is bound to be small."[45]

The issue, however, extended past the individual choices of German fräuleins. German businesses discriminated by race. Prostitutes, men complained to Kester, refused Black customers or charged them higher rates. In 1970, Kester explained, demonstrating the extent of his research, the going rate for Germans was 20 deutsche marks, compared to DM 40 for white GIs and DM 60 for Black. In US dollars that translated to $11.00 for whites and $16.50 for Blacks—equivalent to 8 and 12 percent of an army private's monthly salary. Such discrepancies heightened tension between Black and white GIs.[46]

Bars and clubs in GI districts tended to be segregated by race, in part because they had their origins in the segregated US army of occupation and in part because, by the late 1960s, African American soldiers wanted clubs meant for "brothers," places with a Black vibe. At the Flash-Inn, explained a writer for the *Overseas Weekly*, "soul is the passport for entrance and credentials are closely checked." But outside the seedy GI districts, German bars and clubs frequently turned Black Americans away. According to Kester, some alleged that white Americans were responsible for such actions, that white soldiers had pressured German barkeepers and owners of *Gasthauses* to embrace American racism. Kester, who—though strikingly young for all he had accomplished—was old enough to remember the Second World War, was not convinced. "I would be inclined," he wrote, "to give the Germans a good deal of credit for being prejudiced without any help." Whatever the source, however, the exclusions were real and widespread.[47]

German bars had a variety of ways to discourage Black customers. There was the "so sorry; we are all filled up" move, or a high cover charge that somehow did not apply to whites. Dress code might be invoked, even when white patrons were in equally casual attire. Some clubs became "members only" when Black GIs came to the door. And when the bar-the-door approach failed, there was the "leper treatment," making clear to Black patrons that they were unwelcome. And music. Plenty of German clubs played soul music in the late 1960s and the 1970s; it was widely popular. But a calculated switch to American country and western could quickly change the complexion of a club. If that failed, there were other options. "Nothing, Germans have discovered," *Ebony* noted in early 1974, "will send the brothers running for the exit faster than a few offerings of Country and Western except, perhaps, a 'live' violin and accordion rendition of the *Emperor Waltz*."[48]

*Ebony* played it for laughs, but such blatant discrimination left Black soldiers embittered and alienated. In Frankfurt, Maj. Gen. Frederic Davison made a point of testing clubs himself. Davison covered his short-cropped hair with an Afro wig, donned a turtleneck and corduroy jeans, topped it all off with granny glasses, and set out with a mixed-race group to the bars. The two white men were first in line; they were admitted without question. Davison, third, was stopped and asked for a membership card. Davison did not recount what happened to the "Spanish-speaking American" who followed him, but he used his personal experience to drive home the point when German officials protested that racial discrimination was uncommon.[49]

Davison's experience was confirmed by a group from the National Bar Association, a predominantly Black professional association for lawyers, that launched its own investigation on the conditions in West Germany. James W. Cobb, the president of the association and a DC attorney, reported that his group had been refused entrance to a club in Nuremberg—ironically, one that was playing mostly soul music—and told that police would be called if the men did not leave. This set of accomplished attorneys stood their ground and were eventually allowed in, but such intransigence was not really an option for young soldiers. Cobb emphasized the widespread racism he had found, most notably when the mayor of Bamberg told him that Black GIs were unwelcome because a Black man had raped the daughter of a former mayor. (Cobb—who was, like Kester, all too aware of recent history—informed the mayor that if men were to bear responsibility for the sins of their brothers, he should remember that "genocide was made popular by some of his German brothers.") This group saw itself as a corrective to the too-middle-of-the-road approach of the NAACP, but it found much less traction with army officials even as it got public play.[50]

One long-term American resident of Germany was outraged by the conclusions the group had drawn on its "whirlwind tour," and while her objections demonstrated the "subtle" racism that Black troops attempted to explain to the many military and civilian task forces that came to study "the problem of race" during America's Vietnam era, they at times transcended race and suggested how many perceived the issue. American soldiers in the Seventh Army, "Mrs. J. H." wrote, had been issued a code of conduct for behavior in restaurants and clubs that sounded like "orders a parent would give to a 12-year-old." German restaurants and clubs, she continued, "demand normal behavior," and barring "culprits is not discrimination at all." So far, so good. The manners of American youth needed work.[51]

But, she explained, "in regard to Negro GI's, some of the things [the National Bar Association] called discrimination are a universal rejection of bad manners." Influenced by "extremists" back in the United States, "these Negroes," instead of shaking hands, "go into a long 'dapping session' which averages about one minute: they snap their fingers, wave their hands; wiggle their hips and practically go into a dance." Worse yet, "they may be wearing polka-dotted suits, high red, black, and green boots; a tasseled little cap resting atop a full-blown Afro and a red shirt with the points of the collar reaching halfway to their waist."[52]

An elderly hotel porter in Stuttgart found American GIs wanting, in general. They came to the hotel bar "in rags, or in duty uniforms straight from maneuvers," he said, and they caused trouble when they were turned away. But race, nonetheless, made a difference. Reporting on the techniques German bars and clubs used to exclude Black service members, the author of a 1974 story in *Ebony* also described German bar owners' justifications: "They are tired of having their tables and other furniture carved into, their washroom walls smeared with filthy language and boisterous language used." A fifty-five-year-old master barber told the story's author, "We used to like black soldiers. But today they are so different." When "Pepper" Davison met with local bar owners, offering his own experience of discrimination as evidence, he also promised that he would make sure that Black soldiers "behave[d]" if they were let in.[53]

Army leaders' attempts to end racial discrimination in German bars, clubs, and restaurants more or less paralleled (with the exception of General Davison's Afro wig and granny glasses) their efforts to solve the problem of off-post housing. Here, too, German law was more impediment than asset. German law permitted a business to select the clientele that best enhanced its success. Laws against discrimination were limited in scope, and in this case they were further constrained. The "domestic authority" provision of German civil law, an army report on the racial climate in USAREUR lamented, allowed a business to exclude members of a group if, in the past, other members of that group had caused it difficulty or loss of income.[54]

German courts supported businesses that categorized Black US service members as such a group; in the winter of 1975, courts ruled against Stuttgart mayor Manfred Rommel, son of the World War II general, when he tried to close two bars for discriminating against Black service members. Nonetheless, army leaders—including both Generals Davison—persisted in their attempts to persuade local leaders and business owners to end discriminating by race, even turning to high-level German officials for support. It took the intervention of the Bundestag president to compel the mayor of Mainz to meet with Gen. Frederic Davison to discuss possible solutions to the problem.[55]

Finally, off-limits sanctions had no more effect on bars than on rental housing. Few German establishments relied on American dollars; quite a few saw benefit in keeping potentially disruptive service members off their premises. And because off-limits sanctions were imposed on a service-by-service basis, even the GI bars in seedy "sin strips" could lose soldiers and live off of airmen, or vice versa. And because so many GI bars self-segregated, the actions of German owners were less often the issue. It was the men themselves who took action, often violently, when the unofficial boundaries of race were transgressed.

That violence all too frequently spilled out into German streets, and while army commanders in West Germany emphasized their efforts to combat racial discrimination and improve "communication," the subtext of their efforts was the Cold War itself. US troops in West Germany were on the front line of potential Soviet invasion, but they were also dependent on the acquiescence of West Germany to their presence. That was the argument, at least. The German government was, in fact, not likely to expel American forces.

It had accepted them when US strategy essentially guaranteed the sacrifice of the German nation should the Soviets move through the Fulda Gap, and in the early 1970s German leaders were much more concerned about Sen. Mike Mansfield's repeated and increasingly successful efforts to force the withdrawal of US troops from Germany.[56]

US-German relations were also strained by negotiations over how the massive US military presence was funded. American negotiators argued that Germany was not contributing its fair share to NATO defense. German negotiators insisted that the US was attempting to force Germany to pay for the failed US war in Vietnam. Both the threats of troop withdrawal and the conflict over funding hit their height in 1971.[57] And in this context the turmoil and disruption resulting from the behavior of American troops—and, yes, race was central—threatened American interests in ways that went beyond the implicit risk to combat readiness posed by racially motivated fights in barracks and bars.

The problems of morale that undermined US forces in Vietnam were equally potent in Germany and took shape in a wave of violence and criminality. In February 1969, reported the *Overseas Weekly*, troops assembled for the Reforger I exercise made "this icy North Bavaria area the wild-and-wooly scene of one accidental death, one stabbing, many assaults, five robberies, three vehicle thefts, 10 weapons heists and various other miscellaneous headaches," including "a bloody brawl that flowed out into the street" from the "Soul" bar Flash-Inn, leaving "a tableau of chaos highlighted by a mound of broken glass." Bar districts became either Black or white, unofficial designations but violated at great risk. "As we drive past Bop City, a 'black' club on the outskirts of Baumholder," wrote the author of a 1971 *Rolling Stone* article, "the white sergeant with me says: 'I wouldn't go into that place even if I carried a submachine gun. No white would.'"[58]

Increasingly, German citizens were caught in the conflict. German newspapers began chronicling acts of violence against German civilians. In 1971, the mayor of the garrison city of Ludwigsburg, not far outside Stuttgart, demanded that all soldiers be confined to base at night after a series of violent assaults—four serious physical assaults, four rapes, and eight muggings— had been committed by US soldiers over the space of two months. The town of Neu-Ulm faced similar behavior with a similar reaction.[59]

The *Washington Post* series "Army in Anguish," published that summer, portrayed the US Army in Germany on the verge of collapse, succumbing to drug abuse and criminality and racial violence. The German press amplified that portrait; German officials demanded action. "The people of Nuremberg," wrote an elected official to the army supreme commander in Heidelberg, "have a right to the proper observance of security measures. It is disturbing to have to live in a city where soldiers threaten innocent citizens or brandish weapons often under the influence of drugs."[60]

When German journalists reported soldiers' misconduct, they often specifically pointed to Black soldiers. A report leaked from Gen. Michael Davison's first race relations conference showed Black soldiers as the primary source of crime. The numbers were alarming. Black soldiers, though only 14 percent of US troops in West Germany, were recorded as responsible for 80 percent of serious crimes. That percentage represented 2,984 cases of robbery, assault, and rape, as compared with the 740 similar crimes attributed to white soldiers. Even though Davison tried to play down those numbers, suggesting that crimes by white soldiers were more likely to go unreported and making clear that a single assault by a group of forty individuals counted as forty incidents, rather than as one, Germans drew a lesson. The German press published a litany of Black crime during the summer of 1972: In Neu-Ulm, in early July, eight Black soldiers kidnapped and serially raped a sixteen-year-old German girl. In Stuttgart, Black GIs verbally and physically attacked German pedestrians; in August, Black soldiers attacked a Stuttgart police station and then battled German police with knives and broken bottles for five hours. Women and girls were grabbed on the streets. The list went on.[61]

The point here is not that Black GIs behaved worse than did their white peers. It is likely true, as General Davison suggested, that white crime was less frequently reported than crimes committed by African Americans. It is also true that many Black GIs were angry, quick to join mass actions when they believed a "brother" was unjustly treated or to break up a bar in response to real or perceived insults. It also matters that Germans were not contending only with the internal violence that was spilling from army installations into German streets.

US service personnel committed a series of horrific crimes against German civilians during the early 1970s. Was the low point the army deserter, being brought back to his unit on the Alps Express, who stole a gun from one of his guards and in the course of his escape shot a German rail hostess and threw her body from the moving train? Or was it when fifteen soldiers gang-raped two young girls who had been camping by the Danube River? Or when three soldiers murdered and pulverized the bodies of two German teenagers in the case of a drug deal gone wrong and then kidnapped and raped a young German woman in an attempt to build an alibi?[62]

In the German press, however, *Black* criminality was omnipresent. "Are we now threatened with an escalation of violence by black U.S. soldiers?" asked a Stuttgart newspaper. "Robberies, stabbings, drug addiction, and pitched battles have inevitably given rise to the public perception of the 'criminal American black.'" "Our patience is exhausted," wrote one elected official. "Ami Go Home!" began to echo.[63]

Gen. Michael Davison arrived in Germany in mid-1971, in the midst of the growing public crisis. As he devoted himself to the problem of race within his command, he also looked beyond. He sought assistance from the ministers president of each of the *Länder*, or German states, that housed US army troops. He convinced Chancellor Willy Brandt to make a televised appeal for "tolerance and equal opportunity" from the German people. He persuaded defense minister Helmut Schmidt to make the same televised appeal three times over the course of 1972. He got the German press council to accept that "black sensitivities" matter and to recommend that its members stop referring to the "color" of US servicemen accused of crimes.[64]

But the situation in Germany was in many ways intractable. There were limits to what the US military could claim without presenting itself as an occupying army, acting in defiance of German law. And while German discrimination against Black soldiers exacerbated racial conflict within the army, threatening its combat readiness, the behavior of US military personnel in Germany undermined US-German relations, potentially threatening global security. A confidential memo to Davison from US general Lyman Lemnitzer, the Supreme Headquarters Allied Powers Europe commanding officer, asking that the fact he had discussed "highly sensitive matters" with Chancellor Schmidt be "held very closely," reported that Schmidt was concerned about "the extremely adverse effect that continued stream of press reports dealing with permissiveness, failure to follow orders, mutiny, 'fragging' of officer billets in Vietnam and other breaches of discipline in the US forces may have on the Bundeswehr." Lemnitzer had assured Schmidt that the reports were exaggerated. He made the case that while there *had* been such problems, tightened discipline would make a difference. "I am not sure he was convinced," noted Lemnitzer.[65]

Army leaders in West Germany did best in addressing those things under army control. By definition, German civilians fell outside that realm. Army leaders also did best when addressing clear demands and quantifiable problems. Housing discrimination was subject to policy and process, even when control was incomplete. Discrimination in bars and clubs was more complicated, but there were still mechanisms to employ. Off-post violence, on the

I wish people would quit telling me to be nice to the Vietnamese— —it's hard enough trying to get along with all the colored...

**DOES THE SHOE FIT?**
Understanding breeds understanding...

In Vietnam, Korea, and other Asian nations, US military race relations transcended Black and white. This leaflet, created in 1972 as part of a Military Assistance Command, Vietnam, effort to encourage American servicemen to respect and understand the Vietnamese people, attempted to use one form of prejudice to shed light on another. It was controversial at the time; the inspector general's office declared its use of "colored" to be "offensive and inept." *Courtesy US Army.*

other hand, defied their efforts. American MPs had no independent authority off-post; they could act only in support of German police. And army leaders were often confounded by the force of the rage they confronted. Some were willing to admit that (in Davison's words) the "violent conduct of these soldiers can be viewed as a manifestation of the bitterness and frustration of black soldiers over real or perceived injustices," but recognition was no solution. Efforts to address the issues under army control would make some difference, but high-profile off-post violence in West Germany would continue into the era of the all-volunteer force.[66]

USAREUR confronted one sort of problem; USARPAC—the US Army Pacific—another. In West Germany, off-post racial conflicts were between Blacks and whites, even as the whites were both American and German. In South Vietnam, Korea, and Okinawa, race relations were "tripartite," involving white Americans, Black Americans, and the local Asian population. Often, too, racial conflict was tripartite or triangular, as members of the three groups contested for status and negotiated alliances.

That was particularly true in Korea, where Korean "Augmentation" troops served in US uniform. In 1973, the 2nd Infantry Division was only 57 percent white—as opposed to the US army as a whole, which, at roughly 88 percent white (83.5 percent non-Hispanic white) was still more or less in keeping with the US population as a whole. An army analysis described Black soldiers treating Korean personnel with the same "garden variety of racial prejudice" they had experienced at the hands of whites; the report's Black author had himself witnessed two US Army privates supervising a Korean sergeant—in US uniform—as he dug a ditch. For the US Army, he concluded, Korean Augmentation troops were the "new 'niggers,'" treated as such by both Blacks and whites.[67]

But for those trying to manage "the problem of race" in Korea, off-post relations caused greater headaches. Off-post housing was not the issue. It was the *gi-ji-chon*, or camp towns, where trouble lay. From "Hooker Hill," the It'aewon district of bars and brothels surrounding the Yongsan Garrison in Seoul, to the northern village of Tongduchon, "squatting ugly in the mud" just beyond Camp Casey's gate, racial violence undermined the stability and efficacy of army units and threatened to compromise relations between the United States and South Korea.[68]

Korean camp towns had an ugly history. They had sprung up around US military installations in the early 1950s, seedy collections of bars and brothels dependent on the patronage of American GIs. Following South Korea's military coup d'état in 1961, they were redefined as "special districts" for US military personnel. Korean civilian patrons were banned; the massive prostitution industry was now essentially under state control and operating with the unwritten complicity of the US military command. This system worked to accomplish the Korean government's goal of separating American GIs from (most of) Korean society. It failed to accomplish the usual military justification for supervised prostitution: 57 percent of US troops in South Korea, according to a 1971 army study, had contracted venereal disease. The figure worldwide was 11 percent.[69]

The *gi-ji-chon* were built around the exploitation of Korean women. But they offered economic opportunity to others: a bar owner could clear $200 to $300 a night, but tailors, laundries, even candy shops also prospered. Relations between Koreans in the camp towns and their American customers were often tense. The GIs felt exploited. Bartenders and hostesses frequently contended with cultural insensitivity and arrogance. And violence was always a possibility—most commonly altercations among drunken GIs, but sometimes directed against the Korean workers. A 1964 UPI article, titled without irony "Building Good Will," noted that the Korean press did not "prominently report" assaults on Koreans, whether robbery, beatings, or rape, "except for the particularly bad cases." In general, run-of-the-mill "nastiness" and low-level violence were treated as part of the territory. American GIs were a dependable source of income for thousands of villagers, and camp towns served the goals of the state, keeping foreign military personnel—and the troubles they brought—contained and largely isolated.[70]

In Korea, as elsewhere, racial tensions within the army had become visible and disruptive by the end of the 1960s. An army enlisted man, writing in 1970 for *Pacific Stars and Stripes*, described evidence of racial hate. Lighter fluid tracing the shape of a cross ignited on the bunks of Black soldiers. Partially obscured graffiti on a 7th Infantry Division latrine wall: "I like niggers —everyone should own one." And outside the gate, racial segregation was nearly complete. There were places for whites and places for Blacks. There was some integration in bars that mainly served whites, but most believed it was dangerous for white soldiers to stray into Black areas, especially if on their own.[71]

Violence among US servicemen was increasing, and some of it spilled into the streets and bars surrounding the installation. But it was not just spillover. Black soldiers were angry at the Koreans who ran and worked in the camp towns. They claimed that camp town Koreans discriminated against them, that "black" bars were dilapidated and had poor-quality entertainment, that Korean women would not dance with them, that bar girls and prostitutes refused them. From all accounts, Korean bar workers did not resort to the equivalent of a "live" violin and accordion rendition of the *Emperor Waltz* to make their preferences clear.[72]

Army studies confirmed the charges of discrimination. Korean prejudice existed, manifested in attitudes about skin color and complexion, they concluded, but racial discrimination was primarily an attempt to maximize economic return. In the camp towns, bars catered to either whites or Blacks. So did bar girls, hostesses, and prostitutes. Women who made their living from American GIs mastered what an army report called the "mores" of either Blacks or whites, adopting the vocabulary, dress, and dancing style that appealed to those clients. But all was not equal. White soldiers spent more on drinks than Black soldiers did. White soldiers paid the asking price for company (commonly two dollars for "short time," or one hour, in urban areas), while Black soldiers tended to bargain. And the bottom line: there were many more white customers than Black customers. It was a rational economic decision for a bar or a bar girl to specialize in white GIs. Speaking of Blacks, one "business girl" told an interviewer, "He's a number 10 GI; won't even pay $2."[73]

Army commanders in Korea attempted to manage the racial tensions. They had received the same directives as those elsewhere and had implemented all the new policies and programs. They set up the new race relations training, had PXs restocked, created advisory councils that bypassed the chain of command. One such council persuaded club owners and managers from the Taegu (Daegu) community not only to "counsel" their employees on racial equality but also to approve—by vote—use of off-limits sanctions for clubs that continued to discriminate. The commander of Yongsan Garrison enlisted its psychological operations detachment to create materials for It'aewon clubs. Posters ("Don't Discriminate—Participate") accompanied training sessions on Black culture for club employees, and tape-recorded English lessons taught waitresses "carefully selected words like tolerance and equality."[74]

Whatever difference made was marginal. Women who had sex with foreign soldiers under state supervision were not likely to be moved by these "carefully selected words," and Black soldiers were increasingly alienated from the army and confident in their demands. By 1971, according to an army report on dissidence and racial unrest, some Black soldiers in Korea had begun wearing a "distinctive black uniform" when off duty. It was similar in style to the Vietnam jungle fatigue but in black and worn with a Black Panther–style black beret. "BRO" and the first letter of the soldier's last name replaced the name patch over the right breast pocket. The American flag on the left sleeve was replaced with a tricolor patch, the green, black, and red colors of the Black Liberation Front.[75]

Meanwhile, tensions continued to rise. In April, a Black soldier detonated a hand grenade simulator at the entrance to the Seven-Up Club in the village of Munsan, critically injuring a bar hostess. That same month a hundred Black soldiers stormed a bar that had shifted its focus from Black GIs to white; of the eight in the village, it was the only one that (in the words of *Stars and Stripes*) had "catered to the Negro." Eight white soldiers and ten Korean waitresses were injured.[76]

On July 10, 1971, things blew up in Anjong-ni, a village of about 2,000 located sixty miles south of Seoul. Shortly after 9 p.m. that night, a group of 50 Black soldiers from Camp Humphreys mounted the stage of one of the "plushest" bars on the GI "alley." They shouted at everyone to leave and then demolished the bar. They did the same to another, and another, and another, swinging broken beer bottles and bats, beating up Korean employees, targeting clubs they said discriminated against Blacks. By the time the Korean National Police and US Army MPs arrived, almost a thousand Korean villagers had joined the fray. Camp town residents pursued the soldiers and police to the gates of the base, carrying sickles and throwing rocks, and only when MPs fired tear gas (some reported bullets as well) did they disperse. The next day about 300 camp town residents demonstrated outside camp gates, carrying signs reading "We Don't Need Any Niggers" and "Go Back to Cotton Field."[77]

"Wronged by Whites and Taking It Out on Koreans," headlined the account offered by the leading national daily newspaper *Dong-a Ilbo*. The article described the origins of the riot for its Korean audience: Black soldiers gathered at the Blacks-only Star Club had become "agitated." "Our clubs do not even have a band when the white-only clubs have band music and strip shows," they had complained, according to the article's reconstruction of the event. "These days Koreans discriminate against us too, so we will teach them a lesson." The result was "havoc," reported *Dong-a Ilbo*, a clash between Black soldiers and a thousand stone-throwing locals, extensive property damage, and fifty injured Koreans, including one waiter stabbed with a knife.[78]

Three days later, the same paper argued that the local Koreans living near Camp Humphreys were the "real victims" of racial conflict within the US Army. "Black people are sad," said one Korean restaurant owner, "but the Koreans who live in camptowns are sadder." Representatives of the "Committee of Human Rights of Korea," a group formed in 1961 to manage relations between Koreans and the US military, met with the commander of Camp Humphreys to demand the offenders be punished and the Korean victims be reimbursed for their losses. They called the "riot" an "inhuman act which cannot go unnoticed."[79]

The commander of Camp Humphreys had put the entire town of An-jong-ni off-limits as soon as violence began. (Off-limits powers were already in use; a sign by the main gate signaled which of the town's twelve bars were "on-limits," marked with a black tag, or "off-limits," marked in yellow.)[80] His action had two consequences. It confined the men to base—in effect, if not intention, a punishment for all personnel. And it denied Korean businesses the only patrons they had. In Korea, unlike in Germany, off-limits status was a powerful tool. It gave commanders real economic leverage. But it also created immense frustration and anger among the Koreans whose livelihood depended on American GIs.

Korean coverage of the riot denied Korean responsibility: the fundamental problem was racial conflict between Black and white Americans; Blacks-only clubs had no band or show because Blacks spent "far less money on drinks" than whites; Korean sex workers discriminated only because they were caught in the conflict between white and Black soldiers; camp town bars had been forced to step up competition for white patrons, who spent more money than Black customers, because the US withdrawal of thousands of GIs from Korea left their businesses struggling. There was much truth in those claims. Revealing, however, were the words of the head of the local task force team. "Although our demands" for recompense for the "nigger riot" were "fair and from desperation," he told a reporter, "the U.S. military holds the advantage." As the off-limits policy continued into the fourth week, close to 500 Koreans, most of them prostitutes, began a sit-in outside the camp gates.[81] Off-limits powers did little to combat off-post discrimination when US-Korean tensions ran so high.

As in Germany, American military command in Korea sought the host government's assistance in the wake of racial violence. The riot at Anjong-ni got high-level attention, for Korean press coverage made the conflict difficult to ignore, and intervention from US military command and then from Washington moved camp town issues into the realm of international relations and national security. Relations between South Korea and the United States were uneasy in mid-1971, and as US military involvement in Asia declined under the Nixon Doctrine and South Korea worried about US commitment in the face of North Korean aggression, President Park Chung Hee—a former general who first took power in a military coup and who would declare martial law in his nation within a year's time—understood that the growing camp town tensions had broader consequences. The result was a Blue House committee focused on camp town problems.[82] (The Blue House is the executive office of the Republic of Korea.)

The "Clean Up" campaign that the Blue House committee launched did not focus on race relations, but it did work closely with the Ad Hoc Subcommittee on Civil Military Relations created by the US-Korea "Joint Committee." One of that subcommittee's seven "panels," which focused on "race relations and equality of treatment," recommended that local government authorities encourage club hostesses to dance and converse with all patrons and advise camp town bars to play a "balanced selection" of music. Encourage. Advise. Recommend. There were no teeth to these prescriptions. And no miracles resulted. In 1973, Black soldiers launched a seemingly coordinated series of attacks on camp town bars, with complaints very much like those voiced two years earlier in Anjong-ni.[83]

Off-post discrimination was one of the knottiest problems army leaders faced, whether in the United States or overseas. When Black soldiers were denied service in a restaurant or rejected by the landlord of a clearly vacant apartment, or—in a more problematic realm—charged more by a prostitute, those actions undermined the army's internal policies and programs and initiatives. But the lines between military authority and civilian control matter, even when the ends are just. And those lines carry even greater weight when US troops are stationed in other countries. As they confronted the problem of race, army leaders struggled to exert influence without crossing into the exercise of power. Despite a few landlords and realtors who experienced a change of heart in the steady pressure of commanders' "moral persuasion," it was pressure on their wallets that did the trick. Military off-limits authority, pushed by the Department of Defense, helped force open housing *within* the United States. On the domestic front, the army—when pushed—found the resolve and the tools to make a difference.

Army efforts to end off-post racial discrimination were less successful outside the United States, complicated not only by domestic issues in the host nation but by the demands of international relations and considerations of global security. Army leaders thought off-post discrimination responsible for much of the anger that fueled racial conflict in army units in West Germany and South Korea, but despite very different circumstances in the two nations, efforts to manage off-post race relations had little effect. The racial violence that spilled into the streets and erupted in the bars of those nations continued well into the 1970s.

There is, however, one significant sidebar. In mid-August 1971, the US ambassador to Korea forwarded to Gen. John Michaelis, commander of the US Army in Korea, a copy of a letter he had received through "informal" channels that day, with notice the US military would "be hit with it in official channels soon." Addressed to the president of the United States, the letter from members of the Congressional Black Caucus was written shortly after the violence at Anjong-ni. "We are deeply disturbed," it began, "with continuing racism practiced against minority servicemen stationed throughout the world."[84]

The Congressional Black Caucus made its support for Black service members clear. "When racism rears its ugly head in Germany or Korea," the authors insisted, "black Americans assigned to 'protect freedom' have every right to expect, and indeed demand, the vigorous intervention of our embassies." Given no evidence of such efforts, the caucus members wrote, they could not support appropriations for maintaining troops in nations "where the human dignity of black Soldiers has been violated." They cited precedent set by the House Foreign Affairs Committee, which had—four days after the Anjong-ni riots—blocked $50 million in military aid to South Korea until "Korean leaders deal effectively with the abuse of minority servicemen."[85]

When the Congressional Black Caucus launched its unofficial hearings on racism in the US military the following fall, it began in international territory: classified documents, sent anonymously to caucus members, showed that the United States had agreed to dramatically restrict the number of Black US service members deployed to Iceland. Caucus members suggested that similar "as yet undocumented" arrangements had been demanded by West Germany, Greece, and Turkey. Iceland's ambassador to the United States was so distressed he called Rep. Ron Dellums directly to assure him that Iceland did not practice racism. Caucus statements, however, demanded public response. Secretary of Defense Laird, in reply, declared unequivocally that any "informal agreements" limiting the number of Black servicemen assigned were "no longer in effect," that he was aware of none currently in existence, and that Washington would not agree to any such in the future.[86]

# 8 MILITARY JUSTICE

When civil rights leaders in the Department of Defense decided to film a sample race relations dialogue, a "tell-it-like-it-is discussion" between officers and enlisted men for possible use in race relations training, they focused on what many agreed was 1970's most pressing racial issue: military justice. The resulting film likely would have appalled any competent rap group facilitator, for officers completely dominated the conversation, holding forth at length, overwhelming the session moderator's attempts to turn attention to the enlisted men and women in the room. Nothing especially surprising there; the prerogatives of rank are ingrained, and it is an unusual colonel who would choose to defer to a private, especially in a recorded forum meant for wide circulation. But the officers' prominence was not solely their own doing. The training film was crafted by the Armed Forces Information Office from a longer discussion, and editors downplayed cross-rank dialogue in order to foreground the perspectives of Black and "Spanish-American" leaders.[1]

Whether or not it was by design, the resulting film brought two of the military's key "tools"—leadership and training—to bear on the problem of race and military justice. Army leaders found it useful; the film was the centerpiece of a session featuring Lt. Col. James White—the officer who had first briefed the army secretary and chief of staff—at the 1970 judge advocate general's conference.[2]

For all its rap group failings, the film never downplayed the significance of the problem. Even as editors created a conversation among officers, they used the provocative claim of a young Black sailor for the film's pre-introduction hook. "When a white man is dishing out the punishment," said Seaman

Knox, "I don't believe a black man will get a fair trial." That was the last heard from this sailor, who was edited out of the final dialogue.[3]

But within the film an army lawyer took up Knox's claim, and his words remain. "Knox," said Capt. Togo West, after verifying the sailor's name, "says that he doesn't believe that punishment administered by a white man can ever be fair to him . . . am I incorrect in my characterization? And I suppose that if I just wanted to press him on it, I might get out of him a statement that he doesn't believe that an institution like the army, the air force, navy, Marine Corps, white-administered, white-dominated, white-run—basically—could be fair to him in any [realm]." Captain West (Howard University graduate and future secretary of the army) treated military justice as a bellwether. If young Black enlisted men could not trust the system of military justice, they likely would not trust the institution as a whole.[4]

No one in the room where the race relations dialogue was being filmed felt it necessary to make the case that the military justice system played a key role in the problem of race. That was assumed. Participants in the mandatory army race relations seminars complained about Article 15s (nonjudicial punishment) almost as often as they complained about hair policy. Black soldiers filled prison cells in disproportionate numbers; that was indisputable, even if they did not actually make up the oft-cited 70 percent. And Black lawyers and judges were notoriously scarce. A Black GI who faced a court-martial, whether for murder or for disrespecting an officer, was likely to find himself the only Black person in the room.

Army leaders found little dependable data on race and military justice, as army regulations had prohibited identifying the race of those punished, imprisoned, or court-martialed. But many understood that perception was at least half the problem. The young soldiers who found themselves crosswise in a system they did not fully understand and certainly did not trust would not have been convinced by statistical data. They were more likely to trust their own experiences. They were more likely to rely on rumors, to give credence to stories of military *in*justice that circulated through the ranks.

And they were likely to see the problem in a broader context. The stories passed from brother to brother—about the soldier given an Article 15 for refusing to be called "boy," or the one who was court-martialed for refusing (a lawful order) to cut an Afro—were never just about military justice. Further complicating the problem, soldiers' suspicion of the military justice system was never just about race. By the late 1960s, soldiers—white, Black, brown —had begun to challenge the hierarchical, antidemocratic nature of military life. For many, the military justice system was the face of arbitrary authority.

Even as army leaders recognized that junior enlisted men had little faith in the system, Black ones least of all, they struggled over how best to approach that problem. The first challenge, as with off-post discrimination, was limits on army authority. The implementation of military justice was, of course, largely under army control. But the system itself fell under external authority. And external pressure was, in this difficult era, increasingly unrelenting.

It was Congress that had charge over the Uniform Code of Military Justice (UCMJ), and the legislative branch had passed a major revision to the code in 1968 (an even more extensive one was proposed in 1970). The Supreme Court, which under the leadership of Chief Justice Earl Warren was expanding protections of the accused in the civilian criminal justice system, also issued decisions constraining military authority. Lawyers from the American Civil Liberties Union defended individual soldiers, but the organization also pushed for broader recognition of constitutional rights, particularly when it came to protest and dissent.

In the public sphere, journalists chronicled cases ranging from the momentous trial of 1st Lt. William Calley for the massacre at My Lai to the acquittal of Specialist Emmett T. Doe, a twenty-six-year-old Black soldier from New York facing court-martial for "cursing," pointing out the peculiarities of the military justice system. The pseudo-witty truism that "military justice is to justice as military music is to music" served as the starting point not only for articles but for books—all of which provoked public discussion. And as Black soldiers complained of injustice, external groups took up the cause. The Congressional Black Caucus pushed President Nixon and Secretary of Defense Melvin Laird to address the racial failings of military justice. The NAACP made military justice a key, and public, focus of concern.[5]

Public attention and external pressure guaranteed action, in some form. And army race reformers sometimes benefited from that external force. Nonetheless, the interests and goals of external groups often did not mesh well with army logic, or with prevailing understandings of army needs.

In short, the military justice system did not parallel the civilian justice system. It would take volumes to detail the differences between the two, but in brief, the American military justice system and the system of civilian law had separate origins. Military justice developed as a means to maintain order. Commanders used it as a disciplinary tool, though "discipline," in a military context, was a positive concept ("discipline and order") as much as a punitive one. That rough, practical system had been significantly modified by the time Seaman Knox complained of white justice. But even as the military justice system had incorporated many of the protections of civilian law from World War I forward, particularly following World War II, significant differences between the two remained.[6]

Despite increased protections for the accused, commanders continued to exercise extraordinary authority in the military justice system during the Vietnam era. They could unilaterally impose nonjudicial punishment. They had authority to decide whether the accused was subject to pretrial confinement (there was no bail system). Those who convened the courts (in effect, initiating the charges) also selected the members of the court-martial panel, or jury. And when an institution was (in the words of Captain West) primarily "white-administered, white-dominated, white-run," such authority almost necessarily had racial implications.

As external organizations and institutions, including the Congressional Black Caucus and the NAACP, pushed the army to address the question of race and military justice, they tended to use the civilian system as a model. The results of their external pressure expanded the rights of service members even as those results laid bare the fundamental dilemma that political scientist Samuel Huntington had posed back in 1957: How to reconcile the existence of a military institution based on principles of hierarchy, order, and discipline within a liberal, democratic society?[7]

Army leaders were divided on the topic of military justice. Some saw the need for reform, most particularly when racial disparities were pointed out. But as the institution struggled through the last years of the war in Vietnam, contending with internal dissent and rising indiscipline, even some proto-reformers believed that "permissiveness" had created the crisis and that discipline was its only solution. In that context, they argued, it made no sense to give away commanders' best disciplinary tool just as it was more necessary than ever.

From early 1968, army records noted, "Disciplinary problems have been on the rise in the Army, with increased absenteeism, use of drugs, antiwar agitation, racial tensions, and resistance to discipline." In a move common to discussions of racial conflict, the report deferred responsibility, suggesting that "much of this rise has been a reflection of changing national attitudes and reflects social problems in the civilian society." And as in the case of racial conflict, it concluded that, no matter the problem's origins, "the threat to morale and discipline in the Army has been a matter of grave military concern."[8] It was a problem that had to be addressed.

Just as some leaders saw the military justice system as a partial solution to rising indiscipline and others saw it as a partial cause, the army bureaucracy used it as a measure. And the rising numbers of courts-martial and Article 15s alarmed observers. Court-martial rates rose from 38 per 1,000 in fiscal year 1968 to 50 per 1,000 in fiscal year 1969, an increase of almost 19,000 additional individual cases. Rates of nonjudicial punishment were even more striking. Roughly 301,000 enlisted men received Article 15s in FY 1969; 318,000 in FY 1970. In other words, army leaders used the authority granted them by the UCMJ to punish 196—and then 216—of every 1,000 members of the US Army. Nonjudicial punishment rates topped 20 percent.[9]

Seeking explanations, some senior officers looked to Project 100,000. Since the fall of 1966, recruits and inductees whose "mental test" scores would normally have disqualified them for military service had been channeled into the army. The program had its roots in a Kennedy administration task force but came to fruition when President Johnson took up the notion that the armed forces could function as part of his War on Poverty, providing remedial training, social uplift, and discipline to those who—due to the effects of poverty—failed to meet the standards for induction into the armed forces. To that end, in 1964, Secretary of Defense Robert McNamara proposed the Special Training and Enlistment Program (STEP). The debate over STEP was complicated by the release of *The Negro Family: The Case for National Action*, written by Johnson administration assistant secretary of labor Daniel P. Moynihan. Moynihan identified "the breakdown of the Negro family" as the source of problems ranging from delinquency to the bankrupting of cities and the threat of "political anarchy"; he proposed military service for young Black men as one way to combat the growing crisis.[10]

STEP failed in Congress, but the Johnson administration forged ahead. In 1966, McNamara announced the beginning of Project 100,000 (OHT), which, he argued, would admit low-scoring recruits and return them to civilian life with skills that could "reverse the downward spiral of human decay." But while STEP was proposed in a time of relative peace, Project 100,000 was implemented as the United States committed large numbers of ground troops to the war in Vietnam, and very much against the wishes of military leaders.[11]

It matters that the army was the branch allocated the vast majority of "New Standards" men—71 percent, compared to roughly 10 percent for each of the other services. There *was* a logic there. The army provided the majority of US ground troops in Vietnam. Because New Standards men were largely disqualified from technical training by their low Armed Forces Qualification Test (AFQT) scores, the majority were destined for the infantry. And the army needed the largest number of foot soldiers in this war.[12]

Most army leaders did not find that logic compelling. "The Army was directed to accept the lion's share of personnel under Project 100,000," noted the study on which Colonel White's briefings were based, with concern. "Over 95% of these personnel are in Mental Category IV or V," the lowest categories on a five-part bell curve. And while Project 100,000 drew attention, and provoked concern, statistics seemed to show that Category IV admissions reached well beyond that program. According to a handwritten army chart from 1969, "7.5% of Army content is Project OHT [100,000]"; "22% of Army content is CAT IV." By year's end, 1968, one in five army enlisted men fell into Category IV.[13]

The typical New Standards soldier was a white high school dropout with sixth-grade-level reading and math skills. Nonetheless, Black men *were* dramatically overrepresented in comparison with their percentage of the American population; by mid-1969 they made up 40 percent of New Standards troops. People within and without the military tended to assume that the majority of Project 100,000 men were Black, even as that was not true; SNCC leader Stokely Carmichael condemned the program as an attempt "to get rid of black people in the ghettos." But while Black men accounted for four of ten New Standards men, New Standards men made up three out of every five Black troops.[14]

"McNamara's Morons," some dubbed the OHT recruits, with the sort of cruelty that followed many New Standards men through their time in service. And in Vietnam, army officers linked such "low IQ" men to indiscipline, violence, and militancy. Reporting in September 1970 on rising militancy at Camp McDermott, Vietnam, one senior officer noted that "the participants in general have been low IQ." However, he continued, "some higher intelligence is evidenced by the correlation of local complaints with national racial issues, albeit a distorted association." The assumption here, one frequently voiced in such circumstances, was that less intellectually capable or sophisticated Black soldiers were manipulated by a few men with "higher intelligence." Wrote another officer, on a "potentially serious racial problem" in the 725th Maintenance Battalion, Vietnam, "Dealing with men in the lower A[rmed] F[orces] Q[ualification] T[est] score groups requires patience and compassion on the part of all leaders."[15]

Earlier that same year, as the commanding general of the Americal Division acknowledged that "they could be sitting on a powder keg," the I Corps leadership council (with members from all services) linked Project 100,000 to rising indiscipline and violence. In January, an air force officer told council members that the four men previously reported for a racial assault were enlisted under Project 100,000 and that an overview of racial problems in his unit "indicated that the majority of 'trouble makers'" were OHT men. Two months later, the group requested information on "individuals causing problems in relationship to project 100,000." Some saw the "Vietnamization" reduction in force as a way to get rid of such "troublemakers." Concluded an army task force in 1971: as the army ended its "major participation" in Vietnam, it should impose higher standards for enlistment or induction.[16]

Troublemakers. Militants. Dissent. Indiscipline. Assault. Mass Violence.

Some of the offenses committed, both in Vietnam and elsewhere, were minor. Others were not. Some men were punished for acts that were perfectly acceptable in civilian society—or, if not acceptable, certainly not deemed criminal. Some faced charges that were inherently subjective (what is "conduct befitting an officer and a gentleman," and where is that line crossed? What, exactly, constitutes "disrespect"?). Some soldiers went AWOL. Some smoked dope. Some used heroin. In Vietnam, men refused orders to advance into combat. Fraggings became common. And, as the commander of the MP brigade at Long Binh Jail had felt necessary to remind critics, there were also rapists and murderers and war criminals. "Psychotics," he said. "Sociopaths."[17]

A series of "Blue Bell" reports from the US Army Pacific in the spring of 1969 (preserved in a file on racial discrimination) give a sense for what commanders confronted. On Long Binh Post in March of that year, a "Negro EM assaulted . . . 4 Cau EM using an M16 rifle as a club." Investigation failed to identify the attacker, so no action was taken. On the same post later that spring, a "victim was beaten to death while sleeping in his barracks area." The perpetrators received general courts-martial and were sentenced to 12 months' confinement. At Cam Ranh Bay Army Base Camp, one enlisted man "became enraged" during an argument about a missing tape recorder and "fired approximately 14 rounds from an M14 rifle into a billet area," killing "one EM (Neg)" and wounding six more "(2 Neg and 4 Cau)." He received a general court-martial.[18]

In Korea, an EM fired on a group of Korean children who were following a hunting party; two received "pellet wounds." The soldier, who said that he had fired at a low-flying pheasant, was indicted in the local Korean courts. At Camp Wilson, Korea, a Korean female was "alleged to have been raped by 10 US soldiers," but as she "refused to sustain complaint," no action was taken. In Okinawa, among thirty-five reported disorders was an assault on two enlisted men by four other soldiers because the two had refused to give them twenty-five cents. Two of the attackers received an Article 15. And in Thailand, after an EM "made a remark" to a Thai female who was playing the jukebox, an "unknown number of LNs [local nationals] attacked 4 EM with unidentified weapons." Here, the action taken by the local commander was unknown.[19]

In all cases, the actions of commanders were critical. They, in keeping with the system of military justice, determined how to handle crimes within their units. They had a great deal of autonomy, even as reforms in the system began to circumscribe their authority. But their actions were also scrutinized, both within the army and beyond.

Faced with increasing levels of violence and the threat of open rebellion—some, but not all, of which was linked to race—young commanders struggled to make the right calls. They had been counseled on enlightened leadership and the changing nature of the troops they commanded, but they also knew it was necessary to maintain order and discipline. And within the army, failure to maintain order was usually laid at the feet of command. Thus, when the Office of the Inspector General investigated racial violence in an armored unit in Cu Chi, it blamed the chain of command for failing to impose adequate discipline. In the words of the assistant inspector general, commanders had "allowed a potential dangerous condition to progress without taking early affirmative action to prevent eruption of an incident."[20]

The situation was difficult, but all too familiar. In late 1968 a "troublemaker" (described in the report as "an avowed racist; a follower of Malcolm X; a zealous organizer and leader of a small group of Negro soldiers professing hatred for caucasians," and, for what it's worth, a cook) had been transferred from unit to unit as company commanders broke up troublesome groups and shifted their problem to someone else's doorstep. The fifth transfer in eleven months left Private First Class Gregory Laws in Company D, which was commanded by Capt. Marvin Reneau. Laws was charismatic and angry. He talked about the violence the white man had visited upon the Black race. And he drew a following. In March 1969 someone dropped a gas grenade near the troop billets; a note posted nearby—"Next Time Frags" —made clear it was no prank. Later investigation suggested the note was in Laws's handwriting, but no one was held responsible at the time. Conflict continued to escalate; "disciplinary problems were experienced that did not previously exist," according to Captain Reneau. The group who had coalesced around Laws, he said, had begun "challenging military control openly."

Reneau tried the new techniques of leadership. He counseled Laws, spending "many hours" listening to Laws's take on the superiority of the Black man and trying to convince him that everyone in Company D was treated as an individual, not as a member of a group. But Reneau, likely aware that the situation was about to blow up in his face, also told the investigator that he had met each of Laws's disciplinary challenges "with military control prevailing." Laws *had* received two Article 15s, one for disobeying a direct order and the other for leaving his weapon unsecured.

Counterintuitively, the IG investigation was due to Laws's complaint; there had been a second fragging—a fragmentation grenade, this time—in early April, and Laws had claimed that "white people are trying to kill the Blacks in my unit." The investigator disagreed, citing evidence that Laws himself had planned the fragging in order to create "a racial incident." Captain Reneau, meanwhile, had given up on Laws. He filed papers requesting that Laws be "removed from the Republic of Vietnam as soon as possible" on the grounds that he was "extremely dangerous (physically and otherwise)." And, up the chain of command, the battalion commander transferred Laws once again, thus immediately "eliminat[ing] the leadership of the Negro group" in Company D.

Despite the investigator's skeptical take on Laws's claims, he pointed to failings in the chain of command. When officers and NCOs failed to prevent this small group of Black enlisted men from "flagrantly" carrying weapons and ammunition "for what they called self-protection" within the base camp, the investigator concluded, when they took no action after Laws upended a table during the noon meal at the mess hall or when members of his group overturned the bunks of white soldiers in their billets, they had created the conditions for crisis. Laws and his followers had become "more bold" when they saw that they could get away with such behavior. Commanders, concluded the investigation, had not been decisive enough in their exercise of military authority.

Exercising the authority of military justice, however, was becoming increasingly difficult. In 1970, a highly public discussion of discipline and military justice offered a very different conclusion from the investigator's in Cu Chi. Writing in *Life* magazine, with its vast circulation, veteran war correspondent John Saar offered an almost offhand warrant: "Disciplinary action in the field is disastrous for morale—and ineffective, besides. Military justice has no answer to the grunt's ironic question: 'What can they do to me: send me to Vietnam?'"[21]

Saar's profile of a young (white) company commander and his troops was both sympathetic and cautionary. Even though Saar acknowledged the "alienated view" of a "tall, somber, soul brother," the tensions he traced did not center on race. He instead described a broader conflict between the "Army in evolution" and its leaders in ways that echoed L. Howard Bennett's concern that the division among generations was as significant as the division among races. "Old ideas of dress, behavior, discipline and rank no longer apply," wrote Saar. "Virtually no draftee wants to be fighting in Vietnam anyway, and in return for his reluctant participation he demands, and gets, personal freedoms that would have driven a MacArthur or a Patton apoplectic. . . . Alpha company seethes with problems, but it has not fallen into chaos." That, he claimed, was due to "a special kind of relationship, new in the Army, [that] exists between the 'grunts'—liberated, educated, aware young draftees—and their youthful commander, Captain Brian Utermahlen, West Point class of 1968."[22]

Utermahlen, in Saar's telling, had adapted to the new "permissiveness." "These guys are no longer blindly following puppets," the captain said. "They're thinkers and they want intelligent leadership. It's not a democracy, but they want to have a say. If I ran this company like an old-time tyrant, I'd have a bunch of rebels." Utermahlen's success was in forestalling rebellion; that was the uneasy undertone to the piece. "Resolutely opposed" to marijuana, Utermahlen realized that enforcing regulations would antagonize too many—and, according to Saar, "no commander as perceptive as Utermahlen cares to risk confrontations of that nature in Vietnam just now." Same for the regulations governing appearance. "It's one of the compromises I make," said Utermahlen. "As long as a man does his job, I don't care if he wears peace beads or symbols or if he shaves." And Utermahlen had reason to worry. He had anticipated a "vengeance grenade attack from his own men" earlier that year, and grunts still casually discussed fragging ("If you keep hassling people, tension builds and it has to bring a release," mused one EM, caring little who heard him).[23]

Assignment of a new first sergeant provoked a crisis in Alpha Company; the "big-bellied, 257-pound giant with a bikinied girl tattooed over 12 inches of forearm" had no patience for the evolving army—not for the piles of abandoned ammunition in the firebase, not for the ways the men disregarded Utermahlen's orders, not for the "loose talk about fragging." Two times the NCO drew his pistol to enforce orders; the second time the soldier who had refused to obey returned with an M16. No blood was spilled, but only because others intervened. Captain Utermahlen, in response, requested that the first sergeant be reassigned outside Vietnam.[24]

In Utermahlen's flexibility, Saar saw a positive future for the army—should the army be able to keep him and other young officers like him. But many army "lifers" would have seen neither flexibility nor enlightened leadership. They would have seen an officer afraid of his men. Wrote one such officer, following a series of fraggings in Vietnam that same year, "The positive impact of a hard-nosed commander is dramatic. Knowing that punishment is sure to come is one of the greatest deterrents available to prevent crime."[25]

I n this era of chaos and crisis, the relationship of military justice, race, and order and discipline was increasingly fraught. Two letters that reached the desks of senior leaders in late 1970 illustrate the emerging conflict. The first, written from Vietnam by a West Point graduate, then of field grade rank, was a testament to the frustration of officers attempting to command unwilling troops in a war that was winding down. "I am tired of troops that refuse orders to go to the field," this officer wrote his army superiors; "fed up with the Army's new judicial system that stacks the deck against the commander and adversely affects good order and discipline. I am tired of arrogant blacks who feel they can violate every regulation with impunity and do. Most of all, I am fed up with senior commanders who never question our reason for being, our mission, or the changing nature of [the] environment both socially and tactically. . . . A good infantryman should take delight in staying with the troops. But I have had it."[26]

This officer's primary concern was not the system of military justice. It was a failing war, the shortcomings of senior command, the impossibility of leading his men. "Arrogant blacks," of course, is telling. Perhaps his claim that African American troops under his command refused orders or defied the constraints of military life was accurate. It did happen, especially in units where leadership failed—or when an alternate leader emerged, preaching resistance to the white-dominated army. But even as this officer singled out Black troops, he was not concerned with the underlying "problem of race," not even as a means to improved morale. He was concerned with the breakdown of order, and he attributed growing indiscipline—at least in part—to constraints on commanders' use of the UCMJ.

The second letter, in the form of a memo on "Equity in Military Justice" addressed to Gen. William Westmoreland, put race at the center. In strikingly blunt language for a brigadier general addressing the chief of staff, the acting commander of Fort Carson itemized categories of concern and dictated Westmoreland's response (albeit cushioned by a "please"). The author, DeWitt Smith, was concerned about "discrimination in military justice" against members of minority groups, "especially blacks." These service members, General Smith noted, alleged that they were more likely to be charged with an offense than were whites; were more likely to be placed in pretrial confinement than were whites; were more likely to receive heavier punishment under Article 15, UCMJ, than were whites; and were more likely to receive harsher sentences in courts-martial than were whites.[27]

"These are serious grievances," he wrote. "Real or imagined, they cut away at a principal foundation of morale—equal justice before the law." Smith, initially, wanted better data. "Only when we have the facts in hand can we respond knowledgeably to the allegations," he insisted, before directing Westmoreland to "please have the staff develop and carry out a searching inquiry into the basic allegations cited . . . above," noting in addition that he wished to "be kept informed in this matter so that I, in turn, can inform the Racial Harmony Council" at Fort Carson.[28] In other words, a brigadier general acting commander held the army chief of staff directly accountable to a group of junior enlisted men.

As an aside: there is a backstory to General Smith's memo. Fort Carson, remember, suffered the fallout from Vietnam as intensely as any military installation in the continental United States. Maj. Gen. Bernard Rogers, its commandant, had done more than most to manage alienated Vietnam returnees and explosive racial tensions, creating the fort's Racial Harmony Council and relieving its members from other duties so they could devote themselves to council work. But it was Rogers's second-in-command, Gen. DeWitt Smith, who worked directly with the council. It was Smith who fostered open discussion, insisting that rank be left at the door; it was Smith who listened to complaints and to proposed solutions; and it was Smith who guaranteed "free passage" for Darnell Summers, the elected head of the council, as he conducted Racial Harmony Council "inspections" throughout Fort Carson. Summers, of course, was the Black activist army authorities had sent to Fort Carson following his release from civilian jail in Michigan. And there, against all odds, Summers found a mentor in General Smith.

Smith was a southerner in "demeanor and style," Summers wrote later, but he supported the Racial Harmony Council "without reservation," even when that support strained relationships and threatened his own professional trajectory. These words are not Summers mellowed with age; he re-

On the day that Specialist Darnell Summers completed his term of enlistment in the US Army, Brig. Gen. DeWitt C. Smith gave him this inscribed photograph. Summers returned to his hometown in Michigan to work with Vietnam Veterans Against the War. *Courtesy Darnell Summers.*

mains an activist well into his seventies. And through those years he kept a photograph given him by General Smith as he left Fort Carson and the US Army. It was inscribed, "To Darnell Summers, with respect and deep appreciation for your outstanding contributions to the Fort Carson Racial Harmony Council, with hope that we can continue to work for the brotherhood of man, and with all good wishes." The date: December 9, 1970. It was the following day that Smith penned his memo to the chief of staff.[29] Individual experiences and relationships matter, even in a massive institution.

At the national level, each of these letters—from the frustrated officer in Vietnam; from the acting commander of Fort Carson—joined an ongoing conversation. Each letter captured concerns that kept army leaders awake at night, destroyed careers, threatened the future of the institution itself.

These letters not only demonstrated the different priorities of two men; they epitomized two different ongoing strands of concern and responsibility. And while both men were concerned with failing morale and indiscipline, their solutions pulled in opposite directions. One, casting indiscipline as the result of permissiveness, saw military justice as a disciplinary tool. The other, casting indiscipline as the result of racial military *in*justice, hoped to reform the system.

Those strands were never fully separate. Concerns about race inevitably shadowed broader discussions of discipline and military justice; concerns about indiscipline shaded discussions of racial injustice. And inevitably, they met at the top. Westmoreland could not address those concerns separately, nor could the heads of major commands.

Army leaders had grown increasingly concerned about military justice at the cusp of the 1970s, in the downslope of the US war in Vietnam. That was primarily because they were worried about rising indiscipline and falling morale, about the struggles of junior officers to manage—not to mention lead—their men. But those concerns tangled with others, most particularly the problem of race, but also the mandated move to an all-volunteer force, looming on the horizon; Nixon's conduct of the war in Vietnam; growing anti-war protest and anti-military sentiment; attitudes of youth and the oft-heralded generation gap; and the nation's broader social crisis. They were also shaped by the US Congress's somewhat unorthodox decision to undertake a major reform of the military justice system in the middle of a major war.

It was almost certain that the US war in Vietnam would provoke military justice reform. As various observers pointed out at the time, whenever large numbers of Americans have been forced into uniform, subject to military authority and military disciplinary procedures, they have complained to anyone they thought might listen. During the major twentieth-century wars, they filled congressional mailboxes with stories of the particular injustices visited upon them; they wrote to the president, to the secretary of war or (later) to the secretary of defense.

Normally, however, reform followed the war; it did not happen simultaneously. After World War II, for example, Secretary of War Robert Patterson created a civilian board to investigate GI complaints and revise the system of courts-martial. Racial inequity played a role in the calls for reform; Rep. Adam Clayton Powell termed military courts-martial "America's great shame," and Black leaders heralded the commission to "democratize" military courts-martial as a step toward "rectify[ing] the gross miscarriage of justice" experienced particularly by Black soldiers during the war. In 1950, Congress—which holds constitutional authority to regulate the nation's military forces—enacted the Uniform Code of Military Justice. President Truman signed it the next day, calling it a "modern code" that advanced the "democratic ideal of equality before the law." (Previously, the army military justice system was governed by Articles of War.)[30]

The US war in Vietnam, in this case as in so many others, was a different story. Reform seemed urgent. That was in part because of the sheer volume of complaints, as an increasingly unpopular war demanded large numbers of increasingly unwilling draftees. Civilian pressure also contributed, as highly publicized courts-martial trials, whether for dissent or for war crimes, forced national attention to the intricacies and peculiarities of the military justice system. But reform had been in the works well before ground troops first landed in Da Nang. Influential senators, led by North Carolina's Sam Ervin, had been working to improve the procedural protections offered those in uniform since the early 1960s; their goal, by 1968, was to reconcile the system of military justice with new protections that Supreme Court decisions had written into civilian law.[31]

The 1968 military justice reforms were technical—as legal codes are —and thus often obscure to the men they governed. That soldiers did not always understand their legal options was a problem, and a continuing one. But overall, these reforms expanded the right of the accused to refuse to accept nonjudicial punishment. They required the army to provide free legal representation in a much broader range of circumstances. They replaced "law officers" with military judges and granted them greater legal authority. And they tried to cushion the military justice system from command influence—though not fully successfully.[32]

Congress envisioned greater protections and improved justice. The army's legal officers, on the ground, mainly saw new administrative challenges. In Vietnam, the staff judge advocate's office pulled together a conference on military justice in May 1969, less than two weeks after the act went into effect. Col. John Jay Douglass began this working conference with an exhortation to "think positive." But he did not mince words about the difficulties those military lawyers and judges faced. "I recognize the fact from a planning point of view that we don't know what to plan," he continued. "You say, 'Well, how many people are going to want defense counsel?' or 'How many judges are we going to use?' and so on and so forth." His answer? "I don't know, and nobody else does either."[33]

Everyone in that room recognized the fundamental issue. An already overstretched and understaffed division would be pushed harder. How would it provide the required military judges? How could it come up with enough military lawyers to provide counsel on request? (In Colonel Douglass's words:

"Where are we going to get the bodies?") A newly arrived officer noted that he had been in-country only fifteen days and had "never seen things come at me so fast"; in that time he had served on twelve general courts-martial in six widely separated locations and "marvel[ed]" that, facing such challenges, they had been "operating so good" so far. But institutional culture dictated the group's larger response. Said Douglass, "We've got to plan to prepare the kind of service that Congress and the Judge Advocate General intended and make it work." "Way-out" ideas, he noted twice, were more than welcome.[34]

Implementing major reforms in the midst of a war was no easy task, and the challenge was magnified when NCOs and company-level commanders saw the reforms as undermining their authority. An Army War College study of leadership confirmed the anecdotal complaints. Company grade officers and NCOs saw the new regulations governing military justice, and the JAG Corps that managed them, as a bureaucratic morass that kept them from effectively imposing order and discipline. Another contemporary report was blunter yet. These officer and NCOs, it concluded, overwhelmingly believed that the Uniform Code of Military Justice had "collapsed as an effective disciplinary tool."[35]

Neither study nor report, however, captures the sense of frustration felt by those in direct command. That frustration is much clearer in accounts from the field, such as the "Chronology of Racial Incidents" in C Troop, 1/10 Cavalry. Early (0545 hours) one Friday morning in November 1970, when the troop first sergeant in An Khe checked the troop billets to make sure all soldiers were up for reveille, he found three Black soldiers still in bed. He ordered them to get up. In response, he got a clear refusal to follow a legal order: "Get me up, Mother F——king Swine." The sergeant, in turn, "took hold of the man's bunk." At that point, all three soldiers attacked the NCO, wrestling him to the floor. "We were waiting for you, Mother F——king Swine," said a different soldier. The sergeant—who managed to get free of his attackers—reported the "incident" to both the squadron commander and the JAG office. But the judge advocate general concluded that, by taking hold of the man's bunk, the sergeant had instigated the fight. No action was taken to discipline the three soldiers who had refused his order.[36]

Tensions continued to rise. On January 22, the troop commander and first sergeant sent letters to the headquarters troop commander. The letters were witnessed, instructing that they be read in the case that "bodily harm" came to either of the two men. In his letter, the troop commander described threats made against him by five Black soldiers, all "black power advocates." "If any harm should come to him as a result of actions by the named individuals," the troop commander stated, "he would consider it a direct result of the wholly inadequate US Army legal system in Vietnam." Five days later, he was shot in the head by one of those five soldiers. "All you rabbits take a good look," said the soldier, standing over his commander's corpse. "That's what we are going to do to all you rabbits."[37]

Junior officers and NCOs appealed to Westmoreland in early 1971, as the chief of staff of the army sought out the concerns of small unit leaders. It was more and more difficult to maintain morale and discipline among their men, they told him, and "the administration of military justice at the small unit level has been a contributing factor in an apparent loosening of discipline." In response—and according to common army practice—Westmoreland created a task force. For the record, it is worth noting that DeWitt Smith's "Equity in Military Justice" memo had reached Westmoreland in the final month of the previous year. Perhaps it was not only junior officers who prompted Westmoreland's action.[38]

The group that would be known as the Matheson Committee, after its chair, Maj. Gen. S. H. Matheson, was assigned to interview a broad cross-section of small unit leaders in order to determine whether problems in the administration of military justice did, actually, undermine morale and discipline at the small unit level. Do "genuine defects exist," asked the charge given the group, or are "difficulties encountered . . . related to a lack of training, understanding, or leadership"?[39]

In its report, the Matheson Committee acknowledged the concerns of company grade officers. Article 15s required excessive paperwork. Military judges were too lenient. The requirements of pretrial confinement were too strict and kept company commanders from removing "troublemakers" from the ranks. But those acknowledgments were about as far as the committee's support went. Even as committee members recognized the "frustration" of junior commanders, they laid responsibility at their feet. The problem was not the system of military justice, their report concluded. The problem was leadership. And the solution? Education and training. Better training, they determined, would help junior leaders understand the fundamental concepts of military justice and their own role in its administration: "With understanding will come acceptance, which in turn will lead to a truly effective system of military justice."[40]

The committee declined to offer any detailed consideration of race, discipline, and military justice—a surprising decision, given how many disciplinary problems were deemed racially motivated. Even so, the report acknowledged that a significant minority of junior officers thought Black soldiers were most likely to cause disciplinary problems and that many (pre-sumably white) officers "seemed perplexed" that they could not convince Black soldiers that the military justice system was fair and impartial. Here, too, the committee pointed to education. Better leadership training, mem-bers claimed, would improve "the ability to establish empathy with subordi-nates and the knowledge of when to apply a given disciplinary technique."[41]

Perhaps the military justice committee was right to limit its consider-ation of race. Complaints by small unit leaders were not restricted to racial conflict. The officer who had recently written in frustration from Vietnam saw race as simply one variable in a larger disciplinary crisis. But in so many ways the committee's decision is perplexing. Army officers and NCOs were increasingly forced to contend with racial conflict, racial violence, and racial "militancy," particularly in West Germany. Moreover, the link between race and military justice was drawing the attention of external groups and agen-cies. Most significant, for the army, would be the NAACP.

There is a backstory here, as well. By 1968, the NAACP was in crisis. As the struggle for racial justice had splintered during the course of the 1960s, the traditionalist leadership of the NAACP seemed increasingly out of touch. Many of these older veterans of the civil rights movement rejected the mil-itancy of youth. These leaders saw the growing frustration at how little had changed despite the 1964 Civil Rights Act and significant decisions by the US Supreme Court as a repudiation of their years of hard work and careful strategy. Increasingly, the leadership of the NAACP was challenged by a group of "young Turks," and while executive director Roy Wilkins and the "tradi-tionalists" would prevail, there would be damage.[42]

The organization struggled through the assassinations and uprisings of 1968 with all-too-public internal dissent. In mid-October, Lewis M. Steel, a member of the NAACP legal staff, published "Nine Men in Black Who Think White" in the *New York Times Sunday Magazine*—the site guaranteeing it would be widely read. The title, referring to the US Supreme Court, came from the *Times* editors, but it may have understated the sentiments that ani-mated the piece. Steel, like so many who sought to make a difference in that era of division, had grown more and more frustrated and angry: at the courts, for what he saw as a fundamental conservatism; at the NAACP, hobbled by the traditionalists' narrow vision; at a nation suffused in racism, divided by social inequality, waging an unjust war half a world away.[43]

But if Steel (who was white and a semi-alienated heir to a portion of the Warner Bros. Hollywood-derived fortune) was both young enough and "sufficiently full of [him]self" enough to think his *New York Times* broadside might "pierce the thick hide of the Supreme Court's intransigence," he was not alone. NAACP general counsel Robert L. Carter read his drafts and encouraged him; Carter ordered thousands of copies of the article to distribute, intent on showing that the NAACP legal staff transcended what many saw as Roy Wilkins's accommodationist stance.[44]

Steel's piece was published on a Sunday. The next day, the NAACP board fired him. The board called the article "an indefensible rejection of much of the association's major effort over the last 60 years and the commitment and sacrifice of countless individuals to that effort." Bob Carter was furious. He issued two successive ultimatums to the board, demanding Steel's immediate reinstatement. Both failed. So Carter, the remaining six attorneys, and the seven-member clerical staff acted on the ultimatum. All resigned from their positions.[45]

The former legal staff continued to show up for a while, unpaid and unacknowledged, preparing the hundred or so pending legal suits for others to take over. And while Wilkins's victory confirmed that the NAACP would remain the moderate voice in a sea of growing militancy, it also left the organization less relevant to the struggles of the day. As a local branch condemned the entire affair, calling for a "total purge" of the national board, it argued that Black college students saw the NAACP as "behind the times."[46]

It took months for the NAACP board to replace Carter. The position of general counsel was hugely significant, largely because the NAACP had chosen to pursue its fight for justice primarily through the courts. And Carter had been at its center. He had argued or co-argued—and won—twenty-five of twenty-six of the NAACP cases heard by the Supreme Court.[47]

In October 1969, Carter's replacement was announced. The NAACP's new general counsel, Nathaniel Jones, had served on the President's Commission on Civil Disorders (the Kerner Commission) as a deputy general counsel and spent five years as an assistant US attorney in Ohio's northern district. But perhaps it was equally important that he made it abundantly clear he was in Wilkins's camp. Decisions of the US Supreme Court, he emphasized on the occasion of his appointment, had been "meaningful in unshackling the minds and hearts of black people" and had created the "underpinnings for mounting massive assaults on the bastions of segregation." And though the races were growing more polarized, he said, the NAACP "is the organization that can provide the bridge that can keep the two societies together and prevent a split."[48]

The equally difficult division within the NAACP went unmentioned. Shortly before Jones's appointment, however, the *New York Times Sunday*

*Magazine* had anatomized the precarious hold the venerable civil rights institution had on the ongoing movement for racial justice in a long, not-fully-sympathetic article titled "There Is No Rest for Roy Wilkins."[49]

Jones's task was to rebuild the NAACP's legal division, but it was also to keep the institution visible, to make certain it stayed at the center of the civil rights movement even as younger and more radical actors dismissed it as a "de facto arm of a white-oriented federal government." As the NAACP moved forward under Jones's leadership, that relevance would come from the group's focus on the US military. In early June 1970, the NAACP's deputy executive director had pushed Jones in that direction, making clear that action was urgent not only because of the growing number of complaints the association received from Black troops but because the NAACP needed to claim its place. Perhaps, the deputy director wrote, Jones could try to get the secretary of defense to call a meeting with the NAACP and the service secretaries to discuss the racial problems in the military? And he should not delay. "*Other* organizations," he wrote, "are thinking in the same voice."[50]

In January 1971—the month after those two letters offering opposing takes on the problem of military justice reached the desk of top army leadership—Jones led an NAACP mission to West Germany. Army commanders made themselves and their enlisted troops available, and the NAACP delegation traveled to fifteen military bases throughout the country, covering territory from Berlin to Munich to Mannheim. Jones explained, in each meeting, that the organization had decided to send this small group to Germany because the NAACP had been flooded with requests for help from US service personnel stationed there.[51]

Jones's initial briefing—by Capt. Curtis Smothers—covered many topics, from the failures of leadership to the crisis of off-post housing. But both men were lawyers, and they shared a concern about military justice. Signaling that concern, the NAACP delegation was lawyer-heavy, comprising two members of its legal staff and its head of veterans' and servicemen's affairs (and yes, it specified the "man").[52]

Briefing Jones, Smothers (perhaps surprisingly) emphasized the strengths of the military justice system. "The average GI," he told Jones, "whether black or white gets a hell of a lot more due process than we get in civilian courts, and if you attack them [the military justice system] on that basis you are going to get smeared. You won't make it." The problem, Smothers argued—as would others—was not process. The problem lay in the initial, low-level decisions that junior officers and NCOs made about the men under their authority. Junior officers and NCOs were the ones who initially decided how to handle infractions, and they had a great deal of latitude in those decisions. But once in the system, Smothers insisted, Black soldiers needed better support. Any real change would require people there, on the ground, he told Jones, estimating that it would take two practicing lawyers, two investigators, and a full-time agitator to make a significant difference.[53]

Smothers repeatedly emphasized that the NAACP could do what was necessary "within the existing framework," so long as the group sent people who would "dig in and do the job," not "scholars with their heads in the sky" or those who saw a tour in Europe as just that—tourists in lawyers' clothing, more interested in seeing the sights than in the hard work required. "When you get back there," Smothers told Jones, "you tell them brothers there are 25,000 to 30,000 blacks in Europe. 58 percent of the people confined are blacks. These cats need some help. And I'm not talking about getting your expressions of sympathy, I'm not talking about getting some time on television, I'm talking about being here in direct force." Smothers's passion was persuasive, but Jones was cautious. The NAACP delegation "came over here with our minds pretty open," Jones said, but that "involves a lot of money."[54]

Once home, Jones wasted no time in drawing attention to his trip, and he headlined the problem of military justice. Black soldiers had complained bitterly about "double standards" in military justice, he told reporters, and their "mood was very tense." It made sense that Jones would invoke his "lengthy 'eyeball to eyeball'" sessions with enlisted men in his press conference, for the NAACP delegation repeatedly emphasized that members had gone to Germany in response to pleas for help from Black men in uniform. Nonetheless, it was Smothers's voice that echoed loudest. Jones made no grand calls for change in the system. Instead, he criticized its implementation, often by "frightened" and "inexperienced" commanders.[55]

And, pending release of the delegation's report, Jones offered recommendations for action. Black service members, he claimed, were not receiving the full protection guaranteed by the UCMJ, for, though white military lawyers were available, Black personnel did not trust them, did not have confidence in them, were not able to speak freely to them. White military lawyers saw the same problem; more than a hundred white attorneys, Jones said, had told him of their feelings "of utter frustration in getting Black clients to confide in them."[56]

Jones's solution? Civilian Black lawyers should be sent to West Germany and made available to Black troops. Jones was echoing Smothers's proposal, though with numbers far greater than Smothers had dreamed. After all, Smothers understood how expensive those civilian lawyers would be, how much he was asking. But Jones had an ingenious solution. Because it was the government's duty to provide proper legal counsel to all those governed by the UCMJ, those civilian Black lawyers should be subsidized by the US government.[57] The government would not take him up on the offer.

Following Jones's February press conference, the NAACP would slip into the background as delegation members completed their final report, which they would title "The Search for Military Justice." Meanwhile, on the ground, army leaders continued to struggle with the problem of race.

The report that Westmoreland had commissioned—the one on "the effectiveness of the administration of military justice"—began to bear fruit, and that summer military justice training got a second look. The drill sergeant academy doubled its attention to questions of military justice. Leaders began to "resource" the training of squad and platoon leaders "in terms of what are possible and what are forbidden actions for leaders under UCMJ." None of the documentation mentioned race; after all, this report grew from concern about discipline rather than concern about race. But if Smothers was right and the racial problem lay in implementation, and most particularly at the company level and below, even race-blind training should make a difference.[58]

Half a world away in Vietnam, legal reform was underway. Most changes, given complaints about overwhelming workloads, had to do with improved efficiency. But there, too, officers put faith in education, setting up monthly conferences for special court-martial judges in the hope that such "continuing dialogue" might "impart dynamism and progressiveness to the administration of criminal justice." (Special courts-martial fall between the less-serious summary court-martial and the general court-martial, which is equivalent to a trial for a civilian felony.)[59]

At their first meeting that February at Long Binh, the eight judges present discussed sentencing philosophies and the varying weight they assigned to punishment, deterrence, and rehabilitation, with one judge offering the wisdom of "the late Lebanese poet, Kahlil Gibran," as guidance. As the judges considered hypothetical cases at their monthly meetings, seeking greater uniformity in sentencing, race remained unspoken: according to regulations, the race of the accused could not be identified. Age, education, marital status, army efficiency ratings, awards: all could be taken into consideration. Just not race. The judiciary was aware of the problem, of course, and mandated that special court-martial judges attend "so called 'rap sessions'" led by human resources personnel—though again, written records did not acknowledge that the subject of such rap sessions was race.[60]

*Military Justice*

Even as leaders in Vietnam tiptoed around the problem, it was in West Germany—as so often—that they confronted it directly. Contingency played a role. No one had intended Captain Smothers to focus so unrelentingly on racial injustice when he was assigned to USAREUR's legal system in 1968, but there he was. And the mess created as the US war in Vietnam undermined the once-proud Seventh Army was never by design. But as stories of racial discrimination in West Germany created poor press for the army back in the United States, prompting investigations and delegations, and as racial unrest undermined the army's Cold War mission and threatened United States–West Germany relations, top army leaders insisted that the problem must be managed.

Even before racial violence exploded in USAREUR, however, the Department of Defense was trying to figure out how well its equal opportunity policies were being implemented overseas. In May 1968, a DoD team had begun a tour of US installations in Europe, with a subsequent tour of the "Far East" planned for the fall. The group's leader, Jack Moskowitz, was the third person to fill the slot of deputy assistant secretary of defense for civil rights since McNamara had created it in 1963; L. Howard Bennett was, in effect, his assistant.

Following three weeks of meetings, Moskowitz declared himself pleased by what he had found. "The Army is now the most integrated section of American life," he told reporters, though he did offer a small caveat: "That doesn't mean that we have reached the ultimate solution. People still call each other names." The European *Stars and Stripes*, in turn, reported that "the racial problems which worried the Department of Defense in 1964 have been solved."[61]

Once back in DC, Moskowitz continued to praise the military's "excellent job," though he noted two common complaints. The first, that there was not enough "soul (Negro) entertainment," he saw as good news. "Years ago," he said, "there was real discrimination, and people had more important things to complain about than the type of entertainment they had at clubs." The second complaint, that Black GIs were more likely to get Article 15s than whites, got a bit more credence. "I don't know if there is really any disparity in punishment," Moskowitz told reporters, "but I passed this information on to the appropriate commands."[62]

Capt. Curtis Smothers arrived at the USAREUR judge advocate's office just about the same time as the DoD delegation swept through. The twenty-four-year-old graduate of Georgetown Law had little patience for what he saw as an official "smoke screen," though he seemed most perturbed by

Moskowitz's recommendation that the army include race on its "punishment form." Smothers thought that identifying the accused by race was a gift to a "bigoted commander," though other proponents of racial justice made exactly the opposite case. On the advice of a colonel in the JAG office, Smothers decided to try to dispel the smoke. He contacted the Department of the Army, in DC, and proposed an investigation to answer Moskowitz's question: Was there disparity by race?[63]

That investigation suggested that Black soldiers' complaints were justified. The JAG office determined that Black soldiers received a quarter of nonjudicial punishments, even though they made up less than 12 percent of the command. And investigators did not stop with that headline. They did background checks on 1,400 of those who had gotten Article 15s in the past year, comparing variables, trying to figure out whether there was some predictive constant other than race. Education? Marital status? Rural versus urban origin? Draftee versus volunteer? Intelligence level? Criminal history? (The group's statistician suggested a different variable: one group had more "slackers" than the other. He was replaced.) According to these background checks, Black soldiers who received Article 15s had, on average, more education than whites; white soldiers who received Article 15s scored—on average —about ten points higher on the "mental" exams than Blacks. But, according to Smothers, nothing really panned out. Smothers was certain that the key variable was race.[64]

The commanding general of USAREUR was not thrilled with the investigation's conclusions, but the report went forward to the Department of the Army, which eventually—in Smothers's telling—deemed it a "super duper job" and circulated the results to every staff judge advocate in the army. But the judge advocate general contextualized those results in the army's developing narrative of "the problem of race." Many soldiers, he explained in his accompanying memo, *believed* that commanders discriminated on the basis of race, even though such complaints "were for the most part unfounded." This "erroneous impression" was mostly due to a "failure of communication," one best addressed by improved leadership tactics.[65]

By the time Nathaniel Jones arrived in West Germany in early 1971, military justice reform was well underway. As one JAG officer explained to Jones (in great detail), the office reviewed nonjudicial punishments every month. JAG officers compiled a list of every Article 15 in West Germany, pulled the personnel files of every single soldier who had been punished, combed through those files for context—noting ten to fifteen different factors, from number of siblings to where the soldier had trained—and then compared cases, looking for patterns, for anything that might give the appearance of discrimination. Discipline remained a command prerogative, but monthly reviews offered commanding generals information on which to act.[66]

But actors continued to disagree about the primary purpose of military justice. Most army officers saw military justice as a means to maintain order, even as many believed that only a fair and impartial system could do so. Critics believe that military injustice created disorder and saw racial disparities as evidence of such injustice. When Jones asked whether the review system had reduced the number of Article 15s, army officers were at a loss. "Articles 15's are on the increase, if anything," one replied, clearly thinking of the rising chaos in the ranks. If leaders were to emphasize "making a soldier a soldier," he explained to Jones, "we have got to use disciplinary powers." And Article 15s in his unit, he concluded, with something resembling pride, "have almost come one-third higher since I have been here."[67]

Different assumptions also shaped the solutions proposed. Jones, in a meeting with G-1 (Personnel), asked whether units had complied with instructions to post all Article 15s on unit bulletin boards. "Off and on," said one officer. "Rather haphazardly." But Gen. Harris W. Hollis, the director of personnel, wanted to make a different point. "I must be constrained here, again," said Hollis, "to give you a sense of the soldier." "Curt," he said, had also asked him about compliance. But Curt, Captain Smothers, "has always been a lawyer." And while "there is nothing wrong with lawyers," Hollis said, Smothers "has never been a company commander and understood the sense of the soldier in his almost total aversion to coming close to that bulletin board."[68]

Only a lawyer, went the subtext, would think to combat the EM rumor mill by posting information on a unit bulletin board. Another officer offered his own "sense of the soldier" in the form of a caution. The protections offered by the military justice system were "pretty good," he said, but "in the real world, a 17 year old kid—a 10th grade drop-out"—was not going to be able to negotiate its complexities and was not likely, when faced with an Article 15, to insist that he was entitled to defense counsel.[69]

When Gen. Michael S. Davison arrived in Germany that June, replacing the early-retired Gen. James S. Polk, he understood that he was meant to solve the conjoined problem of indiscipline and race. He tended toward the "race" side of the equation, quickly focusing on the varied forms of discrimination that plagued Black soldiers, intent on making those under his command understand the broader problem and implement the solutions offered. But he may not have expected a crisis quite so soon. In mid-July, what the army's top lawyer in Europe characterized as "a mess hall rhubarb on a Sunday afternoon" created what US journalists termed a cause célèbre, with twenty-nine Black soldiers facing court-martial for willful disobedience of a lawful order.

Publicly, army spokespeople suggested that it was impossible to establish precisely what happened that day. Between army documents and press accounts, however, it is clear that the Sunday afternoon brawl was rooted in ongoing racial conflict and the leadership problems that plagued the Seventh Army. The battalion's previous commander (who, according to newspaper accounts, had kept racial tensions down by "rapping" with Black soldiers) had recently been relieved of command.[70]

The new commander, Lt. Col. David Partin of Troy, Alabama, had been charged with restoring discipline to the battalion; by that Sunday, Partin had been in command for only three weeks. And things were bad. White soldiers were being randomly attacked under cover of darkness. Black soldiers had taken to carrying intimidating "soul sticks" on base, cutting to the front of the mess hall line, blatantly ignoring regulations. A group of white and Hispanic soldiers told a journalist that they blamed "callow officers and NCOs who refuse to assert themselves in the interest of order and discipline" and an "Army establishment where, today, an accusation of racial bias can soil an otherwise spotless record of dedication and devotion." And the battalion's Black soldiers? Like most others stationed in Germany, they pointed—with justification—to widespread racial discrimination, both on- and off-base.[71]

On Sunday, July 18, a group of white soldiers had been hanging out, drinking beer and playing country music on a cassette tape recorder. A few beers in, some of them—"allegedly mimicking the blacks"—got sticks and canes and went into the mess hall to eat. They pulled together tables near the jukebox, in the area usually claimed by Black EMs, turned their music up loud, gave each other "power checks," and made a lot of noise. A Black soldier asked them to turn the music down. They did not. A few minutes later, a group of Black soldiers approached the table where the white soldiers were sitting. A fight broke out. Specialist Lareon Dixon, one of the Black soldiers, was taken into custody, charged with inciting the brawl.[72]

The next day, fifty-three soldiers (forty-nine African American, four white) gathered to protest his arrest. Colonel Partin ordered them to disperse. They did not. All fifty-three were then given Article 15s—though, as was their right, twenty-nine refused to accept the nonjudicial punishment, demanding a trial instead. Meanwhile, Dixon was released for lack of evidence and a white soldier was arrested, charged, and convicted.[73]

The pending trials of the "Darmstadt 29" drew international attention, fitting neatly into ongoing stories of army malfeasance and racial discrimination and the ever-worse news from Vietnam. Tensions escalated as an African American activist from Chicago, seemingly in Germany on her own to investigate another case of alleged military injustice, called in the big guns. Mary Richardson, a twenty-six-year-old woman from Philadelphia whom a *Los Angeles Times* reporter characterized (in language that says much about the era) as "a huge woman whose forensic abilities rival her girth," contacted lawyers from the NAACP and the ACLU.[74]

Trials of the Darmstadt 29 were repeatedly delayed as the accused found, rejected, and renegotiated counsel. But on the eve of the trials' beginning, as the NAACP's Melvin Bolden and the ACLU's Melvin Wulf arrived to join the existing five-lawyer team, General Davison dismissed all charges. The ACLU claimed credit. So did the NAACP. Journalists said that the army was just trying to avoid more publicity. But Davison insisted he had simply taken all relevant factors into account.[75]

Davison meant to defuse unnecessary tension. The NAACP and the ACLU meant to show that they had forced the army to back down, to demonstrate their power and their relevance. Journalists wove the story into a broader narrative, whether it was the *Chicago Defender*'s tale of ongoing racism or the *Los Angeles Times*' story of commanders scared of their men. Congress, of course, had a say. The incident at Darmstadt would play a role in the Congressional Black Caucus's hearings on racial discrimination in the military. And members of the House Armed Services Committee questioned Davison's decision on a whole range of grounds.

In a congressional hearing, several lectured USAREUR's judge advocate, Gen. Wilton B. Persons, on the army's poor management of the press. World War II veterans on the committee rose in defense of traditional leadership. The commander of that Darmstadt battalion, said one, "must have a cast iron constitution to be overruled [by Davison] when he gave a direct order." And Representative W. C. (Dan) Daniel, the subcommittee chair, framed the entire discussion as a hearing on discipline and the problem of permissiveness.[76]

"The Army cannot function as an effective unit of the Military Establishment," Daniel said, "on the theory that when an organized minority, and I am talking about whites, blacks, and all other colors, want something, all it has to do is start a fracas or riot, burn down the barracks, other buildings, or disrupt the orderly process." Daniel drew broader connections, insisting that "this type of permissiveness can only lead to anarchy, both in and outside of the Military Establishment," for "whether at Munich or Attica, the reward for permissiveness is victory for the lawless." General Persons reassured him that Davison was committed to restoring discipline in the army in Europe.[77]

In Germany, under the scrutiny of Congress, the NAACP, the ACLU, a host of journalists, the American public, and the officers and NCOs under his command, General Davison focused his attention on race and military justice. It is perhaps not surprising that members of Congress questioned how resolutely he was focused on discipline, as he frequently—and publicly —argued that military justice should be administered with flexibility and common sense. (Maj. Gen. Frederic Davison, in contrast, was a bit less forgiving. "It's a damn shame," he told *Ebony* in early 1974, "but to tell you the truth, some of these white commanders are too scared of black soldiers to enforce discipline.")[78]

Speaking to reporters soon after he dropped the Darmstadt charges, General Davison insisted that soldiers must be treated "as individuals each with our own bags of problems, limitations, hopes and aspirations." It was true that many officers used the language of individualism to reclaim "only one color," but Davison emphasized the concerns of Black soldiers. "He feels it's a white man's system" said Davison. "He sees the Uniform Code of Military Justice as an example of law written by white men to serve the white system in language that only whites understand." Davison unflinchingly admitted that "subtle racism" was the greatest problem with military justice, as "individuals in the Army who just cannot rid themselves of their prejudices . . . sometimes unconsciously or sometimes very consciously . . . set about in very subtle ways to ignore commands and orders about treating soldiers fairly and vent their prejudices on blacks." His solution? Sensitivity training. Leadership councils. Constant pressure on subordinate commanders.[79]

That does not mean that he ignored the system itself. Davison's Darmstadt decision followed in the path of significant military justice reform, some of it begun under the prior commander. Davison and his new judge advocate, General Persons, figured out a mechanism to keep track of race without including that information in individual case files. They ensured that defendants in special courts-martial were represented by a legal officer and that their trials were overseen by a military judge. They created the "45-day rule": if a case was not brought to trial within forty-five days, it would be dismissed. They opened three law centers—more or less equivalent to the storefront law offices operated in the United States under the Office of Equal Opportunity—to offer soldiers advice from legal experts who were not under the authority of the commander of the unit where the soldier had been accused or disciplined.[80]

In addition, they created a stockade visitation program that sent a legal officer to consult with each new prisoner, not only about his rights but about his specific situation and any personal problems created by his confinement. Pretrial confinement was also under scrutiny, with military magistrates reviewing each case to determine if the accused could be safely released.[81] Nonetheless, both Davison and Persons believed the fundamental problem was individual, not systemic. Not institutional.

In November 1971, just weeks after Davison's controversial Darmstadt decision, the intermingled problems of race, justice, and discipline again made headlines. Davison had scheduled his second big Europe-wide race relations conference at Berchtesgaden (near Hitler's Eagle's Nest) for November 10–12. This time he meant to ensure that commanders were in their seats, and he had brought in big names: Richard Nixon's racial affairs advisor, Robert J. Brown ("Black, beautiful and proud now for 36 years," as he told attendees); Harold Sims, the acting director of the National Urban League; and, not surprisingly, Nathaniel Jones, general counsel of the NAACP. An army press release described Davison's speech as a "firm-jawed stance against prejudice in the military," quoting his claim that "our extraordinary situation demands extraordinary means and actions." A *Washington Post* article quoted Jones: "Military Justice is lily white."[82]

The conference program—with its "Unity is Power" logo—offered attendees a wealth of information. This meeting was not simply for inspiration; Davison had policies and programs and facts to share. But some of those facts were difficult ones, given his agenda, and the presence of journalists from national news media posed a problem. No matter how committed General Davison was to the race relations side of the equation, discipline remained a problem. And the statistics were alarming, especially when it came to race.

The German press, with its frequent focus on Black GIs, was drawn to the discussions of crime and indiscipline. But the race relations conference drew attention within the United States, as well. The *Washington Post* titled its coverage "Black GIs' Crime Up in Europe." The article centered on army efforts to suppress the racial statistics on crime presented at the conference —efforts that were clearly unsuccessful, for even though journalists were forbidden access to the "for official use only" data, the reporter cited them in detail. Crimes of violence by Black soldiers against whites had almost doubled over the past year, the article revealed, with 1,002 reported in the first nine months of 1971 alone. And the number of Black soldiers charged with rape, robbery, and aggravated assault was three times that of white soldiers, even though Blacks represented only 11 to 12 percent of army troops in Europe.[83]

| OFFENSE | CAU vs CAU | NEG vs NEG | CAU vs NEG | NEG vs CAU | TOTAL |
|---|---|---|---|---|---|
| MURDER | 7 | 5 | 2 | 9 | 23 |
| ATT MURDER | 13 | 5 | 4 | 13 | 35 |
| MANSLAUGHTER | 0 | 1 | 0 | 2 | 3 |
| AGGR ASSAULT | 102 | 29 | 28 | 189 | 348 |
| ROBBERY | 4 | 0 | 0 | 48 | 52 |
| DISTURBANCES | 1 | 0 | 1 | 19 | 21 |
| TOTAL | 127 | 40 | 35 | 280 | 482 |

As US Army leaders became concerned about the rising incidence of
interracial violence, units throughout the world were instructed to
gather data. This chart, created by an unidentified unit in Vietnam,
presented crime statistics similar to those in West Germany. The
chart shows all crimes of violence by race but does not identify which
interracial conflicts had "racial content" and does not distinguish
between random attacks and provoked confrontations.
*Courtesy National Archives, College Park, MD.*

This reporter was not sympathetic to Davison, as his reference to the recent case "in which a group of blacks known as the 'Darmstadt 53' challenged
the army establishment and got away with it" made clear. But he also was not
cherry-picking statistics. The original documents show that the percentage of
violent crimes committed by Black soldiers in 1970 and 1971 never dropped
below 72 percent; its height was 87 percent in June 1971. Highly aware of
the implication of those numbers, conference conveners advised caution,
insisting that the statistics were open to "misleading and inflammatory interpretation." General Davison said that the numbers might not be fully valid:
"How many white assaults on Negroes go unreported?" he asked.[84] But such
cautions only went so far, as army units posted armed NCOs in barracks at
night and off-base violence threatened US-German relations. In the end,
Davison's race relations conference was mired in the ongoing and fundamental conflict. Was military justice a way to impose discipline in a difficult
era? Or was military justice, in its undeniable racial disparity, undermining
the very mission of the US Army?

External pressure continued. Just days after the Berchtesgaden conference, the Congressional Black Caucus held its ad hoc hearings on racism in

the US military. Jones was there, too, making a case that "the maladministration of justice is the cancer that erodes America's ability to maintain an effective fighting force." His testimony was followed by that of an air force captain who had served as defense counsel in the Darmstadt case. The "military law system," said Capt. Thomas Culver, "is an arm of discipline of the commander" and is pervaded with "institutional racism." He claimed that its flaws were so fundamental that the only recourse was to follow the example of postwar Germany and "scrap the whole system"; military offenses should be tried in civilian courts, "just the same as any other offenses." "I want you to be very aware," he insisted, "that I choose not to call it the Military Justice System. Justice has no bearing to it."[85]

Justice has no bearing to it.

In early 1972, a civilian attorney staked the life of his Black client on a claim that the entire system of military justice was illegitimate. That his claim was not summarily dismissed by the military judge at Fort Leavenworth, Kansas, says a great deal.[86]

T hose concerned with the problem of race reached no consensus on the role of military justice. Some saw the military justice system primarily as a disciplinary tool, and one essential to restoring good order. Some believed that the administration of the UCMJ fostered the frustration and anger that fueled racial conflict. Some believed that Black soldiers were given Article 15s at higher rates than white soldiers because of institutional racism. Some saw, instead, the conscious or unconscious racism of the individuals who administered the system. Some asked whether, perhaps, disparities actually reflected behavior. Some blamed the army's escalating rates of crime and indiscipline on officers who failed to properly lead their men; some criticized the "permissiveness" that pervaded American society; yet others lamented the "quality" of the men who filled the ranks. But all agreed on one thing: enlisted men had lost faith in the system of military justice. They had no confidence that it was fair or just.[87]

Here, as was most often the case, institutional logic prevailed. The army held to the principle that good order and discipline was fundamental. Reform would take place within the existing system.

That point of agreement provided a possibility, in that it tied to a broader problem the army was confronting. Black soldiers, as each study and task force and investigation discovered anew, believed that the "only one color" seen by the army was not olive drab but white. In the products stocked by PXs worldwide, in regulation haircuts, in stories of past valor, in the men and the few women in positions of leadership, Black soldiers pointed out, the army had long defaulted to white.

These soldiers also, and overwhelmingly, saw military justice as "white." They did not trust the system, didn't trust the white lawyers meant to provide their defense, didn't trust the white officers who sat in judgment, didn't trust the white judges who presided over cases. As analysis after analysis concluded, in order to redeem the system in the eyes of these men, the army must dramatically increase its cohort of Black lawyers and Black judges. To that challenge, the NAACP's Nathaniel Jones had offered an interim solution: civilian lawyers procured and contracted through organizations such as his own. In the end, however, that was not sufficient. For of course it was not only the lawyers and judges who mattered but the officers who imposed discipline in the first place. In order to solve "the problem of race," the army needed more Black officers. And thus it needed a system of "affirmative actions."

# 9 AFFIRMATIVE ACTIONS

The problem of race, army leaders tended to assume, was a problem within the enlisted ranks, the "war within the war" that threatened to tear the institution apart. They were not wrong. It was racial violence that had forced the army to declare race its most critical problem, second only to the US war in Vietnam. And without question, that violence had emerged among men in the lowest ranks. But the problem of race was not restricted to enlisted men, and it was not simply a problem of violence and inarticulate anger. After all, was the uprising at Long Binh Jail or Maj. Lavell Merritt's cri de coeur the more powerful act?

In 1968, Military Assistance Command, Vietnam, *had* seen Major Merritt as a problem. The increasingly frustrated major faced an almost certain court-martial for actions stemming from his "obsessive preoccupation with matters pertaining to racial discrimination and the civil rights movement." He was spared only because Col. Robert Ivey, the staff judge advocate, concluded that a trial would further embarrass the army by amplifying Merritt's voice. That was likely a good call for the army, as well as for Merritt—even if it did not satisfy Colonel Ivey's sense of justice. An army that was rapidly losing public support had no margin for such unforced errors.[1]

Defining Merritt himself as a problem, however, was, well, part of the problem. Even as Merritt did not confront the possibility of incarceration at hard labor, his time as an army officer was coming to an end. In 1948 the army had adopted an "up or out" system, which meant that if Merritt was not promoted to lieutenant colonel, he would be removed from active duty. Merritt had not been selected for promotion twice, and there was no third chance. That was one reason he was so very angry. After more than nineteen years of service, he was on his way out.

And so by early 1969 the army had one fewer Black officer, and it had one fewer potential Black candidate for the senior ranks. Maybe that was fully justified. Maybe not. But while Merritt's case was more dramatic than most, it represented a larger problem. In the army, Black officers were scarce. There were shockingly few Black cadets at the United States Military Academy (USMA) and a relative few rising through university ROTC programs. That initial shortage was compounded by decisions about individual assignments and the intangibles of the promotion system. As a group, Black officers were less likely than their white peers to be promoted beyond the rank of major. Each of those losses mattered disproportionately because there were no lateral hires to senior command. The army had to raise its own. And that took decades.

As Merritt saw his army career dead-end, he had little use for those who had succeeded. The two Black officers (one army, one air force) who wore a star were, in his view, "Uncle Toms." It was clear that by the late summer of 1968 Major Merritt was angry and intemperate. But if a forty-year-old major saw the army's sole Black brigadier general as an Uncle Tom, imagine how that Black general officer likely appeared to young Black draftees. Rising to that rank took extraordinary ability, but it also took someone who could navigate an institution dominated by white men, someone who was acceptable to those who guarded the gates. For those young soldiers who embraced notions of Black pride, the color of the general's skin was not sufficient proof of blackness. Merritt's talk of "House Niggers" made the staff judge advocate angry. It should also have offered him a lesson.[2]

The more significant lesson lay in Merritt's words to his sons, "who have witnessed my debasement and suffered this humiliation and indignity that I was to[o] insensitive to feel all these years." In other times and in other circumstances, Merritt's sons might have joined the next generation of Black officers. Military families beget military service; it was a common pattern in families Black and white. Merritt's sons would possibly have transcended their father's career, entering the army as officers following four years in ROTC or, perhaps, West Point, rather than through officer candidate school (OCS). Major Merritt might have begun a family tradition of military service. Clearly that was not to be, and that was the army's loss.[3]

The army's problem of race was a problem of—and for—Black officers. Bottom line, there were just too few of them. That scarcity created difficulties for Black officers at all ranks. And it harmed the institution of the US

242                                          *Affirmative Actions*

Army, as Black men in authority might have been able to forestall or mitigate some of the escalating racial conflicts. The scarcity of Black officers in senior ranks was due to decisions made by army leaders decades before; it could be addressed only at the margins. But the scarcity of Black officers in the junior ranks and among West Point and ROTC cadets could be—had to be—confronted.

The scarcity of Black officers should have been one of the easiest issues to address. After all, the process of assignment, selection, and promotion was controlled by the army, governed by clear but reformable criteria, cushioned from the violence and uncensored prejudice evident in the enlisted ranks. Solutions might have fit easily into the army's institutional logic.

Instead, solving the problem proved profoundly difficult. Efforts to increase the number of Black officers were initially questioned by the institutional army. For most of the 1960s, white army leaders resisted external pressure, justified by claims of civil rights and equal opportunity, to change army practice. Many put their faith in the reforms of the 1947 Officer Personnel Act, which had replaced promotion-by-seniority with an "up or out" merit system. Many believed that a color-blind process, while not perfect, was the best path to equality. And most believed the number of Black officers would gradually increase, over time, and through regular channels.

But once affirmative action was posed as a solution to the growing racial crisis? It was one thing for senior officers to point to the violence within the enlisted ranks. It was another thing to question the legitimacy of the process through which they had achieved success, or the understandings of merit and accomplishment on which their careers were based. Such resistance was amplified by the military caste system, in which college degrees (something Black men held in very small numbers) increasingly divided the "officers and gentlemen" from the enlisted ranks—despite the democratizing impulses of the 1960s and early 1970s. It would take powerful external pressure to force self-examination and limited change. And as civilian struggles over affirmative action pushed in multiple directions, it frequently lent legitimacy to internal army resistance. Change would require the institutional army to recognize that reform was in its own broader interest. In the end, the army's "affirmative actions" would prove one of its most long-lasting and successful solutions to the problem of race. But the path was not straightforward.

n 1968, African Americans made up 10.5 percent of the US population and 12.6 percent of the US Army. That year, the army had one Black general officer; the other 520 were white. In 1967, there had been none. Of the army's 6,399 colonels, 42 were Black. That was less than 1 percent—0.65 percent, to be precise, which was more than triple the percentage of Black colonels in 1965. Numbers for lieutenant colonels were a bit better: 620 of roughly 16,500. It was not surprising that there were more Black lieutenant colonels than colonels. That is how the system works. The promotion system creates a pyramid. What was surprising—and alarming—was that the army had more Black lieutenant colonels than Black second lieutenants, more majors than first lieutenants.[4]

Lt. Col. James White had used those facts—that lieutenant colonels outnumbered second lieutenants, majors outstripped first lieutenants—when he briefed the chief and the secretary of the army in the summer of 1969. Awareness of the shortage of Black officers was there from the beginning, even as it rarely structured army discussions of the nature of "the problem." That was in part because of the confusing nature of the issue.[5]

Why did it matter that the army lacked a sufficient number of Black officers? Shortages in specific fields mattered. With few Black lawyers and judges, for example, army justice appeared "white." With too few Black chaplains, religious services and counseling seemed less inclusive. But the concern was more broadly based, and it was directly linked to "the problem of race."

Colonel White, in his 1969 briefing, had concluded that "an imbalance in the number of Negro officers assigned to troop units has an adverse effect on race relations." In this version, Black officers were a potential solution: they might mitigate the looming crisis of racial conflict in the enlisted ranks. But White also portrayed Black officers as part of the problem—of the racial conflict that roiled the army. Beginning his briefing with a personal note, White told the chief and secretary of the army, "I can verify from my own experiences that the cries of the Negro soldier, enlisted and in some cases officers, have never been so loud." In other words, just minutes before White suggested Black officers as a partial solution to the problem of race, he acknowledged that some joined their enlisted brothers in frustration, discontent, and even disruption. Perhaps not surprisingly, Major Merritt figured prominently in the report on which White based his briefing.[6]

Moreover, as various elements of the army tried to address the shortage, studies suggested that careers were shortened or derailed by what was already referred to as institutional racism, army practices that systemically failed Black officers. And journalists, chronicling the army's racial crisis, used statistics on race and representation as shorthand evidence of army failings. Thus, as army leaders tried to resolve the conundrum of race and representation, they struggled with the point of their actions: Were Black officers a part of the problem of race? A solution to the problem? Victims of the problem?

That confusion was not fully unique; almost every army attempt to manage the growing crisis was shaped by disagreements over the fundamental goal or appropriate process. Here, though, urgent concerns of the moment intersected with an ongoing program of "affirmative actions" shaped by civilian civil rights and equal opportunity legislation and by the backlash against it.

The army first confronted recommendations that it take "affirmative" action to recruit Black officers in 1963, from the President's Committee on Equal Opportunity in the Armed Forces (also known as the Gesell Committee). True, it had focused on what members saw as the larger, and intractable, problem of off-base discrimination, but it did not ignore evidence of discrimination within the services—most particularly the dearth of Black officers. Committee chair Gerhard Gesell called it a "shocking condition" in correspondence at the time and later acknowledged that committee members debated calling for preferential treatment as a way to achieve greater representation of African Americans in the higher ranks.[7]

The military departments were asked to comment on Gesell Committee proposals, including those calling for reform in recruitment, assignment, and promotions. And the army's response was fairly combative, especially in comparison with the other service branches. When, for example, the committee recommended that each service make "special efforts" and take "affirmative steps" to recruit African Americans with the "special aptitudes" required by the contemporary military, the air force simply ignored the counsel. It instead promoted its plans to encourage "qualified Negroes" to take advantage of educational opportunities. The navy, in turn, claimed a color-blind approach, one that may have been less than persuasive given its dismal record. "Since 1948," read the navy response, "there has been no special assignment category for Negroes. Negroes are not channeled into categories with disregard for aptitude but on the contrary are assigned to technical and other fields on the same basis as members of all other ethnic groups."[8]

The army, in contrast, offered a direct non-concur. "The initiation of a program designed solely to obtain Negroes with special aptitudes denotes preferential assignment of Negro personnel which is undesirable," it stated. "The Army desires to continue to practice principles of sound personnel management," acquiring the "best qualified" personnel and assigning them, based on aptitude, to meet the needs of the army. Current procedures, the response continued, "provide for fair and equal opportunity, and do not permit preferential treatment of any racial group."[9]

The Gesell Committee's recommendation to admit more Black cadets to the service academies prompted a universal response: the services do not control the nomination process. But the army, alone, felt it necessary to explain that it employed a "highly competitive" process for procuring officers in order to acquire "the best qualified personnel." The army had no objection to the committee's proposal, the response declared, so long as "no attempt is made to compromise selection criteria or standards in order to increase Negro representation in the officer corps." And while the army officially concurred with the committee's advice that it periodically review its selection process (as a way to guard against the possibility of discrimination), its response left little doubt about how those reviews would go. Army procedures were already "impartial" and "objective," the response asserted, as they relied on aptitude tests to measure "latent talent" and deliver "the best men available." "It is not recommended," insisted the army, "that standards be lowered to accommodate Negroes or any other group."[10]

The army's responses can be read in various ways: as a commitment to color-blind opportunity; as a fundamentally racist assumption about the capability of Black candidates; as an expression of faith in nonsubjective evaluation processes; as institutional racism; as a defensive response from the service with the least demanding entrance criteria. Likely, there were elements of each.

No matter the rationale or reason, however, it is clear that the Department of the Army was not embracing "special efforts" or "affirmative steps." But with continuing pressure from the Department of Defense and the White House, the army issued a comprehensive equal opportunity regulation—AR 600-21—in July 1964, the day after President Johnson signed the most expansive civil rights act in the nation's history.[11]

While the institutional army's resistance to much of what the Gesell Committee proposed—particularly when it came to officer selection and promotion—suggests what an uphill battle reformers faced, its early-1960s insistence on "color-blind" equality was not out of step with most American institutions. The army's language also allowed it to dodge divisions in Congress, which southern Democrats held hostage over matters of race. And although the Kennedy and Johnson administrations would push for affirmative steps toward racial equity, their policies were initially inchoate and potentially contradictory. It was not until 1965 that President Johnson offered his powerful analogy ("You do not take a person who, for years, has been hobbled by chains and liberate him, bring him up to the starting line of a race and then say, 'you are free to compete with all the others,' and still justly believe that you have been completely fair") and a call for "equality as a fact and as a result," not just as "a right and a theory."[12]

The army's response to the Gesell Committee's calls for equal opportunity and affirmative action cannot be understood in a vacuum; even as it was based in the institutional logic of that era—and the racial and racist assumptions that logic incorporated—it was also fundamentally linked to profound changes in the nation's understandings of equality and opportunity and to the public debates that animated them.

Kennedy had issued Executive Order 10925 in March 1961, establishing the President's Committee on Equal Employment Opportunity (PCEEO). While the administration's order called for a color-blind, racially neutral approach to hiring, it also embraced "affirmative action"—a somewhat ambiguous phrase introduced through Vice President Johnson, who chaired the PCEEO. This administration, the term signaled, would require active and "affirmative" steps toward equal employment, not simply passive avoidance of discrimination.[13]

There were all sorts of problems with Kennedy's executive order and the committee it established. The order never defined discrimination. It failed to stipulate what equal opportunity looked like and specified no way to measure compliance, no number or percentage or quota to be met. The committee had a small budget and a limited staff. It had no jurisdiction over hiring under federal loans and grants, which totaled a then massive $7.5 billion a year. But it did hold authority over defense contractors.[14]

The day after Kennedy's order went into effect, the NAACP's labor secretary filed complaints of "overt discrimination" against Lockheed Aircraft Corporation. At that moment, Lockheed was negotiating a billion-dollar contract with the Department of Defense for work to be done at its Marietta, Georgia, plant. By southern standards, Lockheed was fairly progressive. Five percent of its more than 10,000 employees were Black, and some held skilled, clerical, or professional positions. Like other defense plants in the South, however, Lockheed-Marietta accepted Jim Crow. Even its time clocks were labeled "white" and "colored."[15]

Lockheed's headquarters were in California, but racial segregation in Marietta threatened the entire corporation. Within a month of the NAACP's action, Lockheed had integrated the Georgia plant, and the corporation's president had gone to the White House to sign an agreement that Lockheed would "aggressively seek out" minority candidates for administration, engineering, and other highly skilled positions. Boeing, Douglas Aircraft, Western Electric, and General Electric followed suit. Kennedy's executive order had been limited, but it had a significant effect, for a disproportionate number of defense plants subject to the executive order were in the Jim Crow South.[16]

In 1961, the Department of Defense found itself at the center of the Kennedy administration's push for equal opportunity. And under Robert McNamara, it took up that charge. The civil rights office that the secretary of defense created in the wake of the Gesell report focused on equal opportunity and affirmative action, directing the documentation, for example, of every single "promotable Negro lieutenant colonel" in the US Army and negotiating admission of Black candidates to all the service academies.[17]

The Civil Rights Act that President Johnson shepherded through Congress in 1964 went significantly further than the one Kennedy had proposed, particularly in its efforts to prohibit job discrimination—and the provisions of Title VII were among the bill's most controversial. The House version of the bill passed in February with a 160-vote margin, though not without some fiery debates. And, as expected, it faced a filibuster in the Senate. These were the days of the talking filibuster, a move used primarily to shut down civil rights legislation. The record for the longest filibuster was held by Strom Thurman, South Carolina senator and army veteran, who had held the floor against the Civil Rights Act of 1957 for twenty-four hours and eighteen minutes. (Thurmond filled the time reading the voting legislation of each of the nation's states; no one has yet definitively explained how he managed to go twenty-four hours without using the restroom.)[18]

The 1964 filibuster lasted for sixty working days, including seven Saturdays. Thurmond was once again involved, but this effort to torpedo a civil rights act was launched and led by Sen. Richard Russell (D-GA). Why does this matter? Because Russell was the chair of the Senate Armed Services Committee. The filibuster's other mainstays included not only Thurmond but also Robert Byrd (D-WV), John C. Stennis (D-MS), and Sam Ervin (D-NC) —all members of the Senate Armed Services Committee.[19]

Despite the moral illegitimacy of their cause, southern senators—again, many of them members of the Armed Services Committee—raised issues during their filibuster that would plague national efforts to affirmatively end job discrimination for decades: quotas, "preferential treatment," questions of qualification and merit and the ability to hire "the best man" for the job. Central to that effort were the implications of the recently decided "Motorola Case."

In this decision, Robert E. Bryant, who (according to the *New York Times*) was "a Negro examiner" for the Illinois State Fair Employment Practices Commission, had upheld twenty-seven-year-old "Negro applicant" Leon Myort's case against Motorola, ruling that Motorola had violated Illinois's Fair Employment Act by using a screening test that was unfair to "culturally deprived and disadvantaged groups." Motorola, in turn, argued that such a ruling would create a "double standard for hiring, one standard to be applied to whites, and another to be applied to Negroes." John Tower, the senator who chose to spend his filibuster hours on the Motorola case, claimed that the decision "puts a premium on ignorance for prospective employees, rather than intelligence." Does it mean, he asked rhetorically, "that an employer must hire someone who is not competent by virtue of his environmental and educational background?"[20]

Tower, filling his time reading aloud to the sparsely populated Senate chamber, offered a military connection—a unsigned *Chicago Tribune* column, "The Motorola Rule and Cassius X." The US Army had recently rejected heavyweight boxing champion Cassius Clay. "Boxing Champion Is Unable to Pass Aptitude Tests," the *New York Times* had headlined its front-page story on the decision; "Abilities for Military Duty Are Lacking, Pentagon Says." (Cassius Clay had changed his name to Cassius X in February 1964 and to Muhammad Ali soon thereafter.) Clay's local draft board had directed him to report for preinduction exams on January 24, 1964—a week following his twenty-second birthday and one month and a day before his first scheduled bout with world heavyweight champion Sonny Liston.[21]

Clay's induction exams yielded a 1-Y classification; his "mental test" scores fell below the cutoff for the peacetime army's minimum, which had been raised just eight months earlier. Aware of the likely public outcry—the world champion heavyweight boxer wasn't good enough to fight for the US Army??? —the secretary of the army ordered that Clay be tested again in case "anxiety" over the upcoming match had affected his scores. In the end, following two written exams and evaluation by three psychologists, Clay (by then Muhammad Ali) was deemed a "true failure" rather than "malingerer," someone who did not show the "aptitude and intelligence . . . to contribute to the national defense by fulfilling army needs."[22]

The author of the *Tribune* column was clearly appalled that a man who "picks up a couple of hundred thousand dollars for a few minutes' work and is given to riding around in fancy cars" had been excused from his military obligation. (In case the racist implications of such language are not sufficiently clear, I'll note that he also quoted another writer's claim that this "pugilist" could at least "be trained adequately for 'gorilla' warfare.") Cassius X/Ali was the columnist's proximate target, but his larger focus was the Motorola ruling, the army's rejection of the heavyweight champion simply an "extension of this new doctrine to another flagrant case of what is now termed 'discrimination.'" Ali, after all, had been denied two years as drafted private in the US Army because he had not done well on a screening exam —just as Leon Myort had been denied employment at Motorola because his test scores fell below the hiring cutoff. This columnist made the connection: the "landmark" Motorola decision meant that "justice will . . . only be served when Cassius is given his full rights of citizenship and admitted to that exclusive club known as the army."[23]

In fact, that is what would happen. By late 1966, Secretary of Defense McNamara's ongoing efforts to create a mechanism to "salvage" those from disadvantaged backgrounds by—in effect—implementing the Motorola ruling had come to fruition in the form of Project 100,000. But this was no longer the peacetime army into which McNamara originally sought to incorporate disadvantaged men, those who had been excluded from the benefits of military service by low "mental test" scores. It was instead an army rapidly expanding to meet the demands of the US war in Vietnam.

In 1966, the army lowered its minimum qualification scores from 16 to 10 (out of 100, a score roughly equivalent to an IQ of 80).[24] And world heavyweight champion Ali—now acceptable for service and summoned to serve —refused induction in protest against the US war in Vietnam and in turn was stripped of his title. Ali held firm, but hundreds of thousands of other minimally qualified young men were inducted.

Project 100,000 was restricted to the enlisted ranks. It played no role whatsoever in officer selection or promotion. Nonetheless, experience with New Standards men affected efforts to diversify the officer corps because it brought questions about qualification to the fore. Officers complained about Project 100,000 men throughout the war. New Standards men, the line went, were more difficult to train. Research showed, many argued, that men admitted through Project 100,000 were significantly more likely to have disciplinary issues, to spend time in the stockade, to be court-martialed. And while the majority of New Standards men were white, the majority of Black inductees were New Standards.[25]

As army officers struggled with indiscipline and cratering morale, army officers suggested that McNamara's program bore some of the fault. General Westmoreland directly blamed New Standards men for disciplinary problems and suggested that their presence undermined the war effort. One

*Affirmative Actions*

battalion level commander later recalled, of Project 100,000, that "they were just flooding us with morons and imbeciles. It doesn't mean they couldn't eat and talk and move around, but they couldn't learn well and they'd get frustrated and become aggressive." Struggling with the widespread crisis in the late Vietnam-era army, officers focused on the enlisted men they commanded. Nonetheless, Project 100,000 and the associated discussions of testing and standards and qualifications shadowed debates over how to diversify the officer corps.[26]

Such concerns about standards and qualifications had animated conversations at the Department of Defense's executive seminar on civil rights in the spring of 1966, well before army leaders defined "the problem of race" as a challenge to the institution's fundamental mission. That year, DoD officials brought together representatives from the military branches as part of their increasingly expansive civil rights initiative. In keeping with the national focus on equal opportunity, conveners stressed the shortage of Black officers. An avalanche of statistical data demonstrated "Negro personnel" were dramatically underrepresented in the officer ranks—whether that representation was measured against total proportion in the military, in individual services, or in the US population as a whole. Here the DoD was moving, in the same inchoate fashion as the nation, toward a focus on outcomes and solutions. If Black officers failed to find "equity in career fulfillment," what was to be done? Although the term never appeared, and although DoD conveners always framed their points as questions ("Should special consideration be given for promotion or assignment?"), this executive seminar was a turn to "affirmative actions."[27]

No matter how progressive the DoD framework, individual services were not yet in accord. And the army was, yet again, direct in its opposition. When conveners asked whether services should consciously attempt to "increase the visibility index" of "Negroes in significant assignment slots," the army responded with a definitive "no": "If unqualified Negroes are given assignments merely for the sake of visibility, it could tend to degrade Negroes who have earned significant assignments on the basis of merit."[28]

DoD conveners understood that all the military departments saw a conflict between "standards" and the proposed affirmative actions, and to their credit, they forced participants to confront that issue directly. In workshops on recruiting minority youth, participants discussed how much to consider "cultural and educational differences" in decisions about admission and whether there should be "uniform or comparative (differential) standards." They were asked to weigh the importance of testing and of quantitative measures. (The DoD question read: "If certain quantitative goals are determined for Negroes and there are educational and cultural deficiencies that result in test performances below comparable levels and standards, how do you resolve this conflict between quality of performance required and the quantitative goals set?") Conveners reported that some participants showed "irritation" when asked about the use of "special measures" to compensate for "long-accrued disadvantages," perceiving that proposal as "a threat to the system, to be rejected forthwith." As a written response from the army put it, "A balanced and patient approach to his problems rather than radical solutions to each and every one" offered the Black officer a path to success.[29]

The institutional army did not yet see race as a threat to its mission. Proportional representation of Black officers did not appear as a practical solution to an army problem but as an external demand rooted in the moral claims of the civil rights movement. Even as various individual leaders and men accepted the legitimacy of such claims, that demand threatened army practices; it challenged the army's institutional logic.

But despite powerful resistance on the part of the institutional army, external pressure continued, quietly prompted by Black officers. It is true that Black officers were generally loath to make official complaints of discrimination. Even the most minimally savvy understood that such complaints could derail their careers and that complaints certainly were not seen as evidence of the "balanced and patient" approach endorsed by army leadership. At the DoD seminar, conveners began by reminding participants that Black officers rarely complained about "patterns of discrimination [that] operate against them" because they feared that written complaints might prompt retaliation.[30]

It likely also made a difference that those who complained were rarely found in the right. Forty-six Black soldiers (rank unspecified) complained to the inspector general's office about racial discrimination in the promotion process during fiscal year 1969. The IG found not a single one of those complaints justified. Reluctance to complain officially, however, did not mean that Black officers remained silent. A congressional inquiry into the promotion of Black officers begun in the spring of 1967 offered evidence of that fact, as did a *Washington Post* article, published that same spring, on the challenges Black officers faced in pursuit of promotion.[31]

The most significant pressure on the army, however, continued to come from the Department of Defense. Beginning in 1969, with pressure and support from both Nixon's White House and civil rights groups, Secretary of

Defense Melvin Laird had gradually moved toward expanding federal equal opportunity guidelines. Not only would they apply to civilian contractors, such as Lockheed, but they would also apply to military personnel.[32]

Army leaders were paying attention to external pressure, but they were increasingly coming to understand that change was in the institutional interest of the army. In 1969, the army staff group tasked by Westmoreland with analyzing racial tension "took a hard look" at statistical data on the composition of the officer ranks. Colonel White, in his subsequent around-the-world briefings of key commands on racial tension in the army, made clear that the army's "racial composition" was a continuing problem. In the wake of White's initial briefing, Westmoreland focused on the procurement and assignment of Black officers, devoting two of his seven proposals to that issue. Secretary Stanley Resor, in turn, told the officers assembled at Fort Monroe for the first Department of the Army race relations conference that the army must make recruiting and retaining Black officers a matter of "top priority" and set specific goals as a means to evaluate success.[33]

During the summer of 1970, an internal DoD memorandum stressed "the need for Aggressive Affirmative Action programs that utilize the use of numerical goals and timetables which have not been previously used." And in December, the secretary of defense directed each branch of the military to develop an "affirmative actions" plan. It is worth noting that the term "affirmative action" was more capacious at that point; it encompassed steps to increase minority representation but also tended to include a whole range of other "affirmative," or proactive, efforts. The army's official statement explained it this way: "Affirmative Action is a concept which is a step beyond non-discrimination. It requires positive and planned actions to correct existing deficiencies and inequities."[34]

The 1972 "Affirmative Actions Plan" produced by the Department of the Army was oddly comprehensive but not at all coherent. It was, essentially, a very long list: dozens of pages of discrete actions planned, each accompanied by a milestone for measuring achievement. Practical means of increasing the number, percentage, and promotion rates of Black officers, looking initially to ROTC and West Point and then to admission to the Command and General Staff College—a significant step toward promotion to higher rank —were key. But the list also included such suggestions as "produce worship folders which commemorate ethnic events with religious significance" and "[create a] community action type program" to involve 200,000 to 300,000 young people in "team handball teams."[35]

The Affirmative Actions Plan offered only a brief rationale for these actions —but one that stressed the army's institutional interests. "To remain an effective fighting force capable of defending the nation and providing support in furtherance of national goals," this scant paragraph stated, "the United States Army must maintain a high state of efficiency, discipline, and morale."[36]

But the army attorney general attached a cover letter with a more complete "basic philosophy" for army affirmative action, likely because the plan largely shifted responsibility to local commanders. (Every unit down through brigade level was instructed to develop an individual plan based on its specific circumstances.) That "basic philosophy" began with the army's definition of affirmative action and then turned immediately to the army's ongoing concern with standards and qualifications. Numerical goals or objectives, it cautioned, should be viewed as planning targets, not as "base figures which are to be reached at the expense of requisite qualifications. Standards for performance will not be lowered."[37]

T hus far, this is a bloodless tale of policy and high-level bureaucracy. That, of course, is part of the point. It was enlisted men who had turned to violence and disruption. Black officers—at least those career army officers who had reached field-level rank by the late 1960s—almost always worked within the bureaucratic, institutional culture of the army. But what was it like on the ground? And why was there but a single Black army general in 1968? Why were there but sixty-two full-bird colonels?

One answer was offered in what came to be known as the "Butler Report," a statistical analysis that army leaders worked hard to keep from public view and then scrambled to contextualize when a 1975 Freedom of Information Act ruling left them no recourse. Butler—the author of the 1972 report—was Douthard R. Butler, a thirty-seven-year-old lieutenant colonel and master army aviator recently returned from Vietnam. Growing up during World War II in the small town of Waxahachie, just south of Dallas, Butler had imagined a broader world. His parents hoped he would become a teacher; watching airplanes crossing the Texas sky, he resolved to learn to fly. The official desegregation of the military seemed to offer him a path, and in 1951, at the age of sixteen, he moved out near Houston to attend the Black land-grant university Prairie View A&M—because it offered ROTC.[38]

To Douthard, as to most young Black officers commissioned during the 1950s, the army offered mixed blessings. He moved from a fully segregated Black world at Prairie View to a largely white and clearly white-dominated institution, from the strictures of the Jim Crow South to "total integration" at Fort Benning, all within the space of twenty-four hours. "You would go into the bathroom," he recalled, and "there's a bunch of white guys in there and you'd say WHOA! Where's my bathroom? Where's my fountain?" Such integration was disconcerting as much as liberating, for Black officers quickly learned that while there were, of course, no actual regulations, it was not deemed acceptable to largely "stick with their own." Furthermore, although army life at Fort Benning was integrated, integration ended at post gates, for officers and enlisted men alike.[39]

In the army, Butler had learned to fly. He had been stationed around the world, piloted helicopters in Vietnam. Then, in 1969, he—as a newly promoted lieutenant colonel—was assigned to the Office of Personnel Directorate for army aviation. While that seems an odd assignment for an aviator, key army leaders believed that more Black officers in personnel might help to combat the growing crisis of race. Butler was aware of the problems Black officers faced; sixteen years into his army career, he had lived them for all of his adult life. And he was all too conscious that there were few Black men who made it to field rank and above. It is not clear that his presence influenced race relations in army aviation, but the stint in personnel offered him evidence of disparities that went beyond anecdote and observation. Nonetheless, Butler had no plans to make an issue of the discrepancies he saw between the careers of Black and white officers. His own career was going well. The personnel directorate was not his future. And he, like other successful Black officers, believed that it was "better to evolutionize than to revolutionize."[40]

Butler impressed his commander in personnel, who recommended him for command of an aviation battalion in South Korea. This was a sign of good things to come. Command experience was virtually essential for promotion to the highest ranks, and in the years before selection boards introduced some level of objectivity into the process, such assignments depended greatly on personal connections and the influence of mentors—something Black officers rarely could count on. Butler had the support of his current commander and his branch general; he had been successful in his military career as a pilot. He expected the position would come through. But when he visited branch command to meet with the senior officers who would determine his future, an administrator told him, almost offhandedly, that he would not be awarded command because he had a "weak early file."[41]

Why did that matter? Butler's recent Officer Efficiency Reports were excellent. But the army had adopted a new approach to selection and promotion; the guidance issued to the army selection board that considered officers for promotion to colonel in 1968 read as follows: "No evaluation of demonstrated professionalism or potential for future service can be complete or objective without a review of the entire record; the total man concept should govern." In this new system (which reached beyond promotion boards), Butler's average OER ratings from back when he was a junior officer had scuttled his chances.[42]

Butler kept himself under control, at least in that public space. There were reasons he was a successful officer. But when he burst into his commander's office at Fort McNair, he was no longer so contained. Col. John Marr, seeing the look on his face, tried to calm him down. "I don't know what the hell it is," said Marr, "but we ain't gonna talk about it now." They did, of course, about Butler's own frustrations and about a system in which OERs, even from one's days as a junior officer, could forestall the possibility of promotion or command. Butler, here, made the connections with race.[43]

Colonel Marr, who was willing to acknowledge the larger picture (and who, after all, was head of personnel), suggested that Butler investigate the racial discrepancies he saw. "What would I do?" Butler asked him. And Marr replied, "Knowing you, you'll think of something."[44]

There are two important things to know about Colonel Butler here. First, he was a successful army officer who intended to remain so. Thus, what he thought of fit squarely within army institutional practice: it was bureaucratic, and its result was the 1972 equivalent of a PowerPoint presentation. Second, Butler had been a mathematics major at Prairie View. He understood sampling and statistical analysis. So, with the blessing of his superiors, Butler —using newly available IBM computers—created and analyzed statistical data on promotion rates among Black and white officers. Focusing on OERs generated between 1956 and 1971, he correlated ratings not only by race but also with variables including levels of education (both civilian and military), branch, source of commission, and promotions.[45]

What did he find? That Black officers, in aggregate, almost without exception rated ten points below white officers, in aggregate. And that the top of the ratings curve for Black officers always fell lower than the top of the curve for white officers. In short, Butler offered statistical confirmation of what many Black officers had expected all along. Black officers were rated lower than their white peers, and those ratings undermined their futures in the army.[46]

Butler's findings made a splash, not because he confirmed what most people acknowledged—that racism had marred the 1950s army—but because his analysis challenged both army institutional practice and current assumptions. Most senior leaders who cared about such issues assumed that the racial disparities in junior officers' rankings (a problem for officers like Butler under the "total man" concept) were a legacy of the past, that current rankings would not correlate with race. Butler's statistics showed their error. The ten-point gulf was consistent throughout. The deputy chief of staff for personnel thought that historically Black colleges and universities (HBCUS) might be failing to adequately prepare their graduates; Butler's study found no correlation.[47]

Why, though, were Black and white junior officers rated differently? Butler's study offered no clear answer. Such ratings are subjective, no matter how many institutional guardrails the army introduces. And unstated was the fact that almost all of the "raters" were white. Racism may well have shaped their perceptions. The charts comparing Armed Forces Qualification Test scores by race circulating widely during the late 1960s may have warped expectations. The shadow of (the irrelevant) Project 100,000 may have factored in, as might have heated public debates about affirmative action, race, and merit.[48]

But even many of the most racially progressive white officers were not familiar with the backgrounds and experiences of young Black officers. Few Black officers, at that point, came from West Point or from ROTC at major universities; 75 percent were commissioned from HBCUS. White officers often had never heard of those schools and were less likely to consider their graduates well qualified. Evaluations depended on social factors, too, and not only for the officer himself. How well did the officer and his wife, his family, fit into the broader social world of the post? How well did they manage the inescapable politics? Did the young officer understand how the army worked? Did he come from a line of army officers? Had he found a patron, a mentor, someone to help him move through the complexities of the army and of the age? Someone to steer him toward the right career-building assignments and then make sure he got them?[49]

The army kept the "Butler Report" from public view for three years. That was most likely possible only because it never took the form of a written report, existing only as briefing materials: a set of "vu-graphs" and speaking notes that could not physically be passed into the hands of eager journalists. When, in 1975, the anti-war Center for National Security Studies succeeded in its Freedom of Information Act request, the army was so concerned about the report's public reception that it prepared for a firestorm, arranging a congressional "drop" of documents and preparing a list of potential "dirty" questions and suggested answers for dealing with the press.[50]

Internally, however, the report made a difference. The army began tracking comparative OER scores by race. Racial disparities in ratings began to decline. Promotion and selection boards were briefed on the general results of the Butler study and told to take its findings into account in their decisions, and each board was newly required to include a minority officer. Said one such officer of the Butler Report, "For me it was a license to steal. I got so many people promoted." Not that they did not deserve promotion, he hastened to add, but "they might not have made it had we continued to take the reports [OERs] literally." On the other hand, in 1976 a Black officer dismissed the change as no more than "aggressive rhetoric." "Is equity achieved," he asked rhetorically, in a letter to the *Army Times*, "merely by exposing the promotion and other selection boards to past defects in personnel management?" He argued for a mathematical model that would, "in layman's terms, . . . give the black officer his points back."[51]

Nonetheless, there were institutional changes. On the first day of 1973, the army implemented a revised system of officer evaluation, guaranteeing that each officer received results quickly and making public the average OER scores for each year so that officers could understand where they stood. And a new officer personnel management system grouped all officers into four branches (combat arms, combat support arms, logistics services, and administrative services), guaranteeing that each branch would have the same "promotional selection rate." In other words, the system meant to equalize opportunity. Officers would compete for promotion only with others in their own branch, and the advantage that combat command offered would be at least partially neutralized. This new system was intended to increase the promotion rates of minority officers, who were less likely to hold combat command positions than their white fellow officers.[52]

Turning to a metaphor perhaps best reserved for the navy, the US Army is like a massive ship. Course corrections are gradual. It does not turn on a dime. Butler's study was a gradual course correction, and it could do little about the past. Many Black officers had been retired as captains or majors, certainly not all for good reason. Entire cohorts of Black officers had already missed selection for the Command and General Staff College or the Army War College (whose five Black students enrolled between 1960 and 1968 were five more than at the U.S. Naval College or the Air War College). They had failed to receive the command positions necessary to attain the senior ranks. None of that could be undone. And the military does not do lateral hires; it was not possible to poach a new general from General Motors or Johnson Products Company. Diversifying the top ranks would take time, as well as continued pressure.[53]

If the army had to grow its own officers, of course, the best place to address the problem was at its origins. How best to increase the number of young Black men—and, soon, women!—commissioned as officers in the army? This challenge was, in many ways, more difficult. Black officers, by and large, believed in the institution. They sought success within it. They understood and accepted most of its institutional culture.

Young Black men had no such allegiance. As the *Chicago Defender* put it, writing of the military, "Alert young blacks, who have none of the legacy of slavery in their consciousness and who know that skin color is irrelevant on the firing line, will never understand why whiteness should be an asset and blackness a liability in the climb to success." The "lily-white character" of top command, the column's author asserted, cast doubt on military pronouncements of equality, on the "do-gooder programs [of] brotherhood forums" and "pious and platitudinous lectures," for "the black boy in uniform cannot be made to ignore or forget that he is in a system that seems designed to keep him in a subordinate position even if he had the military genius of Napoleon." Young Black men were more straightforward. "No more ROTC," chanted students at Howard University.[54]

The *Chicago Defender* had a point. That the army had, in 1970, but "1 Black General" with "513 White Mates" (per the column headline) certainly did not encourage ambitious young men who also—suddenly—saw new options in the civilian world. But it was not only the army's poor record on race or the growing competition for talented young Black men and women from the civilian world. Attitudes toward military service had changed, as well. As the war in Vietnam lost support, as headlines told of the massacre at My Lai, of the slaughter of American troops on Hamburger Hill, of racial violence and drug abuse, and of NCOs who refused to go into barracks at night unarmed, the army was at its nadir of public respect. Few young people—of any race —were eager to make a career in the military.

Thus army leaders seeking to increase the flow of Black men into the officer ranks faced three significant challenges. They had to persuade talented young men who had other options to join an institution that even its most ardent supporters saw as struggling. They had to overcome varying levels of internal resistance. And they had to change institutional culture sufficiently to create a path to success for the Black men who were willing to gamble on the army.

There were three possible routes for these young men to become army officers. Officer candidate school, at just twenty-four weeks of training, offered the quickest path. But by 1970, in the process of "Vietnamization,"

**Young. Gifted.
And in charge.**

When you graduate, and you're ready to start your career, you won't want to spend another four years or more as a trainee. You'll want to take charge.

That's where Army Officer Candidate School can put you years ahead of your college class. By giving you immediate management responsibilities.

As an OCS graduate, you could be running your own 200-man company before you're 25. With a monthly operating budget of $100,000. Assets over $2 million. And a payroll approaching $75,000 a month.

You'll have a salary to match your responsibilities. 30 days paid vacation each year. Officer's housing and privileges. And full retirement benefits in only 20 years.

Today's Army is for the young and gifted. If you're ready to take charge of a big job, send the coupon for more about our accelerated management program. Army OCS.

**Today's Army
wants to join you.**

Although the US Army began scaling back enrollment in its
Officer Candidate School in the midst of the Vietnam War, this
advertisement demonstrates the emphasis the institution put on
recruiting college-educated Black men to become army officers.
*Courtesy N. W. Ayer Advertising Records, Archives Center,
National Museum of American History, Smithsonian Institution.*

OCS was scaling back. Its enrollment dropped 350 percent in 1970 alone. Besides, there were public questions about the overall quality of the officers it produced, as army leaders debated whether inferior OCS-training had contributed to the war crimes at My Lai. Few saw OCS as the best way to build an eventual cohort of senior Black officers.[55]

Then there was ROTC. During the Cold War 1950s, Army ROTC was producing 12,000 new lieutenants every year. ROTC (not all army) had been established at 313 colleges or universities, and in every state. Harvard and Stanford had units, as did most major and minor public institutions. Two years of ROTC was compulsory for male students at many of them. But students resented compulsory ROTC—not particularly because they opposed military service or a military presence on campus but because the training put additional demands on their time. Between 1961 and 1965, compulsory Army ROTC was abolished at sixty colleges and universities.[56]

As ROTC enrollment dropped dramatically, the military tried to rescue the program. Significant scholarships were offered from 1964 on. ROTC reforms, however, coincided with the escalating US war in Vietnam. And while the anti-war sentiments of American college students have long been overclaimed, even a relatively small opposition can have great impact. As the war in Vietnam grew increasingly unpopular on university campuses, ROTC was the most visible symbol of American military might. In the space of a single year, from October 1968 to October 1969, overall ROTC enrollment dropped more than 25 percent. And its very presence came under attack. During the 1969–70 academic year, the ROTC building at the University of Michigan withstood an explosion, a three-day sit-in, a fire, and a demonstration that left forty broken windows. Faculty at a range of institutions voted to withdraw academic credit for ROTC courses. Many campuses banished ROTC. It voluntarily withdrew from others. Over the five-year span that began in 1967, army ROTC lost 80 percent of its enrollment.[57]

Nonetheless, ROTC seemed the best source for Black officers. Black colleges and universities had historically furnished the majority of Black officers. Twelve army ROTC units existed at HBCUS in 1967; collectively, that year, they provided 278 new lieutenants to the US Army. In contrast, the United States Military Academy class of 1967 had only two Black graduates. But like their white peers, students at HBCUS had begun to reject compulsory ROTC. Some began to call for its expulsion from campus. In early 1967, Stokely Carmichael's visit to Morgan State sparked student demands that ROTC be banished (it was not, but compulsory ROTC was ended). That same year, at Howard University, student protesters interrupted a talk by Selective Service head Lewis Hershey. The Howard administration soon abolished compulsory ROTC, amid much hand-wringing about the rudeness of the protesters, but two years later students set the ROTC office on fire. Overall, from 1966 to 1971, ROTC enrollment at HBCUS dropped by 45 percent.[58]

In response, the army turned to the NAACP and the Urban League, seeking advice on how to appeal to the young men who might be future officers; the NAACP referred to the relationship as a "contractual agreement" with the various ROTC commands in the continental United States. Army leaders also sought a foothold at smaller, more conservative HBCUS, places where Afros were still banned and coeds' parietals were not under assault. There they found some success. Only at HBCUS did Army ROTC programs increase during this era, from twelve in 1969 to eighteen in 1972. In a more controversial move, the Army ROTC launched a pilot program at Baltimore's Morgan State. There, "highly motivated" juniors whose test scores kept them out of ROTC were admitted with probationary status. By 1972, eleven institutions were participating in what came to be known as the Expanded ROTC Opportunities Program. Eight of them were HBCUs. About half of the professors of military science (a title many regular faculty had difficulty with) at HBCUs opposed the program, fearing that it would foster the belief that Black officers were unqualified. Project 100,000 loomed in the background.[59]

Here, of course, was the heart of the struggle. The army needed more junior Black officers. But every year fewer young Black men saw the army as their best opportunity. As sources of new officers, OCS increasingly raised concerns and ROTC was struggling for its life. What to do? Should the army remove what might well be artificial stumbling blocks? Federal rulings had thrown the role of testing into question: Were such screening tests directly relevant to the task at hand? Did they discriminate against "culturally deprived and disadvantaged groups"? Was the army losing qualified men by ignoring other sources? Thus the turn to smaller, less visible HBCUs. Thus the tentative toe in the water: Maybe the ROTC admissions test should not have so much power?

One of the senior personnel officers who had supported Butler's study, however, had seen HBCUs as part of the problem. Not all of them, of course, but he believed that overall their graduates were less well prepared than graduates of other public and private universities. He thought that went a long way toward explaining why Black officers were promoted at lower rates than their white peers. Butler had directly contested that claim in his report, but that concern reflected a widely held assumption.[60] Was this, many white leaders wondered, the best path to equal representation?

And what of West Point?

The US Military Academy at West Point did not have a good record on race. By 1968, over the 166 years of the academy's history, only 68 Black cadets had been graduated from West Point. An additional 11, over the course of those 166 years, had not made it to graduation. During the 1950s, there were never more than 20 African American cadets in all four classes combined; those 20, factored into the total enrollment of roughly 3,200, represented sixth-tenths of 1 percent. That percentage *dropped* in the 1960s.

But it was not simply numbers. From the beginning, Black cadets had struggled to find a place in the academy. James Webster Smith, the first African American to enter West Point, was ostracized by the white cadets. They refused to share a room with him, to eat with him, to engage him in any form of what was, at the time, labeled "social intercourse."[61]

Smith had carried the weight of great expectation to West Point; he had been selected and prepared and nominated by men who believed that Black cadets at West Point would make a powerful symbolic point. Smith, who had been born into slavery, was spotted in Columbia, South Carolina, by northern philanthropist David Clark, who—seeing his promise—had prepared him for this future, enrolling him in high school in Hartford, Connecticut, and then securing his nomination to West Point. Smith was one of four young Black men nominated for a cadetship in 1870. Two were denied admission on medical grounds. A third, Michael Howard, roomed briefly with Smith but soon failed the entrance exam—along with forty-six of the eighty-five white nominees. Smith claimed that academy officers had made the entrance exams brutally difficult in hopes of excluding the Black nominees: "They had prepared it to fix the colored candidates, but it proved most disastrous to the whites," he wrote.[62]

Smith and the other Black nominee who survived long enough to sit the academic exams were described by a tactical officer at West Point in language suggesting the struggles they would face. Smith, wrote Capt. Rufus L. King, was "a tall, slim, loose-jointed cadaverous party, with arms and legs of extraordinary length, and indescribable complexion, chalky white except in spots where the tan struck through and occasional deeper splotches of brown; little beady, snakelike eyes, high cheek bones and kinky hair . . . the personification of pulsive gloom." The other young man, Michael Howard, appeared to King as "a chuckling bullet-headed little darkie, whose great eyes . . . wander."[63]

As the sole Black cadet at West Point, forced to drill alone to avoid standing "too near" a white cadet, left without the support of a roommate in the difficult plebe year, Smith also faced an organized campaign to drive him from the academy. Those who vowed to exclude "colored" men from West Point enforced a pledge to "silence" Smith, to speak not a word to him beyond the unavoidable. Over the course of his first year at West Point, Smith withstood three recommendations for courts-martial and two trials, both for confrontations with white peers. He survived all, though was turned back a full year. From home, Smith's father wrote words that may have seemed less encouraging than demanding: "The rebels will devil you so much you can't stay," wrote Isaiah Smith, but "you must not resign on any account, for that is what the democrats want."[64]

Smith was determined but also unwilling to simply put his head down and persevere. During his first months at West Point he had pushed back against his harassers, and he had complained of constant harassment to his patron, David Clark. Clark, in turn, made the ill-calculated decision to publish a version of Smith's letter of complaint in the *Hartford Courant*. Clark meant to gain sympathy for Smith by publicizing the harassment he faced.

Instead, he virtually guaranteed that Smith would not join the Long Gray Line of West Point graduates. Faculty joined with cadets in opposition to Smith. Wrote Professor George L. Andrews (class of 1851), "Probably a worse selection for the first colored cadet could not have been made. He was malicious, vindictive and untruthful. Instead of contenting himself with manfully meeting trouble when it came, he diligently and successfully sought it." "Low, tricky, vindictive," was the verdict of tactical officer King.[65]

Clark turned next to President Ulysses S. Grant, pointing out in a personal visit to the commander in chief Smith's excellent academic record but insisting that the harassment was becoming intolerable. "Don't take him away," said Grant, seeing Smith more as a symbol than as a young man. "The battle may as well be fought now as any time." But Grant's son Fred, in his final year at West Point, was also in the room. He objected to his father's words. The time had not come, he said, "to send colored boys to West Point." And when Clark pointed out that there were now Black men in the Senate, Fred Grant made clear what opposition Smith faced: "Well, no damned nigger will ever graduate from West Point," said the president's son.[66]

Smith did not graduate. He was dismissed for deficiency in Natural and Experimental Philosophy (physics), and when his appeals failed, he left the academy in July 1874. Angry and embittered, he nonetheless completed his college degree and took a position as mathematics instructor at South Carolina Agricultural and Mechanics Institute. Just sixteen months after he left West Point, at the age of twenty-six, Smith died of tuberculosis.[67]

In 1877, Henry Ossian Flipper became the first Black cadet to graduate from West Point. Like Smith, he had been born into slavery. Like Smith, he was academically talented. But unlike Smith, Flipper endured the silencing in silence. Still, harassment at the academy continued, with institutional support. In 1880, Black cadet Johnson Chesnut Whittaker was found tied to his bed, bleeding from his head, ears, hands, and feet. West Point, in a travesty of a trial, judged that the wounds were self-inflicted, that Whittaker had staged the scene to avoid taking his end-of-term exams and to bring discredit on West Point. The nation's commander in chief overturned the verdict, but West Point dismissed Whittaker for academic deficiency.[68]

From 1870 through the end of the century, twenty-three young Black men were nominated for cadetships at West Point. Only twelve passed the entrance exams. Of those twelve, only six remained for more than one semester. Of those six, only three graduated. Following Charles Young's graduation in 1889, no other Black cadet would graduate from West Point for forty-seven years. That cadet—Benjamin O. Davis Jr., who would become the air force's first Black general—was silenced . . . for four full years.[69]

By the 1960s, much had changed. Black cadets remained exceedingly rare, but they faced no organized harassment. There was individual racism, certainly, and unthinking slights. But by 1968 the army had been officially desegregated for twenty years—more than a lifetime for the eighteen-year-old plebes. In the late 1960s, however, as in the years following the US Civil War, Black cadets at West Point had assumed a symbolic importance. The Black press pointed to the shortage of Black officers as evidence that the army's commitment to equality was hypocritical, at best. The NAACP and the Urban League said much the same. Pressure came from the Department of Defense—though the House and Senate Armed Services Committees, both led by segregationist southerners who served on the academy's Board of Visitors, played little role in the push for equal opportunity. The DoD announced that any school that practiced racial discrimination would lose its ROTC funding, and the three military academies—at West Point, Annapolis, and Colorado Springs—launched what *Ebony* characterized as a "massive national recruitment campaign." Even so, the author of the *Ebony* article made clear his skepticism, portraying the campaign as yet another example of the "national quest for the bright, highly trainable, 'instant Negro.'"[70]

By late 1967, the Department of Defense was seeking statistics on minority enrollment from West Point. That request was soon followed by directions from the Department of the Army to study recruiting techniques for Black applicants. West Point, army leaders suggested, should have at least the same percentage of minority students as did the civilian college population.[71]

Significantly, that same year West Point's superintendent replaced the admissions officer who had served since 1955. The new admissions officer, Lt. Col. Manley Rogers, launched what he called "a vigorous program to encourage minority group candidates," one that would eventually come to resemble headhunting—"an executive search type of operation," with telephone calls, letters, and visits to their homes.[72]

In 1968, though, the process was more modest. Manley created a public relations program that emphasized equal opportunity. And he finagled an appointment of a minority group recruiting officer to the admissions staff. That year West Point sent a mass mailing to potential minority candidates. And it restored the question about racial identity to the application form—now seeking (in the words of the commandant) to "recognize immediately minority group applicants" in order to give them "whatever assistance is appropriate." Results followed quickly. While the class of 1972 (entering in 1968) included nine Black cadets, 1969's class of 1973 increased those numbers fivefold, to forty-seven. This, noted West Point's superintendent, "has been accomplished without the use of a double standard."[73]

In some ways, West Point's addition of minority cadets was painless. In civilian society, as equal opportunity legislation required access for members of racial minorities and for women, those applicants dramatically increased the competition for each slot—especially as jobs began to disappear in the 1970s. White male construction workers or firefighters (or law students or middle managers) saw a zero-sum game. Incorporating those who had previously been excluded meant excluding someone else. Promoting someone who had previously been marginalized meant not promoting someone who had been on that promotion track. That was not the case at West Point. As the United States moved into combat in Vietnam, Congress required the USMA to almost double its enrollment. In 1965, every single qualified applicant was admitted to the class of 1969. As the class size expanded each year through 1971, increasing minority representation had no impact on other qualified candidates.[74]

Between 1965 and 1971, the USMA would increase the size of its corps from 2,500 to 4,417. Equal opportunity admissions—or even affirmative actions— was thus a much easier sell, even if it had not been mandated from above. But the rapid expansion was not easy. Barracks, classrooms, equipment, faculty —all presented a challenge. And so did the acquisition of qualified cadets. Writing in 1967, West Point's superintendent noted that his "central concern" was maintaining standards of intellectual excellence "in the face of this expanding student population."[75]

In 1971, a new superintendent went further, claiming that "all activities" of the USMA "continued, methodically and resolutely, to insure that as many as possible of only the best qualified young men of our nation will one day join the Long Grey [sic] Line." As the war in Vietnam had grown ever more unpopular, as young men increasingly rejected not only the purported "indoctrination" offered by military academies but also systems of hierarchy, uniformity, and arbitrary authority, and as colleges and universities competed for the outstanding young men the academy sought, West Point was struggling to find enough qualified applicants.[76]

That was especially true of the young Black men who qualified for admission. They now had other options, courted by civilian colleges and universities as well as by businesses and corporations. And the no-strings-attached scholarships offered by civilian universities made West Point's all-expenses-paid education look a lot less "free." West Point's minority admissions officer Art Hester (class of 1965) faced that challenge.

Hester's path to West Point had been much the same as many of his peers', save for the fact that he had been born on a sharecropper's farm in Mississippi. His family moved to Chicago while he was small, and he had graduated from Chicago's Marshall High School with high marks. In 1960, the military seemed a good option. His family could not afford to pay for college, and the service academies were free. He had five uncles who had served, two in World War II and three in Korea; they were all well respected for their service. And Hester had always wanted to fly. He easily secured a nomination from his congressman, Frank Annunzio . . . for the Air Force Academy. But Hester had flat feet and his vision was not 20/20. Back to square one, he took Annunzio's advice and turned to West Point, where he was admitted the following year.[77]

The experience of Black cadets at West Point had changed profoundly since the graduation of Benjamin O. Davis Jr. Hester saw no difference between how he and his white classmates were treated. Four of the six Black cadets who entered in 1961 graduated; while loss of a third sounds terrible, that was pretty much the expected rate of attrition overall. Hester went to airborne and to ranger school and then to Vietnam with the 101st Airborne. After a year in West Germany, the young captain was on track to return to Vietnam when he got a call from personnel. He had a potential assignment to teach at West Point but needed to get a master's degree in the space of a year in order to fill that slot. An intense four quarters at Stanford later, Hester had an MA in industrial engineering and a position in West Point's admissions office.[78]

Hester found plenty of support from the top but did not want the equal admissions opportunity program to remain dependent on superintendents' attitudes or shifting priorities. His goal was to institutionalize the program. The cadet corps, argued Hester, should look like the nation. That meant dramatically increasing the number of African American cadets. In the army bureaucratese that was approved by both the USMA and the Department of the Army, the admissions plan read, "The goal of this program is to increase the number of minority cadets so that their ethnic distribution in the Corps of cadets is commensurate with that of the national population."[79]

But Hester went further. In March 1970, he submitted what he titled "An Argument for Changing the Admissions Systems at the United States Military Academy in Order to Increase the Enrollment of Minority Students." Hester argued that the army faced a growing problem. Young Black soldiers, he wrote, "just as their civilian counterparts, are becoming increasingly sensitive about their cultural identity and heritage." And, he continued in the language of a loyal army officer, although the army has "long enjoyed a good reputation for fairness and equal opportunity among Negroes," that good reputation was undermined by the fact that "there is only one black general officer in the entire Army." Perceptions of unfairness, Hester claimed, would only be intensified by the coming move to an all-volunteer force, in which the percentage of Black enlisted men would likely increase dramatically.[80]

Hester then proposed something he acknowledged seemed "quite radical," an idea that "would undoubtedly be opposed by some in the Army's hierarchy": he wanted the academy to accept minority students "of high potential" who did not "measure up to the established academic standards." Here was the superintendent's "double standard," proposed just as the academy's class size had stabilized and admissions became, once again, zero-sum. But Hester also offered an institutionally acceptable solution. What if minority students whose academic preparation was less than it might be were admitted to the USMA Preparatory School, which since 1946 had offered a year's worth of intensive training to enlisted soldiers who sought admission to the academy? It was not immediate, but that institutionally savvy recommendation would later be adopted.[81]

The question of minority admissions, of course, did not exist in a vacuum. The West Point superintendent and Board of Visitors had been worrying about how to maintain quality as the academy more or less doubled the size of the Corps of Cadets. More broadly, the army had been confronting challenges to its evaluation and promotion system; such questions were not exactly welcomed by those who had found success in that system, for suggestions that it was not fair likewise implied that their success was not fully legitimate. And public conversations about "reverse discrimination," quotas, qualifications, and standards shaped responses within the academy, as well. Top leadership supported Hester's efforts, but his memo set off debates about whether admissions standards should be absolute or flexible and about what, exactly, the purpose of the academy was.[82]

The stakes rose in the spring of 1971 when President Nixon, embracing a "southern strategy" in his attempt to hold on to the White House in the 1972 election, ordered West Point's superintendent to build a monument to the "West Pointers who lost their lives serving on the Southern side" on academy grounds. Making his political calculation clear, Nixon wanted the monument completed before the Republican nominating convention the following year.

*Affirmative Actions*

The USMA superintendent, Maj. Gen. William A. Knowlton, tried to finesse the demand (he could not exactly refuse instructions from his commander in chief), planning instead to create an exhibit on West Point and the Civil War. That was definitely not what Nixon had in mind; Nixon wanted a major public monument to the Confederacy, which he could use to build support among white voters in the South. He vetoed Knowlton's plan.[83]

Nixon, however, had not provided funds for the monument. Knowlton knew there was not really time to appeal to Congress, nor any assurance that Congress—in 1971—would fund such a project. So Knowlton appealed to West Point's alumni association, the only organization allowed to raise money for this federally funded institution. And there Capt. Arthur Hester —the youngest member of the executive board and its only African American member—took a stand. West Point must not build a monument to traitors, he argued; it must not celebrate those who fought against the United States. Hester was supported by former astronaut Frank Borman, but he found himself—as a twenty-eight-year-old captain—directly confronting both a recent army chief of staff and a former chair of the Joint Chiefs. Hester lost, but not by much. The vote was eighteen to sixteen in favor of funding Nixon's monument.[84]

Amazingly, Nixon's demand and the conflict it provoked had not leaked to the press or to the current cadets. The first they heard was when Knowlton —in a politically savvy move—asked the elected president of the de facto Black student union (race-based organizations were not officially allowed at West Point) his opinion of the planned monument. As Knowlton had anticipated, things blew up. There were 119 Black cadets by that point, and while the entering classes of 1968 and 1969 had been slow to embrace claims of Black identity or to push against USMA practices, the younger cadets saw the world differently—and Percy Squire, the group's president, saw their point. The younger cadets argued for mass resignation, for demonstrations, for public sit-ins. Squire thought more strategically. In the end, he crafted a "manifesto" that was signed by every Black cadet and—in a decision that they knew might put at risk their future careers—by all but one Black officer at the academy.[85]

The manifesto went beyond the proposed monument, though that was its immediate provocation. Squire pointed to the larger stakes. The Black cadets had come to West Point, the manifesto explained, "with aspirations of improving the quality of leadership being given to Black military men." And in service of that goal, they had stayed silent in the face of repeated offenses.

The Behavioral Science Club, pictured here in a yearbook photograph, became a de facto Black student union at the US Military Academy at West Point. In 1971, all 119 Black cadets joined together to sign a six-page "Manifesto" that condemned "blatant racism" at the academy. *Courtesy USMA Archives.*

But no longer. "A long train of abuses and usurpations . . . evinc[ing] a design of racism," they wrote, now demanded "the presentation of a history of repeated injuries . . . to a candid America."[86]

The cadets' thirteen itemized grievances reached back to the silencing of Black cadets and forward to the academy's failure to recruit "gifted young black high school graduates" to fill the officer ranks of the future. They included the shortage of Black instructors, the lack of Black leaders in the cadet chain of command, the academy's unwillingness to create an "equitable haircut policy for blacks." And, most significantly, cadets highlighted the planned Confederate monument to officers who had "abrogated their oath." "This last grievance," read the manifesto, "more so than any other, has seriously weakened the faith we had in the administration to understand our racial pride. For if, as black officers, we were ever associated with an institution that endorsed this type of action, it would gravely hamper our ability to reach the black soldiers we hope to command after graduation." Making clear that they were acting to fulfill their own "moral obligation," they called upon those in positions of authority to "employ their moral courage."[87]

As cadet leaders maneuvered the threat of public unrest internally, they also gave a hint of the public turmoil they could create. *Ebony* magazine's "Getting It Together at 'The Point'" was an implicit threat. While the author,

*Affirmative Actions*

a young associate editor at the magazine who was both an army veteran and a pallbearer at Malcolm X's 1965 funeral, played up the conflict between the "rising tide of black consciousness" and the "total loyalty" demanded at West Point, he briefly noted the "quiet uproar" over the plans to build a Confederate monument. More than a million households subscribed to *Ebony*. The cadets were making clear that they knew how to use the press, that they had connections they would tap if they deemed it necessary.[88]

Superintendent Knowlton—an extraordinarily accomplished officer (three Silver Stars; eight languages; strong networks in the Pentagon)—skillfully managed the cadets' threat of unrest to derail Nixon's order. Imagine, he suggested, cadets staging mass protests at the monument's dedication. Outrage from the Black press. Fury from the Congressional Black Caucus.

The still-quiet threat of "a massive rebellion" at West Point was enough to get Nixon to back down. But the conflict was not quiet within the academy. The manifesto prompted real change. Most visible were the Afros—real Afros, not "army Afros"—that Black cadets began to wear. And as cadets embraced the symbols of Black identity, the administration worked harder to provide Black instructors and to recruit the "gifted young black high school graduates" that would make West Point look like the nation it served.[89]

These young Black cadets had combined two strands of protest that had commanded army attention: the (threat of) disruption and violence; the clearly stated demands for change. And their approach showed how well they understood the institution. They emphasized that the West Point graduates who fought for the Confederacy had betrayed the oath sworn by all in the Long Gray Line, not the fact that officers who led Confederate forces had fought on behalf of those who owned these cadets' ancestors. They made clear that the monument, if built, would undermine their ability to lead young Black enlisted men in the future. They played to West Point's culture and to the army's interests. And they won.

The army's move to an all-volunteer force in 1973 presented a new set of challenges, just as it lessened others. Over the years immediately following the end of conscription, the army's enlisted force grew more and more disproportionately Black. For both the army and for American society, that presented a conundrum.

Faced with filling 20,000 to 30,000 pairs of boots a month, and without the pressure of the draft to spur volunteers, the beleaguered army had begun portraying military service as a "good job." And many young Black men, still contending with disproportionately limited opportunities in civilian life, signed up. In 1974, Black Americans made up more than 27 percent of new accessions. And Black soldiers reenlisted at much higher rates than did their white peers—at roughly half, as compared with less than one-third. By 1977, more than a quarter of the army's enlisted ranks were Black.[90]

Some critics wrote about "tipping points," envisioning a number or percentage that would begin to discourage white men from enlisting. A few, as calls for armed revolution still echoed, worried about Black men with guns. But others were legitimately concerned that disproportionate representation meant disproportionate risk. If Black soldiers made up more than 30 percent of the 2nd Infantry Division in Korea—which they did—combat casualties would likely be 30 percent Black. Claims that the United States was using Black men as cannon fodder in Vietnam had not faded, despite statistical evidence to the contrary; a 30 percent Black infantry division left army leaders lying awake at night. But at the same time, in a nation that had long restricted the opportunities available to Black men, how could it justify closing off what the army was, directly, now promoting as "an opportunity"?[91]

By 1974, when people discussed quotas for Blacks in the army, they were talking about quotas to *limit* the number of Black enlisted soldiers, not the aspirational quotas for the acquisition and promotion of Black officers. Secretary of the Army Bo Callaway, who served for just over two years, overseeing the move to the all-volunteer force, rejected such quotas, even as he shifted recruiters from inner cities to primarily white suburbs. But Callaway also argued that Black men and women were enlisting and reenlisting because of the opportunities they found in the army, that "percentages are the least important indicators of representativeness when you view them in relation to justice, opportunity, individual work, advancement by merit and the other real indicators of our Army's strength." And the enlisted ranks of the army grew increasingly Black.[92]

Callaway, a southerner who had voted against civil rights legislation as a congressman from Georgia, did not seem the ideal candidate to carry forward affirmative actions. But under his watch, as questions about race shaped almost all discussions of the future of the all-volunteer force, his office focused intently on the issue. Callaway himself walked a fine line when it came to racial issues, but he pushed the institutional army to clarify—and expand —its affirmative actions program.

In early 1974, Callaway created an ad hoc general officers' steering committee on equal opportunity, chaired by the deputy chief of staff for personnel. This group, assigned to review army equal opportunity policies and procedures, was soon overtaken by events, when President Nixon—concerned about reports that religious or ethnic identity had been used to disqualify American Jews from assignment to Saudi Arabia—directed the DoD to conduct a complete review of equal opportunity policies and practices in the military. Under DoD direction, the committee's charge expanded to a worldwide review, considering policy, practice, and implementation.[93]

This group worked from the army's 1972 Affirmative Actions Plan, which members characterized as going "further than equal opportunity" by requiring "recognition of sociological factors." Committee members, not surprisingly, emphasized the bureaucratization of equal opportunity. They recommended that the life of the ad hoc committee be extended. They called for statistical data—"essential to the management of equal opportunity"—from all levels of command and assigned the Office of the Deputy Chief of Staff for Personnel to create guidelines for collecting it. They acknowledged that implementation still "lagged behind full achievement of army goals and objectives" but cited studies demonstrating that it had improved during the prior two years, particularly through the creation of unit-based, local affirmative action plans. They also endorsed "proper discriminating actions." Those "discriminating actions" included permission for army agencies to request that files of minority officers be included when nominations for specific positions were sent forward. In a major shift, however, the steering committee focused on gender as well as on race.[94]

Callaway, as secretary of the army, fostered the bureaucratization of equal opportunity, weaving it into army institutional process and practice and, eventually, logic. In one of his final actions in office, this Republican appointee and prior civil rights opponent implemented a new army affirmative action plan, complete with detailed, specific, time-linked goals.[95]

Simply judging by the numbers, the army's affirmative actions (emphasis on the s) made a difference. By 1975, members of racial minorities (primarily African American) made up almost a quarter of ROTC cadets and more than 9 percent of those at West Point. Today, the "diversity" of cadets at West Point closely mirrors the nation's racial/ethnic population. The army's officer corps went from 3.9 percent Black in 1972 to 11.3 percent Black by the end of the millennium, a percentage it has more or less maintained ever since. In 2020, only one—or 8 percent—of the twelve four-star generals was Black, but 17 percent of three-star generals were, as were 14 percent of two-star and 16 percent of one-star. In 2021, 12.3 percent of army active-duty officers were Black; that almost exactly mirrors the US population (even as the percentage of first lieutenants is higher than the percentage of lieutenant colonels). The success measured in that 12.3 percent, however, is complicated by another statistic: as enlisted troops, Black Americans almost double their portion of the US population.[96]

Should the percentage of Black officers equal the percentage of African Americans in the US population? The percentage of Black soldiers serving in the army? The percentage of those who possess the basic qualification of a college degree? And what of the fact that Black women serve at much higher rates than Black men? (In 1995, almost half of all enlisted women in the active army were Black.) Or that Black men make up only 4.6 percent of all postsecondary enrollments (with a college degree necessary for officer status)? Or that Hispanic enlisted men now outnumber Black enlisted men?[97]

Fundamental questions remain. New questions have emerged. But the affirmative actions to which the US Army committed itself in the 1970s continue to provide the institutional framework for solutions.

# CONCLUSION

Did it work?

That depends on what "it" is. For the US Army, "it" was managing the racial crisis that threatened to tear the institution apart. Sure, some leaders argued that the army should be a model for the nation when it came to race. Many within the army or who spoke on its behalf condemned racism; many made clear their commitment to racial equality. That mattered—even if some of the statements were more performative than heartfelt. Nonetheless, the institution would not have addressed the problem of race with such focus and intensity were it not for the sense of crisis, were it not for the fact that key leaders believed racial conflict undermined the ability of the US Army to fulfill its mission of national defense.

Those leaders were fundamentally most worried about the violence that set the army afire. But they also understood the disruptive power of more measured actions, the manifestos and demands and proposals that engaged outside pressure, from the Black press and the NAACP to members of Congress and presidential administrations. They meant to manage that, as well. Their key goal was stability—the stability they deemed necessary for the army to successfully defend the nation.

Did they succeed? Yes, in the sense that the army stabilized. Yes, in the sense that the crisis passed.

The actions that army leaders at all ranks took—the actions described in the previous pages, from affirmative action programs to the incorporation of Black culture and history into army programs—helped defuse the crisis. And the army's broader move from purported race blindness to race consciousness mattered enormously. But broader historical changes that were beyond army control also contributed: the end of the US war in Vietnam, the move to an all-volunteer force, the Black freedom movement's shift in focus, and significant changes in the demographics of the army. By the late 1970s, while race remained a problem, army leaders no longer saw "the problem of race" as a threat to the army's stability or as the central crisis the institution must confront.

By the mid-1970s, the army was no longer full of men who did not want to be there. The draft was over. If individuals did, in fact, hate the US Army, at least they themselves had made the decision to join. Army life was still army life, the promises of "no more chickenshit" in the all-volunteer force not fully realized, but reforms linked to the all-volunteer force did improve the daily lives of enlisted soldiers. Perhaps equally important, this was no longer an army mired in a failing war, with the demands of Vietnam reaching far beyond the conflict in Southeast Asia. And while we cannot simply accept army leaders' frequent claim that the problem of race was simply imported from American society, a claim that too easily let army practices and policies off the hook, as revolutionary claims of Black separatism and Black nationalism faded from classrooms and street corners, they faded from army barracks as well.

It also mattered that army demographics changed. By the late 1970s, African Americans made up almost 30 percent of the enlisted ranks. Black Americans were still in the minority, in the army as in the nation, but the institution felt—and was—less white. The percentage of Black enlisted soldiers did begin to drop in the 1990s, and it declined further during the US wars in Iraq and Afghanistan. Still, in 2020, a full one-third of active duty enlisted soldiers were not white, with Black troops making up close to a quarter of the whole. That meant not only a less white army but also a less Black-and-white army. In 2020, 20 percent of active duty enlisted troops were Hispanic/ Latino (some of whom were also counted, in army records, as "white").

The army also had become increasingly female. Faced with recruiting shortfalls following the move to an all-volunteer force, army leaders saw women as a way to fill more boots and, in turn, to fill positions that were not traditionally open to women. The separate Women's Army Corps was dissolved in 1978. Perhaps unsurprisingly, gender integration was in some ways more complex than racial integration. And of course, race still played a role. In 2020, 15.5 percent of the active duty army was female, up from 1.2 percent in 1971—and that cohort of soldiers was majority-minority: 38 percent were Black, 22 percent Hispanic (again, some of whom were also counted as "white").[1] The bigger point is that adding women to the mix altered the dynamic. Within the army, during this period of crisis, almost everyone had defined "the problem of race" as male, and equal opportunity as (in the words of Curtis Smothers) a "male problem exclusively oriented to race relations." Few had thought about female soldiers.[2] Shifting demographics changed the problem at hand.

And, finally, while the US Army may be an institution apart, it exists in and draws its members from American society. That society is vastly different, when it comes to race, than it was in the 1960s and early 1970s. It is not necessary to pretend that racism has been vanquished or that structural inequities have disappeared in order to insist on—speaking as a historian—just how much has changed, and for the better. The actions of the US military contributed to those changes.

Much of what the army did in response to the problem of race was disorganized and stopgap—a "crisis managed program," as the evaluation of the second "affirmative actions" program described it.[3] Many army actions were highly contingent, specific to time and place. But that makes sense. Problems are manifest in time and place. They are specific to their moment. Efforts to solve those problems must be historically specific to have any prayer of success.

The army's most creative efforts to manage "the problem of race" usually were the most closely linked to the sensibilities and sensitivities of the era. Some of these were more successful than others (based on army goals), but few survived beyond that historical moment. Nonetheless, historically specific actions had long-term impacts, and many evolved into long-term programs and policies.

Even as individual policies and practices fell away or were replaced by approaches more appropriate to a changing world, the US Army's focus on "the problem of race" fundamentally changed the institution. Race—as a problem, but also as a significant category—became part of the army's institutional logic. It was bureaucratized. It was woven into the fabric of army organizational charts and regulations; included in education and training and evaluation; the subject of data collection and of affirmative action targets and goals. "Race" is now measured, analyzed, reported. Regulations and paperwork stifled much of the creativity and flexibility that marked early efforts to solve the problem—to save the army, as many saw the task. But an institutionalized problem is one that does not easily disappear.

**A**gain, did it work? What if "it" was, as those who fought for change desired, creating racial equality in the army?

The army's bottom line remained military efficiency and combat readiness, its moves toward racial justice always framed, largely, in those terms. Changing a massive bureaucratic institution is slow work, always subject to failures of implementation and to conflict over priorities and over methods. As US ground troops were withdrawn from Vietnam and the US military transformed into an all-volunteer force, many who had fought for change remained frustrated and disappointed. Their revolution was far from complete—incomplete enough that some believe, today, that little has changed, that Black soldiers are still fighting the very same battles that were fought half a century ago. In that, they are wrong. When it comes to racial justice in the US Army, or in almost any American institution, much remains to be done. That is clear. But looking back from today to 1969, the year the army first identified the problem of race, it is also clear how much has been accomplished.

Those who fought for racial equity and social justice in the US Army found incomplete success—but it *was* success. To paraphrase the words of Congressman Ron Dellums: As powerful as the army is, it did change.

# ACKNOWLEDGMENTS

Writing my first book on the US Army felt like exploration, the combined joy and unease of traveling to a new and fascinating place where I had to learn to make sense of a complex culture and a sometimes-counterintuitive logic. That experience yielded the intellectual framework that structures this book. But while I saw *America's Army* through metaphors of travel and exploration, writing *An Army Afire* seemed akin to the profoundly domestic process of making a quilt. I'm sure that's in part because I wrote most of this book during the relative isolation imposed by a global pandemic; it had been half a century since I'd spent so much time so close to home, and in the midst of widespread suffering and loss I discovered new pleasures in that domestic life—quilting included. More than that, though, telling this story—creating this story—felt like piecing scraps (of research rather than fabric) into a pattern I didn't fully appreciate until I saw it complete.

This project was launched with an Oscar Handlin Fellowship from the American Council of Learned Societies, and a Carnegie Foundation fellowship along with a National Endowment for the Humanities Public Scholars fellowship gave me freedom to focus on completing it. I am profoundly grateful for the gift of time to think, to research, and to write. I thank Temple University and—most especially—the University of Kansas, which offered me generous funding as a Foundation Distinguished Professor and through the Balfour Jeffrey-Higuchi Research Award that made extensive research travel possible. I have had extraordinary levels of financial support in researching and writing this book, and I know exactly how fortunate I've been.

I'm thrilled to get a chance to work with Debbie Gershenowitz and the excellent staff at the University of North Carolina Press. And the insightful comments offered by the press's three anonymous readers were invaluable. Their engagement with this work means a lot to me, most especially if my guesses about their identities are correct.

Presenting my work-in-progress to a wide variety of audiences—scholarly, military, and public—also helped me sharpen my arguments and see new connections. I'm grateful for invitations from and conversations following talks at Texas Christian University; the American Studies program at Leeds University; the Faculty of Law, University of Tokyo; the Logics of War Series, Brown University; the Vanderbilt History Seminar "Freedom since the Sixties/The Free and the Unfree"; the US Army Heritage Center Foundation; the World War I Museum and Memorial; the US Army Webinar and TRADOC Leaders Professional Development Session, Combined Arms Center, Fort Leavenworth; the Gender Seminar at the Hall Center for the Humanities, University of Kansas; and the Dale Center's Richard McCarthy Lecture, University of Southern Mississippi. I also benefited from the comments of anonymous readers for the *Journal of American History*, where I published a version of the material in chapter 6.

I can't say (or write) it often enough: archivists, librarians, command historians, and those charged with writing official histories have made this book possible. I appreciate the assistance of the archivists, librarians, historians, and research staffs at the US Army Center of Military History; the US Army Heritage and Education Center; the National Archives and Research Administration, College Park; the Defense Equal Opportunity Management Institute; the US Army Cadet Command; and the Library of Congress. Thanks in particular go to William Donnelly, Nicholas Schlosser, MaryKay Schmidt, Andrei Adaryukov, and Leo J. Daugherty III.

This book is built on research in historical archives, but conversations with those who lived the history reminded me, once again, of how much difference individuals make in determining its path. Thank you to John Aljets, Charles Becknell, Jose Bolton Sr., Will Gravely, Robert E. Gregg, Chuck Heiden, Arthur Hester, Richard O. Hope, Robert Killebrew, Robert Nuchow, David Pankey, A. Carl Segal, William Shkurti, Darnell Summers, and Bill Yates.

For assistance in obtaining images, my thanks go to Gail Yoshitani, chair of the Department of History, US Military Academy at West Point; René Stevens, Defense Equal Opportunity Management Institute; Catharine Giordano, *Stars and Stripes*; Judith Andrews, Smithsonian National Museum of African American History and Culture; Nicholas Schlosser, US Army Center of Military History; Gary A. White and the family of James S. White; and Darnell Summers.

For translations from Japanese, Korean, and German, thank you to Shoji Nakamura, Mina Lee, and Marjorie Galelli; for using their networks of connections on my behalf, to Mike Perry, Ty Seidule, Don Wright, Charles Bowery, and Jose Guzman; for attention to detail, to Scott Hedberg and

Karin Gresham; for depth of knowledge, to Brian Linn; for inspiration, to Greg Daddis and Kara Vuic; and to David Farber, for reminding me that "it's complicated" is not an argument and for talking this project through with me, time and time again. As always, he made it all so much better.

Each time around I am indebted to more people: family, friends, students, and colleagues (in overlapping categories) throughout the nation and the world. To all of y'all—thank you.

And most particularly, for this book:

My friend David Pankey died in 2018, and writing this book was much harder without him. David did three tours in Vietnam, one as a LRRP, followed by something top secret and nuclear in early-1970s Germany. He finished out his army career as a recruiter for the then-new all-volunteer force—the first gold-star recruiter in the nation. Years down the road, David turned up, age fifty-nine, in my "war and culture" class at the University of New Mexico. "I understand war," he wrote on the initial class survey I handed out, "but I have no idea what you mean by culture." Over the following fourteen years, David tried to explain the army to me. "Yes, I know that's what it *says*," he wrote me, more than once, about some document or the other, "but that's not what it *means*." And in what provided a moment of epiphany: "You keep trying," he told me, "to make sense of the army like it's a university. It's not."

One never knows what hardship will bring, but I know I wouldn't have made it through the past two years without the friendship of Ann Schofield, the kindness of Richard Godbeer, and the generosity of my brother, Richard Bailey. Or without Kara Vuic, Debbie Gershenowitz, Greg Daddis, and Bob Brigham. In the summer of 2020 we were texting each other so often that our families said, with not entirely good nature, that we might as well be in high school. Greg made the T-shirt: High School Friends, 2020.

And, as always, Max and David fill my heart. I'm so proud of the man Max has become. And David has inspired me since the day we met; he has made my life an adventure. I owe him everything.

# NOTES

ABBREVIATIONS USED IN THE NOTES

AHEC  US Army Heritage and Education Center, Carlisle, PA

Bennett,  L. Howard Bennett, "Command Leadership: Avoiding Racial
"Command Leadership"  Conflict and Maintaining Harmony, Unity and Strength in the
Armed Forces," January 8, 1970, in "Equal Opportunity, 1970–
1972" folder, box A70, Melvin R. Laird Papers, Gerald R. Ford
Presidential Library, Ann Arbor, MI

Bennett Report  "Report of the Joint Office of the Secretary of Defense—
White House–Military Departments Base Visits to Southeast
Asia," Racial Literature, 1971 file, box 4, DCoS Pers & Adm
(G-1) Human Relations Br, RG 472, National Archives and
Records Administration at College Park, MD

"Bennett Visit"  "Visit of Mr. Howard Bennett (28 Nov 1969)" file, box 1,
DCoS Pers & Adm (G-1) Human Relations Br, RG 472,
National Archives and Records Administration at
College Park, MD

CDD  *Chicago Daily Defender*

CMH  US Army Center of Military History, Fort McNair,
Washington, DC

Cortright Papers  David Cortright Papers, Swarthmore College Peace Collection,
Swarthmore, PA

CT  *Chicago Tribune*

Davison Speeches  "Speeches" file, box 5, Michael S. Davison Papers, US Army
Heritage and Education Center, Carlisle, PA

DCSPERS Discrim  Deputy Chief of Staff for Personnel Policy Files on
Discrimination in the Army, US Army Heritage and
Education Center, Carlisle, PA

"Fort Monroe  Race Relations Conference," Department of the Army,
Conference"  Fort Monroe, VA, November 17–20, 1970, US Army Heritage
and Education Center, Carlisle, PA

Jones-Smothers  Transcript of Nathaniel R. Jones discussion with Curtis R. Smothers, January 27, 1971, folder 1, box 2705, NAACP Papers, Library of Congress, Washington, DC

Laird Papers  Melvin R. Laird Papers, Gerald R. Ford Presidential Library, Ann Arbor, MI

Merritt Files  "MIV-29-68 MAJ. MERRITT," box 13, Military Assistance Command Vietnam, Inspector General Investigations Division, RG 472, National Archives and Records Administration at College Park, MD

Merritt Statement  Major Lavell Merritt, statement to press, October 9, 1968, distributed in press briefing Sunday, October 13, 1968; included in "MIV-29–68 MAJ. MERRITT," part 3 of 3, box 13, Military Assistance Command Vietnam, Inspector General Investigations Division, RG 472, National Archives and Records Administration at College Park, MD

NAACP Papers  NAACP Papers, Library of Congress, Washington, DC

NARA-CP  National Archives and Records Administration at College Park, MD

*NYT*  *New York Times*

P&A/HR  Deputy Chief of Staff (Personnel & Administration) (G-1) Human Relations Br, RG 472, National Archives and Records Administration at College Park, MD

Resor, Keynote Address  Secretary of the Army Stanley R. Resor, Keynote Address, Annual Meeting of the Association of the United States Army, October 13, 1969, in Historical Reference Collection, Speeches: Stanley R. Resor, US Army Center of Military History, Fort McNair, Washington, DC

RVN  Republic of Vietnam

*S&S*  *Stars and Stripes*

*S&S-P*  *Pacific Stars and Stripes*

Sussman Report  Arthur M. Sussman, Memorandum for Assistant Secretary of the Army (Manpower & Reserve Affairs), "Race Relations in the Army—Vietnam and Thailand," January 14, 1970, in SEA-RS 272 file, US Army Center of Military History, Fort McNair, Washington, DC

USARV IG Invstgn  USARV, IG Section/Invstgn & Cmplnt Div, RG 472, National Archives and Records Administration at College Park, MD

*WP*  *Washington Post*

White Briefing  Briefing Officer LTC James S. White, Text of ODCSPER,
DA Briefing for the CINCUSAREUR, "An Assessment
of Racial Tension in the Army," October 27, 1969, "Race"
permanent file, HRC 228.01, US Army Center of Military
History, Fort McNair, Washington, DC

INTRODUCTION

1. The phrase took various forms; it most commonly appeared as "the problem of race," "the race problem," and "the racial problem." For an early use, see Westmoreland's statement on Equal Opportunity and Treatment of All Military Personnel, October 17, 1969: "The roots of the race problem lie outside the army." In "Equal Opportunity and Racial Unrest 1970" file, box 1, P&A/HR.

2. "43 Negro Soldiers Jailed for Refusing Riot Standby," *Baltimore Sun*, August 25, 1968; for discussion of events at Long Binh Jail, see chapter 1.

3. James E. Westheider, *Fighting on Two Fronts: African Americans and the Vietnam War* (New York: New York University Press, 1997), 112; CGUSATHREE FT MCPHERSON GA to RUEPWD/TAG WASH DC, Blue Bell, February 8, 1969, folder 14, box 2, Series II Official Papers: Blue Bells, DCSPERS Discrim.

4. "Race Relations Briefing for Secretary of the Army," Fort Carson, January 27, 1971, "Race Relations in the Army" folder, box 1, Charles R. Wallis Papers, AHEC; Wallace Terry, "Bringing the War Home," *Black Scholar* 2 (November 1970): 11; Davison CG II FFV to LTG McCaffrey DCG USARV, November 13, 1970, "Vietnam Incidents" file, SEA-RS 140b, CMH.

5. "7 GIs Held in Pyongtaek Racial Brawl," *S&S-P*, April 16, 1971; "Chronology of Racial Incidents, 6 January–6 April 1971," "Race Relations Survey 1971" file, box 3, P&A/HR, RG 472, NARA-CP. It appears from the detailed description of events that the same man addressed the first sergeant and shot the troop commander, but two enlisted men were present at both incidents. See further discussion in chapter 8.

6. William Shkurti, email to author, June 9, 2019; Daniel J. Nelson, *A History of U.S. Military Forces in Germany* (Boulder, CO: Westview Press, 1987; reissued by Routledge University Press, 2018), 116, citing *Stuttgarter Zeitung*, August 15, 1972.

7. "The War within the War," *Time*, January 25, 1971.

8. Thomas A. Johnson, "'I'll Bleed for Myself,' Says Black U.S. Soldier in Europe," *NYT*, October 11, 1970.

9. White Briefing, 1, 16.

10. MG John C. Bennett to All Iron Horsemen, Subject: Racial Harmony Among Young Americans, Dec. 6, 1971, 1, "Racial Harmony Council" file, box 1, Charles R. Wallis Papers, AHEC.

11. David H. Frazier, "Mountaineer a minority, too," letter to the editor, *S&S*, April 1, 1976.

12. On Women's Army Corps history, see Bettie J. Morden, *The Women's Army Corps, 1945–1978* (Washington, DC: Center of Military History, 1990), 248, 304. On total enlisted strength of the army, see William Gardner Bell, *Department of the Army Historical Summary, Fiscal Year 1969* (Washington, DC: Center of Military History, 1973), 34.

13. Hon. Louis Stokes, "Racism in the Military: The Congressional Black Caucus Report, 15 May, 1972," 92nd Cong., 2nd Sess., 118 Cong. Rec. 36582 (October 14, 1972).

14. Stokes, "Racism in the Military," 36582.

15. Stokes, "Racism in the Military," 36595.

CHAPTER 1

1. "Discrimination Charge," *Irish Times*, October 14, 1968.

2. See, for example, Regulation No. 600-7, HQ US Army Hawaii, "Equal Opportunity and Treatment of Military Personnel," Hawaii Army file, Equal Opportunity Box 1, OSD (MRA), RG 330, NARA-CP. This regulation, dated April 7, 1965, specifies that army personnel may not "under any circumstances" participate in civil rights demonstrations because of "the requirement to achieve maximum readiness for military operations," which is "necessarily paramount over the right of individuals to participate in non-military activities."

3. All headlines are from newspapers.com, with articles published on October 14, 1968. Merritt's story seems not to have been carried by the *Stars and Stripes* (likely in accord with directive number 360-1, Public Information Policies and Procedures, dated March 19, 1967). Perhaps more interestingly, although Merritt's charges were the subject of an editorial a week later in the *Chicago Daily Defender*, they received no immediate coverage in the Black press.

4. "Ambushed G.I. Honored in Death" and "Army Denounced by Negro Major," both *NYT*, October 14, 1968.

5. "Gen. Frederic Davison," *Pittsburgh Courier*, October 5, 1968; Richard Pyle, "U.S. Army Racist, Negro Major Says," *Pittsburgh Post-Gazette*, October 14, 1968 ("unbelievable progress" is the *Post-Gazette*'s characterization of Davison's comments).

6. Gene Grove, "The Army and the Negro," *NYT*, July 24, 1966; Julian Hartt, "Army Cited as Example of Integration's Success," *WP*, August 30, 1966.

7. Hartt, "Army Cited"; "The Integrated Society," *Time*, December 23, 1966, 26; on Black leaders, James E. Westheider, *Fighting on Two Fronts: African Americans and the Vietnam War* (New York: New York University Press, 1997), 2; "MACV J-1 U.S. Forces Morale," from briefings given the Secretary of Defense, Saigon, South Vietnam, July 7 and 8, 1967, 1 (p. 280 of full briefing), SEA-RS 300a, CMH.

8. On army strength, see Defense Manpower Data Center, Office of the Secretary of Defense, US Department of Defense (specific numbers are 858,633 in 1961; 1,570,343 in 1968), as shown in David Coleman, "U.S. Military Personnel, 1954–2014," History in Pieces website, accessed September 16, 2022, https://historyinpieces.com/research/us-military-personnel-1954-2014; on global deployment, see Tim Kane, "Global U.S. Troop Deployment, 1950–2003," Heritage Foundation website, October 27, 2004, www.heritage.org/defense/report/global-us-troop-deployment-1950-2003.

9. Quote from "'Racialism' in U.S. Services," *Guardian* (London), October 14, 1968.

10. "Negro Major Charges U.S. Army Is Racist," *Los Angeles Times*, October 14, 1968. Merritt had, in fact, not been "passed over." He was found "fully qualified, not recommended" in both 1966 and 1967; in 1968 he was selected for retention in grade. Information from "Facts Concerning Major Lavell Merritt," attached to memo from Director of Military Personnel Policies to Vice Chief of Staff, USA, October 30, 1968, folder 1, box 11, DCSPERS Discrim.

11. Merritt Statement.

12. Merritt Statement, 4.

13. Merritt Statement, 5.

14. Merritt Statement, 2, 7–8.

15. For discussion, see Steve Estes, "'I Am a Man!': Race, Masculinity, and the 1968 Memphis Sanitation Strike," *Labor History* 41 (2000): 153–70; Merritt Statement, 8.

16. Merritt Statement, 1; information on Merritt's military record from COL Robert H. Ivey, Staff Judge Advocate to CG, USA Element, USMACV, "Misconduct of Major Lavell Merritt," November 7, 1968, and copy of Army Commendation Medal Citation, both in "MIV-29-68 MAJ. Merritt (Corrective/Follow-Up Action)" file, part 1 of 3, Merritt Files; Merritt Statement, 8 (on Chicago); testimony of 1SG Anthony J. Thomas to Clifford I. Wagner, IG, October 17, 1968, 265, Merritt Files.

17. MG Charles A. Corcoran, CSA-MACV, to IG MACV, "Directive for Investigation," October 14, 1968, in part 1 of 3, Merritt Files. I constructed the following narrative from the comprehensive investigation of Major Merritt. I cite the location of all direct quotes, but the Merritt investigation files, while voluminous, were not complete. The documents were often contradictory in their numbering, with pages unnumbered or not in sequential or original order.

18. Lavell Merritt, Major, INF, to Command, MACV, "Request for Command Assistance," October 7, 1968, 1, in part 3 of 3; also cited in "Report of Investigation Concerning Allegations of Misconduct on the Part of Major Lavell Merritt," Inspector General to Chief of Staff, MACV, October 29, 1968, part 1 of 3, both in Merritt Files.

19. Ivey to CG, "Misconduct of Major Lavell Merritt."

20. For example, Merritt faced charges of ethics violations in 1983 after he, as Montgomery County's minority purchasing officer, created a controversial "Leadership Assembly" to demonstrate the economic muscle of Black business and community leaders. Keith B. Richburg, "Montgomery Controversy Splits Black Leadership," *WP*, June 15, 1983.

21. Testimony of LTC Wray E. Bradley, conducted by LTC Stanley W. Brooks, IG, October 21, 1968, exhibit B-24, 423, 434, part 2 of 3, Merritt Files. All Bradley quotes are from this sequence.

22. Bradley testimony, 447, 448, 439, 446; "Facts Concerning Major Lavell Merritt."

23. Bradley testimony, 446.

24. Bradley testimony, 423, 448.

25. "Report of Investigation," 5–6; testimony of MAJ James Charles Irving to LTC Clifford I. Wagner, IG, October 16, 1968, exhibit B-2, 24; testimony of LTC Angelo Perri to LTC Clifford I. Wagner, IG, October 16, 1968, 11, both in part 1 of 3, Merritt Files.

26. Perri testimony, 4, 11.

27. Testimony of SGT Jackie L. Bivens to LTC Clifford I. Wagner, IG, October 26, 1968, exhibit B-30, 504; To Commander, MACV, attn: Chief of Staff, from MACIG; investigation conducted by Colonel Robert W. Marsh, Chief, Investigations Division, "Misconduct of Major Lavell Merritt," 3, both in Merritt Files.

28. Testimony of CPT Richard D. Heroux to LTC Clifford I. Wagner, IG, October 17, 1968, exhibit B-9, 201–2; testimony of SFC Robert L. Hall to LTC Clifford I. Wagner, IG, October 17, 1968, exhibit B-10, 252, part 2 of 3, both in Merritt Files.

29. Heroux testimony, 200–201.

30. Testimony of CPT Rodney J. Miller to LTC Clifford I. Wagner, October 16, 1968,

exhibit B-5, 115–16, part 1 of 3, Merritt Files; Bivens testimony, 503. There are various accounts of this incident throughout the witness interviews.

31. Description of this event is compiled from multiple testimonies. Chair descriptions include Thomas testimony, 270 ("slammed" and "underhanded toss"); testimony of SGT Henry R. Daniel to LTC Clifford I. Wagner, October 17, 1968, exhibit B-12, 279, part 2 of 3, Merritt Files; quotes from Bivens testimony, 520, and Thomas testimony, 268.

32. Bivens testimony, 510, 502; "Report of Investigation," 2; Hall testimony, 249.

33. Bivens testimony, 513.

34. For Hall's version, Hall testimony, 247; Bivens testimony, 501–2; Heroux testimony, 217–18; testimony of SFC James D. Giles to Clifford I. Wagner, IG, October 16, 1968, 127–31, part 1 of 3, Merritt Files; testimony of MAJ Thomas R. Stanton to LTC Clifford I. Wagner, IG, October 16, 1968, 48–49, part 1 of 3, Merritt Files.

35. "Certificate" (statement by CPT Rodney J. Miller), August 28, 1968, 1, part 3 of 3, Merritt Files.

36. "Report of Investigation," 6; Stanton testimony, 64.

37. "Certificate" (Miller), 1.

38. Miller testimony, 114.

39. Irving testimony, 44–45; letter from BG Robert E. Connor to MAJ Lavell Merritt, n.d., part 3 of 3, Merritt Files.

40. Merritt to Command, "Request for Command Assistance."

41. "Report of Investigation," 2.

42. Perri testimony, 1, 14.

43. For example, questioning in Daniel testimony, 282–85; Thomas testimony, 266, 273; Hall testimony, 254; Giles testimony, 142; and Nelson testimony, 68.

44. Daniel testimony, 282.

45. "Unbecoming" comments from Hall testimony, 256; testimony of SFC Willie M. Nelson to LTC Clifford I. Wagner, October 16, 1968, exhibit B-4, 82; 115, part 1 of 3, Merritt Files; Irving testimony, 26, 32, 33–35; Miller testimony, 115, Merritt Files.

46. Bivens testimony, 509 (Paulson); Miller testimony, 99 (physical action); Irving testimony, 32 (mutiny).

47. Irving testimony, 26; MAJ Stanton's comments relayed by LTC Perri in Perri testimony, 10.

48. Nelson testimony, 71; Irving testimony, 23–24.

49. Testimony of TSgt William D. Connery (USAF) to LTC Clifford I. Wagner, IG, October 24, 1968, exhibit B-29, 497, part 3 of 3, Merritt Files; Stanton quoted in Perri testimony, 10; Stanton testimony, 55, 53.

50. Irving testimony, 21, 26, 24, 27.

51. Irving testimony, 43, 36.

52. Irving testimony, 46.

53. Comparison of "Report of Investigation" summaries, 5–16, with transcripts of Wagner's interviews.

54. "Report of Investigation," 16.

55. "Report of Investigation," 2, 3.

56. Ivey to CG, "Misconduct of Major Lavell Merritt," 1.

57. Ivey to CG, "Misconduct of Major Lavell Merritt," 2.

58. Merritt to President Johnson, letter, November 10, 1968, in folder 1, box 11, Series II Official Papers, DCSPERS Discrim.

59. Lavell Merritt, "A Shield of Grace," typescript accompanying Merritt's letter to President Johnson, November 10, 1968.

60. A brief overview of the event appears in Joe Kolb, "Long Binh Jail Riot during the Vietnam War," *Vietnam Magazine*, December 2004, accessed on Historynet website, www .historynet.com/long-binh-jail-riot-during-the-vietnam-war.htm.

61. "Vietnam War Deaths and Casualties by Month," American War Library website, 1988, www.americanwarlibrary.com/vietnam/vwc24.htm.

62. Ryan Moore, "Long Binh Post and the Vietnam War," *Worlds Revealed: Geography and Maps at the Library of Congress* website, August 2, 2017, https://blogs.loc.gov /maps/2017/08/long-binh/; on Long Binh Post, see Meredith H. Lair, *Armed with Abundance: Consumerism and Soldiering in the Vietnam War* (Chapel Hill: University of North Carolina Press, 2011), 32–38; on calls from DC, oral history of Eugene Murdock, quoted in Cecil Barr Currey, *Long Binh Jail: An Oral History of Vietnam's Notorious U.S. Military Prison* (Washington, DC: Brassey's, 1999), 134. Extended quotes from oral histories conducted by Cecil B. Currey make up the majority of Currey's volume, with Currey's commentary interwoven. In this book, I cite Currey when referring to his analysis or the unfootnoted information he includes; I cite each oral history or letter as "[individual's name] in Currey, *Long Binh Jail*, p. x."

63. For a version of the Associate Press story, see "U.S. Military Prisoners Stage Riot," *Jackson (TN) Sun*, August 30, 1968; "The War: Riot at the LBJ," *Time*, September 6, 1968. UPI stories cited "reliable military sources" in attributing the fight that "touched off the riot" to "racial tensions." See "U.S. Soldiers in Vietnam in Stockade Riot," *Daily Northwestern* (Oshkosh, WI), August 30, 1968. "Chucks" was a derogatory term for whites.

64. Currey, *Long Binh Jail*, xv. In this work, Currey assembled portions of more than fifty oral histories of or written communications with those who played various roles at Long Binh Jail. As he points out, often by juxtaposing portions of various accounts, not all participants remember the events the same way.

65. Currey, *Long Binh Jail*, 49; Gerald B. Vessels (name not fully legible), Chaplain (MAJ), "Report and Personal Analysis of Riot in USARV Confinement Facility, Long Binh Post, Vietnam," to Chief of Chaplains, Department of the Army, September 9, 1968, unpaginated (2, 3, 14), in "1968: Confinement Facilities" folder, box 3, General Records, 1968–1971, RG 472, NARA-CP.

66. Oral history of Terrence Gough, conducted by Ronald Spector, February 24, 1982, 3, 6, in SEA-RS Collection, CMH; Currey, *Long Binh Jail*, 37. The MACV chief of staff ordered the inspector general to investigate "unspecified incidents of brutality" alleged by the bureau chief of CBS, Saigon, on January 11, 1969. See "Report of Investigation Concerning Alleged Brutality and Maltreatment at the US Army, Vietnam Installation Stockade," Confinement Facilities Files, USARV/Staff Advct Gen Sec, Admin Ofc, General Records, 1968–1971, RG 472, NARA-CP.

67. Norwood Jackson in Currey, *Long Binh Jail*, 41–42; George Deringer to Cecil B. Currey, November 29, 1990, in Currey, *Long Binh Jail*, 41.

68. Tom Guidera in Currey, *Long Binh Jail*, 29; William Keyes in Currey, *Long Binh Jail*, 80.

69. Kolb, in "Long Binh Jail Riot," cites the 90 percent figure as fact; 70 percent from Wayne Price in Currey, *Long Binh Jail*, 56; and Gough oral history, 21.

70. Currey, *Long Binh Jail*, 53, 52. These metal containers were small, and while they were painted silver to deflect the sun and shaded by a tarp, if it was 110 degrees outside, it was all of that *and* stifling within. Dimensions from Ronald H. Spector, *After Tet: The Bloodiest Year in Vietnam* (New York: The Free Press, 1993), 254; "The Box" from Herbert Green to Cecil B. Currey, April 24, 1990, in Currey, 121.

71. Keyes in Currey, *Long Binh Jail*, 66; characterization of Johnson from oral histories of Keyes, Murdock, and Jackson, quoted in Currey, 65–66; Vessels, "Report," 2; Gough oral history, 4. The 1938 film *Boys Town* was based on the work of Father Edward Flanagan, who founded a home for underprivileged boys in Nebraska. Spencer Tracy played Flanagan in the film.

72. Johnson's actions from Currey, *Long Binh Jail*, 65–66, 83–84 (including Jackson); Gough oral history, 4; Vessels, "Report," 2; testimony of Charles W. Griswald (clinical psychologist technician), Witness Statement, September 2, 1968, "USARV Installation Stockade Riot, Long Binh," box 10, CMH Refiles, RG 319, NARA-CP.

73. Jackson in Currey, *Long Binh Jail*, 65–66; Mike Doherty in Currey, 66. Similar testimony from guard SGT Gerald Treece, Witness Statement, September 2, 1968, "USARV Installation Stockade Riot, Long Binh," box 10, CMH Refiles, RG 319, NARA-CP.

74. Inmate Frank Troutman in Currey, *Long Binh Jail*, 112; Joshua Williams in Currey, 111.

75. Currey, *Long Binh Jail*, 111–14, 2; oral histories or testimony of Joshua Williams and inmates Frank Troutman, Payton, David Coppege, and Jimi Childress in Currey, 111–14.

76. Vessels, "Report," 2, 3.

77. Testimony of Antonio Aguinaldo Gibel, Witness Statement, September 3, 1968, "USARV Installation Stockade Riot, Long Binh," box 10, CMH Refiles, RG 319, NARA-CP.

78. Gibel testimony.

79. Overview in Kolb, "Long Binh Jail Riot"; cigarette filters from Jeremiah James in Currey, *Long Binh Jail*, 114; guards overpowered in Currey, 115; Gough oral history, 5; escape efforts from inmates Gerald Stovall and Nathaniel Fort Jr. in Currey, 105–9; improvised weapons in Currey, 115; inmates flee from inmate Leonard L. Thrumes and Claude K. Fouad in Currey, 119, 127; guards and wire from Doherty in Currey, 115.

80. Overview in Kolb, "Long Binh Jail Riot"; Currey, *Long Binh Jail*, 3–4; and Gough oral history, 20; freeing prisoners from Louis Zarrelli in Currey, 116; kerosene from Green in Currey, 121; bound hands from Vessels, "Report," 5; unnamed inmate quoted in Currey, 120; Haskett's murder in Currey, 120–21; "stupid fools" from inmate Dennis M. Sullivan in Currey, 119.

81. Accounts of Johnson's attack from Doherty; inmates Gerald Stovall, David Coppege, and Frank Troutman; and Ernest B. Talps in Currey, *Long Binh Jail*, 124–25; and Vessels, "Report," 4. Talps accompanied Johnson into the compound.

82. Map of Long Binh Post from Moore, "Long Bình Post and the Vietnam War"; Currey, *Long Binh Jail*, 130.

83. Vessels, "Report," 11; for Black inmates rescuing guards, Green on Charles Planter in Currey, *Long Binh Jail*, 121; Stovall in Currey, 116.

84. Vessels, "Report," 6.

85. Currey, *Long Binh Jail*, 130; Herman Trop, Eugene Murdock, Frank T. Mildren in Currey, 130–32.

86. Murdock, Trop in Currey, 131.

87. Rosaries in Vessels, "Report," 9; Mildren, Trop, Murdock in Currey, *Long Binh Jail*, 131–32.

88. Murdock in Currey, *Long Binh Jail*, 134–35.

89. Vessels, "Report," 9, 10.

90. Vessels, "Report," 12, 13.

91. Murdock in Currey, *Long Binh Jail*, 134.

92. Vessels, "Report," 15.

93. Mildren in Currey, *Long Binh Jail*, 136.

94. Currey, *Long Binh Jail*, 137; Kolb, "Long Binh Jail Riot." Damages from the initial riot were calculated at $97,529 in 1968 dollars (Currey, 138).

95. Departure and quotes from Doherty and McCotter in Currey, *Long Binh Jail*, 139, 141, 142.

96. "Section 2 Lessons Learned" in "Operational Report of Headquarters, 18th Military Police Brigade, for Period Ending 31 October 1968," November 15, 1968, 15, "18th MP BDE ORLL 31 Oct 1968" file, box 121, USARV/Command Historian, RG 472, NARA-CP.

97. Vessels, "Report," conclusion.

CHAPTER 2

1. Resor, Keynote Address, 1. The AUSA is the large nonprofit professional organization for the US Army; its members are civilian, veteran, and military.

2. Resor, Keynote Address, 2. "Vietnamization" was the policy of gradually withdrawing US troops and shifting responsibility for the war to the government of the Republic of Vietnam. Resor also briefly discussed an investigation of the Army & Air Force Exchange System for financial improprieties and the improper handling of nonappropriated funds.

3. Resor, Keynote Address, 5.

4. David Cortwright, "Black GI Resistance during the Vietnam War," *Vietnam Generation* 2 (1990): 54, https://digitalcommons.lasalle.edu/vietnamgeneration/vol2/iss1/5.

5. Resor, Keynote Address, 5.

6. Resor, Keynote Address, 8. "Marine Commandant's Message on Racial Tension," *NYT*, September 4, 1969; Bennett, "Command Leadership"; James Stanley White, "'Crisis in Black': An Assessment of Alienation among Black Vietnam-Era Veterans" (master's thesis, George Washington University, May 9, 1976).

7. Samuel Zaffiri, *Westmoreland* (New York: William Morrow, 1994), 197; William C. Westmoreland, *A Soldier Reports* (New York: Doubleday, 1976), 25–27, 226.

8. Bennett, "Command Leadership," 2. Bennett is discussing actions taken in 1968 and 1969, which he characterized as "necessary and prudent . . . but . . . neither adequate nor sufficient."

9. Morris J. MacGregor Jr., *Integration of the Armed Forces, 1940–1965* (1981; repr., Washington, DC: Center of Military History, US Army, 2001), 576. The DoD and US Army struggled over whether including racial IDs enhanced or hindered equal opportunity, and regulations changed over the course of the Cold War era. For example, an IG investigation into charges of racial prejudice concluded that "there are no racial prejudice practices in

D Company" while also recommending that "those individuals who use the terms 'Nig-ger', 'Black SOB', and any others with racial connotations" should be informed that "such practices will not be tolerated in the Company." Case 68-34, box 7, Investigations, USARV IG, RG 472, NARA-CP.

10. Quote from "After Action Report," 15, "Fort Monroe Conference."

11. The summary that follows is dramatically abridged from the account given in Mac-Gregor, *Integration*, and so loses both historical detail and the nuances of the argument he makes in this excellent official army history. The number of Black units was cut to four in 1869.

12. MacGregor, *Integration*, 7. On World War I, see Adriane Lentz-Smith, *Freedom Struggles: African Americans and World War I* (Cambridge, MA: Harvard University Press, 2009).

13. Editorials, "Our Special Grievances" and "The Reward," *The Crisis*, September 1918, 217, quoted in Ulysses Lee, *The Employment of Negro Troops* (1962; repr., Washington, DC: Center of Military History, US Army, 2001), 4.

14. George S. Schuyler, *Pittsburgh Courier*, December 21, 1940, quoted in MacGregor, *Integration*, 8.

15. MacGregor, *Integration*, 12.

16. MacGregor, *Integration*, 13, 15, 24.

17. MacGregor, 11; COL Eugene R. Householder, TAGO, Speech before Conference of Negro Editors and Publishers, December 8, 1941, AG 291.21, quoted in MacGregor, 23.

18. MacGregor, 38–39. On World War II, see Thomas A. Guglielmo, *Divisions: A New History of Racism and Resistance in America's World War II Military* (New York: Oxford University Press, 2021).

19. MacGregor, *Integration*, 291–92. On the post–World War II era, see Christine Knauer, *Let Us Fight as Free Men: Black Soldiers and Civil Rights* (Philadelphia: University of Pennsylvania Press, 2014); on desegregation, Sherie Mershon and Steven Schlossman, *Foxholes and Color Lines: Desegregating the U.S. Armed Forces* (Baltimore: Johns Hopkins University Press, 1998).

20. Quoted in MacGregor, *Integration*, 292 (quote is from statement to a Black audi-ence, 1940); on Russell, 307.

21. Executive Order 9981, Milestone Documents, National Archives website, revised February 8, 2022, www.archives.gov/milestone-documents/executive-order-9981.

22. Executive Order 9981; McGregor, *Integration*, 430, 457, 347, 354, 648.

23. "Services Abolish All-Negro Units," *NYT*, October 31, 1954; "Integration in the Services," *NYT*, November 1, 1954.

24. James E. Westheider, *Fighting on Two Fronts: African Americans and the Vietnam War* (New York: New York University Press, 1997), 2. Such comments appear frequently in the mainstream Black press and in army discussions of racial conflict. On attitudes toward the military, see William Brink and Louis Harris, *Black and White* (New York: Simon and Schuster, 1966), 162–75.

25. Roy Wilkins to Harris Wofford, April 5, 1961, JFK Presidential Library, www.jfk library.org/Asset-Viewer/RbvfZID58EujvNxPmXnBPQ.aspx.

26. Tim Weiner, "Robert S. McNamara, Architect of a Futile War, Dies at 93," *NYT*, July 6, 2009. Though it comprised more than 4,500 words, the obituary never mentioned

McNamara's civil rights efforts. An undated list of "Secretary McNamara's Achievements in Civil Rights," created by the office of the assistant secretary of defense for manpower (OASD[M]), is in "Achievements in Civil Rights" file, Subject Files Re: Civil Rights, box 1, OASD(M), RG 330, NARA-CP.

27. "The Mob in Alabama," *WP*, May 23, 1961.

28. MacGregor, *Integration*, 530; "Job Equality Order Issued by M'Namara," *NYT*, March 28, 1961.

29. Quotation from "Military Shows No Segregation," *CDD*, July 2, 1960.

30. "Race Inquiry Unit Urged for Military," *WP*, August 26, 1961; Lara Zade, "Before DC, Robert S. McNamara Called Ann Arbor Home," *Michigan Daily* (Ann Arbor), July 9, 2009.

31. MacGregor, *Integration*, 536.

32. Bart Barnes, "Adam Yarmolinsky Dies," *WP*, January 7, 2000; Neil A. Lewis, "Adam Yarmolinsky Dies at 77," *NYT*, January 7, 2000; MacGregor, *Integration*, 536.

33. Quotations from John G. Norris, "GI Race Discrimination Off Base Being Tackled," *WP*, July 7, 1963.

34. John F. Kennedy, "Televised Address to the Nation on Civil Rights," June 11, 1963, John F. Kennedy Presidential Library, www.jfklibrary.org/learn/about-jfk/historic-speeches /televised-address-to-the-nation-on-civil-rights#:~:text=It%20ought%20to%20be%20 possible%2C%20in%20short%2C%20for%20every%20American,his%20children%20 to%20be%20treated, accessed September 7, 2022.

35. Jack Raymond, "Report Ordered on Negro G.I.'s," NYT, June 23, 1963.

36. MacGregor, *Integration*, 548; "An Anti-Bias Order Given to Services," *Des Moines Register*, from New York Times News Service, July 27, 1963.

37. Marjorie Hunter, "Vinson Asks Curb on Military Drive to End Color Line," *NYT*, September 18, 1963; MacGregor, *Integration*, 550–51. Hébert attributed that zeal to Yarmolinsky, who was not in fact responsible for the directive.

38. Robert S. McNamara, "Social Inequities: Urban's Racial Ills," speech to National Association of Educational Broadcasters, 43rd Convention, Denver, CO, November 7, 1967, in *Vital Speeches of the Day* 34 (December 1967): 98–103.

39. "Trigger of Hate," *Time*, August 20, 1965, 17. According to James Landers, *The Weekly War: Newsmagazines and Vietnam* (Columbia: University of Missouri Press, 2004), 12–13, *Time* was the highest circulation newsmagazine during the Vietnam War, circulating 3.2 million copies a week in 1965. Newsmagazines reached approximately one-sixth of the nation's households during this era.

40. Malcolm McLaughlin, *The Long, Hot Summer of 1967: Urban Rebellion in America* (New York: Palgrave Macmillan, 2014), 6, offers the list of urban uprisings. His discussion of the inaccuracy of the term "race riot" and the relationship between riot and rebellion (12–16) is useful.

41. McLaughlin, *Long, Hot Summer of 1967*, vii–viii, 6.

42. "Frank's Made It: A Steady Job," *Sumter (SC) Daily Item*, December 19, 1970; Farnsworth Fowle, "Frank McGee of N.B.C. Dead," *NYT*, April 18, 1974.

43. All descriptions and quotes in this and the following paragraphs come from Frank McGee, *Same Mud, Same Blood*, NBC News, 1967, first aired December 1, 1967, 50 minutes, from transcript on www.nbclearn.com/portal/site/k-12/flatview?cuecard=72264.

44. "Integration in the Military," *Los Angeles Sentinel*, March 24, 1966; "Military Leads the Way in Race Relations," *Los Angeles Sentinel*, December 28, 1967; "Negroes in Vietnam: 'We, Too, Are Americans,'" *Ebony*, August 1968, 90.

45. Joseph Alsop, "Matter of Fact . . . The Negro and the Army," *WP*, May 25, 1966.

46. "Democracy in the Foxhole," *Time*, May 26, 1967, 21+.

47. Thomas A. Johnson, "The U.S. Negro in Vietnam," *NYT*, April 29, 1969.

48. "Democracy in the Foxhole"; R. W. Apple Jr., "Negro and White Fight Side by Side," *NYT*, January 3, 1966; Gene Grove, "The Army and the Negro," *NYT*, July 24, 1966; Donald Mosby, "Our Man Mosby Finds No Prejudice in Viet Combat," *CDD*, May 23, 1968; Julian Hartt, "Army Cited as Example of Integration's Success," *WP*, August 30, 1966.

49. Apple, "Negro and White"; Gretchen Livingston, "Profile of U.S. Veterans Is Changing Dramatically as Their Ranks Decline," Pew Research Center, 2022, www.pewresearch .org/fact-tank/2016/11/11/profile-of-u-s-veterans-is-changing-dramatically-as-their-ranks -decline. The two forms were, respectively, the Enlisted Qualification Record and the Officer Qualification Record.

50. MacGregor, *Integration*, 576. Racial designations would remain on biostatistical, criminal, and casualty records. Alfred B. Fitt was the civil rights deputy at that point; later that year he would become the army's general counsel.

51. Marion S. Barry Jr. and Betty Garman, "SNCC: A Special Report on Southern School Desegregation, Student Nonviolent Coordinating Committee," Atlanta, GA, 1965, on Civil Rights Movement Archive website, Duke University Archives, accessed September 16, 2022, www.crmvet.org/docs/65_sncc_school-rpt.pdf.

52. Table B-42, "Civilian Unemployment Rate, 1965–2011," U.S. Government Publishing Office, accessed September 16, 2022, www.gpo.gov/fdsys/pkg/ERP-2012/pdf/ERP -2012-table42.pdf.

53. Quote from Milton Viorst, *Fire in the Streets: America in the 1960s* (New York: Simon and Schuster, 1980), 375.

54. Carmichael explained his understanding of Black Power in a long feature article in *Ebony* magazine in 1966: Lerone Bennett Jr., "Stokley Carmichael: Architect of Black Power," *Ebony*, September 1966, 25–32; letter from Roy Wilkins, NAACP Special Contribution Fund, October 17, 1966, Civil Rights Movement Archive website, crmvet.org; "The Politics of Power" editorial, *Afro-American* (New York), June 4, 1966.

55. *Face the Nation* interview, June 19, 1966, transcript available on Civil Rights Movement Archive website, crmvet.org; Bennett, "Stokely Carmichael," 26.

56. Stokely Carmichael, "Black Power" speech, UC Berkeley, November 19, 1966, transcription from taped remarks published in Joanne Grant, *Black Protest: 350 Years of History, Documents, and Archives* (New York: Ballantine Books, 1966), available on Civil Rights Movement Archive website, crmvet.org. Carmichael played out this logic in his *Face the Nation* interview; he used the "insidious subterfuge" quote in that interview and in other public statements, including a version in Stokely Carmichael, "What We Want," *New York Review of Books*, September 22, 1966, 5–6, 8.

57. Stokely Carmichael, "Watts Speech," Will Rogers Park, Los Angeles, November 29, 1966, transcription available on Civil Rights Movement Archive website, www.crmvet.org /info/661126_sncc_bp_watts.pdf.

58. "Detroit Crowd Warmly Greets H. Rap Brown," *CDD*, August 28, 1967; "Rock Throwing Follows Brown's Talk in Detroit," *CDD*, August 29, 1967. This article continued,

with commentary on Brown's quote: "Forty-three persons were killed in the disorder." Wallace Turner, "A Gun Is Power, Black Panther Says," *NYT*, May 21, 1967.

59. Judy Klemesrud, "Saundra Williams Is First Miss Black America," *Oshkosh (WI) Northwestern*, from New York Times News Service, September 9, 1968. Soul ad from William L. Van Deburg, *New Day in Babylon: The Black Power Movement and American Culture* (Chicago: University of Chicago Press, 1992), 196; he cites *Sepia* magazine, October 1968; quote on Afros from a later *Ebony* cover story chronicling the history of the Afro: Phyl Garland, "Is the Afro on Its Way Out?," *Ebony*, February 1973, 128.

60. All materials contained in "Report of Inquiry Alleging Racial Friction in 3d Battalion, 8th Infantry, 4th Infantry division," November 27, 1967, Case 68-60, box 9, USARV IG Invstgn.

61. Case 68-60.

62. Bennett, "Command Leadership," 2.

63. Alan Thomas Jr. interviewed by James Westheider, March 22, 1995, quoted in Westheider, *Fighting*, 98.

64. "Incidents of Racial Friction," file 710-08, Congressional Investigations, Corrections Division Selected Permanent Subject Files, 1964–1969, box 3, Office of Provost Marshal General, RG 389, NARA-CP; the incident in Germany is described in Curtis Daniell, "Germany: Trouble Spot for Black GIs," *Ebony*, August 1968, 127; and is also cited in Westheider, *Fighting*, 98.

65. Westmoreland and Abrams from George Lepre, *Fragging: Why U.S. Soldiers Assaulted Their Officers in Vietnam* (Lubbock: Texas Tech University Press, 2011), 21. Lepre cites MG Kerwin to GEN Abrams, 0402Z, April 6, 1968; and GEN Abrams to LTG Palmer et al., MAC 04599, April 6, 1968, Abrams Messages, CMH.

66. Perry Flippin, "Military Race Relations Studied," *S&S*, May 9, 1968; James Gunter, "Race Progress Good in Army, Probers Say," *S&S*, May 11, 1968; Marc Huet, "Europe GI Integration Is Praised," *S&S*, July 12, 1968.

67. "Incidents of Racial Friction."

68. John T. Wheeler, "Black-Power Tension Has Come to Vietnam," *S&S*, May 6, 1969. General Abrams created a "watch group," comprising representatives from all services in the region, to monitor racial tensions and incidents. See Graham A. Cosmas, *MACV: The Joint Command in the Years of Withdrawal, 1968–1973* (Washington, DC: Center of Military History, US Army, 2007), 235.

69. Bennett Report.

70. Carl T. Rowan, "Pentagon Ignored Racial Warnings," *Kansas City (MO) Times*, August 27, 1969. Rowan, who was African American, wrote a nationally syndicated column from 1966 through 1998.

71. Elaine Sciolino, "Carl Rowan, Writer and Crusader, Dies at 75," *NYT*, September 24, 2000.

72. Rowan, "Pentagon Ignored"; George C. Wilson, "Viet Race Fights to Increase," *Arizona Republic* (Phoenix), from Washington Post News Service, November 15, 1968.

73. "Rights Controversy Brewing in Defense Department," *Jet*, December 9, 1965, 3. Rowan and Bennett had crossed paths in the elite African American community in Minneapolis during the 1950s. Bennett moderated a three-person panel discussion that included Rowan in 1951, for example. "U.S. Called Picture of 'Unrealized Ambition,'" *Minneapolis Star*, November 28, 1951.

74. William M. Hammond, *Public Affairs: The Military and the Media, 1968–1973* (Washington DC: Center of Military History, US Army, 1996), 177.

75. "Incidents of Racial Friction."

76. Paul J. Scheips, *The Role of Federal Military Forces in Domestic Disorders, 1945–1992* (Washington, DC: Center of Military History, US Army, 2005), 359; on general anxiety see, for example, John T. Wheeler, "Black Power Comes to Vietnam as Racial Tensions Increase," *WP*, April 20, 1969.

77. Daniell, "Germany," 126; Gerald F. Goodwin, "African American Soldiers and Race Relations in the 'Nam" (PhD diss., Ohio University, 2014), 172.

78. "Tensions of Black Power Reach Troops in Vietnam," *NYT*, April 13, 1969; William Greider, "Black Ire Erupts on Military Posts," *WP*, August 16, 1969.

79. U.S. Congress, House, Special Subcommittee to Probe Disturbances on Military Bases of the Committee on Armed Services, *Inquiry into the Disturbances at Marine Corps Base, Camp Lejeune, N.C., on July 20, 1969*, 91st Cong., 1st Sess., December 15, 1969, H.A.S.C. 91-32, 5055.

80. U.S. Congress, House, Special Subcommittee, *Inquiry into the Disturbances*, 5053; Paul Good, "A Proud Esprit Soiled," *Life*, October 17, 1969, 47; "Three Marines Hurt in Fight with Negroes," *Chicago Tribune*, July 24, 1969. See also John Hanrahan and Ural B. Adams, "Race Problems Confront Quantico Marines," *WP*, August 18, 1969.

81. U.S. Congress, House, Special Subcommittee, *Inquiry into the Disturbances*, 5051, 5059; U.S. Congress, House, Committee on Armed Services, "Full Committee Consideration of . . . Résumé of Report of Special Subcommittee to Probe Disturbances on Military Bases," 91st Cong., 1st Sess., December 11, 1969, H.A.S.C. 91-34, 5077.

82. "Race and the Military," *WP*, August 22, 1969.

83. Martin D. Gottlieb, "The Army's Efforts to Ease Racial Tension," *San Antonio Express*, September 20, 1970; "Department of Defense–Human Goals (Personnel), 1969" folder, box A67, Laird Papers; "Black, Confident, Cocky," *Atlanta Black Star*, June 6, 2016.

84. On Hamburger Hill, see Gregory A. Daddis, *No Sure Victory: Measuring U.S. Army Effectiveness and Progress in the Vietnam War* (New York: Oxford University Press, 2011), 166–67.

85. "Faces of the American Dead," *Life*, June 27, 1969, cover story; Howard Jones, *My Lai: Vietnam, 1968, and the Descent into Darkness* (New York: Oxford University Press, 2017), 182–84.

86. Westmoreland was briefed by White on September 18, 1969. Resor was briefed by White, with Westmoreland in attendance, on September 27, 1969. Both briefings appear on Westmoreland's daily schedule in Army Chief of Staff History Files 34–36 for July 1, 1968, to December 31, 1969, box 48, Series II Official Papers, William C. Westmoreland Collection, AHEC.

87. Resor, Keynote Address. Resor was briefed by White (based on the Westmoreland-ordered assessment). T. Rees Shapiro, "Stanley R. Resor, Former Army Secretary, Dies at 94," *WP*, April 19, 2012.

88. Resor, Keynote Address, 4, 5.

89. Resor, Keynote Address, 5.

90. Resor, Keynote Address, 6.

91. Resor, Keynote Address, 5–6.

92. Resor, Keynote Address, 9 (this is the final sentence of the speech).

### CHAPTER 3

1. T. Rees Shapiro, "Stanley R. Resor, Former Army Secretary, Dies at 94," *WP*, April 19, 2012.

2. Dennis Hevesi, "Melvin Laird, Defense Secretary Who Challenged Vietnam Policy, Dies at 94," *NYT*, November 16, 2016.

3. Richard A. Hunt, *Melvin Laird and the Foundation of the Post-Vietnam Military, 1969–1973* (Washington, DC: Historical Office of the Secretary of Defense, 2015), 524–26. Also, Robert J. Brown, White House memorandum on "The Status of Minority Groups in the Armed Forces," March 19, 1969 (followed by White House staff responses and recommendations); Secretary of Defense, Memorandum for the White House, May 2, 1969 (response to White House request); Secretary of Defense, Memorandum for All Military Personnel, "Equal Opportunity and Treatment in the Armed Forces," May 2, 1969; Whitney M. Young (Urban League) to Melvin Laird, May 9, 1969 (referencing conversation of March 24, 1969), all in Equal Opportunity and Race Relations folder, box C6; "People Objectives" (draft), circulated July 28, 1969, in Department of Defense–Human Goals (Personnel), 1969 folder, box A67; "Department of Defense Human Goals," in "Human Goals, 1969–1972" folder, box A74, Laird Papers.

4. White Briefing, 1.

5. White Briefing, 5.

6. This paragraph draws on Vanessa Williams, "Jim White Is a Long Shot Buoyed by a Successful Past," *Philadelphia Inquirer*, May 10, 1991; "Temple Community Relations under Peter Liacouras," *Temple News* (Philadelphia), March 25, 2008; "James White: An Active Kappa Man for Four Decades," *Philadelphia Tribune*, November 9, 1990; "Wins Pace Award," *Cincinnati Enquirer*, May 17, 1970; "Man Joins Staff," *Orlando Sentinel* (Negro edition), August 1, 1960; and conversation with White's son, Gary A. White (May 13, 2022). Morgan State University is a historically Black institution that was opened to members of all races when it became a public college in 1939.

7. This paragraph draws on Williams, "Jim White"; "James White," *Philadelphia Tribune*; conversation with Gary A. White. Quotation is from "Temple Community Relations under Peter Liacouras," *Temple News*.

8. Richard C. Gross, "Uniforms New Order of the Day at Pentagon," April 18, 1981, UPI Archives, accessed September 16, 2022, www.upi.com/Archives/1981/04/18/Uniforms-new-order-of-the-day-at-Pentagon/2437356418000; Ralph Cipriano, "Last Patrol Aids Vietnam Memorial Groundbreaking," *Philadelphia Inquirer*, June 28, 1987.

9. White Briefing, 2.

10. White Briefing, 1, 12, 16, 11, 1. I have not been able to locate a written version of the briefing delivered to Westmoreland and to Resor, but army documents confirm that the briefing White presented "throughout the army" was "essentially the same briefing" he presented to the chief of staff of the army and the secretary of the army in the fall of 1969, making clear that Resor's phrases come from White's report, rather than the other way around. Information from "Pace Award Won by Officer, Civilian," *S&S-P*, May 15, 1970; DCSPER-SARD to Acting Deputy Assistant Secretary of Defense (Civil Rights), "Fact Sheet," undated (c. 1970), in folder 2, box 29, DCSPERS Discrim.

11. White Briefing, 1, 2.

12. White Briefing, 2–3.

13. White Briefing, 18, 16, 4.

14. White Briefing, 13, 15, 16.

15. Westmoreland Sends, Subj: Equal Opportunity and Treatment of Military Personnel, October 17, 1969, "Equal Opportunity and Racial Unrest 1970" file, box 1, P&A/HR.

16. Jack Anderson, "Military Chiefs Accused of Race Trouble Coverup," *Orlando (FL) Sentinel*, September 24, 1969.

17. Haines message, January 10, 1970, "Visit with LTC White 1970" file, box 1, P&A/HR.

18. MG Ben Sternberg to GEN Ralph E. Haines Jr., November 24, 1969, in "Bennett Visit."

19. On Sternberg, historical newspaper clippings ("Col. Sternberg Has New Duties" and "Lt. Col."), posted without attribution on Find a Grave website, www.findagrave.com /memorial/49355717/ben-sternberg#view-photo=153528086.

20. Sternberg to Haines, November 24, 1969.

21. BG Verne L. Bowers, DCoS (P&A), memo for G-1, December 8, 1969, in "Bennett Visit"; Sternberg to Haines, November 24, 1969.

22. Responses to G-1 memo on Sternberg letter from LTC William B. Stallings, Deputy Information Officer, December 24, 1969; W. K. Wittwer, Colonel, MPC, Provost Marshal, January 11, 1970; Wilton B. Persons Jr., Colonel, Staff Judge Advocate, January 11, 1970, all in "Bennett Visit."

23. Response to G-1 memo from COL Willard W. Hawke, Inspector General, January 13, 1970, in "Bennett Visit."

24. COL William C. Dosson Jr., Chief, Investigation and Complaints Division, IG, Memo for IG, "Equal Opportunity and Treatment of Military Personnel," in "Case 70-20" file, box 22, USARV IG Invstgn.

25. The report did note that the "small percentage of complaints" related to the issues discussed in Sternberg's letter could "indicate a communications breakdown between minority groups and superiors" and proposed that such communication channels be improved. IG, "Equal Opportunity and Treatment of Military Personnel."

26. Hawke Response.

27. Hawke Response.

28. COL Willard W. Hawke, IG, "Proposed Article—Racial Understanding," provided in response to request from DCoS (P&A) for a 200- to 250-word piece to publish in *USARV Commander's Notes*, January 14, 1970, in "Case 70-20" file, box 22, USARV IG Invstgn.

29. See Case 68-34, box 7, USARV IG Invstgn.

30. William Whitesel, Colonel, Chief, PPAD, response to G-1 memo on Sternberg letter, January 27, 1970; A. S. Allen, Colonel, AGC, Deputy Adjutant General, response to G-1 memo on Sternberg letter, January 8, 1970, both in "Bennett Visit" file.

31. "U.S. Forces Bias Study in Viet Starts," *Palm Beach (FL) Post*, November 24, 1969; "So This Is Washington" column, *Pittsburgh Courier*, November 15, 1969; HQ MACV, "Visit of Mr. L. Howard Bennett (GS-18)" memo, November 20, 1969, in "Bennett Visit"; Ethel Payne, "Bar Bars Nixon's Black Aide," *CDD*, October 21, 1969.

32. Bennett biography compiled from Curt Brown, "Judge L. Howard Bennett," *Minneapolis Star Tribune*, April 29, 2017; "Reports Say Bennett Set for Defense Post," *Minneapolis Star Tribune*, November 2, 1963; "Defense Aide Alabama State Finals Speaker," *Pittsburgh Courier*, August 15, 1964; "Va. State Collegians Hear Rights Employee," *CDD*, October 2, 1965.

33. C. Brown, "Judge L. Howard Bennett"; "U.S. Official's Daughter Booked," *Akron (OH) Beacon Journal*, July 6, 1965.

34. "Violent Protests Hit," *Times and Democrat* (Orangeburg, SC), May 26, 1964; "Grads Told to Help Build Nation into an Integrated, Free Society," *CDD*, June 15, 1968.

35. Talking Paper, Subject: Equal Opportunity: Visit to RVN by Mr. L. Howard Bennett, in "Bennett Visit."

36. Preface to Bennett Report. The report includes comments on each site the team visited. It was distributed to commanders in Southeast Asia in July 1970.

37. L. Howard Bennett, "Equality of Opportunity and Race Relations in the Armed Forces," 2, circulated to the Secretaries of the Military Departments and the Joint Chiefs of Staff by Roger T. Kelley, ASD (M&RA), on January 26, 1970, in "Equal Opportunity, 1970–1972"folder, box A70, Laird Papers.

38. Based on search for the term "generation gap" in Newspapers.com; Bennett Report, 4.

39. Bennett Report, 4.

40. Bennett Report, 6.

41. Bennett, "Equality of Opportunity," 2; "Command Leadership: Avoiding Racial Conflict and Maintaining Harmony, Unity and Strength in the Armed Forces," January 8, 1970, in "Equal Opportunity, 1970–1972" folder, box A70, Laird Papers. This is an eleven-page document that summarized his key points and seems to have been made available to the press.

42. Bennett, "Command Leadership," 1.

43. Bennett, 10, 7; "Pentagon on Race Tiff: 'Sing' Troubles Away," *Alton (IL) Evening Telegraph*, February 13, 1970; see also "Racial Song Switch Liked," *Orlando (FL) Evening Star*, February 13, 1970. This proposal, often credited directly to Bennett, appeared in newspapers throughout the nation. A few noted that he offered other proposals as well, but the focus was always on singing and dancing.

44. Bennett, of course, didn't create the term "New Breed Black"; his use legitimated it. In July 1966, Adam Clayton Powell described Black Power as "a new philosophy for a new breed of cats." UPI, "Quotes in the News," *Marysville (OH) Journal-Tribune*, July 19, 1966. Stokely Carmichael, speaking in Watts, said, "There is a new breed of black people in the country today." "New Attack by Carmichael on 'Our Plight,'" *Daily Independent Journal* (San Rafael, CA), November 28, 1966. By 1969 the term had been used to describe Ron Dellums and John Conyers, as well.

45. Bennett, "Command Leadership," 3, 5, 8, 6.

46. "Arthur M. Sussman," uchicago news, August 13, 2016, https://news.uchicago.edu /story/arthur-m-sussman-former-uchicago-general-counsel-and-vice-president-1942-2016; Sussman Report, 11.

47. Sussman Report, 1, 12, 8, 11.

48. Sussman Report, 3, 7, 13.

49. Sussman Report, 2.

50. Sussman Report, 2.

51. Sussman Report, 2.

52. Handwritten notes on Q&A following twelve briefings or meetings (all in same hand) and "Recommendations Made by LTC James S. White after Visit," typed memo with no further information, both in "Visit with LTC White 1970" file, box 1, P&A/HR.

53. Ralph Blumenthal, "Army Finds Rise of Racial Tension in Study of Bases," *NYT*, January 25, 1970.

54. The *Courier-Journal* carried Blumenthal's piece with the pull-out title "Negro Losing Faith?": Blumenthal, "Racial Tension Rising in Army, Survey Shows," *Louisville (KY) Courier-Journal*, January 25, 1970; "Army Race Problem 'Serious': Blacks Have Lost Faith," *WP*, January 25, 1970; "Racism in the Army," *CDD*, January 28, 1970.

55. "Crimes of Violence by Race," in "Equal Opportunity Reporting thru 1970" file, box 5, P&A/HR; "African Americans in the Vietnam War" chart in David Farber and Beth Bailey, *The Columbia Guide to America in the 1960s* (New York: Columbia University Press, 2001), 385. That figure refers to total military, not only to the US Army.

56. Thomas A. Johnson, "G.I.'s in Germany: Black Is Bitter," *NYT*, November 23, 1970.

57. Johnson, "G.I.'s in Germany."

58. Johnson, "G.I.'s in Germany."

59. Paul Delaney, "Nixon Orders GI Race Probe in Europe," *S&S*, September 1, 1970. On the Nixon administration and Secretary of Defense Melvin Laird's actions, see Hunt, *Melvin Laird*, 524–36.

60. "3 Groups Honor Render at Dinner," *Syracuse Post-Standard*, June 20, 1970; "Cincinnati Native in Civil Rights Post," *Cincinnati Enquirer*, July 21, 1970; "Render Promises Total Commitment," *Syracuse Post-Standard*, July 21, 1970.

61. George Grim, "GI Racial Tensions Studied," *Star Tribune* (Minneapolis), September 20, 1970 (son); "L. Howard Bennett Resumes U.S. Post," *Star Tribune*, July 29, 1970 (black Republican); "Top Black Civilian in Defense Department Is Sworn In," *Jet*, August 6, 1970, 5.

62. Grim, "GI Racial Tensions."

63. Frank W. Render II, Memorandum for the Secretary of Defense, "U.S. Military Race Relations in Europe – September 1970," November 2, 1970, 6, US Army Heritage and Education Center, Carlisle, PA (Render Report); notices of promotions in the armed forces, *Minneapolis Star*, April 8, 1970; "Specialist Reenlists," *Anniston (AL) Star*, June 1, 1967.

64. Render, Memorandum, cover memo.

65. Render, Memorandum, 7.

66. Render, Memorandum, cover memo.

67. Render, Memorandum, 8.

68. Render, Memorandum, 7–8.

69. Render, Memorandum, 10, 9, 15, cover memo, 2, 12, 16.

70. Render, Memorandum, 12, 24, 16; Delaney, "Nixon Orders GI Race Probe in Europe."

71. Render, Memorandum, 9, 16.

72. "Fort Monroe Conference."

CHAPTER 4

1. Hugh A. Mulligan (Associated Press correspondent), "Service Has 'Legal Orders' and Open Doors," *Manhattan (KS) Mercury*, May 26, 1971.

2. John M. Goshko, "Race Rifts Follow the Flag," *WP*, September 27, 1970; Michael S. Davison, "In Europe, the Focus Is on People," *Army*, October 1971, 49.

3. GEN Michael S. Davison, "Address at the Command and General Staff College," April 10, 1972, 103, in Davison Speeches; Maria Höhn and Martin Klimke, *A Breath of*

*Freedom: The Civil Rights Struggle, African American GIs, and Germany* (New York: Palgrave Macmillan, 2010), 144; Daniel J. Nelson, *A History of U.S. Military Forces in Germany* (Boulder, CO: Westview Press, 1987; reissued by Routledge University Press, 2018), 103–4, 106; Davison, "In Europe."

4. Goshko, "Race Rifts."

5. Amerikkka quote from *Voice of the Lumpen*, May/June 1971, as it appears in Höhn and Klimke, *Breath of Freedom*, 149. The authors tie this language to the group's November 1970 broader discussion of its "role in the revolutionary struggle."

6. Goshko, "Race Rifts."

7. Goshko, "Race Rifts"; Bob Umphress, "Sgt. Talked of Retaliation, Grenade Trial Told," *S&S*, October 29, 1970.

8. Goshko, "Race Rifts"; Umphress, "Sgt. Talked."

9. Hank Franz, "10 Face Trial in Grenade Incident," *S&S*, September 18, 1970; Umphress, "Sgt. Talked."

10. Goshko, "Race Rifts."

11. Goshko, "Race Rifts"; William Currie, "'Got Wrong Man,' Viet Hero Jailed in Germany Says," *CT*, June 17, 1970; Flynn McRoberts, "Hobson's Choice," *CT*, November 8, 1992.

12. Goshko, "Race Rifts."

13. Goshko, "Race Rifts"; "Judge Moves to Help GI Hero in Army Jail," *CT*, June 16, 1970; "City Honors Former Street Gang Leader," *CT*, January 20, 1970.

14. Alice Siegert, "Chaplain Testifies for Chicago GI," *CT*, November 3, 1970; McRoberts, "Hobson's Choice."

15. Goshko, "Race Rifts"; transcript of NAACP delegation meeting, "Colonel Dooty tape," 4–6, folder 2, box 2705, NAACP Papers.

16. Goshko, "Race Rifts."

17. Goshko, "Race Rifts" (see account of same event in "Black Explosions in West Germany," *Time*, September 21, 1970, 53); Hubert J. Erb, "Army 'Doing Its Best' to Bridge Racial Gap," *S&S*, September 9, 1970.

18. William Shkurti email to author, June 9, 2019.

19. Höhn and Klimke, *Breath of Freedom*, 114–16, 147, 149.

20. Maria Höhn, "The Black Panther Solidarity Committees and the Voice of the Lumpen," *German Studies Review* 31, no. 1 (2008): 133–54; "On Revolutionary Justice" and "In Defense of Brother Billy Smith," *Voice of the Lumpen*, October 1971, African American Involvement in the Vietnam War website, www.aavw.org/served/gipubs_voice_lumpen _abstract01.html, accessed September 16, 2022.

21. Höhn and Klimke, *Breath of Freedom*, 149–53; "How Come? And Why?," *About Face* (published by Unsatisfied Black Soldiers, Heidelberg, Germany), July 4, 1970, African American Involvement in the Vietnam War website, www.aavw.org/served/gipubs_about face_abstract01.html; Shkurti email, June 9, 2019.

22. Maria Höhn, "Solidarity Committee and the Trial of the Ramstein 2," in *Changing the World, Changing Oneself: Political Protest and Collective Identities in West Germany and the United States in the 1960s and 1970s*, edited by Belinda Davis et al. (New York: Berghahn Books, 2010), 222–28; Rhonda Williams, in *Concrete Demands: The Search for Black Power in the 20th Century* (New York: Routledge University Press, 2015), 213, says that there were four men in the car.

23. Ken Loomis, "Polk Closing Out Army Career of 37 Years with 'Hat Trick,'" *S&S*, February 28, 1971, 10; "Davison Named to Succeed Polk," *S&S*, February 25, 1971.

24. "Davison Named to Succeed Polk"; Nelson, *U.S. Military Forces in Germany*, 110; "Army to Spot-Check in Europe for Bias," *NYT*, October 14, 1970. All major commands in Europe were directed to create such inspection teams. See statement from Department of the Army, included in memorandum from Carl S. Wallace, Special Assistant to the Secretary of Defense, to BG James D. Hughes, Military Assistant to the President, June 17, 1971, in "Equal Opportunity and Race Relations, 1969–1973" folder, box C7, Laird Papers.

25. Render Report, 7, 9, 15.

26. George C. Wilson, "Black Unrest Found among GIs in Europe," *WP*, December 18, 1970; GEN Walter Kerwin to X-O, October 14, 1970, in folder 24, box 22, DCSPERS Discrim.

27. "A Day of Solidarity," *About Face*, September 12, 1970, African American Involvement in the Vietnam War website, www.aavw.org/served/gipubs_aboutface_abstract02 .html. "1st shirt" is a first sergeant (E-8).

28. On Smothers's background: "Curtis Randolph Smothers," obituary, *Baltimore Sun*, July 1, 2012; "Black U.S. Army Officer to Be Transferred Home," *Evening Sun* (Hanover, PA), April 8, 1971 (SNCC); Nathaniel R. Jones, *Answering the Call: An Autobiography of the Modern Struggle to End Racial Discrimination in America* (New York: New Press, 2016), 108.

29. Jones-Smothers, 39.

30. Jones, *Answering the Call*, 108.

31. Jones-Smothers, 32.

32. Jones-Smothers, 32, 33.

33. Jones-Smothers, 34–35, 4.

34. Jones-Smothers, 19–27, 8; "Army Denies Judge's Plea for Inquiry into Race Bias," *NYT*, April 1, 1971; "Black U.S. Army Officer to Be Transferred Home"; Thomas A. Johnson, "Monitors Urged for Army Reform," *NYT*, March 21, 1971. For further information about this event, see chapter 7 in this book.

35. "Davison Named to Succeed Polk." Thomas A. Johnson, in "Pentagon Said to Penalize Officers on Racial Policy," *NYT*, July 28, 1971, noted that there was speculation that Polk had been retired prematurely because of "months of racial tension and major outbreaks of racial violence" in Germany.

36. Hon. William Clay, "Defense Department Retires General Polk—A Racist in High Command," 92nd Cong., 1st Sess., 117 Cong. Rec., part 6, 8230–31 (March 25, 1971); "Black U.S. Army Officer to Be Transferred Home."

37. Westmoreland Sends, Subj: Equal Opportunity and Treatment of Military Personnel, October 17, 1969, "Equal Opportunity and Racial Unrest 1970" file, box 1, P&A/HR; Resor recaps his points from the 1969 Association of the United States Army speech in his "Memorandum for the Secretary of Defense; Subject: Department of the Army Actions to Improve Race Relations," March 17, 1970, in "Equal Opportunity, 1970–1972" folder, box A70, Laird Papers.

38. Michael S. Davison, "Remarks for the Commanders' Equal Opportunity/Human Relations Conference," Garmisch, Germany, June 6, 1972, 166, in Davison Speeches.

39. "Gen. Davison: 'Toughest Period . . . Ever,'" *WP*, September 12, 1971; General Hollis meeting with Nathaniel Jones, January 1971, unpaginated transcription, folder 2, box 2705, NAACP Papers.

40. "Human Relations," letter prepared for signature of deputy commanding general (apparently by USARV Human Relations Council), n.d. [fall 1970], "Visit with LTC White 1970" file, box 1, P&A/HR.

41. Charles Wallis, "Draft of Report to DA," typescript with penciled corrections, 2, 7, in Race Relations in the Army folder, box 1, Charles R. Wallis Papers, AHEC.

42. Nathaniel Jones, notes on visit to Mainz, Germany, February 10, 1971, unpaginated, folder 1, box 2705, NAACP Papers.

43. Michael S. Davison, interviewed by Douglas H. Farmer and Dale Brudvig, April 9, 1976, section 5, 5; Wilton B. Persons, interviewed by Herbert J. Green and Thomas M. Crean, 1985, vol. 2, 351, both in Senior Officer Oral History Program, AHEC.

44. David Minthorn, "Army Black General Says Pressure On for Equality," *Colorado Springs Gazette-Telegraph*, November 14, 1971.

45. "General's Stars Pinned on Negro," *Spokesman-Review* (Spokane, WA), September 16, 1968; "Black General—Viet Duty Made History," *San Francisco Examiner*, May 27, 1969; Drew Middleton, "First Black U.S. Division Chief," *NYT*, May 19, 1972; Don E. Mallicoat, "Coping with People Problems," *Soldiers* 26 (May 1972): 10; Merritt Statement, 5.

46. Haynes Johnson and George C. Wilson, "The Army: Its Problems Are America's," last in the series, *WP*, September 20, 1971; Johnson, "Pentagon Said to Penalize Officers on Racial Policy"; "GI to Study Race Relations," *S&S*, July 29, 1971.

47. Statement of Wallace Terry, "Racism in the Military: Congressional Black Caucus Report, 15 May, 1972," as it appears in 92nd Cong., 2nd Sess., 118 Cong. Rec., #166-part 2, unpaginated (October 14, 1972).

48. "3 Services Will Rate Views toward Race," *NYT*, May 22, 1971; "Race Relations to Go on the Record," *S&S*, February 20, 1972. Secretary of Defense Melvin Laird issued DoD Directive 1100.15, "Equal Opportunity within the Department of Defense," on January 14, 1970; one major provision was that "leadership in operating successful Equal Opportunity Programs" be made a "criterion in the evaluation for promotion of military and civilian officials." See "Department of Defense Accomplishments in the Area of Equal Opportunity during the Nixon Administration," June 17, 1971, "Equal Opportunity and Race Relations, 1969–1973" folder, Box C7, Laird Papers; and Richard A. Hunt, *Melvin Laird and the Foundation of the Post-Vietnam Military, 1969–1973* (Washington, DC: Historical Office of the Secretary of Defense, 2015), 533–34.

49. For one example, Goshko, "Race Rifts."

50. Davison, "Remarks for the Commanders' Equal Opportunity/Human Relations Conference," 159, in sequence of speeches. The full quote is: "The company is the real Army for our men."

51. Report of seminar, "Racial Tension and Equal Opportunity for Treatment of Military Personnel," Fort Leavenworth, December 29, 1969, folder 6, box 22, DCSPERS Discrim; MG Ben Sternberg to GEN Ralph E. Haines Jr., November 24, 1969, in "Bennett Visit," 3.

52. "Special Study: Racial Harmony in the Army," June 1, 1969, 7, 13, folder 3, box 28, DCSPERS Discrim; notes from MACV briefing, "Visit with LTC White 1970" file, box 1, P&A/HR.

53. Davison, "Remarks for the Commanders' Equal Opportunity/Human Relations Conference," 161, 165. For "lessons learned" and an additional example: memorandum for the USARV Ad Hoc Committee, "Lessons Learned Concept Applied to Racial Matters," "Equal Opportunity Reporting thru 1970" file, box 1, P&A/HR: "However, in many cases,

developing racial problems are not recognized early enough due to the lack of experience on the part of young commanders and the fact that little guidance is available on the identification and effective solution of this type problem in its early stages."

54. Bennett Report, 8; "Recommendations Made by LTC James S. White after Visit," in "Visit with LTC White 1970" file, box 1, P&A/HR; European Theater's Equal Opportunity and Human Relations Handbook from "Fact Sheet: Department of Defense Equal Opportunity Programs and Affirmative Actions in the Area of Race Relations," "Equal Opportunity and Race Relations, 1969–1973" folder, box C7, Laird Papers.

55. Ethel L. Payne, "Negro Soldiers Still Face Discrimination," *CDD*, March 20, 1967; also appears in the *Philadelphia Tribune*, March 25, 1967.

56. For example, "Starting a Racial Harmony Program," undated memo from Office of the Brigade Chaplain, Fort Carson, CO, in "Racial Harmony Council" file, box 1, Wallis Papers, AHEC: "Some commanders will get real tense about program. No commanders need have any fear who is honestly seeking to do right."

57. "Lessons Learned—Case #4," "Equal Opportunity Reporting thru 1970" file, box 1, P&A/HR.

58. Memo to G-1 from office of the Deputy Chief of Staff (Personnel and Administration), USARV, "Equal Opportunity Reporting thru 1970" file, box 1, P&A/HR.

59. See Bennett Report, 6, 7.

60. AWC, *Study on Military Professionalism*, Carlisle Barracks, PA, June 30, 1970, i, v.

61. John T. Wheeler, "Black Power Comes to Vietnam as Racial Tensions Increase," *WP*, April 20, 1969.

62. "Positive Actions Taken by Member Units to Ease Racial Tensions, December 1969–January 1970," reports for meeting of ICTZ Leadership Council, January 21 and February 18, 1970, in "Council Meetings 1970" file, box 1, P&A/HR; Mulligan, "Service Has 'Legal Orders.'"

63. Information Sheet (on how one battalion commander has "successfully employed" his race relations council), "Racial Harmony Council" file, box 1, Wallis Papers, AHEC.

64. Bennett Report, 9, 5. Material from the Bennett report appears, word for word or slightly altered, in David I. Cooper, "Race in the Military: The Tarnished Sword," typed manuscript, 4, found in Race Relations in the Army folder, box 1, Wallis Papers, AHEC. Cooper was, at the time of the Bennett trip to Southeast Asia, a staff assistant in the office of the deputy assistant secretary of defense for civil rights. He was a member of the team that toured Southeast Asia and may well have drafted portions—or more—of the report.

65. For description of command challenges and situation at Fort Carson, see Charles R. Wallis, manuscript labeled by hand as "draft for report to HQ DA," "Racial Harmony Council" file, box 1, Wallis papers, AHEC. Wallis was the deputy chief of staff at Fort Carson.

66. Bernard Rostker, *I Want You!: The Evolution of the All-Volunteer Force* (Santa Monica, CA: Rand Corporation, 2006) 153–54; Matt Schudel, "Army General Introduced Major Reforms," *Los Angeles Times*, November 10, 2008.

67. "Race Relations Briefing for Secretary of the Army," Fort Carson, January 18, 1971, point g (no page numbers), in "Race Relations in the Army" folder, box 1, Wallis Papers, AHEC; Persons oral history, 350, Senior Officer Oral History Program, AHEC.

68. Summers portrait, events of August 1968, and subsequent trial compiled from Darnell S. Summers, former chair of Fort Carson Racial Harmony Council, posting and attached documents on Fort Carson: Post "Racial Harmony Council" 1970 website, July 22,

2003, www.angelfire.com/jazz/stwb/FTCARSONRHC_.html; "Council Oks Black Demands," *Hillsdale (MI) Daily News*, July 17, 1968; "GI Accused in Shooting of Policeman,"
*Times-Herald* (Port Huron, MI), December 9, 1968; "2 Face Trial in Shooting," *Ironwood
(MI) Daily Globe*, December 19, 1968; "Sentenced in Inkster Shootings," *Traverse City
(MI) Record-Eagle*, June 18, 1969; "Darnell 'Stephen' Summers," Dictionary of War website,
accessed September 16, 2022, http://dictionaryofwar.org/node/723; Darnell Summers,
telephone interviews with author, May 16 and 24, 2022.

69. Darnell Summers, telephone interviews with author, May 16 and 24, 2022.

70. Description of posttrial experience and time at Fort Carson in subsequent paragraphs based on author's interviews with Darnell Summers.

71. Patricia Sullivan, "Gen. DeWitt C. Smith, 84, Dies," *WP*, July 30, 2005.

72. "Race Relations Briefing for Secretary of the Army," Fort Carson, point *h* (no page
numbers).

73. "Race Relations Briefing for Secretary of the Army," Fort Carson, point *c*. See also
points *g, h.*

74. "We Need to Make Changes in . . . Army," *WP*, September 13, 1971; this piece was
in the form of questions and answers, with the quotation coming from an army officer
with a "high staff job in Europe." "Race Relations Briefing for Secretary of the Army," Fort
Carson, point *g.*

75. General Mildren was responding to L. Howard Bennett's visit and concluding rec-
ommendations. GEN Frank T. Mildren, "Subject: Complaints and Requests for Assistance,
Advice or Information," in "Bennett Visit"; Michael S. Davison, "Address at the CGSC,"
April 10, 1972, 107, in Davison Speeches.

76. Wallis, "Draft of Report to DA," typescript with penciled corrections, 11–12, Wallis
Papers, AHEC. No date on document; appears to be 1970, August or later.

77. Herbert Mitgang, "Chaplain Is Revealed as Author of Book on Vietnam," *NYT*,
May 4, 1981; Cecil B. Currey ("Cincinnatus"), *Self-Destruction: The Disintegration and Decay
of the United States Army during the Vietnam Era* (New York: W. W. Norton, 1981), 56.

CHAPTER 5

1. Ralph M. Pope, deputy assistant chief of staff G-1, memorandum for Colonel Foster,
March 25, 1970, "Equal Opportunity Reporting thru 1970" file, box 1, P&A/HR.

2. For Vietnam-era military occupational specialty (MOS) codes, see MOS Codes in the
Vietnam Era website, July 2012, ed-thelen.org/MOS-Vietnam-era.html; see also Office of
the Chief of Information, US Army, *The Spirit of Fort Benning*, 1970, on YouTube, youtube.
com/watch?v=87SRfcCoppk.

3. Resor, Keynote Address, 9; Conrad C. Crane et al., *Learning the Lessons of Lethality:
The Army's Cycle of Basic Combat Training, 1918–2019* (Carlisle, PA: US Army Heritage and
Education Center, 2019), 43; *The Spirit of Fort Benning*.

4. Additional training centers: Ellen R. Hartman et al., *Vietnam and the Home Front:
How DoD Installations Adapted, 1962–1975* (n.p.: US Army Engineer Research and De-
velopment Center, 2014), 55, apps.dtic.mil/dtic/tr/fulltext/u2/ab14648CSA.pdf; William
Gardner Bell, ed., *Department of the Army Historical Summary, Fiscal Year 1969* (Washing-
ton, D.C.: U.S. Army Center of Military History, 1973), 34; *The Big Picture: Basic Training,
Part 1*, (1966?), on YouTube, youtube.com/watch?v=F5yMlaoD83A.

5. US Army Research Institute for the Behavioral and Social Sciences, *Race Relations and Equal Opportunity in the Army: A Resource Book for Personnel with Race Relations/Equal Opportunity Responsibility* (by contract, Human Sciences Research, Inc., December 1973), 82–83.

6. Crane et al., *Learning the Lessons*, 43.

7. Office of the Chaplain, Headquarters 3rd Ordnance Battalion, USASUPCOM, Saigon, Subject: Afro-American Culture Society, November 15, 1969, in Case 70-20, box 22, USARV IG Invstgn; Martin D. Gottlieb, "The Army's Efforts to Ease Racial Tension," *San Antonio Express*, September 20, 1970; A. Carl Segal, MD, Columbia, MD, interview with author, December 5, 2014, recording in author's possession, and Segal, "Race Relations—Fort Benning 1967–70," 3, talking points document that Segal prepared for author, November 15, 2014.

8. Segal interview.

9. Segal interview.

10. Segal interview.

11. Bert R. Estlow, "1962 Clinic Yearbook" (1962), Jefferson Medical College Yearbooks, Paper 109, http://jdc.jefferson.edu/jmc_yearbooks/109; Segal appears on page 184. It is worth noting that over half the class was married.

12. Segal interview.

13. Segal interview; Segal, "Race Relations"; 1LT William Marshall and SPC Michael Pearson, Race Relations Coordinating Group, Fort Benning, GA, "Race Relations at Fort Benning: Report on an Ongoing Program," 2, "Fort Monroe Conference."

14. Segal interview; Segal, "Race Relations."

15. Segal interview.

16. Segal interview.

17. Segal interview.

18. Segal interview.

19. Jim Baker, "Who Decided to Keep Calley Is Being Asked," *Colorado Springs Gazette-Telegraph*, February 2, 1970; Howard Jones, *My Lai: Vietnam, 1968, and the Descent into Darkness* (New York: Oxford University Press, 2017), 200.

20. "Army Orders Court-Martial in 'Massacre,'" (UPI) *Miami Herald*, November 25, 1969. One charge was the premeditated murder of "not less than 70 Oriental human beings." Jones, *My Lai*, 225.

21. Baker, "Who Decided to Keep Calley Is Being Asked"; Bill Montgomery, "Talbott Racial Idea Works at Benning," *Atlanta Journal-Constitution*, June 25, 1972; Paul J. Scheips, *The Role of Federal Military Forces in Domestic Disorders, 1945–1992* (Washington, DC: Center of Military History, US Army, 2005), 289; Segal interview; on potential violence of Black GIs, see Sol Stern, "When the Black G.I. Comes Back from Vietnam," *NYT Magazine*, March 24, 1968.

22. Beth Bailey, *America's Army: Making the All-Volunteer Force* (Cambridge, MA: Belknap/Harvard University Press, 2009), 42.

23. Lauren Wiseman, obituary, *WP*, May 9, 2011; Chief of Staff, US Army, to Commandant, AWC, "Subject: Analysis of Moral and Professional Climate in the Army," April 18, 1970, included in AWC, *Study on Military Professionalism*, Carlisle Barracks, PA, June 30, 1970, 53; George C. Wilson and Haynes Johnson, "Retraining the Leaders of Today's GI," *WP*, September 18, 1971.

24. Segal interview; Marshall and Pearson, "Race Relations at Fort Benning," 4–5.

25. Marshall and Pearson, "Race Relations at Fort Benning," 4–5, includes note that seminars are "primary focus"; Segal, "Race Relations."

26. US Army Research Institute for the Behavioral and Social Sciences, *Race Relations and Equal Opportunity in the Army*, 81.

27. Resor, address, 6, November 18, 1970, INCL 2, "Fort Monroe Conference."

28. Segal interview.

29. Segal interview.

30. Segal interview; Segal, "Race Relations"; "After Action Report," 10–11, "Fort Monroe Conference."

31. United States Department of the Army Command Information Division, "Commanders Call Support Materials," 4th Quarter, 1971, https://books.google.com/books?id=dSe PUPEyFGUC&pg=PP5&dq=DA+PAM+%22Commanders+call+support+materials%22 +1971+%22Better+Race+Relations%22&hl=en&newbks=1&newbks_redir=0&sa=X&ved =2ahUKEwj8scWUmZz6AhVwFjQIHRO0AF0Q6AF6BAgCEAI#v=onepage&q=DA%20 PAM%20%22Commanders%20call%20support%20materials%22%201971%20%22 Better%20Race%20Relations%22&f=false.

32. Bailey, *America's Army*, 52.

33. On sensitivity training, see the highly critical Elisabeth Lasch-Quinn, *Race Experts: How Racial Etiquette, Sensitivity Training, and New Age Therapy Hijacked the Civil Rights Revolution* (Lanham, MD: Rowman and Littlefield, 2001), esp. 76–109; and Jessica Grogan, *Encountering America: Humanistic Psychology, Sixties Culture and the Shaping of the Modern Self* (New York: Harper Perennial, 2013).

34. "Human Potential: The Revolution in Feeling," *Time*, November 9, 1970; Jane Howard, *Please Touch: A Guided Tour of the Self-Help Movement* (New York: McGraw Hill, 1970), 262–67.

35. Marshall and Pearson, "Race Relations at Fort Benning," 15, 29.

36. "Army Sets Up Race Relations Courses," *Daily Journal* (Fergus Falls, MN); Thomas A. Johnson, "200 Trainees at Ft. Dix Get Course in Race Relations," *NYT*, February 5, 1971.

37. Johnson, "200 Trainees."

38. Leadership Department, United States Army Infantry School, "Leadership Aspects of Race Relations: Advance Sheet," INCL 4, "Fort Monroe Conference." This is the material furnished to students prior to completing the four-hour instruction block.

39. George C. Wilson and Haynes Johnson, "Army Leaders Struggle to Cope with Racial and Social Problems," *WP* series, in *Courier-Journal* (Louisville, KY), September 18, 1971.

40. Wilson and Johnson, "Army Leaders Struggle to Cope."

41. Gottlieb, "Army's Efforts to Ease Racial Tension."

42. MG John C. Bennett to All Iron Horsemen, Subject: Racial Harmony Among Young Americans, December 6, 1971, "Racial Harmony Council" file, box 1, Charles R. Wallis Papers, AHEC; Charles Wallis, "Draft of Report to DA," 6–7, Wallis Papers, AHEC.

43. David Pankey, personal correspondence with author, March 14, 2010, describing period in early 1971.

44. "Not All Education Films Are 'Studies in Boredom,'" *The Robesonian*, June 21, 1970.

45. *Black and White: Uptight*, written, produced, and directed by Max Miller, 1969, Avanti Films, in NARA II AV Collection; also available on YouTube.

46. *Black and White: Uptight*; discussion questions included in United States Department of the Army Command Information Division, "Commander's Call Support Materials."

47. Subject: Minutes of Meeting with CPT Mitchell concerning the Human Relations Program at DBTTB, items 2, 10, February 13, 1972, Dong Ba Thin Training Battalion, in "Racial Incidents" file, box 5, P&A/HR. According to commanders attending Fort Benning race relations training in 1972, *Black and White: Uptight* was no longer authorized for use in race relations training.

48. Gottlieb, "Army's Efforts to Ease Racial Tension"; survey material included in III Corps & Fort Hood Commander's Conference Notes, October 24, 1972, George P. Seneff Papers, AHEC.

49. "Army Sets Up Race Relations Courses." During Render's visit to Europe, he announced that the DoD was considering mandatory race relations education for all military personnel; this article explicitly noted that the army was nonetheless moving ahead with its own program.

50. Melvin Laird, Memorandum for Monday Staff Meeting Group, Subject: People in the Defense Department, July 28, 1969, and William C. Westmoreland, Memorandum for Secretary of Defense, Subject: People in the Defense Department, August 5, 1969, both in "Department of Defense–Human Goals (Personnel), 1969" folder, box A67, Laird Papers.

51. Robert F. Froehlke to Secretary of Defense, Memo: People in the Defense Department—your memo of 28 July, marked "personal," in "Department of Defense–Human Goals (Personnel), 1969" folder, box A67, Laird Papers; U.S. Congress, House, Special Subcommittee to Probe Disturbances on Military Bases of the Committee on Armed Services, *Inquiry into the Disturbances at Marine Corps Base, Camp Lejeune, N.C., on July 20, 1969*, 91st Cong., 1st Sess., December 15, 1969, H.A.S.C. 91-32, 5055.

52. "Major General Lucius Theus," Air Force Biographies website, accessed September 17, 2022, www.af.mil/About-Us/Biographies/Display/Article/105440/major-general-lucius-theus; Richard O. Hope, *Racial Strife in the U.S. Military: Toward the Elimination of Discrimination* (New York: Praeger, 1979), 40–41. The following section draws on Richard O. Hope, telephone interview with author, January 12, 2021.

53. News Release, Office of Assistant Secretary of Defense (Public Affairs), Washington DC, March 5, 1971, no. 196-71; budget in "Memorandum for Secretaries of the Military Departments, Subject: Defense Race Relations Institute," June 24, 1971, both in "Equal Opportunity and Race Relations, 1969–1973" folder, box C7, Laird Papers.

54. Isaac Hampton II, "Reform in Ranks: The History of the Defense Race Relations Institute, 1971–2014," in *Integrating the U.S. Military: Race, Gender, and Sexual Orientation Since World War II*, ed. Douglas W. Bristol and Heather Marie Stur (Baltimore, MD: Johns Hopkins University Press, 2017), 126; Jo Nordheimer, "Armed Forces School Seeks to Cut Racial Tension," *NYT*, March 19, 1972; Bob Thomas, "Human Harmony Is Goal," *Florida Today* (Cocoa), February 12, 1974. On DRRI, see also Say Burgin, "'The Most Progressive and Forward Looking Race Relations Experiment in Existence': Race 'Militancy', Whiteness, and DRRI in the Early 1970s," *Journal of American Studies* 49 (3): 557–74.

55. News Release, no. 196–71; Hampton, "Reform in Ranks," 127; "Richard Hope," The History Makers website, July 16, 2017, www.thehistorymakers.org/biography/richard-hope; Hope, *Racial Strife*, vii; Hope interview.

56. Hope interview.

57. Hope, *Racial Strife*, 50; Bob Gregg, in telephone interview with author, October 6, 2020, says one woman—a naval officer—was part of the initial group but resigned after the pilot program.

58. Hope, *Racial Strife*, 45–51; William Gary McGuire, *The Evolution of DEOMI* (Deomi Press, online, no date, post-2015), 9, 13–14, https://apps.dtic.mil/dtic/tr/fulltext/u2/1039313 .pdf.

59. Laird to Volpe, October 13, 1971, "Equal Opportunity and Race Relations, 1969–1973" folder, box C7, Laird Papers; Nordheimer, "Armed Forces School"; Eric Sharp, "Race Seminars," *S&S*, November 20, 1972.

60. Bill Craig, "All Left with Better Feelings, Captain Says," *S&S*, February 9, 1972; Walt Trott, "One White Officer's Reaction: 'I Feel a Little Blacker . . . ,'" *S&S*, February 9, 1972; Gregg interview.

61. Bill Yates, telephone interview with author, October 13, 2020; Gregg interview; Jose Bolton, telephone interview with author, October 6, 2020; Hope interview; DEOMI, *Celebrating Fifty Years: Past, Present, Future*, 2021, www.defenseculture.mil/Portals/90 /Documents/AboutDEOMI/Anniversary/50th%20Anniversary%20Booklet.pdf?ver=Fx Tokqwfk9PJGUPMXX3cGA%3d%3d.

62. Trott, "One White Officer's Reaction"; Sharp, "Race Seminars"; Hope, *Racial Strife*, 51; McGuire, *Evolution of DEOMI*, 16.

63. Sharp, "Race Seminars."

64. "Smile" from Sharp, "Race Seminars."

65. Sharp, "Race Seminars"; Gayle White, "The Changing Role of Army Women," *Journal and Constitution Magazine* (Atlanta, GA), May 5, 1974.

66. "Human Potential"; Bruce L. Maliver, "Encounter Groupers up against the Wall," *NYT Sunday Magazine*, January 3, 1971.

67. 115 Cong. Rec., part 12, H15331 (June 10, 1969) (comments by Hon. John R. Rarick); "Psychological Manipulation," *Indiana (PA) Gazette* (Associated Press), February 11, 1971; Paul Scott, "Compulsory Sensitivity Training," *Indianapolis News*, August 2, 1971.

68. Hon. John R. Rarick, "Military Brainwashing by the Numbers—Race Relations," in "Extensions of Remarks," Cong. Rec. 6553 (March 15, 1971); article included in Cong. Rec. is Oziel Garza, "DOD Launches Race Education Program," *Pentagram News* (DoD), March 11, 1971.

69. Carl C. Craft, "Federal Employees Yell 'Foul' at Touch-and-Tell Sessions," *S&S*, September 4, 1971.

70. Hope, *Racial Strife*, 52, 53; US Army Research Institute for the Behavioral and Social Sciences, *Race Relations and Equal Opportunity in the Army*, 88; Nordheimer, "Armed Forces School."

71. Hope, *Racial Strife*, 55; B. Thomas, "Human Harmony Is Goal."

72. James A. Thomas, ed., *Race Relations Research in the U.S. Army in the 1970s: A Collection of Selected Readings* (Alexandria, VA: United States Army Research Institute for the Behavioral and Social Sciences, 1988); Sharp, "Race Seminars"; handwritten notes on "Human Relations Training for Commanders," in "USARV Human Relations Briefing (Chaplain)" file, box 5, P&A/HR.

73. Curtis Smothers, Subject: "Compliance Monitoring Visit to Pacific Command Installations," July 28, 1972, "Equal Opportunity, 1970–1972" folder, box A70, Laird Papers; "Course That 'Gets It Together,'" *S&S-P*, November 6, 1972; "New School to Focus on

Race Matters," *S&S*, August 18, 1972; "Anti-Bias Class Graduates," *S&S-P*, March 19, 1972; GEN Michael Davison, "Remarks at the USAREUR Race Relations School Graduation," Oberammergau, Germany, December 15, 1972, 255, in Davison Speeches.

74. Hope, *Racial Strife*, 52, 54.

75. Davison, "Remarks at the USAREUR Race Relations School Graduation," 256–57.

76. Charles Moskos, "How Do They Do It?," *New Republic*, August 5, 1991, cover story; J. Thomas, *Race Relations Research*, 233; Hope, *Racial Strife*, 52.

77. House Committee on Appropriations, Department of Defense Appropriation Bill, 1974, November 26, 1973, Cong sess. 93-1, serial #13020-7, 51.

78. Marc Huet, "House Panel Criticizes DoD Race Relations Training," *S&S*, December 1, 1973; see also House Committee on Appropriations, Department of Defense Appropriation Bill, 1974, 60.

79. Mary Neth, "Rapping on Race Relations," *S&S*, October 16, 1974.

80. Hope, *Racial Strife*, 58–59; Bob Hoyer, "New Look at Race, Drug Problems," *S&S*, December 25, 1973; Moskos, "How Do They Do It?"

81. Hope, *Racial Strife*, 58.

82. J. Thomas, *Race Relations Research*, 47.

83. J. Thomas, 42.

84. J. Thomas, 271.

85. "About: History," Defense Equal Opportunity Management Institute website, accessed September 17, 2022, www.defenseculture.mil/About-DEOMI/History.

86. Hope, *Racial Strife*, 98–99.

### CHAPTER 6

1. Thomas A. Johnson, "G.I.'s in Germany: Black Is Bitter," *NYT*, November 23, 1970.

2. Beth Bailey, *America's Army: Making the All-Volunteer Force* (Cambridge, MA: Belknap/Harvard University Press, 2009), 78.

3. This is from the list of materials available for dependent schools, furnished following a concerted effort on the part of military families in Germany. Subject: Black Studies Program, Department of the Army Directorate, United States Dependent Schools, European Area, June 20, 1970, included with material from "Military Conferences U.S. Army, Europe and Seventh Army, Berchtesgaden, Germany (West) 1971," folder 7, box 2703, Part V, NAACP Papers.

4. "John G. Kester," biographical entry, Historical Society of the District of Columbia Circuit website, accessed September 17, 2022, https://dcchs.org/sb_pdf/biographical-sketch-john-g-kester/; John G. Kester, Memorandum for the Assistant Secretary of the Army (M&RA), Subject: Haircuts, September 5, 1969, in SEA-RS 249, CMH.

5. Kester, Subject: Haircuts.

6. Kester, Subject: Haircuts.

7. Seminars discussed in COL Charles K. Nulsen Jr., "Rap It Out," *Army Digest*, November 1970, 8, copy contained in "Racial Literature 1971" file, box 4, P&A/HR. Nulsen was deputy chief of staff, G-1, Fort Bragg, NC. "Race Relations Briefing for Secretary of the Army," Fort Carson, January 27, 1971, in "Race Relations in the Army" folder, box 1, Wallis Papers, AHEC. Some 25.3 percent of non-whites listed hair as their top complaint; 17.6 percent of whites did the same.

8. Statement of Wallace Terry, "Racism in the Military, The Congressional Black Caucus Report, 15 May, 1972," as it appears in 92nd Cong., 2nd Sess., 118 Cong. Rec., #166-part 2, unpaginated (October 14, 1972).

9. Martin D. Gottlieb, "The Army's Efforts to Ease Racial Tension," *San Antonio Express*, September 20, 1970; "Die Armee schafft sich immer neue Neger," *Der Spiegel*, June 21, 1971.

10. "Hair Situation in Nation's Armed Forces Varies with the Location," *Brownsville (TX) Herald*, May 20, 1970; same UPI article also appears as "The Long and Short of Service 'Hair' Rules," *S&S*, May 30, 1970.

11. Charles Howard, "Afro Hair: Symbol of the Times," letter to the editor, *S&S*, July 29, 1970.

12. "People Are Talking About," *Jet*, May 1, 1969, 42, quoted in Lawrence Allen Eldridge, *Chronicles of a Two-Front War: Civil Rights and Vietnam in the African American Press* (Columbia: University of Missouri Press, 2011), 200; "Race Relations Briefing for Secretary of the Army," Fort Carson, 6–7; Terry testimony; Howard, "Afro Hair."

13. Donald R. Evans, Wiesbaden, "Likes 'Afro' Style," letter to the editor, *S&S*, August 9, 1969. See also "Are Hair Regs Unfair?," *S&S*, June 4, 1971.

14. Nulsen, "Rap It Out," 7.

15. Record of Trial, Special Court-Martial, Airman First Class August Doyle, December 8–10, 1969, p. 120, untitled folder; Doyle v. Koelbl, Fifth Circuit Court of Appeals, DC Docket No. CA-a-446, November 30, 1970, 37, untitled folder, both in box 1348, ACLU Papers, Princeton University Library, Princeton, NJ.

16. Doyle trial (1969); Charles Becknell, interview with author, October 1, 2015, Albuquerque, NM.

17. "Army OKs 'Neat' Afro Haircuts, but Hippie Hair Styles Are Out," *Alexandria (LA) Daily Town Talk*, May 6, 1970; "Afros OK for Negro Soldiers," *Ottawa (ON) Journal*, January 8, 1970; Bennett Report, 4.

18. Peter G. Nordlie et al., *Improving Race Relations in the Army: Handbook for Leaders* (prepared for the Department of the Army Motivation and Training Laboratory by Human Sciences Research, Inc., October 1972), 56; seminar discussion of key problems held at Fort Leavenworth on December 8 and 15, 1969, in folder 6, box 22, DCSPERS Discrim. Emphasis in original.

19. "Black Marines May 'Go Afro' within Limits," *Delta Democrat-Times* (Greenville, MI), September 3, 1969. The USMC commandant also recognized the Black Power salute as a gesture of "recognition and unity," while banning it from official ceremonies; "Official OK on Afro Haircuts Makes It Rough on Black Marines," *Index-Journal* (Greenwood, SC), September 4, 1969; James T. Wooten, "Marines Divided by Order Allowing Afro Hair Styles," *NYT*, September 15, 1969.

20. "Official OK on Afro Haircuts"; Sussman Report, 5; "Medium 'Afro' Haircuts OK," *Army Times* (n.d. [1969]), clipping in HRC 727 Hair Styles/Beards, CMH.

21. "After Action Report on Visit of Acting Deputy Assistant Secretary of Defense (Civil Rights)," November 30, 1969; "After Action Report on Mr. L. Howard Bennett," December 8, 1969; BG Verne L. Bowers, DCoS (P&A), memorandum approving policy, December 8, 1969; MG Ben Sternberg to General Ralph E. Haines Jr., November 24, 1969, 2, all in "Bennett Visit"; "Army OKs 'Neat' Afro Haircuts."

22. Use of "whitewalls" in Hubert J. Erb, "Army in Europe Disturbed by 'Racial Confrontations,'" *Fond du Lac (WI) Commonwealth Reporter*, September 8, 1970.

23. Ad for Halo shampoo, MeTV website, accessed September 17, 2022, www.metv.com/stories/shampoos-of-the-1960s; on the expansion of AAFES during this era, see Meredith H. Lair, *Armed with Abundance: Consumerism and Soldiering in the Vietnam War* (Chapel Hill: University of North Carolina Press, 2011), chap. 4.

24. Colonel John D. Florio, "Army–Air Force Exchange Service Programs," p. 1/slide 1, INCL 5, "Fort Monroe Conference."

25. Walter Rugaber, "PX System: One of the Most Powerful and Least Visible Retailing Enterprises," *NYT*, February 27, 1970.

26. Rugaber, "PX System"; Walter Pincus, "$3.7 Billion PX System Faces Probe by House," *WP*, February 10, 1969; Lair, *Armed with Abundance*, 165–67.

27. Exhibit No. 358, "Affidavit of LT. COL. John G. Goodlett, Jr.," sworn July 30, 1970, in U.S. Congress, Senate, "Fraud and Corruption in the Management of Military Club Systems," Hearings before the Permanent Subcommittee on Investigations, Committee on Government Operations, 92nd Cong., 1st Sess., Cong. Rec. 912–13 (1971); Pincus, "$3.7 Billion PX System."

28. "Commissary and PX Study Starts in June," *S&S*, May 25, 1969; Richard Holloran, "Rubicoff Says Rep. Rivers Tried to Block Inquiry on Army PX's," *NYT*, March 13, 1971; "Senate Investigators Probe Deeply into Cole's Dealings," *S&S*, March 9, 1971.

29. Walter Rugaber, "PX's: Hands in the Till at the 'Big Store,'" *NYT*, November 7, 1971; "Fraud and Corruption," Permanent Subcommittee on Investigations, 912.

30. On research, Florio, "Army–Air Force Exchange Service Programs," 2; initial list of items appears in "Pacex Stock Assortment Ethnic Products" (attached to document with September 24, 1970, date stamp that in turn refers to September 2, 1969, documents, "Merchandise in Support of Negro Customers"), "Equal Opportunity Reporting thru 1970" file, box 1, P&A/HR.

31. "Pacex Stock Assortment"; Lacy Banks, "The Military Meets the Afro," *Ebony*, September 1970, 86, 90.

32. Florio, "Army–Air Force Exchange Service Programs," 4, 5; Banks, "Military Meets the Afro," 86.

33. Banks, "Military Meets the Afro," 8. The AP story appeared in various versions; quotes drawn from "Afro Cuts Shown to Marines," *Kansas City (MO) Times*, September 27, 1969, and "Marine Corps Studying Afro Hair Styles," *Daily Inter Lake* (Kalispell, MT), September 26, 1969.

34. Hazel Guild, "Are the Complaints Justified?," *S&S Daily Magazine*, February 16, 1970.

35. Quote is from typed collection of AP news snippets, along with handwritten query and response from COL R. V. Foster, April 5, 1970, in "Equal Opportunity Reporting thru 1970" file, box 1, P&A/HR.

36. AP news snippets; Bob Guthrie, "Afro Stylist Gives Pointers at PX," *S&S-P*, June 6, 1970.

37. "At AAFES Shops: Afro Cut Is In," Army News Features, US Army Command Information unit, August 20, 1973, in HRC 72 Hair, CMH; a survey conducted at Fort Hood on race relations found that 91 percent of black enlisted men and 95 percent of white enlisted men had heard members of the same race complain often or occasionally that they "could not get a good haircut from an Army barber." "Enlisted Personnel Questionnaire on Race

Relations Programs in the Army," questions 63 and 64 under VI: Services and Products, Fort Hood, AHEC.

38. Thomas A. Johnson, "'I'll Bleed for Myself,' Says Black U.S. Soldier in Europe," *NYT*, October 11, 1970; Ted Brooks, "The 'Dap'—It Says 'He's My Brother,'" *S&S*, April 21, 1971. On dapping and its significance, see Gregory A. Freeman, *Troubled Water: Race, Mutiny, and Bravery on the USS* Kitty Hawk (New York: St. Martin's Press, 2009), 73–74.

39. "After Action Report," 18, "Fort Monroe Conference."

40. "Report of Inquiry into a Racial Incident at Camp Baxter, Da Nang," May 14, 1971, 5, ROI Racial Incident at Camp Baxter, Da Nang, folder 1 of 2, box 8, MACV–Inspector General, RG 472, NARA-CP.

41. Nordlie et al., *Improving Race Relations in the Army*, 57; Kimberley L. Phillips, *War! What Is It Good For? Black Freedom Struggles and the U.S. Military from World War II to Iraq* (Chapel Hill: University of North Carolina Press, 2012), 222.

42. "Long and Short of Service 'Hair' Rules"; CG 23d INF DIV CHU LAI RVN to RUMDAVA/CG USARV LBN RVN, Subject: Race Relations, April 14, 1971, in "Race Relations Survey 1971" file, box 3, P&A/HR; Brooks, "The 'Dap.'"

43. Michael S. Davison, "Opening Remarks," Equal Opportunity Conference, Berchtesgaden, Germany, November 10, 1971, 18, in Davison Speeches.

44. Marc Huet, "Army May OK 'Cultural Items' with Uniform," *S&S-P*, November 9, 1972, appears in *Stars and Stripes* (Europe) as "Army May Approve Wearing Trinkets," November 4, 1972. In the early 1970s, AR 670-5 prohibited "the wearing of unauthorized items of clothing and or ornamentation with the military uniform."

45. CO 2d BDE 25th INF DIV (CFJ) to CG USARV LBN RVN, Subject: Race Relations, April 12, 1971, in "Race Relations Survey 1971" file, box 3, P&A/HR.

46. For an account of a controversy concerning First Marine Aircraft Wing in Vietnam and protest from Rep. W. S. Stuckey (D-GA), see "Stars and Bars Can Fly in Viet," *S&S*, May 18, 1968; and AP article by military reporter Fred S. Hoffman, "Confederate Flag Shall Fly Again," *Abilene (TX) Reporter-News*, May 17, 1968; and "It Should Fly Anywhere . . . ," *Scott County Times* (Forest, MS), June 19, 1968. On army tolerance of such flags, see "Negro, Later Killed, Wrote: Some U.S. Army Units Fly Confederate Flags in Viet," *Cincinnati Enquirer* (from Chicago Daily News Service), March 17, 1968.

47. "After Action Report," 16, "Fort Monroe Conference"; Thomas A. Johnson, "200 Trainees at Ft. Dix Get Course in Race Relations," *NYT*, February 5, 1971.

48. Nordlie et al., *Improving Race Relations in the Army*, 57; MG John C. Bennett to All Iron Horsemen, Subject: Racial Harmony among Young Americans, December 6, 1971, 1, "Racial Harmony Council 1970, 1971, 1972" file, box 1, Charles R. Wallis Papers, AHEC; "Race Relations Briefing for Secretary of the Army," Fort Carson.

49. Quotes from "Small-Unit Leader's Pamphlet," MACV Dir 600-12, April 17, 1972, p. 6 of Annex C, in "MACV Publications" file, box 5, P&A/HR. According to Graham A. Cosmas, in *MACV: The Joint Command in the Years of Withdrawal, 1968–1973* (Washington, DC: Center of Military History, US Army, 2007), 236, this directive was first issued in 1970; the pamphlet for small-unit leaders was adapted from one created by the Marine Corps.

50. "Small-Unit Leader's Pamphlet," p. 4 of Annex C; CG 23d INF DIV CHU LAI RVN, Subject: Race Relations.

51. Kester, Subject: Haircuts, 2, 3.

52. Admiral Zumwalt addressed hair, along with twelve other topics of concern, in Z-57 on November 10, 1970. Zumwalt had originally wanted to title this "Zinger" "Mickey Mouse, Elimination of," but his vice chief convinced him to use "Demeaning and Abrasive Regulations" instead. Zumwalt, who tended to use the words "fun" and "zest" when he considered regulations governing personal behavior, was popular with younger sailors, but senior officers and civilian authorities developed an "anti-Zumwalt fervor." Larry Berman, *Zumwalt: The Life and Times of Admiral Elmo Russell "Bud" Zumwalt* (New York: Harper-Collins, 2012), 244–50.

53. Bailey, *America's Army*, 242.

54. See AR 600-20 in its evolving forms; a full set is available through the NCO Historical Society (www.ncohistory.com); most are held at the Center of Military History.

55. On the army efforts to manage the move to the all-volunteer force, see Bailey, *America's Army*, chap. 2; on the N. W. Ayer advertising campaign and this 1971 ad, see Beth Bailey, "The Army in the Marketplace: Recruiting the All-Volunteer Army," *Journal of American History* 94 (June 2007): 47–74; on Westmoreland's response, Jack Anderson, "Long Hair in Army Ad," *Las Cruces (NM) Sun-News*, October 28, 1971.

56. "Army's Hair War Jabs Old Wounds," *Pantagraph* (Bloomington, IL), December 22, 1974; "Aspin Asks for Congressional Investigation into 'Petty Harassment' of GIs in Europe," Press Release, December 9, 1974, USAREUR—Drugs, Hair folder, box 1, DG101; and correspondence between Secretary of the Army Bo Callaway and Representative Patricia Schroeder, Haircut folder, box 1, DG101, both in Cortright Papers.

57. On timing, see William L. Van Deburg, *New Day in Babylon: The Black Power Movement and American Culture* (Chicago: University of Chicago Press, 1992), 294; and correspondence between Callaway and Schroeder, May 9, 1975, quote from attachment, 2.

58. Matthew Carroll petition, May 1, 1974, USAREUR—Drugs, Hair folder, box 1, DG101, Cortright Papers; Bailey, *America's Army*, 87.

59. Dan Synovec, "Confrontation Era Over, Expert Says," *S&S*, July 25, 1974.

60. Fred C. Weyland to Maj. John T. Rollinson, November 11, 1974, HRC 727 Hair Styles/Beards, CMH. This letter was included as the army's sample reply to complaints about army hair policy in response to a request from Deputy Assistant Secretary of Defense John G. Finneran in January 1975; Finneran requested information on army hair policy to answer a congressional request for "the rationale of each Military Service concerning the length of haircuts."

61. "CMA Upholds Hair Regs," *Army Times*, July 19, 1976; Andy Plattner, "Hair Style Regs Could Get Clipped," *Army Times*, n.d. (clipping; probably July 1976); "Top Court OKs Haircut Policy," *Army Times*, n.d. (clipping, probably April 1976), all in Haircut folder, box 1, DG101, Cortright Papers. See also Gael Graham, "Flaunting the Freak Flag: *Karr v. Schmidt* and the Great Hair Debate in American High Schools, 1965–1975," *Journal of American History* 91 (September 2004): 522–43.

62. Devon Suits, "Army Announces New Grooming, Appearance Standards," Army News Service, January 27, 2021, www.army.mil/article/242536/army_announces_new _grooming_appearance_standards; for AR 670-1, see Army Publishing Directorate website, accessed September 17, 2022, https://armypubs.army.mil/ProductMaps/PubForm /Details.aspx?PUB_ID=1020639.

CHAPTER 7

1. Len Brown, "Army Tackles Racial Polarization Problem," *S&S-P*, February 1, 1970; report of seminar, "Racial Tension and Equal Opportunity for Treatment of Military Personnel," Fort Leavenworth, December 29, 1969, folder 6, box 22, 2 (multiple page 2s in report), DCSPERS Discrim.

2. Quoted in Rawn James Jr., *The Double V: How Wars, Protest, and Harry Truman Desegregated America's Military* (New York: Bloomsbury Press, 2013), 52–53; John Vernon, "Jim Crow, Meet Lieutenant Robinson: A 1944 Court-Martial," *Prologue Magazine*, Spring 2008, National Archives and Records Administration, www.archives.gov/publications /prologue/2008/spring/robinson.html.

3. On WAC history, see Bettie Morden, *The Women's Army Corps, 1945–1978* (Washington, DC: Center of Military History, US Army, 1990). I calculated the approximate number of African American trainees based on an average 13 percent representation in the corps during that era. The Women's Army Corps was assigned to Fort McClellan in 1954, along with the Army Chemical Corps; this major World War II training center had been shut down for a few years following the war.

4. Raymond Arsenault, *Freedom Riders: 1961 and the Struggle for Racial Justice*, abridged ed. (New York: Oxford University Press, 2011), 93–98.

5. "Required Information for Trainees," P & P Manual, WAC Training Battalion, January 21, 1960, p. B-XVI-1, in "Behavior, Social" file, box 7, Women's Army Corps, NARA-CP.

6. Lon H. Smith to All Incoming Military Personnel, October 21, 1961, in "Behavior, Social" file, box 7, Women's Army Corps, NARA-CP.

7. Arsenault, *Freedom Riders*, 93–98.

8. Arsenault, *Freedom Riders*, 93–98.

9. "Law Ground Underfoot," editorial, *Anniston (AL) Star*, May 15, 1961.

10. Smith to Personnel, October 21, 1961.

11. Quote taken from "Truman Order Started Services Integration," *Birmingham News*, August 7, 1963. The paper ran the full Gesell report in five parts, describing it as "increasingly controversial."

12. Robert S. McNamara, "Social Inequities: Urban's Racial Ills," speech to National Association of Educational Broadcasters, 43rd Convention, Denver, CO, November 7, 1967, in *Vital Speeches of the Day* 34 (December 1967): 99–100; Jack Raymond, "Pentagon Finds Housing Discrimination against Negro Servicemen in North and South," *NYT*, March 26, 1964; "Military Leaders Told to Aid in School Mixing," *Birmingham News*, August 7, 1963.

13. Department of Defense Directive 5120.36, July 26, 1963, copy located in "DoD Executive Seminar on Civil Rights" folder, box 32; Army Regulation 600-21, "Equal Opportunity and Treatment of Military Personnel," folder 3, box 28, both in Official Papers, DCSPERS Discrim.

14. "Presentation on the History and Problems of Equal Opportunity in the Army," ca. 1964, 18, folder 2, box 3, Official Papers: Briefings, DCSPERS Discrim.

15. "Presentation on the History and Problems of Equal Opportunity in the Army," 19–20.

16. "Presentation on the History and Problems of Equal Opportunity in the Army," 19–20.

17. Morris J. MacGregor Jr., *Integration of the Armed Forces, 1940–1965* (1981; repr., Washington, DC: Center of Military History, US Army, 2001), 550.

18. Initial quotes from army responses to question at "Department of Defense Executive Seminar on Civil Rights," April 22–23, 1966, in "DoD Executive Seminar on Civil Rights" folder, box 32, DCSPERS Discrim; "S.O.P. for Dinner Meetings," memorandum from John G. Kester to MG Harry J. Engel, DA Housing Coordinator, August 3, 1967, in folder 3, box 3, Official Papers, DCSPER Discrim. "Off-Base Equal Opportunity Status Report," December 31, 1966, for Fort Gordon, GA, and Fort Leavenworth, KS, are two of a full set of reports on all off-base issues from all installations with 500 or more personnel, in Equal Opportunity, OSD (MRA), "Off-Base Equal Oppt'y Status Reports '62–65" file, box 1, RG 330, NARA-CP. Dana Adams Schmidt, "Pentagon Widens Rules to Prevent Racial Inequities," *NYT*, December 18, 1970.

19. "DoD Executive Seminar on Civil Rights."

20. "DoD Executive Seminar on Civil Rights."

21. McNamara, "Social Inequities."

22. McNamara, "Social Inequities," 100; Phil Casey, "Clifford Forbids GIs to Lease Space in Biased Housing," *WP*, June 21, 1968; "Army Charges Bias Near Base," *WP*, November 17, 1967.

23. Casey, "Clifford Forbids GIs to Lease Space in Biased Housing"; "Rental Units Open to Negro GIs Doubles," *WP*, January 1, 1969. Clark Clifford's replacement, Melvin Laird, supported equal opportunity and open housing; his major initiative as secretary of defense was a new Pentagon focus on "Human Goals." Laird, however, was more concerned about undermining the necessary mutual support between military installations and their neighboring communities than McNamara had been. And after Congress passed the Fair Housing Act in 1968, Laird, unlike McNamara, could rely on federal legislation and enforcement. See Melvin Laird response to Roy Wilkins, October 8, 1970, in "Equal Opportunity and Race Relations, 1969–1973" folder, box C6, Laird Papers. Roy Wilkins, as chair of the Leadership Conference on Civil Rights, had asked Laird to encourage compliance testing (which the Pentagon prohibited) to make sure that landlords were living up to their written assurances. In response, Laird agreed that the assurances were not sufficient but nonetheless prohibited sending out individuals to test compliance because it was necessary to "preserve a constructive relationship between the installation commander and the community."

24. "Constructive relationship" from Melvin Laird to Roy Wilkins, October 8, 1970; report of seminar, "Racial Tension and Equal Opportunity for Treatment of Military Personnel," 2 (multiple page 2s in document); Schmidt, "Pentagon Widens Rules to Prevent Racial Inequities"; "Army Pushes Reform on Off-Base Housing Bias," *WP*, March 20, 1971. (The Pentagon acted first, followed by army changes in March.)

25. "Germany Meets the Negro Soldier," *Ebony*, October 1946, 5–6.

26. Petra Goedde, *GIs and Germans: Culture, Gender, and Foreign Relations, 1945–1949* (New Haven, CT: Yale University Press, 2003), 108–9; Goedde quotes from both the *Ebony* article and *Last of the Conquerors*. See also Adam Shatz, "'How Does It Feel to Be a White Man?': William Gardner Smith's Exile in Paris," *New Yorker*, August 11, 2019.

27. Nathaniel Jones's notes from briefing for NAACP representatives by Colonel Chalmers, January 28, 1971, file 3, box 3705, NAACP Papers; Gene Oishi, "The GI in

Germany," *Baltimore Sun*, September 3, 1972; Hans J. Massaquoi, "A Battle the Army Can't Afford to Lose," *Ebony*, February 1974, 120.

28. Sylvan Fox, "War and Prejudice," *NYT*, March 23, 1968; Curtis Daniell, "Germany: Trouble Spot for Black GIs," *Ebony*, August 1968, 126.

29. Robert D. McFadden, "G.I. Housing Bias in Germany Cited," *NYT*, April 23, 1971; "Negro GIs Rate Germany Hostile Nation—NAACP" and "Calls Bias Reports Magnified," both in *S&S-P*, April 25, 1971.

30. Memo, Gloster B. Current to Nathaniel Jones, June 4, 1970, folder 6, box 2703, NAACP Papers, on active attempts to create these relationships given the number of complaints the NAACP was receiving from African American military personnel. Melvin Laird to Roy Wilkins, May 1, 1971, and Harris W. Hollis, DCSPER, to Roy Wilkins, June 10, 1971, both in folder 9, box 2704, NAACP Papers.

31. Thomas A. Johnson, "Army Judge Fighting Bias in Germany Is Called Home for Talks at Pentagon," *NYT*, March 14, 1971.

32. Johnson, "Army Judge Fighting Bias"; "Army Denies Judge's Plea for Inquiry into Race Bias," *NYT*, April 1, 1971; Daniell, "Germany," 126.

33. "Presentation on the History and Problems of Equal Opportunity in the Army," 19.

34. For a detailed study of the US Army's social crisis in Germany, see Alexander Vazansky, *An Army in Crisis: Social Conflict in the U.S. Army in Germany, 1968–1975* (Lincoln: University of Nebraska Press, 2019).

35. "Discrimination in Off-Base Housing," folder 28, box 29, DCSPERS Discrim.

36. "Appendix D: Condition of Troop Billets" and "Appendix F: USAREUR Family On-Post Housing," both from Conference on Equal Opportunity and Human Relations, November 10–12, 1971, in folder 7, box 2703, Part V, NAACP Papers.

37. "Discrimination in Off-Base Housing"; Oishi, "GI in Germany."

38. McFadden, "G.I. Housing Bias in Germany Cited"; Nathaniel Jones to Frank W. Render II, February 26, 1971, in folder 8, box 2704, NAACP Papers; "Appendix O: Conditions in USAREUR," Conference on Equal Opportunity and Human Relations, NAACP Papers.

39. "Appendix N: Assessment of Racial Climate in USAREUR"; "Appendix F: USAREUR Family On-Post Housing"; "Appendix G: Status of Housing Referral Offices and Off-Post Housing," all from Conference on Equal Opportunity and Human Relations, NAACP Papers.

40. Kurt Loder, "Reforger: Boondoggle, Boon Docks & Boredom," and "Graf Sin Strip's a Joke," both in *Overseas Weekly*, n.d. (February 1969, during Reforger I); "Violence Marks Graf Exercise," *Overseas Weekly*, February 23, 1969.

41. Oishi, "GI in Germany"; Davison to Palmer, August 16, 1972, in CINC/US/AR/EUR Declassified Documents, September 1–December 27, 1972, box 2, Michael S. Davison Papers, AHEC; Craig R. Whitney, "Bias against Black G.I.'s," *NYT*, March 29, 1975.

42. John G. Kester, "Memorandum for the Secretary of the Army: Report: Trip to USAREUR," October 23, 1970, 20, in folder 7, box 2701, NAACP Papers.

43. Kester, "Trip to USAREUR."

44. Kester, "Trip to USAREUR," 35; Charles Alverson, "GI Blues: Today's Action Army in Germany," *Rolling Stone*, December 23, 1971; Melvin W. Bolden Jr. to Nathaniel R. Jones, "Memorandum: Suggestions & Observations of *Time Magazine* Interview on Military Race

Relations in Europe," February 22, 1971, in folder 8, box 2704, NAACP Papers. Original included typo: "Americab."

45. Kester, "Trip to USAREUR," 35; Bolden to Jones, "Suggestions & Observations."

46. Kester, "Trip to USAREUR," 36; historical currency converter website, accessed September 17, 2022, https://fxtop.com/en/historical-currency-converter.php?A=60&C1=DEM&C2=USD&DD=23&MM=10&YYYY=1970&B=1&P=&I=1&btnOK=Go%21; Military Pay Chart 1970 website, accessed September 17, 2022, www.navycs.com/charts/1970-military-pay-chart.html.

47. "Graf Sin Strip's a Joke"; Kester, "Trip to USAREUR," 21.

48. Massaquoi, "Battle the Army Can't Afford to Lose," 123. Even though this description is from early 1974, other less detailed accounts show similar actions by the late 1960s.

49. "Black U.S. General Testing German Racism in Person," WP, July 30, 1973; Massaquoi, "Battle the Army Can't Afford to Lose," 123. Davison began such periodic tests soon after he arrived in Germany.

50. Larry Phillips, "Group Raps Racism in Europe," Army Times, August 2, 1972.

51. Mrs. J. H., "Bell's Report on Germany Challenged," letter to the editor, Detroit News, July 29, 1972, folder 11, box 2703, NAACP Papers.

52. Mrs. J. H., "Bell's Report."

53. Whitney, "Bias against Black G.I.'s"; Massaquoi, "Battle the Army Can't Afford to Lose," 124; "Black U.S. General Testing German Racism in Person."

54. "Appendix N: Assessment of Racial Climate in USAREUR," N-4, Conference on Equal Opportunity and Human Relations, NAACP Papers.

55. "Appendix N"; Whitney, "Bias against Black G.I.'s"; Alexander Vazansky, "'Army in Anguish': The U.S. Army, Europe, in the Early 1970s," in GIs in Germany: The Social, Economic, Cultural, and Political History of the American Military Presence, ed. Thomas W. Maulucci Jr. and Detlef Junker (Washington, DC: German Historical Institute/Cambridge University Press, 2013), 286; Vazansky cites Davison's interview, Senior Officer Oral History Program, AHEC.

56. See Brian Linn, Elvis's Army: Cold War GIs and the Atomic Battlefield (Cambridge, MA: Harvard University Press, 2016); Daniel J. Nelson, A History of U.S. Military Forces in Germany (Boulder, CO: Westview Press, 1987; reissued by Routledge University Press, 2018), 98–99.

57. Nelson, U.S. Military Forces in Germany, 100–101.

58. "Graf Sin Strip's a Joke"; Alverson, "GI Blues."

59. Nelson, U.S. Military Forces in Germany, 105, citing Stuttgarter Zeitung, August 7, 1931 [sic; should be 1971], and Stuttgarter Zeitung, August 20, 1971. I rely heavily on the primary source research and the translations of German newspapers done by Daniel Nelson throughout the remainder of this section on West Germany and include his citations for readers' reference.

60. Nelson, U.S. Military Forces in Germany, 107–8, citing Nürnberger Nachrichten, September 16, 1971.

61. Nelson, U.S. Military Forces in Germany, 111, citing Frankfurter Rundschau, November 3, 1971, and 116, citing Stuttgarter Zeitung, August 15, 1972.

62. Nelson, U.S. Military Forces in Germany, 188, citing Saarbrücker Zeitung, October 28, 1972; 118, citing multiple sources, including Stuttgarter Zeitung, August 14 and 16, 1972; 117, citing Die Welt, October 21, 1972.

63. Nelson, *U.S. Military Forces in Germany*, 117, citing *Stuttgarter Nachrichten*, August 14, 1972, and *Stuttgarter Zeitung*, August 31, 1972; 119, citing *Augsburger Allgemeine*, October 27, 1972.

64. "Leading Today's Soldier in Europe," remarks by GEN Michael S. Davison before the Woodrow Wilson International Center for Scholars, Washington DC, March 25, 1972, 8, FOIA release posted online, www.foia.cia.gov/sites/default/files/document_conver sions/5829/CIA-RDP80R01731R001900030015-7.pdf; Michael S. Davison, "Opening Remarks," Equal Opportunity Conference, Berchtesgaden, Germany, November 10, 1971, in Davison Speeches. Davison notes that references to the race of those accused of crimes had dropped 40 percent since the agreement was made.

65. Lemnitzer to Davison, Confidential Correspondence, October 22, 1971, CINC/ US/AR/EUR Declassified Documents, September 1–December 27, 1972, box 2, Davison Papers, AHEC.

66. Davison to Palmer, August 16, 1972, confidential eyes only, CINC/US/AR/EUR Declassified Documents, July 5–August 31, 1972, box 2, Davison Papers, AHEC; post–All-Volunteer Force, see Nelson, *U.S. Military Forces in Germany*, 119–27.

67. Richard Halloran, "U.S. Army Division in Korea Combats Racial Flare-Up," *NYT*, December 4, 1974; for army demographics, see Hal Sider and Cheryl Cole, "The Changing Composition of the Military and the Effect on Labor Force Data," Bureau of Labor Statistics, 1984, 11, www.bls.gov/opub/mlr/1984/07/art2full.pdf. In 1970, non-whites were slightly underrepresented in comparison to the total US population but fairly quickly became overrepresented in the first decade of the all-volunteer force. Examples are drawn from a partial document, which appears to be correspondence sent to Ms. Susan Human, beginning with page 5 of a report on racial conflicts in South Korea, dated January 7, 1974, in "Korean Incident 10/73" file, box 1 of 8, Acc. 87A-003, DG101, Cortright Papers. Original quotation included typo: "graden."

68. David Vine, "My Body Was Not Mine, but the U.S. Military's," *Politico*, November 3, 2015, www.politico.eu/article/my-body-was-not-mine-but-the-u-s-militarys; Bob Guthrie, "Racial Problems in the 7th Inf. Div. Area," *S&S-P*, September 5, 1970.

69. For a richly detailed history of the camp towns, in the context of her study of the US military and prostitution in Korea, see Katharine H. S. Moon, *Sex among Allies: Military Prostitution in U.S.–Korea Relations* (New York: Columbia University Press, 1997). On VD rates and official status of prostitution, see Tim Shorrock, "Welcome to the Monkey House," *New Republic*, December 2, 2019; on "special districts," see Vine, "My Body Was Not Mine."

70. Moon, *Sex among Allies*, 68, 69; Albert E. Kafe (UPI), "Building Good Will," *S&S*, June 17, 1964.

71. Guthrie, "Racial Problems."

72. George M. Hampton, *Race Relations Research in Korea: Technical Report* (Arlington, VA: prepared under contract for the US Army Research Institute, December 1973). Hampton describes "waitresses and entertainers" giving Black soldiers "sullen and sometimes outright discourteous service."

73. Hampton, *Race Relations Research in Korea*, 36, 51, G-11, 33; Moon, *Sex among Allies*, 30.

74. Guthrie, "Racial Problems"; Joseph Hitt, "Human Relations Seminar Airs Club Bias Incidents," *S&S-P*, July 20, 1970; Moon, *Sex among Allies*, 71.

75. Described in "Consolidated Report on Dissidence and Racial Unrest within the Army" file, box 1, Korea Operations Files, 1971–1972, RG 550, NARA-CP.

76. "7 GIs Held in Pyongtaek Racial Brawl," *S&S-P*, April 16, 1971.

77. For descriptions of incident, see Jim Freeland and Jim Lea, "Riot-Torn Anjong-Ni—Why It Happened," *S&S-P*, July 16, 1971; "Wronged by Whites and Taking It Out on Koreans," *Dong-a Ilbo*, July 10, 1971, 7; Moon, *Sex among Allies*, 73–74. For protest and signs, *Kyunghyang Shinmun*, July 10, 1971, 7 (article quotes [in Korean] "Blacks Go Back to Cotton Field" and "Blacks Go Home"); and Moon, *Sex among Allies*, 72 (Moon cites *Overseas Weekly*, August 14, 1971, for signs I quoted in text).

78. "Wronged by Whites and Taking It Out on Koreans."

79. See articles on p. 6, *Dong-a Ilbo*, July 13, 1971, and p. 7, *Kyunghyang Shinmun*, July 12, 1971.

80. Freeland and Lea, "Riot-Torn Anjong-Ni"; the "kicker" that ran above the story's title was "Black GIs on Rampage."

81. *Dong-a Ilbo*, July 13, 1971; "Women Storm Army Camp," *S&S*, August 11, 1971.

82. Survey of press coverage in major Korean newspapers conducted for the author by Mina Lee, PhD student, Department of History, University of Virginia: three major newspapers, the *Dong-a Ilbo*, the *Maeil Business Newspaper*, and the *Kyunghyang Shinmun*, published thirty-eight articles on racial violence in military *gi-ji-chon* between 1971 and 1973. On relations between the United States and the Republic of Korea, see Moon, *Sex among Allies*, chap. 3.

83. Moon, *Sex among Allies*, 77; "Korean Incident 10/73" file, box 1, DG101, Cortright Papers.

84. Congressional Black Caucus to President Nixon, July 22, 1971, transmitted to General John H. Michaelis from Francis T. Underhill with accompanying note, August 17, 1971, in "Underhill, Francis T." file, Correspondence, Personal 1969–1972, John H. Michaelis Papers, AHEC.

85. Congressional Black Caucus to President Nixon.

86. Michael Getler, "Quota Barred on Black GIs Sent Overseas," *WP*, November 18, 1971; Ethel L. Payne, "So This Is Washington" column, *CDD*, November 27, 1971.


CHAPTER 8

1. Office of the Secretary of Defense, *Dialogue on Race Relations (UCMJ)* (film), NARA-CP. The film is moderated by CPT Gary Myers, USA; participants include Roger Kelley, ASD (M&RA); L. Howard Bennett, and LTC James White. There appear to be eighteen participants. One is female. The majority are people of color.

2. *Dialogue on Race Relations (UCMJ)*; Memorandum, Subject: 1970 The Judge Advocate General's Conference, in folder 28, box 22, Official Papers, DCSPERS Discrim.

3. *Dialogue on Race Relations (UCMJ)*.

4. *Dialogue on Race Relations (UCMJ)*; "Togo D. West Jr." (obituary), *Los Angeles Times*, March 11, 2018.

5. Jack Nelson, "Negro GI Charged in Cursing," *WP*, February 13, 1968; Blue Bell, February 16, 1968, Ft. McPherson, GA, in folder 13, box 2, Official Papers, DCSPERS Discrim. The basis for the charges: Capt. Larry Tyree, of Raleigh, NC, had intervened as Doe explained he was simply discussing Black history after Spec 4 Jimmy Chandler, of

Commerce, GA, had told him to "stop talking black power in front of inductees." Tyree told Doe to "shut up" and left the room. Doe then said, "I can't speak my mind without some white bastard telling me to shut up."

6. On US military law during this era, see Elizabeth Lutes Hillman, *Defending America: Military Culture and the Cold War Court-Martial* (Princeton, NJ: Princeton University Press, 2005); and William T. Allison, *Military Justice in Vietnam* (Lawrence: University Press of Kansas, 2007). Hillman pays little attention to issues of race, suggesting the imbalance that existed at the time: racial disparities were of minor concern to those concerned with the system of military justice, while military justice was of great concern to those concerned about racial inequities. See also Marc Huet, "Drastic Changes in Military Justice Studied," *S&S*, August 17, 1970.

7. Samuel P. Huntington, *The Soldier and the State: The Theory and Politics of Civil–Military Relations* (Cambridge, MA: Belknap/Harvard University Press, 1957), 346; for awareness at the time, see William L. Hauser, *America's Army in Crisis: A Study in Civil-Military Relations* (Baltimore: Johns Hopkins University Press, 1974), 61.

8. William Gardner Bell, ed., *Department of the Army Historical Summary Fiscal Year 1969* (Washington, DC: U.S. Army Center of Military History, 1973), 61.

9. Quotations and statistics from Bell, *Department of the Army Historical Summary*, FY 1969, and William Gardner Bell, ed., *Department of the Army Historical Summary Fiscal Year 1970* (Washington, DC: U.S. Army Center of Military History, 1973), 60–63. Fiscal years begin in October (thus fiscal year 1968 ran from October 1, 1967, to September 30, 1968), which means analysis based on fiscal years lag in reflecting the events of the chronological years (FY 1968 underrepresents the escalating crises of 1968). Some variant of the category "Military Justice" appears in DAHSUM reports across this era.

10. On Project 100,000, see Geoffrey W. Jensen, "Project 100,000: A Parable of Persisting Failure," in *Beyond the Quagmire: New Interpretations of the Vietnam War*, ed. Geoffrey W. Jensen and Matthew M. Stith (Denton: University of North Texas Press, 2019), 145–80; and "McNamara Plans to 'Salvage' 40,000 Rejected in the Draft," *NYT*, August 24, 1966, 1–2. Jensen also analyzes the original and retrospective debates about the legitimacy and effectiveness of the controversial Project 100,000 program. Daniel P. Moynihan, *The Negro Family: The Case for National Action* (Washington, DC: Office of Policy Planning and Research, U.S. Department of Labor, 1965).

11. Jensen, "Project 100,000," quote from 153.

12. Handwritten chart, "CAT IV Input," in folder 6, box 35, DCSPERS Discrim, with no date; material through 1969 is included.

13. Handwritten chart, "CAT IV Input"; "Special Study: Racial Harmony in the Army," June 1, 1969, 9, 10, folder 3, box 28, DCSPERS Discrim.

14. Jensen, "Project 100,000," 176, 160, 162. On the typical New Standards soldier and percentages, see Isaac Hampton II, *The Black Officer Corps: A History of Black Military Advancement from Integration through Vietnam* (New York: Routledge, 2013), 144.

15. "Defense: Refilling the Pool," *Time*, November 11, 1966; BG MacFarlane to MG Dolvin, September 16, 1970, "Equal Opportunity and Racial Unrest 1970" file, box 1, P&A/HR; AVDCSP CO to CSA, "Racial Tension in the Maintenance Battalion," January 2, 1970, in SEA-RS 140b, CMH.

16. "Monthly Report of I Corps Leadership Council," January 24, 1970, and March 1, 1970, "Council Meetings 1970" file, box 1, P&A/HR; report to General William C.

Westmoreland by the Committee for Evaluation of the Effectiveness of the Administration of Military Justice (Matheson Report), June 1, 1971, 52, SEA-RS 294, CMH.

17. Tom Guidera in Cecil Barr Currey, *Long Binh Jail: An Oral History of Vietnam's Notorious U.S. Military Prison* (Washington, DC: Brassey's, 1999), 29; William Keyes in Currey, 80.

18. Descriptions from Blue Bells, folder 17, box 2, Series II Official Papers, DCSPERS Discrim.

19. Descriptions from Blue Bells.

20. Description of this incident, including the following paragraphs, from MAJ Thomas J. Ashley, Assistant Inspector General, "Report of Investigation," with exhibits, April 20, 1969, SEA-RS 255, CMH. Description drawn from six-page report and exhibits B-5, B-12, B-15, and E.

21. Description that follows from John Saar, "You Can't Just Hand Out Orders," *Life*, October 23, 1970, 35.

22. Saar, "You Can't Just Hand Out Orders," 33, 31.

23. Saar, "You Can't Just Hand Out Orders," 32, 36, 34.

24. Saar, "You Can't Just Hand Out Orders," 36–37.

25. AVDAIG, "Report of Investigation Concerning Alleged Fragging Incidents in the 1st Battalion, 7th Cavalry Rear Area, February 23, 1970," in SEA-RS 140b, CMH.

26. William M. Hammond, *Public Affairs: The Military and the Media, 1968–1973* (Washington, DC: Center of Military History, US Army, 1996), 370. Hammond cites "Memo, Robert F. Froehlke, ASD Admin, for Secretary of Defense, 8 Dec 70, 330-76-067, box 92, Viet 330.11, Laird Papers, WNRC."

27. "Equity in Military Justice," BG DeWitt Smith to CSA William Westmoreland, December 10, 1970, in "Race Relations in the Army" folder, box 1, Charles R. Wallis Papers, AHEC.

28. "Equity in Military Justice."

29. Darnell Summers, telephone interviews with author, May 16 and 24, 2022; Summers's website, Fort Carson: Post "Racial Harmony Council" 1970, www.angelfire.com /jazz/stwb/FTCARSONRHC_.html, includes an account of events, scanned photograph of Smith, and a newspaper clipping documenting RHC election and duties.

30. Fred P. Graham, "Reforms Sought in Military Code," *NYT*, May 18, 1967; "Army to Revise Courts-Martial," *CDD*, April 6, 1946; "Rep. Powell Asks Complete Overhaul of Army Justice," *CDD*, June 1, 1946; "Truman Signs Code of Service Justice," *NYT*, May 7, 1950.

31. "G.I. Discharges Facing Scrutiny," *NYT*, November 17, 1961; "General Praises Military Justice," *NYT*, January 20, 1966; Graham, "Reforms Sought in Military Code."

32. See Robinson O. Everett, "The New Look in Military Justice," *Duke Law Journal*, 1973, 649–701, for an overview and analysis of the reforms. See also Joseph W. Bishop Jr., "The Quality of Military Justice," *NYT*, February 22, 1970.

33. Transcript of Staff Judge Advocate Military Justice Conference, May 24, 1969, Long Binh Post, in file 401–02, box 6, MACV, Staff Judge Advocate/Advisory Division, RG 472, NARA-CP.

34. Transcript of Staff Judge Advocate Military Justice Conference.

35. On the leadership study, see MAJ John M. Zdeb, "Restoring the Shield: Westmoreland and the Recovery of Military Professionalism" (MA thesis, US Army Command and

General Staff College, 2016), esp. 77–78. For "collapsed" quote, fragment of SAMVA (Special Assistant for the Modern Volunteer Army), "The American Soldier of Vietnam, 1971," 34, included with DCSPER-SED to Commanding General, Continental Army Command, on "Military Justice Training," n.d. (summer 1971?), in 1002-02 (NCOA/DSS 71), Training Programs 1967–71, USCONARC, HQ, RG 546, NARA-CP.

36. "Chronology of Racial Incidents, 6 January–6 April 1971," in "Race Relations Survey 1971" file, box 3, P&A/HR.

37. "Chronology of Racial Incidents."

38. DA Memo, ODCSPER-SARD, seeking authorization for task force, March 1, 1971, and CSA Memorandum, establishing task force, March, 16, 1971, with Matheson Report, CMH.

39. CSA Memorandum.

40. Matheson Report, 9–10, 33–34, 48; quotation from 54–55.

41. Matheson Report, 41–42.

42. For an overview of the incident, see Thomas A. Johnson, "NAACP Facing Rupture," *Dayton Daily News* (New York Times News Service), November 24, 1968; and Lewis M. Steel, *The Butler's Child: White Privilege, Race, and a Lawyer's Life in Civil Rights* (2016; Columbia: University of South Carolina Press, 2020), esp. xi–xii, 126–36.

43. Steel, *Butler's Child*, 134, 129.

44. Steel, *Butler's Child*, 134, 131.

45. Johnson, "NAACP Facing Rupture"; Steel, *Butler's Child*, 135.

46. "New NAACP Branch Boss Starts Unity Drive," *Sacramento Bee*, December 17, 1968; Steel, *Butler's Child*, 136; Emil Dansker, "Greene NAACP Calls for Purge of National Board," *Dayton Daily News*, October 29, 1968.

47. "NAACP Names New Counsel," *Pittsburgh Courier*, October 11, 1969.

48. "N.A.A.C.P. Picks General Counsel, *NYT*, October 2, 1969.

49. Martin Arnold, "There Is No Rest for Roy Wilkins," *NYT Sunday Magazine*, September 28, 1969.

50. Johnson, "NAACP Facing Rupture"; Glouster B. Current to Nathaniel Jones, June 4, 1970, folder 6, box 2703, Part V, NAACP Papers.

51. Transcript, Jones delegation meeting, "Col Dooty" tape, 2, folder 2, box 2705, NAACP Papers; Thomas A. Johnson, "Black Legal Help for G.I.'s Is Urged," *NYT*, February 15, 1971.

52. Transcript, Jones delegation meeting, 2.

53. Jones-Smothers, 57.

54. Jones-Smothers, 59.

55. Johnson, "Black Legal Help for G.I.'s Is Urged."

56. Johnson, "Black Legal Help for G.I.'s Is Urged."

57. Johnson, "Black Legal Help for G.I.'s Is Urged."

58. ATIT-At to Commandant, US Army Infantry School, on "Military Justice Training," July 27, 1971, and DCSPER-SED to Commanding General, Continental Army Command, on "Military Justice Training."

59. Supervisory Judge, 17th Judicial Circuit, to Staff Judge Advocate, HQ, US Army Vietnam, on "Model Plans and New Concepts for the US Army Judiciary in USARV," April 12, 1971, and Transcript of Military Judges Conference, February 15, 1971, Long Binh Post, both in file 402–08, box 15, MACV, Staff Judge Advocate/Advisory Division, RG 472, NARA-CP.

60. Transcript of Military Judges Conference, February 15, 1971.

61. "Race Relations Team Named by Pentagon," *S&S*, April 30, 1968; James Gunter, "Race Progress Good in Army, Probers Say," *S&S*, May 11, 1968; Morris J. MacGregor Jr., *Integration of the Armed Forces, 1940–1965* (1981; repr., Washington, DC: Center of Military History, US Army, 2001), 559n14.

62. Marc Huet, "Europe GI Integration Is Praised," *S&S*, July 12, 1968.

63. Jones-Smothers, 19.

64. Jones-Smothers, 20–21, 25–26.

65. Jones-Smothers, 23–34; Judge Advocate General to All Staff Judge Advocates, Memo on "Nonjudicial Punishment," March 25, 1969, in folder 1, box 22, Official Papers, DCSPERS Discrim.

66. Transcript, Jones delegation meeting, 5–8.

67. Transcript, Jones delegation meeting, 9.

68. Transcript, Jones delegation with USAREUR DCSPER office (?), unpaginated, folder 2, box 2705, NAACP Papers.

69. Transcript, Jones delegation with USAREUR DCSPER office (?), unpaginated; identification of Hollis as DCSPER, Wikipedia, accessed September 17, 2022, https:// en.wikipedia.org/wiki/Harris_W._Hollis; for a similar concern about the capacity of en-listed men to manage the system, see "Special Study: Racial Harmony in the Army," June 1, 1969, 10, folder 3, box 28, DCSPERS Discrim, the document that served as a basis for White's briefing. The authors asked: "Should the commander expect Mental Category IV personnel as a group to articulate suspicions (real and imagined) of subtle discriminatory practices in the standards and content desired by the chain of command or the inspector general?"

70. U.S. Congress, House, Special Subcommittee on Recruiting and Retention of Military Personnel of the Committee on the Armed Services, Hearings, 92nd Cong., 1st and 2nd Sess., Cong. Rec. 8748.

71. Joe Alex Morris Jr., "U.S. Army in Germany: Vexing Racial Picture," *Los Angeles Times*, November 21, 1971.

72. U.S. Congress, House, Hearings before the Special Subcommittee on Recruiting and Retention of Military Personnel, 8753 (Mr. Ichord quotes from an army "fact sheet"); information on Dixon and subsequent charges against white soldier from Morris, "U.S. Army in Germany." Morris described Dixon as a private; the fact sheet indicated he was a Specialist 4.

73. Morris, "U.S. Army in Germany."

74. Morris, "U.S. Army in Germany."

75. Bob Umphress, "Trial of 6 GIs Accused in Darmstadt Fracas Is Delayed Once Again," *S&S*, October 5, 1971.

76. Mr. Daniel, in Persons's testimony, Hearings before the Special Subcommittee on Recruiting and Retention of Military Personnel, 8775–76.

77. Daniel in Persons's testimony.

78. Hans J. Massaquoi, "A Battle the Army Can't Afford to Lose," *Ebony*, February 1974, 118.

79. John M. Goshko, "Black Troops Distrust U.S. Military Justice," *WP*, October 31, 1971, for all quotes; other evidence of Davison's positions comes from Persons's testimony be-fore Congress, Persons's oral history (Wilton B. Persons, interviewed by Herbert J. Green and Thomas M. Crean, 1985, Senior Officer Oral History Program, 1985, AHEC), 367–75,

and Davison's testimony before Congress (U.S. Congress, House, Special Subcommittee on North Atlantic Treaty Organization Commitments, Hearings, 92nd Cong., 1st and 2nd Sess., Cong. Rec. 13288–89 [1972]). While this hearing was on other issues, the chair of the Subcommittee on Recruitment and Retention, Mr. Daniels (VA), had sent questions to be posed to General Davison.

80. Goshko, "Black Troops Distrust U.S. Military Justice" for specific actions; for more, see "Appendix H: Judge Advocate Equal Opportunity Programs," in "Conference on Equal Opportunity and Human Relations, November 10–12, 1971," folder 7, box 2703, Part V, NAACP Papers; see also Persons oral history, 376, 370, and Persons testimony before Congress, 8745.

81. Goshko, "Black Troops Distrust U.S. Military Justice."

82. General Michael S. Davison Speech, November 10, 1971, US Army press release. This document, along with other material on the conference, including the full program with appendixes, is in folder 7, box 2703, Part V, NAACP Papers. Joe Alex Morris Jr., "Black GIs' Crime Up in Europe," WP, November 12, 1971.

83. Morris, "Black GIs' Crime"; program, Conference on Equal Opportunity and Human Relations, November 10–12, 1971 (logo on cover; statistics not included in WP article are from appendix K, p. K-5), in folder 7, box 2703, Part V, NAACP Papers. Morris was a Los Angeles Times reporter who had covered the Darmstadt trials and attended the conference, along with three reporters each from CBS and ABC television networks and other newspaper and magazine reporters, including one from Ebony.

84. Morris, "Black GIs' Crime." The USAREUR internal statistics are mirrored by the "Crimes of Violence by Race" statistics from the US Army, Vietnam, July 1970–May 1971. Removing the category of "disturbances," there were 261 "NEG vs CAU" violent crimes and 34 "CAU vs NEG" violent crimes (murder, attempted murder, manslaughter, aggravated assault, and robbery). "Equal Opportunity Reporting thru 1970" file, box 5, P&A/HR.

85. Hon. Louis Stokes, "Racism in the Military: The Congressional Black Caucus Report, 15 May, 1972," 92nd Cong., 2nd Sess., 118 Cong. Rec. 36585, 36587, 36588 (October 14, 1972). The transcript contains many typos, including in this quote: "not" for "no."

86. On this trial, see B. Drummond Ayers Jr., "Military Justice Assailed at Trial," NYT, February 9, 1972; Ayers, "Defense Loses Two Key Motions in Kansas Rape Court-Martial," NYT, February 11, 1972; Ayers, "Guilty Plea Ends Army Test Case," NYT, February 12, 1972. A Black former army specialist, incarcerated for a rape conviction at Fort Leavenworth, was charged with rape and attempted murder committed while, as a trusty, he had freedom to move about the post. His attorney withdrew his challenge to the UCMJ following an adverse ruling by the judge, following his consideration of a written brief on the topic, "rather than risk making a new law at the possible expense of a man's life."

87. Not discussed in this chapter is the Department of Defense Task Force on the Administration of Military Justice, created in April 1972 at the direction of Secretary of Defense Melvin Laird (January 1972) and in response to President Nixon's "direction to take a fresh look at the question of racial discrimination in the military justice system." The task force was cochaired by Nathaniel Jones and GEN Clair Hutchin Jr. The final report did not achieve consensus, though all members affirmed that racial discrimination was a problem within the US military. Of the four service judge advocate generals (there were five military officers on the task force, including its cochair), three joined two of the remaining nine members in a limited dissent. They rejected the notion of systemic racism, indicating that

they believed there were multiple explanations for the existing disparities and that they were not due to racism alone. General Prugh, the army judge advocate general who had preceded Persons as judge advocate in Germany, explained his reservations (and support) in detail in a subsequent lecture to the New York City Bar Association. Department of Defense, "Report of the Task Force on the Administration of Military Justice in the Armed Forces," November 30, 1972, 4 vols., HRC 319.1, CMH, quote on Nixon from vol. 1, p. 2; MG George S. Prugh, speech to the Bar Association of the City of New York, March 15, 1973, Speech File Service, US Army Command Information Unit, Washington DC, p. Z-1.

CHAPTER 9

1. "Report of Investigation Concerning Allegations of Misconduct on the Part of Major Lavell Merritt," Inspector General to Chief of Staff, MACV, October 29, 1968, part 1 of 3, 2, 3, Merritt Files.

2. "Misconduct of Major Lavell Merritt," "MIV-29-68 MAJ. Merritt (Corrective/Follow-Up Action)" file, part 1 of 3, Merritt Files.

3. Merritt Statement, 8.

4. "Negro Participation in the Armed Forces by Grade, Race," April 28, 1969, folder 12, box 16, DCSPERS Discrim; White Briefing, 3. "Humps" at more senior ranks are periodically created by wartime expansion, but in the case of Black officers, whatever "hump" there was at major or lieutenant colonel rank was not due to an excessive number or percentage of Black officers at that rank. See the info in Brian McAllister Linn, *Real Soldiering: The U.S. Army in the Aftermath of War, 1815–1980* (Lawrence: University Press of Kansas, forthcoming), chap. 4.

5. White Briefing, 3.

6. White Briefing, from "Conclusions" slide, and p. 2; he drew on "Special Study: Racial Harmony in the Army," June 1, 1969, 7, 12, folder 3, box 28, DCSPERS Discrim.

7. Morris J. MacGregor Jr., *Integration of the Armed Forces, 1940–1965* (1981; repr., Washington, DC: Center of Military History, US Army, 2001), 539.

8. "Comments of the Military Departments on the Recommendations of the President's Committee on Equal Opportunity in the Armed Forces," 1, folder 2, box 41, DCSPERS Discrim.

9. "Comments of the Military Departments," 1.

10. "Comments of the Military Departments," 1, 4.

11. John Sibley Butler, "Affirmative Action in the Military," *Annals of the American Academy of Political and Social Science* 523 (September 1992): 202.

12. Lyndon B. Johnson, "Commencement Address at Howard University," June 4, 1965, The American Presidency Project website, www.presidency.ucsb.edu/documents/commencement-address-howard-university-fulfill-these-rights.

13. Terry H. Anderson, *The Pursuit of Fairness: A History of Affirmative Action* (New York: Oxford University Press, 2004), 59–64.

14. Anderson, *Pursuit of Fairness*, 62–63.

15. Anderson, *Pursuit of Fairness*, 63.

16. Anderson, *Pursuit of Fairness*, 63–64.

17. Anderson, *Pursuit of Fairness*, 63; Secretary of Defense, Memorandum for the White House, May 2, 1969, "Equal Opportunity and Race Relations, 1969–1973" folder, box C6,

Laird Papers; MacGregor, *Integration*, 569. LTC White's briefing material drew from a report titled "Reference Material on Negro Officers Considered for Promotion to Colonel, AUS in 1967–1968," which not only listed all twenty-seven "Negro Colonel Promotable DA" candidates but included an overview of the armed forces by race, rank, and branch of service from 1965 to 1968 (folder 12, box 16, DCSPERS Discrim).

18. Executive Order 11246, issued by President Johnson in 1965, required federal contractors to create affirmative action plans to ensure that equal opportunity programs yielded results. That requirement was extended to include the US military in 1970. See Joseph James DeFranco, "Blacks and Affirmative Action in the U.S. Military" (master's thesis, University of Illinois, 1987), 76; "About Filibusters and Cloture," and "Civil Rights Act of 1964," both on United States Senate website, accessed September 17, 2022, www .senate.gov; Jon Kelly, "The Art of the Filibuster: How Do You Talk for 24 Hours Straight?," *BBC News Magazine*, December 12, 2012, www.bbc.com/news/magazine-20672974.

19. "Committees of the 88th Congress," Congressional Resources, C-Span website, https://www.c-span.org/congress/committee/?61182&congress=88#, accessed September 17, 2022; NCC Staff, "The Filibuster That Almost Killed the Civil Rights Act," *Constitution Daily*, April 11, 2016, National Constitution Center website, https://constitutioncenter .org/blog/the-filibuster-that-almost-killed-the-civil-rights-act.

20. Anderson, *Pursuit of Fairness*, 75; Proceedings and Debates of the 88th Cong., 2nd Sess., Cong. Rec. 9024–42 (April 24, 1964), including "Dispute in FEPC Arises in Illinois," *NYT*, March 22, 1964, 9024, 9025.

21. "The Motorola Rule and Cassius X," *CT*, March 19, 1964, 16, read aloud by filibustering Senator Tower, in Proceedings and Debates of the 88th Cong., 2nd Sess., 9037.

22. "Cassius Clay Rejected by Army," *NYT*, March 21, 1964, 1; Department of the Army, "Fact Sheet Pertaining to Cassius Clay's Rejection by the Army," in U.S. Congress, Senate, Committee on Appropriations, Foreign Assistance and Related Agencies Appropriations for 1965: Hearings before the Committee on Appropriations, 88th Cong., 2nd Sess., Cong. Rec. 640–41 (1964).

23. "Motorola Rule and Cassius X."

24. "Defense: Refilling the Pool," *Time*, November 11, 1966.

25. Handwritten chart, "CAT IV Input," in folder 6, box 35, DCSPERS Discrim, with no date (material through 1969 is included); "Racial Harmony in the Army," 9, 10.

26. Geoffrey W. Jensen, "Project 100,000: A Parable of Persisting Failure," in *Beyond the Quagmire: New Interpretations of the Vietnam War*, ed. Geoffrey W. Jensen and Matthew M. Stith (Denton: University of North Texas Press, 2019), 155; see also Gregory A. Daddis, *No Sure Victory: Measuring U.S. Army Effectiveness and Progress in the Vietnam War* (New York: Oxford University Press, 2011), 185–86. Both Jensen and Daddis contest the negative evaluations.

27. "Department of Defense Executive Seminar on Civil Rights," April 22–23, 1966, "DoD Executive Seminar on Civil Rights" folder, box 32, DCSPERS Discrim; "Equity in Career Fulfillment" is the title of Session 1; quote is from Session 1, part D, "Questions from Agenda Subjects," #5-d.

28. "DoD Executive Seminar," Session 1, part C.

29. "DoD Executive Seminar," Session 1, part D, #5; Session 1, unpaginated and unnumbered; Session 1, part C, #9b.

30. "DoD Executive Seminar," Session 1, part A ("Definition of the Problem"), item 1.

31. TIG to DCSPER (in response to request from LTC White), "Racial Discrimination Cases Received in OTIG," n.d., folder 1, box 29, DCSPERS Discrim. Of a total of 326 complaints about racial discrimination, the Office of the Inspector General found only 6, or 1.84 percent, to be justified. That was slightly down from 1.92 percent in FY 1968; Memorandum for Deputy Under Secretaries of the Military Departments (Manpower) from Assistant Secretary of Defense, Subject: Congressional Inquiry on Promotion Opportunities, April 15, 1967, folder 2, box 4, DCSPER Discrim; Jesse W. Lewis Jr., "The Negro in Vietnam—II: Some Still Feel Race Figures in Promotion," WP, April 3, 1967.

32. "People Objectives" (draft), circulated July 28, 1969, in "DoD Human Goals (Personnel), 1969" folder, box A67; "Department of Defense Human Goals," in "Human Goals, 1969–1972" folder, box A74; Memorandum for Secretary of Defense from ASD (M&RA), Subject: Equal Opportunity Within the Department of Defense," August 28, 1970, in "Equal Opportunity and Race Relations, 1969–1973," folder, box C6; Department of Defense Directive Number 1100.15, December 14, 1970, in "Equal Opportunity and Race Relations, 1969–1973" folder, box C7, all in Laird Papers; Interview of Melvin R. Laird, 9–10, Historical Office, Office of the Secretary of Defense website, September 2, 1986, https:// history.defense.gov/Portals/70/Documents/oral_history/OH_Trans_LairdMelvin%209-2 -1986.pdf?ver=2015–06-30-110159-040 (origins ASD [M&RA]). For a more detailed discussion of Laird's actions, especially in relation to the Nixon administration, see Richard A. Hunt, *Melvin Laird and the Foundation of the Post-Vietnam Military, 1969–1973* (Washington, DC: Historical Office of the Secretary of Defense, 2015), 524–36.

33. White Briefing, 3; William Westmoreland, "Actions to Be Accomplished," and Resor to Sec Def, Subject: "Department of the Army Actions to Improve Race Relations," in "Equal Opportunity, 1970–1972" folder, box A70, Laird Papers; Resor, address, 4, November 18, 1970, INCL 2, "Fort Monroe Conference."

34. Office of the Adjutant General, DA, Memorandum, Subject: Race Relations and Equal Opportunity Affirmative Actions Plan, September 1, 1972 (cover memorandum for distribution of *Department of the Army Affirmative Actions Plan*).

35. *Department of the Army Affirmative Actions Plan*, July 14, 1972, unpaginated.

36. *Department of the Army Affirmative Actions Plan*.

37. Cover memorandum, *Department of the Army Affirmative Actions Plan*.

38. The great majority of material on Douthard Butler and the Butler Report comes from Isaac Hampton II, *The Black Officer Corps: A History of Black Military Advancement from Integration through Vietnam* (New York: Routledge, 2013). Hampton, who credits Butler as friend and mentor, incorporates material from Butler's private collection of documents and from an oral history interview. For this paragraph, see p. 70. See also "Local Man Promoted to Colonel," *Waxahachie (TX) Daily Light*, December 29, 1976. On FOIA, Memorandum for Deputy Chief of Staff for Personnel from Director of Army Equal Opportunity Programs, Subject: "Release of the 'Butler Study,'" July 31, 1975, in "Racism Clips" folder, Cortright Papers.

39. Hampton, *Black Officer Corps*, 17.

40. Hampton, 67–68, 36.

41. Hampton, 68.

42. "Guidance," furnished to selection board, June 23, 1968, p. 17, filed with list of "Negro Colonel Promotables," in folder 40, box 18, DCSPERS Discrim.

43. Hampton, *Black Officer Corps*, 68.

44. Hampton, *Black Officer Corps*, 68.

45. "Release of the 'Butler Study'" memorandum; "Local Man Promoted to Colonel"; Hampton, *Black Officer Corps*, 79, 73.

46. Hampton, *Black Officer Corps*, 72–90; "Release of the 'Butler Study'" memorandum.

47. Hampton, *Black Officer Corps*, 79, 101–3.

48. For example, DCSPER-SARD, "DoD Study of Promotion Opportunity and Disciplinary Actions Affecting Negro Servicemen" (1969–70?), compared disciplinary violations of those with AFQT scores between 21 and 30 by race and by rank. In "Memorandums, 25 Mar 1969–17 Nov 1970, n.d.," box 22, and "Cat IV Input," handwritten chart, n.d., in folder 6, box 35, both in DCSPERS Discrim.

49. Hampton, *Black Officer Corps*, 101–3; DeFranco, "Blacks and Affirmative Action," 67.

50. "Release of the 'Butler Study'" memorandum.

51. "Release of the 'Butler 'Study'" memorandum; Hampton, *Black Officer Corps*, 94; "Black Officer," letter to the editor (titled "Little Progress Seen in OER Racism"), *Army Times*, September 24, 1976.

52. US Army Research Institute for the Behavioral and Social Sciences, *Race Relations and Equal Opportunity in the Army: A Resource Book for Personnel with Race Relations/Equal Opportunity Responsibility* (by contract, Human Sciences Research, Inc., December 1973), 52.

53. "Negro Officers Selected for Senior Service Colleges, 1960 to 1969," in folder 24, box 27, DCSPERS Discrim; on Black businessmen, Derek T. Dingle, "Then and Now," *Black Enterprise*, August 1, 2005.

54. Louis Martin, "1 Black General in U.S. Army Has 513 White Mates," *CDD*, July 4, 1970; Hugh Warner, "Demonstration against ROTC Disrupts Assembly," *The Hilltop* (Howard University), November 10, 1967.

55. Linn, *Real Soldiering* (forthcoming), chap. 5; Michael S. Neiberg, *Making Citizen Soldiers: ROTC and the Ideology of American Military Service* (Cambridge, MA: Harvard University Press, 2000), 167.

56. Paul N. Kotakis, "Army ROTC at One Hundred," *Military Review*, May–June 2016, 107; Neiberg, *Making Citizen Soldiers*, 36, 58.

57. Neiberg, *Making Citizen Soldiers*, 100, 114, 116, 121, 123–26; Harold J. Logan, "ROTC Applicants Rise as Unit Totals Fall," *WP*, May 20, 1977 (figures that yield the 80 percent statistic). Neiberg emphasizes that faculty criticism provided the opportunity for reform and that opposition to ROTC's presence on campus was by no means universal among students.

58. Charles Johnson Jr., *African Americans and ROTC: Military, Naval and Aeroscience Programs at Historically Black Colleges, 1916–1973* (Jefferson, NC: McFarland, 2002), 180–91, 176. See issues of *The Hilltop*, Howard University, April 7, 1967, and April 28, 1967. USMA Black graduates from "Negro United States Army Military Academy Graduates, 1961 to 1970," folder 24, box 27, DCSPERS Discrim.

59. Draft of letter, Julius E. Williams, NAACP, to General Rodgers, USA, n.d. (with 1978 material), and invitation to minority recruiting conference, BG Melvin A. Goers to Julius Williams, August 18, 1971, both in "Correspondence, 1971–78," Part VI: B4, NAACP Papers; C. Johnson, *African Americans and ROTC*, 178; DCSPER-SARD to Acting Deputy Assistant Secretary of Defense (Civil Rights), "Fact Sheet," undated (c. 1970), in folder 2, box 29, DCSPERS Discrim.

60. Hampton, *Black Officer Corps*, 72.

61. William S. McFeely, *Grant: A Biography* (New York: W.W. Norton, 1981), 375–76; Matt Oliver, "Society's Sacrifice: The First Black Cadet at West Point, James Webster Smith," unpublished paper, United States Military Academy, December 1993, 3–8 (http://digital-library.usma.edu/digital/collection/p16919coll1/id/23).

62. Oliver, "Society's Sacrifice," 7–8.

63. Oliver, "Society's Sacrifice," 2.

64. McFeely, *Grant*, 376–78; Oliver, "Society's Sacrifice," 9–13, 7, 5–6.

65. Oliver, "Society's Sacrifice," 8, 7.

66. McFeely, *Grant*, 376.

67. Oliver, "Society's Sacrifice," 15–16.

68. Rory McGovern, *Black Cadets at West Point, 1870–1890* (video), Black History Project at West Point, February 9, 2021, www.youtube.com/watch?v=zqaxwedHz7w&list=PLWW ulOrrh9EjUnXmprl24ktMKZ6UdgdcZ&index=3.

69. McGovern, *Black Cadets at West Point; Gen Benjamin O. Davis Jr Destined to Lead High*, West Point video, February 18, 2021, www.facebook.com/watch/?v=474631476877800.

70. Harriet Griffiths, "Segregated Schools to Lose Funds for ROTC Programs," *Evening Star* (Washington, DC), May 7, 1965; "Bugle Call for Negro Cadets," *Ebony*, June 1966, 73.

71. Jeffery K. Toomer, "A Corps of Many Colors: The Evolution of Minority Recruiting Efforts at the United States Military Academy," unpublished paper, USMA, November 14, 1997, 6; he cites Alfred B. Fitt, December 27, 1967, and July 23, 1968, both in USMA Archives, West Point, New York.

72. 1968 Annual Report of the Superintendent, United States Military Academy, July 1, 1967–June 30, 1968, 11, USMA Library Digital Collection, http://digital-library.usma.edu /digital/collection/superep/id/79/rec/1.

73. 1968 Annual Report, 11; "The New Look at West Point," *Boy's Life*, July 1969, 44; James Feron, "West Point Goes Hunting for Recruits," *NYT*, May 7, 1985; 1969 Annual Report of the Superintendent, United States Military Academy, July 1, 1968–June 30, 1969, 6, USMA Library Digital Collection, http://digital-library.usma.edu/digital/collection /superep/id/80/rec/1.

74. Arthur Hester, interview by author, September 6, 2021.

75. 1966 Annual Report of the Superintendent, United States Military Academy, July 1, 1965–June 30, 1966, 1, USMA Library Digital Collection, http://digital-library.usma.edu /digital/collection/superep/id/77/rec/1; 1967 Annual Report of the Superintendent, United States Military Academy, July 1, 1966–June 30, 1967, 1, USMA Library Digital Collection, http://digital-library.usma.edu/digital/collection/superep/id/78/rec/1.

76. 1969 Annual Report, 6; 1967 Annual Report, 1–2; 1971 Annual Report of the Superintendent, United States Military Academy, July 1, 1970–June 30, 1971, 13, USMA Library Digital Collection, http://digital-library.usma.edu/digital/collection/superep/id/82/rec/1, 2; 1968 Annual Report.

77. Hester interview.

78. Hester interview.

79. Hester interview; "Equal Admissions Opportunity Program," United States Military Academy, document furnished to author by Arthur Hester, September 6, 2021.

80. Arthur Hester, "An Argument for Changing the Admissions Systems at the United

States Military Academy in Order to Increase the Enrollment of Minority Students," March 10, 1970, 5, document furnished to the author by Arthur Hester, September 6, 2021.

81. Hester, "An Argument," 6–7.

82. Toomer, "Corps of Many Colors," 7–8.

83. This account is based on Ty Seidule, "Black Power Cadets: How African American Students Defeated President Nixon's Confederate Monument and Changed West Point, 1971–1976," *Hudson River Valley Review*, 55–82; quote from p. 59.

84. Seidule, 60.

85. Seidule, 61–64.

86. "Manifesto from Black Cadets," undated (November 8, 1971), provided to author by Arthur Hester, September 6, 2021.

87. "Manifesto from Black Cadets."

88. Peter Bailey, "Getting It Together at 'The Point,'" *Ebony*, December 1971, 136–44; Seidule, "Black Power Cadets," 67; James West, "*Ebony Magazine*, Lerone Bennett, Jr., and the Making and Selling of Modern Black History, 1958–1987" (PhD thesis, University of Manchester, 2015), 54.

89. Seidule, "Black Power Cadets," 66–68, 70–71.

90. Beth Bailey, *America's Army: Making the All-Volunteer Force* (Cambridge, MA: Belknap/Harvard University Press, 2009), chap. 4; ODCSPER, DA, "Equal Opportunity: Second Annual Assessment of Programs," 1978, chap. 2, pp. 3–4, HRC 319.1, CMH; Drew Middleton, "Army in Rebuttal on Blacks' Ratio," *NYT*, March 11, 1975.

91. B. Bailey, *America's Army*, chap. 4; "2d Div Is 30% Black," *Army Times*, December 17, 1975, 15, and Defense Manpower Commission, memo on "Public Hearing on Race in the Military," January 26, 1976, "Racism Clips" File #2, Cortright Papers.

92. B. Bailey, *America's Army*, chap. 4; George M. Coleman, "Blacks Get 'Square Deal' in Army, Callaway Avows," *Atlanta Daily World*, July 7, 1974, 1, 4; "'Race Is No Longer Key Issue in Modern Army,' Secretary Callaway Says," *Atlanta Daily World*, January 18, 1974; Callaway to Dellums, May 22, 1975, 2–3, in CD accompanying Bernard Rostker, *I Want You!: The Evolution of the All-Volunteer Force*" (Santa Monica, CA: Rand Corporation, 2006).

93. Memo CSA to SA, Subject: "Final Report," n.d., accompanying Department of the Army, *Final Report of the Ad Hoc General Officers' Steering Committee on Equal Opportunity*, n.d. (ca. May 1975).

94. Department of the Army, *Final Report of the Ad Hoc General Officers' Steering Committee on Equal Opportunity* (accompanying memo dated May 20, 1975), 17, 5, 76, 15.

95. Fred S. Hoffman, "Minority Advance Planned by Army," *WP*, July 2, 1975.

96. Hampton, *Black Officer Corps*, 104; Tom Vanden Brook, "Where Are the Black Officers?," *USA Today*, September 1, 2020; Department of Defense, "2020 Demographics: Profile of the Military Community," charts 2-24, 2-25, Military One Source website, accessed September 17, 2022, https://download.militaryonesource.mil/12038/MOS/Reports/2020 -demographics-report.pdf. "Where Are the Black Officers?" shows that the percentage of Black officers in the US Army matches or exceeds the proportion of the population, while at the same time bemoaning the lack of Black officers; the article depends either on the unstated goal of parity with enlisted ranks or confusion about the demographics of the United States. The author points out that Black commanders in the combat arms are exceedingly rare; as an article in the *Christian Science Monitor* notes, only 10 percent of Black

officers elect to join the combat arms, compared with about a quarter of white officers (Anna Malrine Grobe, "ROTC at Black Colleges? How Pentagon Aims to Diversify Military Brass," *Christian Science Monitor*, March 17, 2020). "Cadet Diversity," US Military Academy at West Point, accessed January 31, 2022, www.westpoint.edu/about/cadet-consumer-information/cadet-diversity. For discussion—now dated—about the relative success and failure of Black officers, see Irving Smith, "Why Black Officers Still Fail," *Parameters* 40, no. 3 (2010), https://press.armywarcollege.edu/parameters/vol40/iss3/12.

97. "Blacks in the U.S. Army," 2010 (?), 15, https://api.army.mil/e2/c/downloads/572478.pdf; "Distribution of Active-Duty Enlisted Women and Men in the U.S. Military in 2019, by Race and Ethnicity," Statista website, accessed September 17, 2022, www.statista.com/statistics/214869/share-of-active-duty-enlisted-women-and-men-in-the-us-military; "Fact Sheet: Men of Color," Postsecondary National Policy Institute, January 26, 2020, https://pnpi.org/men-of-color/.

CONCLUSION

1. "2020 Demographics: Interactive Profile of the Military Community," Military OneSource website, 2020, https://demographics.militaryonesource.mil/chapter-2-race-ethnicity for statistics; David J. Armor and Curtis L. Gilroy, "Changing Minority Representation in the U.S. Military," *Armed Forces and Society* 3 (January 2010): 223–46. White women made up 49.1 percent of enlisted female troops; Beth Bailey, *America's Army: Making the All-Volunteer Force* (Cambridge, MA: Belknap/Harvard University Press, 2009), 133.

2. Curtis Smothers, Subject: "Compliance Monitoring Visit to Pacific Command Installations," July 28, 1972, "Equal Opportunity, 1970–1972" folder, box A70, Laird Papers.

3. Department of the Army, *Final Report of the Ad Hoc General Officers' Steering Committee on Equal Opportunity*, n.d. (ca. May 1975).

# INDEX

Abrams, Creighton, 60, 62, 65, 87, 113
affirmative action, 7, 93; and Butler Report, 254–58; and Bo Callaway, 272–73; civilian struggles over, 242, 248–50; and defense contractors, 247–48, 253; and DoD initiatives, 247–48, 251–52, 253, 265, 273; and Gesell Committee, 245–47; history of in military, 245–47; and Motorola case, 249–50; and program achievements, 243, 273, 275–78; and Project 100,000, 250–51, 257; and qualifications, 249, 251–52, 254; and quotas, 248, 253, 254, 272; and shortage of Black officers, 241–46, 251, 253, 258, 273–74; as solution, 243–44, 252; at USMA, 267–68
Affirmative Actions Plan, 253–54, 273
Afro, 195, 197, 210; and AAFES, 162–66, 168; army regulation of, 158–61, 168, 172–73, 176–77; controversy over, 158–59, 168, 196; and Marine Corps, 160–61, 164–65; and Willie Morrow, 164–66; as symbol, 58, 76, 153–76 passim
Ali, Muhammad, 249
all-volunteer force, 201, 178; Black percentage of, 271–72; concerns about, 134, 174, 222, 268; and hair policy, 157, 173–74; planning for, 69, 82, 120, 134, 157, 222; and recruiting, 134, 155, 173; as source of reform, 157, 173–74, 276
American Civil Liberties Union (ACLU), 211, 235–36
Armed Forces Qualification Test (AFQT), 214, 257
Army & Air Force Exchange Service

(AAFES): and consumer goods for Black servicemembers, 76, 162, 164, 176; and corruption charges, 154, 163; and haircuts, 162, 164–66; and Willie Morrow, 164–66; seizing opportunity, 154, 162, 163, 166; size and impact of, 162–63; as solution, 162, 163, 166–67, 176
Article 15, 20, 97, 216, 217, 234; complaints about, 74, 210; as disciplinary tool, 40, 212, 233; disproportionate rates of, 220, 231–32, 239; and reform, 74, 223, 232–33, 239, 255; statistics on, 213. *See also* military justice; Uniform Code of Military Justice
Association of the United States Army (AUSA), 38, 65

bars, 1, 37, 154, 162, 178; in South Korea, 2, 202–7; in United States, 145, 187, 188; in Vietnam, 17, 19, 22, 26; in West Germany, 89, 102, 188, 193–99, 207, 231
Bennett, L. Howard, 93; analysis of racial crisis, 60–62, 82–83, 91, 92, 114, 117–18, 122, 140–42, 160–61; attitude toward Black Power, 81; biography, 80, 83; DoD inspection tours, 59–62, 79–86, 91–92; role in DoD, 59, 62, 79, 80, 90, 140, 231
*Black and White: Uptight* (documentary), 138–40
Black Liberation Front, 109, 204
Black Panthers, 28, 58, 98, 102–4, 109, 115, 204
Black power, 10, 20, 139, 224; claims of, 2, 18, 56–58, 139; as context, 58, 81;

Department of Defense (DoD): directives, 50, 93, 105, 112, 125, 140, 148, 180, 183, 189, 207, 246, 252, 265; investigations and studies, 40, 48, 92–93, 110–11, 141, 231; policies, 54–55; race relations initiatives, 6, 39, 50, 54–55, 68, 80, 84–85, 90, 107, 141, 148, 209, 231, 247–48

Diggs, Charles, 47–48

Du Bois, W. E. B., 42

education and training, 7, 76, 93, 204; approaches to, 126, 142–43, 150–51, 209; and army as educational institution, 124–25; and claims of authenticity, 126–27, 133, 134, 138, 143; and congressional concerns, 147–48, 149–50; content of, 136–40, 142–45; and DoD, 84, 140–41, 147–48; and DRRI, 141–49; and Fisk University, 143; for leaders, 113–14, 124, 125, 136–37, 225–26, 230; mandated, 132, 133, 135–36, 137, 148; post-training education, 125, 138–40, 148–49; role of Fort Benning, 127–32, 133, 135, 143; as sensitivity training, 127, 134–37, 143–47, 149; as solution, 26, 84, 92, 113–14, 124–25, 132–33, 149, 150, 151–52, 171, 225–26, 236, 277

equal opportunity: in Department of Defense, 9, 39–50 passim, 54, 60–61, 65, 69, 75, 79, 85, 90, 93, 105–10, 179, 231, 248, 251–53, 265, 273; in US Army, 14–15, 39–41, 65, 69, 75, 79, 85, 107, 109–12, 136, 144, 151, 177, 183, 200, 236, 243, 245–48, 277, 280; and USMA, 265–73; in US policy, 45. *See also* regulations, US Army (AR)

Ervin, Sam, 146–49, 223, 248

"Faces of the American Dead" (photographs), 65

Fanon, Frantz, 115

Flipper, Henry O., 264

Fort Benning, 125–35, 143, 151, 182, 255

Fort Bragg, 10, 38, 71, 126, 137, 156, 157, 182; 82nd Airborne Division, 51, 71

Fort Campbell, 125, 182; and 101st Airborne Division, 51, 54, 267

Fort Carson, 2, 4, 38, 62, 87, 109, 117–23, 138, 157–58, 170, 220–21; and Racial Harmony Council, 119–22, 220

Fort Dix, 38, 136, 170

Fort Gordon, 77, 185

Fort Hood, 1, 62, 140, 179, 182

Fort Leavenworth, 35, 113, 122–23, 160, 185, 239

Fort McClellan, 2, 180–82

Fort Monroe Conference, 93, 132–33, 151, 253

Fort Riley, 38, 62, 71, 156–57, 179, 182

fraggings, 41, 60, 99, 101, 135, 200, 215–19

Garth, Marshall B., 98–102, 117, 122

generation gap, 58, 84, 95–96, 110, 116–18, 178; and AVF, 155, 173; and hair, 157–58, 172–73; as problem, 73–74, 79, 82, 90–92, 95–96, 106, 157, 218, 222; and suspicion of Black officers, 90, 96, 118, 242

Gesell, Gerhard, 48, 245

Gesell Committee, 48–49, 180, 183–84, 245

graffiti, racist, 59, 85, 97, 115, 203

Grant, Ulysses, 264

Haines, Ralph, 75–79

Hall, Robert L., 18–20

Hamburger Hill, 65, 157, 259

Hawke, Willard, 77–79

Hester, Arthur, 267–69

Historically Black College or University (HBCU), 257, 261–62; Howard University, 210, 259, 261; Jackson State University, 115, 174; Morgan State University, 71, 105, 261

Hobson, James, 99–101, 119

Hope, Richard O., 142–49. *See also* Defense Race Relations Institute; education and training

House Armed Services Committee, 39, 50, 64, 70, 75, 146, 163, 235, 248, 265

Howard, Michael, 263

Humphrey, Hubert H., 34, 80

Vietnam War: Black service members within, 53–54, 71, 87, 89, 222, 250; as primary focus of leadership, 96, 162; racial conflict within, 60, 100, 212–15, 241; as unpopular, 10–11, 38, 46, 58, 72, 82, 115, 120, 130, 142, 163, 172, 174–75, 186, 222, 226, 250, 257, 259–61, 266; as unsuccessful, 1–3, 6, 64, 69, 75, 168, 191, 219, 221, 223, 231, 276. *See also* fraggings; Long Binh Jail; Merritt, Lavell

Voting Rights Act of 1965, 55

Wagner, Clifford, 21–24

Walter Reed Army Medical Center, 127–28, 132

Warren, Earl, 211

Westmoreland, William, 59; biography, 40; concerns about race, 60; and Fort Monroe Conference, 93; and hair policy, 174; message, 74–75, 81, 108; and military justice, 219–20, 222, 223, 230, 250, 253; and race education, 126, 132, 157; and racial harmony study, 40, 65, 70–71, 253; and *Study on Military*

*Professionalism*, 116, 131; and White briefing, 65, 71, 74, 81

White, James S., 3, 65, 71–75, 78, 81–82, 86–88, 93, 113–14, 125, 156, 178, 209, 214, 244, 253

Whittaker, Johnson C., 264

Wilkerson, Lieutenant, 52

Women's Army Corps (WAC), 5, 146, 180–81, 276. *See also* soldiers, female

World War I, 42, 44, 212, 280

World War II, 39, 48, 76, 80, 106, 187, 197, 212, 222, 235, 254, 267

X, Malcolm, 57, 103, 119, 216, 271

Yarmolinsky, Adam, 47–48

Young, Whitney, 53, 69

youth, 82–83, 85, 95–96, 110, 117–18, 125, 134–35, 139, 158, 161, 171, 196, 222, 226, 251; Black, 58, 81–83, 85–86, 95–96, 106, 110, 113, 117–19, 122, 161, 171; German, 104; white, 83, 86, 106, 110, 113, 171, 174. *See also* generation gap; soldiers, Black; soldiers, white